The Bitter Landscapes of Palestine

First published in the UK in 2024 by
Intellect, The Mill, Parnall Road, Fishponds, Bristol, BS16 3JG, UK

First published in the USA in 2024 by
Intellect, The University of Chicago Press, 1427 E. 60th Street, Chicago, IL 60637, USA

Production completed in November, 2023

A catalogue record for this book is available from the British Library.

Cover Image: ʻEin ar-Rashash, December 2018. Photograph: Margaret Olin.
Cover Designer: Tanya Montefusco
Frontispiece 1: Abandoned Palestinian village, Al-Baqaʻa, Occupied West Bank, 2023. Photograph: Margaret Olin.
Frontispiece 2: Margaret Olin and David Shulman. Photograph: Guy Hirshfeld.
Frontispiece 3: The view from an Israeli outpost at dawn, occupied Palestine, April, 2018. Photograph: Margaret Olin.
Production Manager: Debora Nicosia
Copy-editor: MPS Unlimited
Typesetting: Debora Nicosia
Series Editor: Alfredo Cramerotti

Paperback ISBN 978-1-78938-909-8
ePDF ISBN 978-1-78938-911-1
ePUB ISBN 978-1-78938-910-4

Part of the Critical Photography series
ISSN 2041-8345 | Online ISSN 2042-809X

Printed & bound by Short Run Press Ltd, Exeter EX2 7LW

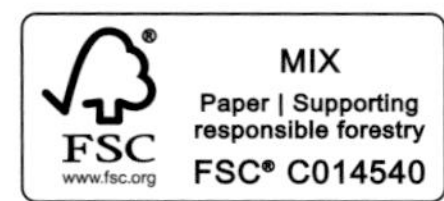

The Bitter Landscapes of Palestine

Margaret Olin and David Shulman

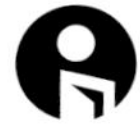

Intellect Bristol, UK / Chicago, USA

Critical Photography

Series Editor: Alfredo Cramerotti

Print ISSN: 2041-8345 | Online ISSN: 2042-809X

Since 1986, Intellect has provided a vital space for widening critical debate in new and emerging subjects. As a leading academic publisher in the fields of creative practice and popular culture, Intellect has a strong list of visual culture and contemporary art focussed publications. We aim to offer a platform for photographers, writers and creative artists to present and critically reflect on their work and to produce original, adventurous projects.

Critical Photography seeks to encourage visual and textual reflection on/with contemporary photography; to marry photographic work and critical texts, representing a balance between the two forms. The series is at the forefront in expanding the notion of critical debate: each book investigates a theoretical issue via two systems of representation, placing them at equal level. Neither text that 'explains' pictures nor photography that 'illustrates' text, the series addresses aspects of our being and becoming in a thought-provoking and aesthetically stunning form and content.

In this series:

The Bitter Landscapes of Palestine, by Margaret Olin and David Shulman (2024)
Fortunes of War: Photography in Alter Space, by Eric Ledesma (2021)
Photography as Critical Practice: Notes on Otherness, by David Bate (2021)
Theater of War, edited by Meredith Davenport and Daniel A. Kelin, II (2015)
The Culture of Photography in Public Space, edited by Anne Marsh, Melissa Miles and Daniel Palmer (2015)
The Blind, edited by Alfredo Cramerotti (2015)
Photography, Narrative, Time: Imaging our Forensic Imagination, edited by Greg Battye (2014)
On Perfection: An Artists' Symposium, edited by Jo Longhurst (2013)
Photocinema: The Creative Edges of Photography and Film, edited by Neil Campbell and Huw Davies (2013)
Contingency in Madagascar: PHOTOGRAPHY • ENCOUNTERS • WRITING, by Stephen Muecke, Photographs by Max Pam (2012)
Photography and Landscape, by Rod Giblett and Juha Tolonen (2012)
Unmapping the City: Perspectives of Flatness, edited by Alfredo Cramerotti (2011)

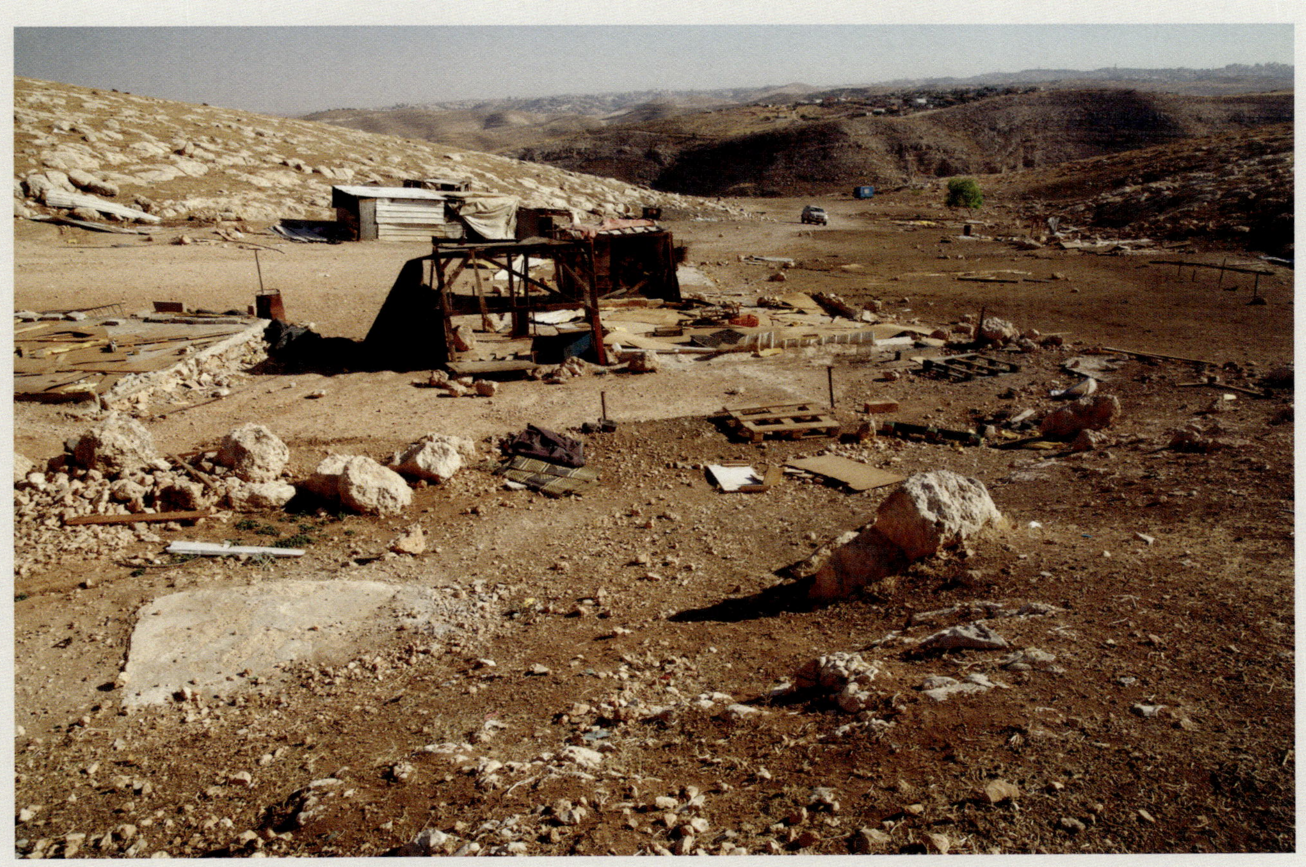

Abandoned Palestinian village, Al-Baqa'a, Occupied West Bank, 2023.

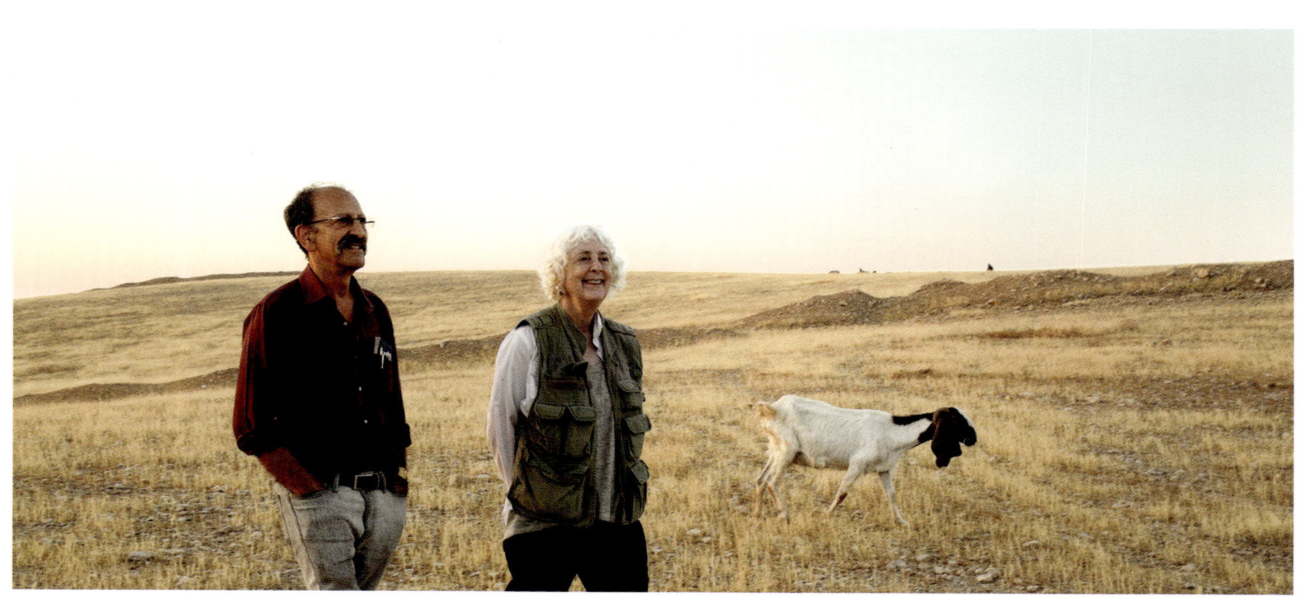

Authors' Statement

As we write, in late October, 2023, a war has broken out in the wake of horrendous, murderous attacks by Hamas on the Israeli communities in the Gaza periphery followed by terrible destruction wrought by Israel in Gaza. We cannot foresee what will come next. But in the West Bank, Israeli settlers have seen a golden opportunity for ethnic cleansing. The pace of destruction, encouraged by the right wing government formed after last year's election, has now increased to intolerable levels. Village after village, including several portrayed in photographs and words in this volume, are being destroyed, their inhabitants driven out by settler violence with the support of the army—what looks like the beginning of a second Nakba. It breaks our hearts to think that this volume may be the last documentation of the way of life we have tried to convey.

Margaret Olin & David Shulman

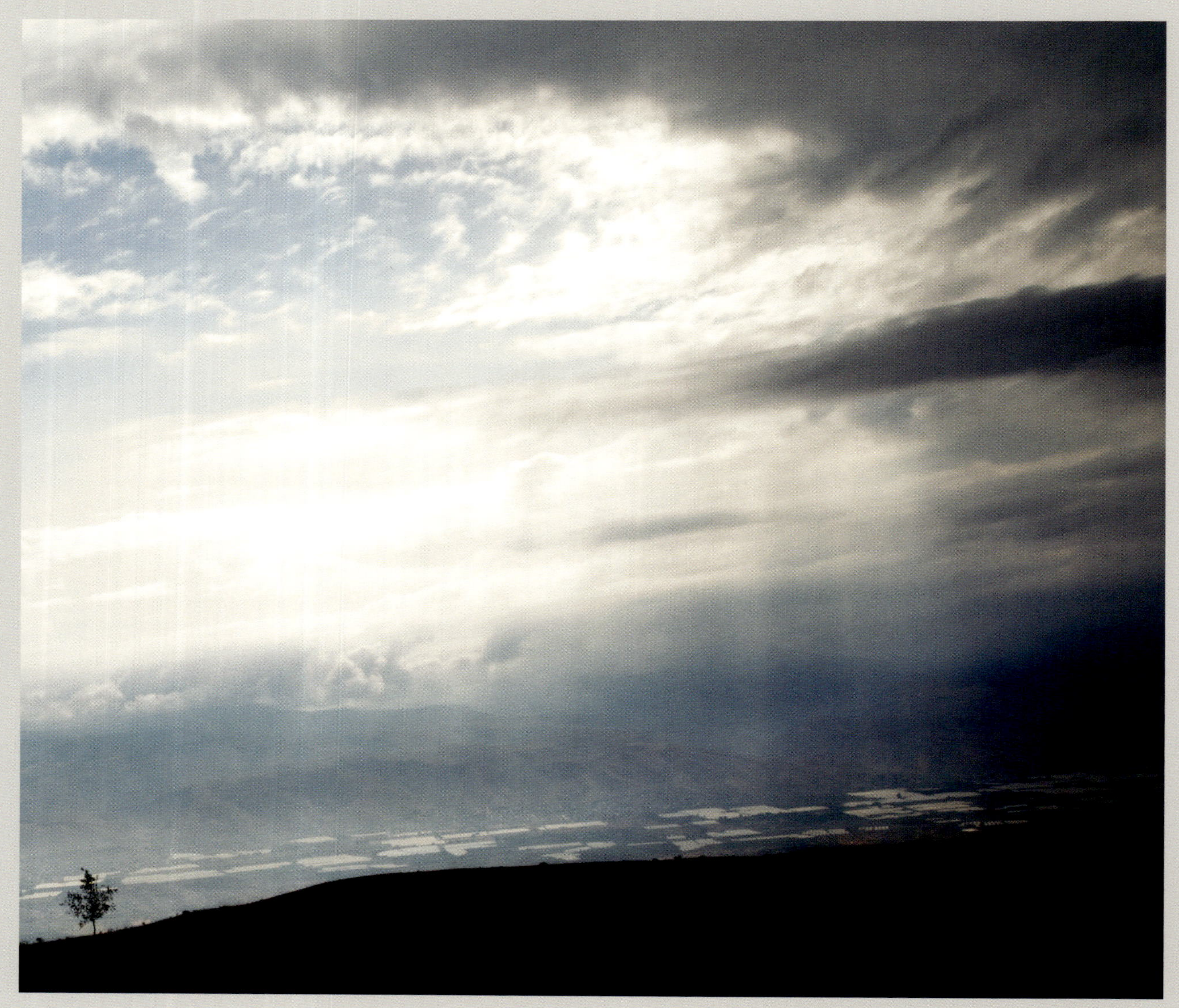

Toward the End of Winter, the Skies Open and Light Comes Raining Down—
On Sheep, Goats, Shepherds, also on Thieves, Soldiers, and Police.

For Fatma, Nasser, and Sa'id,
three exemplars of the activist spirit in the South Hebron Hills
and the Jordan Valley, in honor of their courage and our friendship
and in memory of Ezra Nawi and Hajj Suleiman.

Contents

Figures

Photographs

Maps

Acknowledgements

The authors wish to thank all those who helped this book come into being.

A preview was an exhibition of pictures and text, “Can Rocks Feel Pain?” at the Whitney Humanities Center, Yale University (January–March 2020). We are grateful to the then Director, Gary Tomlinson, to Mark Bauer, Associate Director, and to Sara Carrigan, Program Coordinator. Maurice Samuels and Renee Reed at the Judaic Studies Program offered their support, logistic, and financial, to the exhibition and to the booklet we were able to produce in conjunction with it. Martin D. Jean, Director of the Institute of Sacred Music, generously helped fund the exhibition, the catalogue, and the book. Timothy Barringer, Chair of the History of Art Department, also provided a generous subsidy for the publication. From the bottom of our hearts, we thank all of these friends for their encouragement, material and moral, from the beginning.

Special thanks to Gabriel DaSilva, Vanalyne Green, David Massey, Jen Morris, and Laura Wexler, for much-needed advice at many critical stages; Stefan Nicolescu, who taught us about rocks; Ralph Nelson, who encouraged Margaret to consult Stefan; James Ponet, our guru, who insisted that we meet each other and who commented movingly on the early drafts; Guy Hirshfeld, Amiel

Vardi, Arik Ascherman, and the other astonishing volunteers of Ta'ayush and Torat Tzedek who have dedicated themselves to the struggle for life and freedom in the South Hebron Hills and the Jordan Valley; Guy Butavia, selfless activist, who made himself available many times to shepherd us all over the South Hebron Hills; Daniil Brodsky and Yael Moav, who arranged Margaret's visit to Al-Khan al-Ahmar and brought her there, respectively; Ada Bilu, Rita, and Paul Mendes-Flohr, for nurturing Margaret in the field and in Jerusalem, also binding up the occasional wounds; Yigal Bronner, who first brought David to South Hebron and steadfastly continues the fight; the late Aaron Siskind, who provided visionary sustenance and mentorship to Margaret at the beginning, and Robert Storr, for re-igniting her photographic trajectory. The photographs are by Margaret Olin, except where credited to David Shulman or others. For permission to use their photographs, we are grateful to Michal Hai (Figs. 2.7 and 10.3), Amir Bitan (Fig. 11.4), Yigal Bronner (Fig. 12.9), and Istvan Perczel (Fig. 13.4). We are grateful to Tamar and Reuven Sofer, creators of the maps on pp. 223–25. Finally, Blake D. Ogden, of the School of Visual Arts, shared his expertise and helped us see the book through the printing process.

The readers of our blog, touchingphotographs.com, for their ongoing engagement; the devoted staff of Intellect, especially Jelena Stanovnik, Debora Nicosia, Tim Mitchell, the two anonymous readers for Intellect Press, and all those who helped bring this book into being: our families, who put up with innumerable absences in the field and were prepared to live with some measure of fear; and above all, the shepherds and farmers of the South Hebron Hills, the Jordan Valley, and elsewhere in Palestine, who hold fast to *sumud*, persistence, resilience, at immense cost, and who have put their trust in us.

From the Series Editor to the Reader

On the Concept of Dissonance

Alfredo Cramerotti

The concept of dissonance in the realm of human experience is akin to the entangled threads of a complex tapestry, where contradictions and incongruities create a fabric that is at once bewildering and enlightening. Dissonance is, in many ways, the crucible where the raw materials of life are melted down, mixed, and re-forged into our understanding of the world.

One such manifestation of dissonance lies in the interplay between beauty and horror. We have all been struck, at least in one occasion, by the jarring juxtaposition of the grace of a blossoming flower against the backdrop of a decaying, forgotten building. Or the proud gaze of a parent amongst the most debilitating environment for their offspring. This type of dissonance forces us to confront the capricious nature of existence, where the sublime and the abhorrent coexist, blurring the boundaries of our emotional responses. It is in these moments that we, as individuals, must grapple with the complexities of our feelings, our perceptions, and our understanding of the world.

The dissonance between simplicity and complexity is another facet of life that I have personally grappled with. It is in the delicate balance between the straightforward and the convoluted that I have found the most compelling narratives. The simplicity of a child's laughter juxtaposed with the complexity of adult anxieties, for instance, reveals the multidimensional nature of our lives. It challenges us to embrace both the straightforward and the intricate, recognizing that life's beauty often lies in the harmonious coexistence of the two. And often, the disagreement between the insider and outsider on a specific issue resonates deeply beyond our immediate comprehension. As an academic, I have often found myself straddling the line between being an insider, privy to the intellectual inner circle, and an outsider, navigating the labyrinth of unfamiliar discourse. This dissonance is a constant reminder of the dynamic nature of belonging and exclusion. It forces me to question the boundaries that divide us, compelling me to seek a more inclusive perspective.

Dissonance, in short, becomes the fulcrum of moral and ethical dilemmas. It is in the space between personal bias and the pursuit of objectivity that we confront the fundamental questions of integrity and fairness. The desire for discovery often grapples with the need for impartial evaluation. It is through navigating this tension that I have come to appreciate the profound implications of dissonance in decision-making. I would go here to the extent of claiming that it is the discordant symphony of life, where opposing forces, ideas, and emotions collide to create a rich and multifaceted human experience and, more specific to the case, academic inquiry. Embracing these contradictions is to engage in a continuous dance with the complexities of the human condition, where dissonance, in all its forms, enriches our understanding of the world and ourselves.

October, 2023

Foreword

Rev. Prof. Dr Mitri Raheb
President, Dar al-Kalima University,
Bethlehem, Palestine

The Bitter Landscapes of Palestine echoes voices of people who are seldom heard. Its photographs shed light on faces hidden from the mainstream media and who have names, dreams, and hope.

Their aspirations are basic: they want to live on the land of their ancestors; to have the freedom to lead their flock to areas where they find the minimum to survive on in a harsh environment. The Palestinian communities in the South Hebron Hills, like the larger Palestinian people, are facing a settler colonial state. The main feature that distinguishes settler colonialism from classical or neo-colonialism is the fact that settler colonialists come to settle in an occupied land permanently. They exercise state sovereignty and juridical control over the indigenous land, while ultimately aiming to eliminate the native people. To do so, settler colonialism developed different mechanisms, ideological constructs, and social narratives. The indigenous land is described as *terra nullius*, empty or barren land that is just waiting to be discovered, thus becoming the private property of the settlers. The native people are depicted with racist constructs as primitive, savage, and violent, while the settlers are portrayed as the civilized and brave pioneers. To defend the settled property from the savage, a police state is created and is granted extraordinary power over the native people, including power over their civil affairs.

The book reveals the nature of the settler colonial state that uses its military might to terrorize the native Palestinian people, implementing policies with the clear aim of occupying the bulk of the Palestinian geography with the minimum of the Palestinian demography. Historic Palestine looks therefore much like a piece of Swiss cheese, where Israel gets the cheese (the land with its resources) while pushing the Palestinians into holes, overpopulated areas with no resources.

However, this book is not only about Israeli settler colonialism but also about Palestinian *sumud*, Palestinian resilience, resistance, and hospitality. It is a story of a people that do not give up easily but keep clinging against all odds to their right to live on their land in dignity and freedom.

The area on the South Hebron Hills is indeed a bitter landscape, where the injustice cries to heaven. However, it is also a story of a people who do not give up hope but continue to be resilient, thus struggling for a better future. Besides the face of the Israeli soldiers and settlers, this book shows the face of a small segment of Jewish Israelis who do not agree with their government nor with the ideology and practice of the Jewish settler; they exercise their own form of activism and resistance to the occupation of Palestinian land and they believe in a different future characterized by justice, freedom, equality, and neighborly relations.

Yet, the authors are not naive to believe that this future is to be realized easily or soon. They hope, however, that by telling what they have seen with their own eyes and what they have heard with their own ears, they might raise awareness, challenging a numb Israeli and international consciousness, thus contributing to the end of Israeli occupation of Palestinian land and people.

Foreword

Seeing, Reading, Breathing

W. J. T. Mitchell

> My task which I am trying to achieve is, by the power of the written word, to make you hear, to make you feel—it is, before all, to make you see. That—and no more, and it is everything.
>
> —Joseph Conrad

As I read these words and view these photographs, I find myself noticing my breathing. Many kinds of breath, some of them unnameable, unbearable.

Gasps, at the beauty of the South Hebron hills and Jordan Valley captured in Margaret Olin's photographs taken from early morning to dusk.

Sobs, catches of breath at the sight of the ruined, murdered houses of the Palestinian shepherds, monuments of twisted corrugated metal, shattered stone walls, punctured water tanks, bulldozed stone walls, scattered pieces of furniture.

Panting, out of breath in sympathy at the labor of rebuilding, caught in photographs of men struggling to move a boulder a few feet, gathering shattered furniture, torn walls and broken dishes.

Growls of fury and rage at the thuggish settlers who descend on peaceful shepherds, throwing rocks at them, chasing their sheep, smashing their cars, threatening their children. More growls at the indifferent soldiers and police who wave papers at the shepherds, push and shove them, threatening them with arrest, insisting that they "are just doing their job," writing meaningless reports, handcuffing elderly men and carting them away, and then complaining that photographing their activities is "impolite."

Sighs of relief as the shepherds make tea and offer it to the soldiers as a peace offering. A sigh as the moments of *zulem* (cruelty, dishonor, humiliation) wrought by violence, hate, and cynical indifference are followed by Gandhian non-violence and *sumud* (perseverance).

Holding the breath while drinking the tea and feeling the ceremonial moment out of time, the suspended *epoché*, when Allah is creating and re-creating the world anew, as the shepherds rest before re-building.

The breath of speech, stuttering, inarticulate, shuttling between a shout of "NO!" and a whisper of "YES!" The big inhalation, to gather breath for a long speech describing the terror and beauty conveyed by this book; to analyze the geopolitics that makes it possible for this to go on day after day, year after year; to theorize the psycho-politics of fascism that can make one people perform a variation on the persecution and extermination that are so central to history; to appeal to the better angels of Israel and Palestine, some of them appearing on these hillsides as activists, witnesses, peacemakers, helpers; to shout out to the world that is oblivious to this reign of subtle, well-concealed terror just one more "NO!"

And then to exhale with that whispered "Yes" to children playing barefoot among the stones, the sheep and goats devouring the thorns, the donkeys waiting patiently for their burdens, the women sewing, cooking, cleaning, reading, and arguing about going to school or staying at home, the men standing firm, patient, refusing to move, waiting to be pushed, shoved, arrested, and carted away.

Cries of pain as a murdered shepherd, shot through the spine, is carted away to the hospital where he will not arrive in time because of the roadblocks and checkpoints. Cries of women over their children, arrested for picking cherries from the orchard of an illegal settlement. Cries of command called out to the sheep and the dogs who help to guide them, leading them to the tenderest thorns and greenest patches on the stony hillsides.

Gags of disgust at the settlers' attempts to poison the landscape, even by piping their sewage onto the hillsides below their settlements, poisoning the shepherds' wells, burning their olive trees. The feeling of strangulation, involuntary loss of breath as the physical counterpart to the slow, inexorable, seemingly irresistible choking off of a people and an ancient way of life where the people belong to the land as much as it belongs to them.

Time to take a breath, make some tea, and go on reading.

Breath gathered, then a longing for shouts and chants of protest, for dances of endurance and resistance: how long, O Lord, how long? Let my people go—to their homes, their flocks, their land.

I.1 Umm al-Amad, Ramadan,
South Hebron Hills, June 2018.

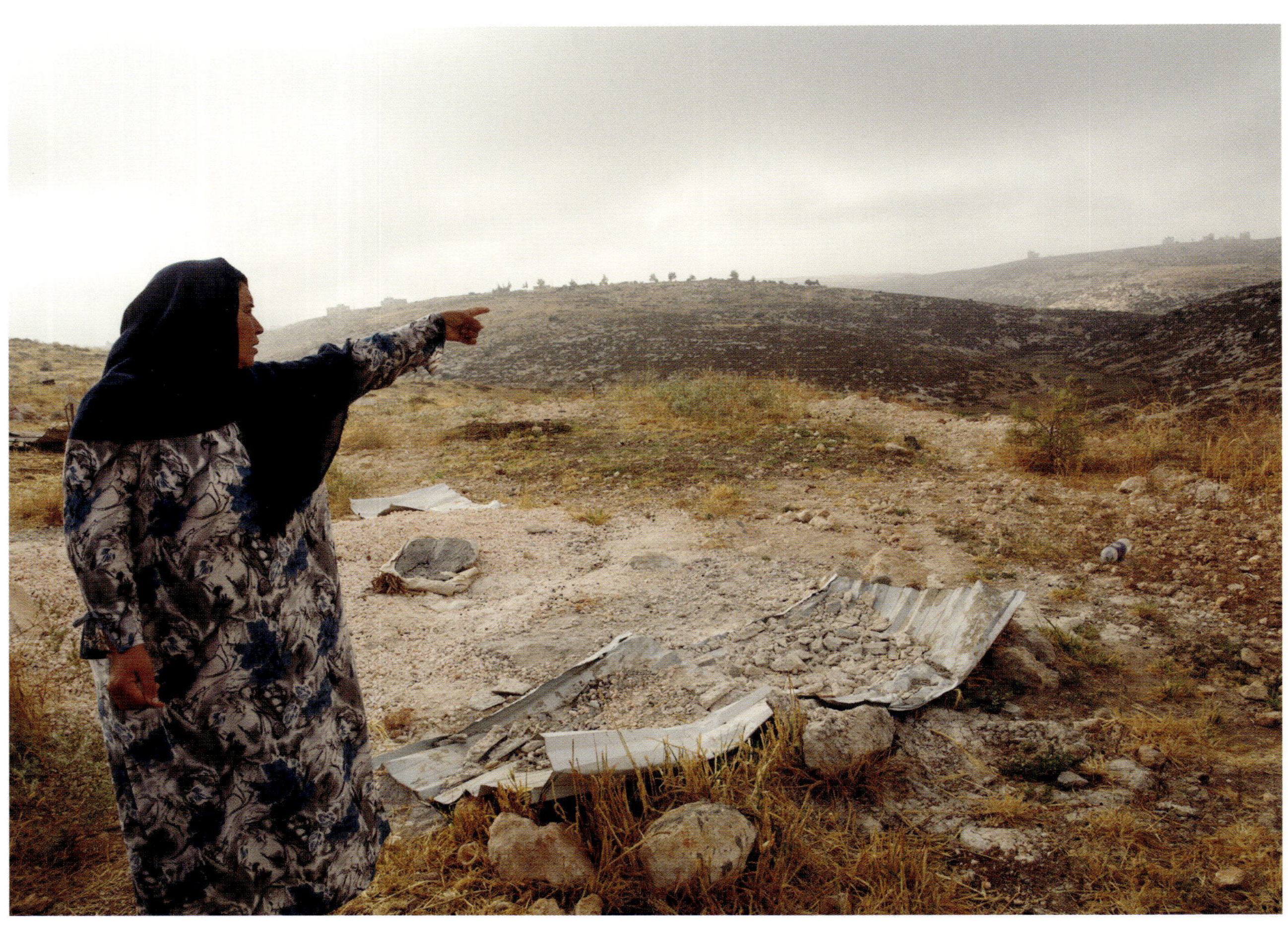

Introduction

We will speak only of what we have seen and heard directly and what we have experienced in our bodies.

1.

We first met in New Haven in April 2014, through our good friend, James Ponet. Peg wanted to get involved with an activist group in Palestine–Israel; she was traveling to Israel for a conference in May and didn't want to pretend that everything was normal. David was a long-time activist with Ta'ayush, Arab-Jewish Partnership, an all-volunteer organization working mainly in the South Hebron Hills. So Peg was introduced to this group and, on May 31, 2014, she had her first taste of action.

Peg: My plan was academic. I wanted to study the photographic practices of anti-occupation activists. But what I encountered the first day changed everything: the overwhelming loveliness of the South Hebron Hills in the early light; soldiers running down a slope in their heavy boots and full combat gear, to confront a farmer who is plowing a minuscule field; five soldiers guarding a small, kidnapped tractor as though it were a pack of dangerous prisoners of war threating to foment an uprising; the bearded owner of the newly confiscated tractor, fingering his beads; another group of soldiers who surrounded and leered at me, telling me to "take my friends" (I'd just met them that day), "and go"; and the last straw, those same soldiers bragging about the day, a few days earlier, when they hauled off to the police station four little girls, one of them handicapped, and detained them there for ten hours. Their crime? Picking and eating cherries on the way home from school.[1]

I was hooked. I began a series of blog posts to search for a visual story-telling style that could convey the

1. Chaim Levinson, "Palestinian Girls Detained for Picking Settlers' Cherries," *Haaretz*, 27 May, 2014.

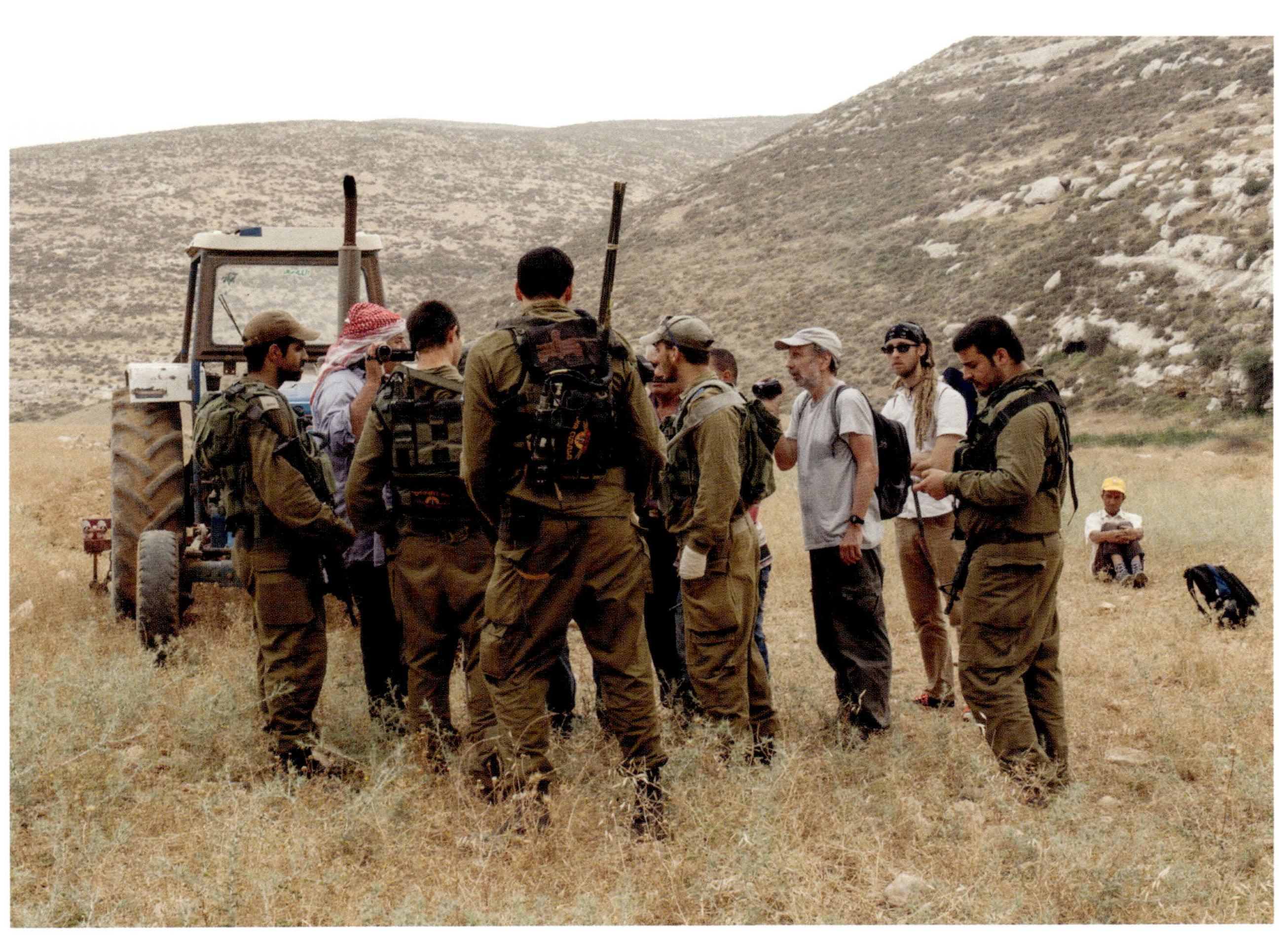

I.2 Wadi Sumsum,
South Hebron Hills, May 2014.

strange ways of this beautiful and alien planet. The search continues to this day.

David: My first day in the South Hebron hills was January 11, 2002. I was just back from the better part of a year in Berlin, and I was searching for some way for me and my conscience to survive in Israel. I had just become a grandfather. We were a large group—about 250 activists, in a long caravan of cars—and our mission was to bring blankets to the Palestinians near Jinbah whose homes (most of them caves) had been demolished by the army; the army also confiscated the tents the Red Cross had donated, and the villagers were spending their nights in the open air. It was bitter cold in the hills. The soldiers, obedient as always to the settlers, had set up a series of staggered roadblocks to keep us from reaching Jinbah. Each of us clutching a blanket wrapped in plastic, we washed over the roadblocks, one after another. There were arrests, there were beatings, there were the inevitable threats and growls and verbal abuse, and there was the sweet intoxication of doing the right thing, of defiance. By late afternoon we reached the Palestinians. We embraced one another like brothers. I knew I was where I had to be.

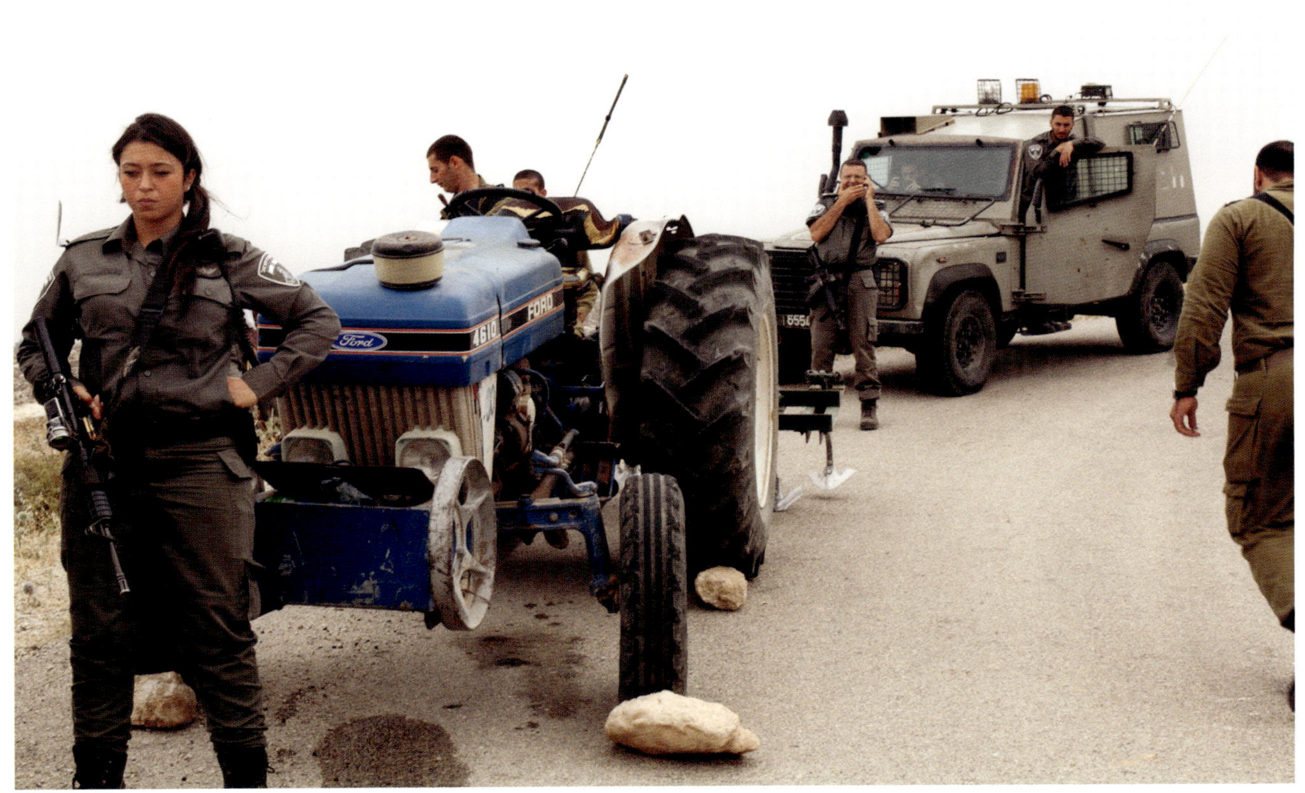

I.3 Wadi Sumsum, May 2014.

We would meet in the field from time to time. On March 14, 2015—a hard day, with arrests and much pain, in Zanuta—David wrote a report and asked Peg if she had photos to go with it. She did. Soon we were producing the blog reports together. You can see them at www.touchingphotographs.com. We have been driven by the need to share what we have known in Palestine, also to document a way of life that is hanging by a thread.

Sometimes—rarely—one can read in newspapers about incidents that take place on the West Bank. They don't tell you about the shock one gets each time you enter into that reality. It's that shock that we want you, our readers, to feel.

Palestinians throughout the West Bank live in terror. That they have survived at all on their land is a wonder, a tribute to their stubborn perseverance, *sumud* in Arabic. They are fighting every hour to preserve their way of life—fighting not with guns and clubs, the settlers' and soldiers' weapons of choice, but by getting up every morning, taking the sheep and goats out to graze, harvesting their olives when the army lets them, baking bread, churning butter, sending their children to school even when there is danger, standing up to those who have come to attack and destroy. Nothing in this life can be taken for granted.

Over years, we have shared the goodness and the danger. Of course, for us it was much easier. Usually, after a day in the field, we come home to safety, warmth, food in plenty, a glass of wine, a shower, music. Often we begin immediately after arrival to search for words and pictures that will hold the memory of that day.

Many days, hundreds of hours, perhaps more than hundreds. Typically, we leave before dawn. There's a certain magic to walking to the Liberty Bell Park, where we rendezvous, in that hour: the day still trying to be born. Then it's an hour in the minibus from

Jerusalem to Umm al-Khair or Susiya or Twaneh in the hills, and a little less or a little more than an hour to the various sites in the Jordan Valley. Sometimes we manage to sleep a few minutes more on the way down. Then the landscape changes. The hills become steeper, and the vistas of the desert open up. On the left, you can see all the way to the Dead Sea and beyond into Jordan. As we go farther south, gradually there are flocks of sheep and goats on the slopes, with a lone shepherd or two guiding them. Another world. Tiny hamlets or villages that don't look like other West Bank villages: they are sparse, simple, close to the ground, clustered around tents and shacks and sheep-pens, nestled into the open spaces between the hills. Morning scenes: coffee on a stove or wood fire; a breakfast of olives and labaneh or omelet; gathering the flocks to head out for grazing. Morning sounds: the throaty language the shepherds use to speak to, or yell at, the sheep, and the rather different dialect for the goats; the wind smoothing the wild grass; a raucous chorus of donkeys; the voices of children crying, running, playing, going to school. And the colors have changed: in the early morning light, the slopes go from red to dark brown to tan and yellow; the light itself rains onto the golden rough topsoil, teeming with pebbles and bigger stones and thorns; in the distance, one sees the blue outline of the hills in Jordan across the river. Always the immense, wide-open, ever-changing sky.

Then work begins. We join whoever needs us—shepherds, farmers trying to plow their fields, olive-pickers (in the fall), women minding the tabun stove and the children and also often going out with the flocks. Usually we break into smaller units of two or three, spread out over the hills. At some point during the day, after whatever events have overtaken us separately, we reunite, tell our stories, and go off to some new task feeling fortified by these oases of friendship. Eventually there will probably be tea and maybe something to eat—the flakey, gossamer pita of the Jordan Valley Bedouins or the rough-and-ready thick pita of South Hebron, with a little of the rock-hard salty cheese they make, perhaps some hummus and tomatoes with zaatar and olive oil.

By late afternoon, the colors change dramatically. The hills, once golden-brown, become first blue, then darker blue, then purple. When Ezra Nawi was alive, that was often the moment when he would be struck by some wild revelation, a good deed waiting to be done, an act of solidarity, usually in some inaccessible or dangerous place where the soldiers are waiting to pounce upon us. And then it starts all over again, however exhausted, or cold, or burned by sun, we may be. And sometimes when we are already on the way back to Jerusalem there will be an emergency call, like when settlers were shooting in Khirbet Safa and we raced back to defend the villagers. There are days that end in the police station at Kiryat Arba, waiting to be released after arrest.

Though our testimony is here to be read and seen, we have no intention of speaking for our Palestinian friends. We want to give those of you who have no first-hand experience of the occupation, and perhaps not even of Palestine, a sense of how you might feel if you went there. We want to convey the wonder, sorrow, and anger that one feels in the face of the beauty and cruelty of these landscapes.

But we do want you to hear Palestinian voices. This book includes interviews with Palestinian and Israeli activists. These are selections, often from conversations that unfolded over the years, in Arabic, Hebrew, sometimes English, in homes, outside on the hills, in the desert, over tea, or maybe standing in a newly plowed field. This kind of work, and this kind of friendship, lends itself to reflection. Whatever else we may manage to do, we hope we have, at least a little, taken the edge off the loneliness.

2.

The hills and valleys of the occupied West Bank are dotted with Israeli settlements. Almost no Palestinian village in Area C, under direct Israeli military and civil control, is out of sight of these settlements and the so-called illegal outposts (illegal even under Israeli law). The older ones were established by the government beginning in the late 1970s and early 1980s, not long after the 1967 war. More recent ones, including the outposts now mushrooming everywhere in the territories, are usually private initiatives by the settlers, backed up, however, by the army, the police, and all the instruments of the Israeli system. In general, nothing in Israel is as permanent as an illegal outpost in Palestine.

All the settlements rest on stolen Palestinian land with the possible exception of the original Etzion Bloc south of Jerusalem. All are concentrated in Area C, that is, over 60% of the West Bank, which is slotted for annexation in the vision of a large part of Israel's population. Through a series of legal ruses, the Israeli civil and military courts allowed the government to take these lands and give them to Jewish settlers.[2] Nearly all attempts by the original owners and users to reclaim possession have been denied by the courts. Over the years, the settlement project has grown to monstrous proportions. Today there are close to half a million Israeli settlers on the West Bank, in the midst of a Palestinian population of some two and a half million. The settlements are, without doubt, one of the major obstacles to the very possibility of establishing a Palestinian state or reaching a comprehensive peace agreement. In practice, Areas B and A (the latter under full Palestinian control) are also subject to more or less continuous incursions by Israel soldiers.

2. Michael Sfard; *The Wall and the Gate: Israel, Palestine, and the Legal Battle for Human Rights* (New York: Metropolitan Books, 2018); also David Kretzmer and Yaël Ronen, *The Occupation of Justice: The Supreme Court of Israel and the Occupied Territories*, 2nd ed. (Oxford: Oxford University Press, 2021).

The harsh reality documented in this book has a prehistory. The Occupation in its present form derives from the 1967 Six Day War, which ended with Israel in control of the entirety of historic Palestine, from the Jordan River to the Mediterranean Sea. Before that, the dominant political idea, embodied in the United Nations resolution (181) of November 29, 1947, was that the land would be partitioned between the Jews and the Arabs. The Zionist leadership accepted this principle on pragmatic grounds, although the dream of settling and possessing the entire territory never died. The Palestinian leadership, and the Arab states, rejected partition altogether. In any case, the intended Palestinian state never happened. After the 1948 war, the West Bank was taken over by Jordan (despite widespread protest in the Arab world), and the Gaza Strip became part of Egypt.

In the years immediately following the 1967 war, the newly controlled territories were, in theory, being held in reserve as bargaining chips for an eventual peace agreement. That idea, which was still in place when the Oslo accords between Israel and the new Palestinian Authority were signed in 1993–95, has by now become obsolete. What we see, over the century-long history of the conflict, are two ruthless national movements, each intent upon holding all the territory and destroying one another. Within these terms, the primary mechanisms that served the Jews in Palestine during the British Mandate, before the State of Israel existed—that is, acquiring land by creating settlements with their surrounding fences and water towers—continue unabated, underwritten by successive Israeli governments, as if inseparable from the Zionist project. However, the settlements put in place by the present generation come imbued with a new religious, messianic ideology blind to considerations of practical or political utility. The religious Zionists who have pioneered these settlements, once a tiny minority but by now an integral part of the mainstream, have, in effect, kidnapped the state and are holding it to ransom for their annexationist program.

Palestinian resistance to Zionism, and of course to the Occupation, has often been extremely violent. It is, however, important to remember that the Occupation itself is an act of severe state violence. The continuities with the pre-state and early-state policies are all too apparent. Attacks on Palestinian communities, the poisoning of their wells, and ultimately expulsion from their lands were well documented during the 1948 war and adumbrated by earlier acts in the Mandate period.[3] For two decades after that war, Arabs living in Israel, now citizens of the state, were under military rule with its constant disruption of normal life, just as we see, in a far more extreme form, in Area C in the occupied territories today.

The Palestinians with whom we have worked closely over the past many years have long since abandoned the idea of violent resistance and adopted, in its place, the Gandhian principle of non-violent civil disobedience. This is not to say that violent groups such as Hamas and the Islamic Jihad are not active both in Gaza and the West Bank. It is also important for us to say that the Israeli settlers in Area C are not a unified, homogeneous group. The ones we tend to meet in the field belong to the most fanatical factions among the settler communities; many of them are simply thugs. But among the settlers generally one also finds idealists interested in co-existence with their Palestinian neighbors. Moreover, the great majority of Israeli settlers in the territories are only there because the government subsidizes their housing and provides public services. Many of them have no idea they are part of the problem or have blocked that thought from their awareness.

3. On wells: see Ofer Aderet, "'Place the Material in the Wells': Docs Point to Israeli Army's 1948 Biological Warfare," *Haaretz*, October 14, 2022; on the Nakba generally, see Benny Morris, *The Birth of the Palestinian Refugee Problem, 1947–1949* (Cambridge: Cambridge University Press, 1988).

A number of human-rights and peace-oriented organizations work in Israel and Palestine, among them Ta'ayush, founded at the outbreak of the Second Intifada in 2000. All these groups aim, among other things, at protecting the Palestinian civilian population from the settlers and the soldiers and at keeping alive the dream of a future peace. The pages that follow emerge from this kind of work and owe a huge debt to many of these organizations and especially to Ta'ayush and its devoted activists.

We have divided the book into a series of short thematic chapters interspersed with what we call *laḥzāt*. *Laḥza* is Arabic for "a moment." You can also think of these laḥzāt as providing a chorus of voices telling their own stories. Sometimes a picture stands wordless, alone. Some of the moments are simply a pause, a tea break, as happens regularly in the course of a day in the field.

Although as we write things look dark, and it is hard to predict how or when a viable symbiosis will emerge or what form it will take, someday, one way or another, Palestinians and Israeli Jews will find a way to live together. We see our own work as contributing, on some level, to that future.

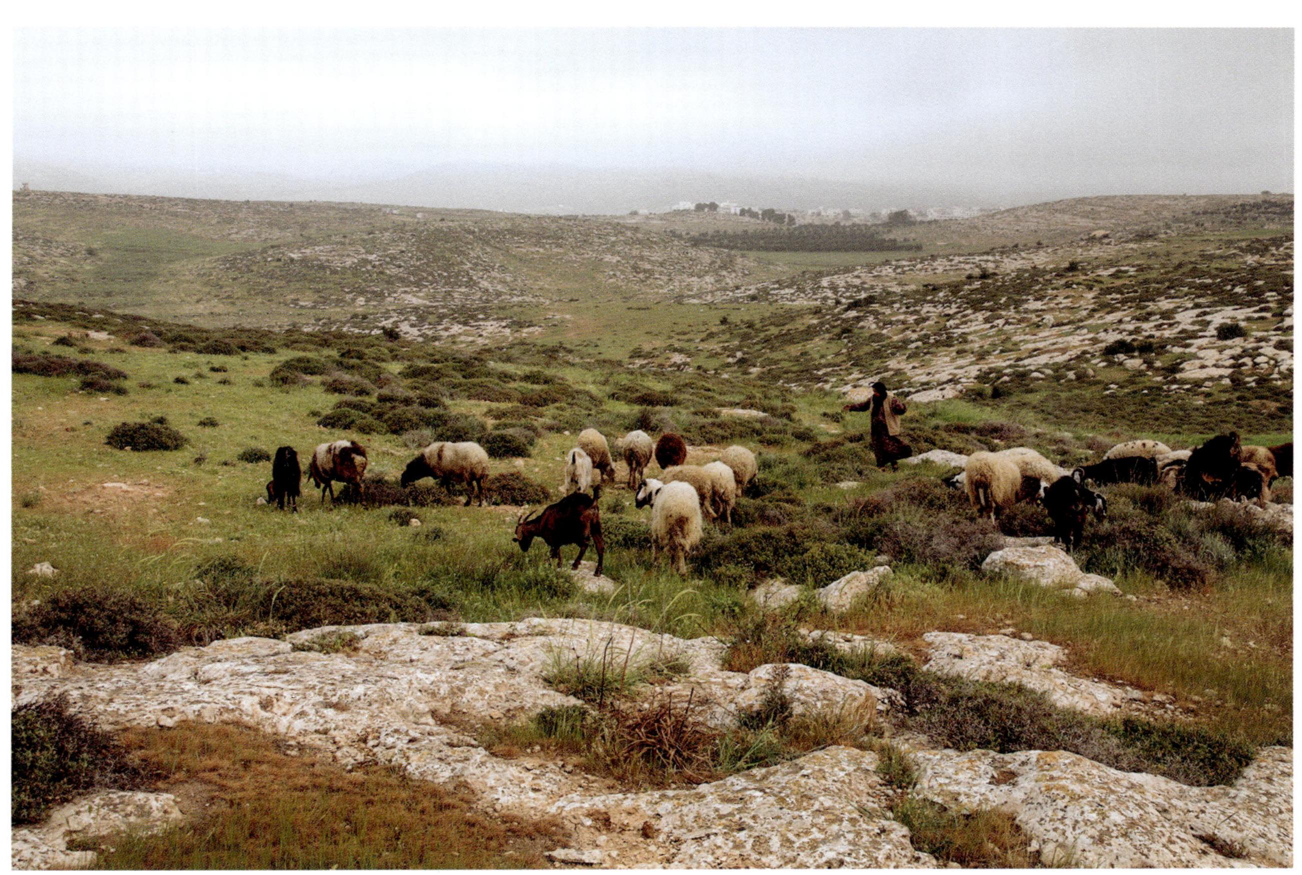

I.4 Umm al-Amad, March 2018.

1.1 Road from Umm al-Ara'is to Susiya , March 2015.

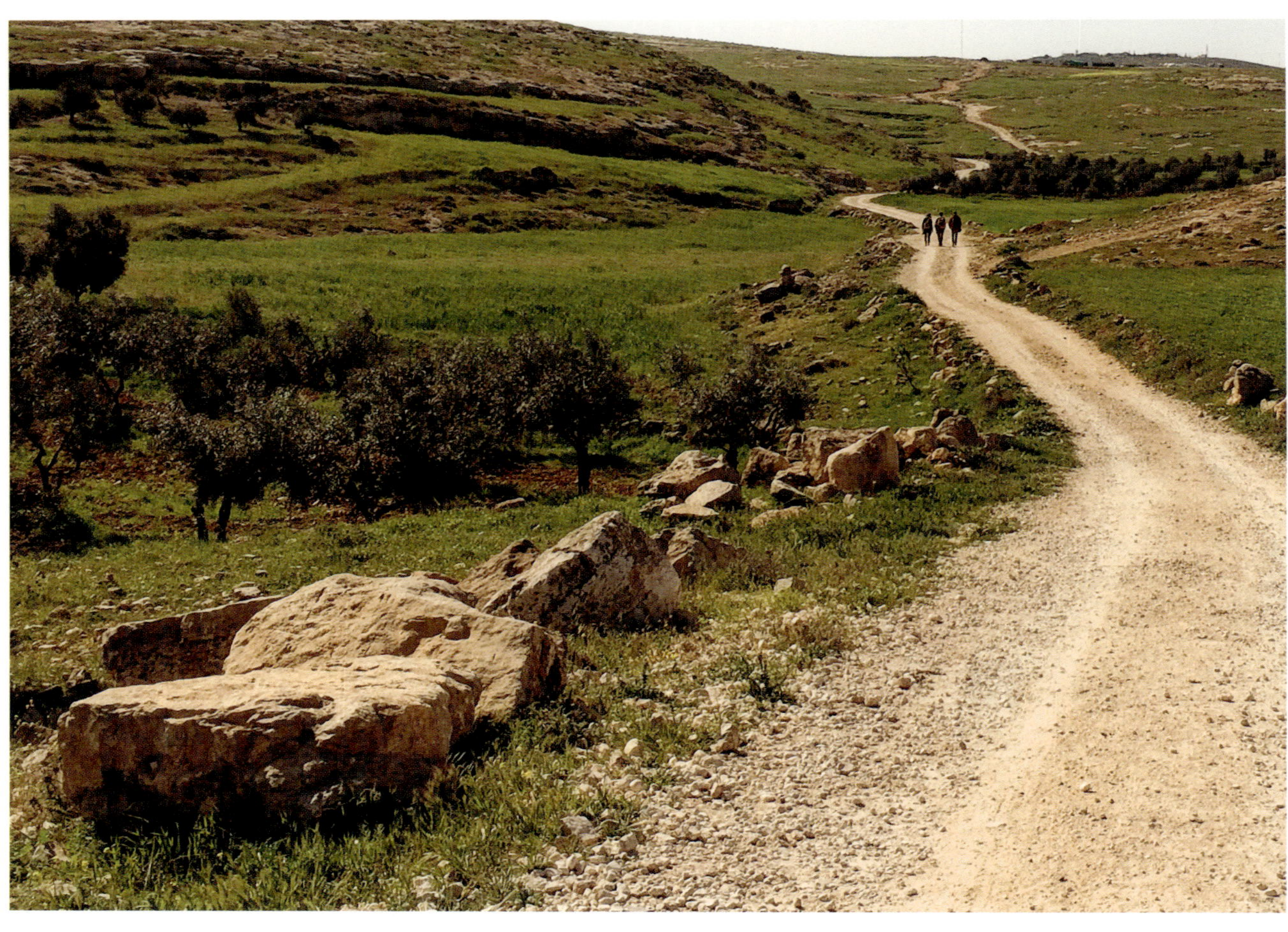

1.

Can Rocks Feel Pain?

Sheep, shepherds, rocks, and hills. We can see for some miles.
We breathe in the open spaces.
Behind us, the hills taper off into the desert.

Wherever we step, there are rocks, in all sizes and shapes, interspersed with green patches of wild zaatar, sage, asphodels, and thorns, the sheep's favorite delicacy.

The ground is caked dry and yellow in summer, a wet morass in winter, if the rains have come.

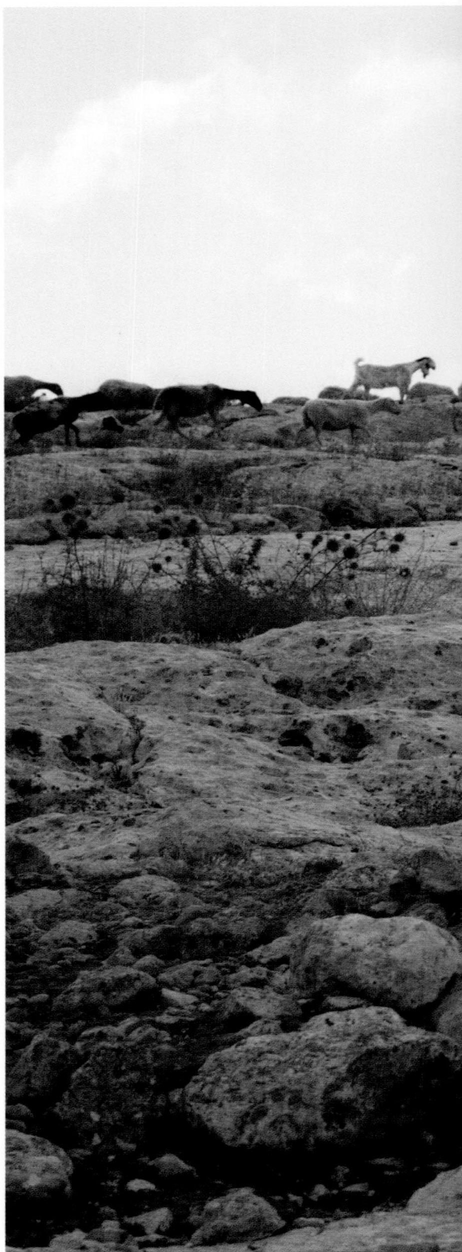

1.2 Umm al-Amad, June 2014.

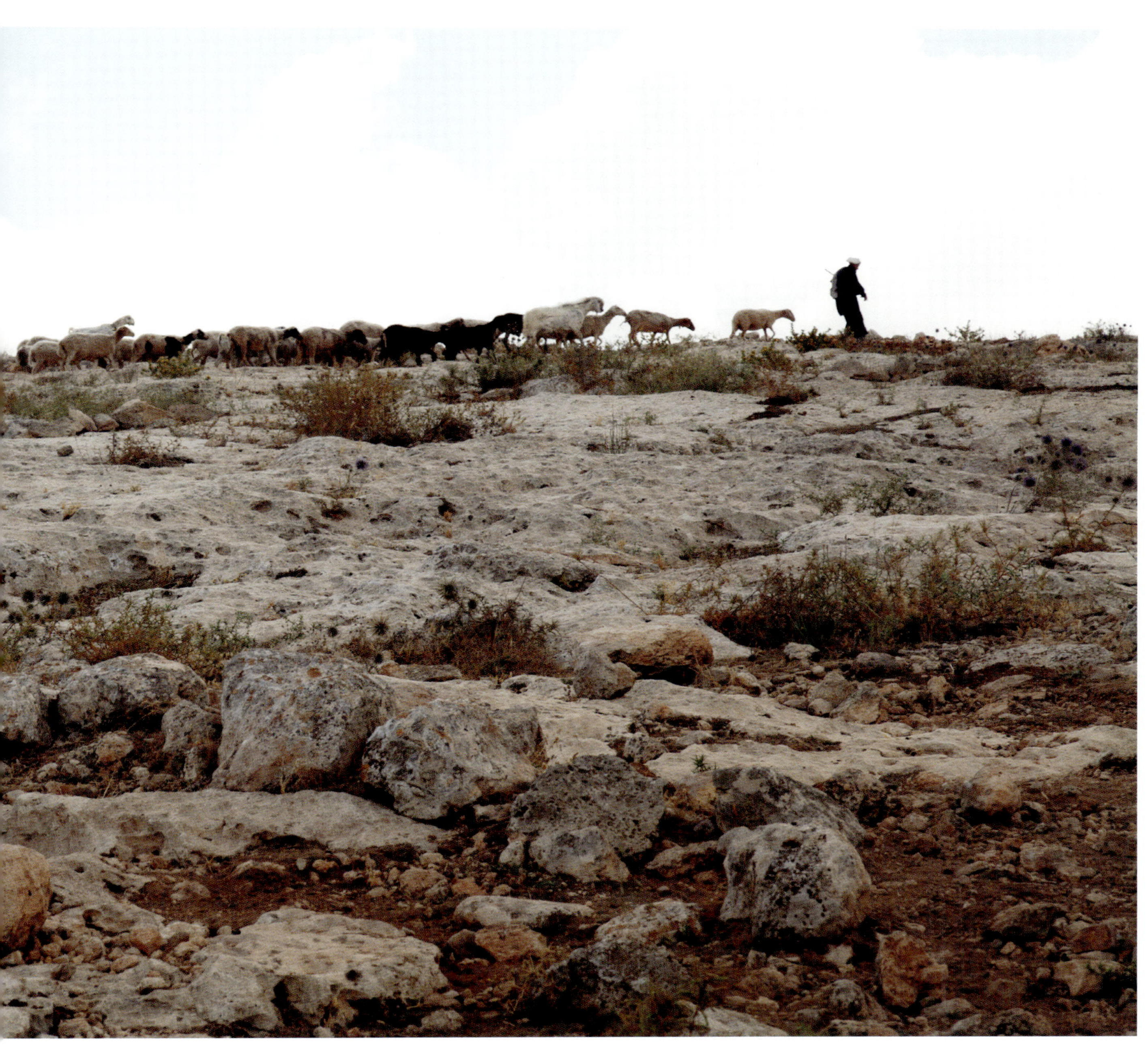

These rocks have an eloquent depth, like living beings. Sometimes they come huddled together like a tribe. Sometimes they rest on the massive rock floor, eroded over centuries.

1.3 Magha'ir al-'Abid. Nahal Harduf, South Hebron Hills, January 2022.

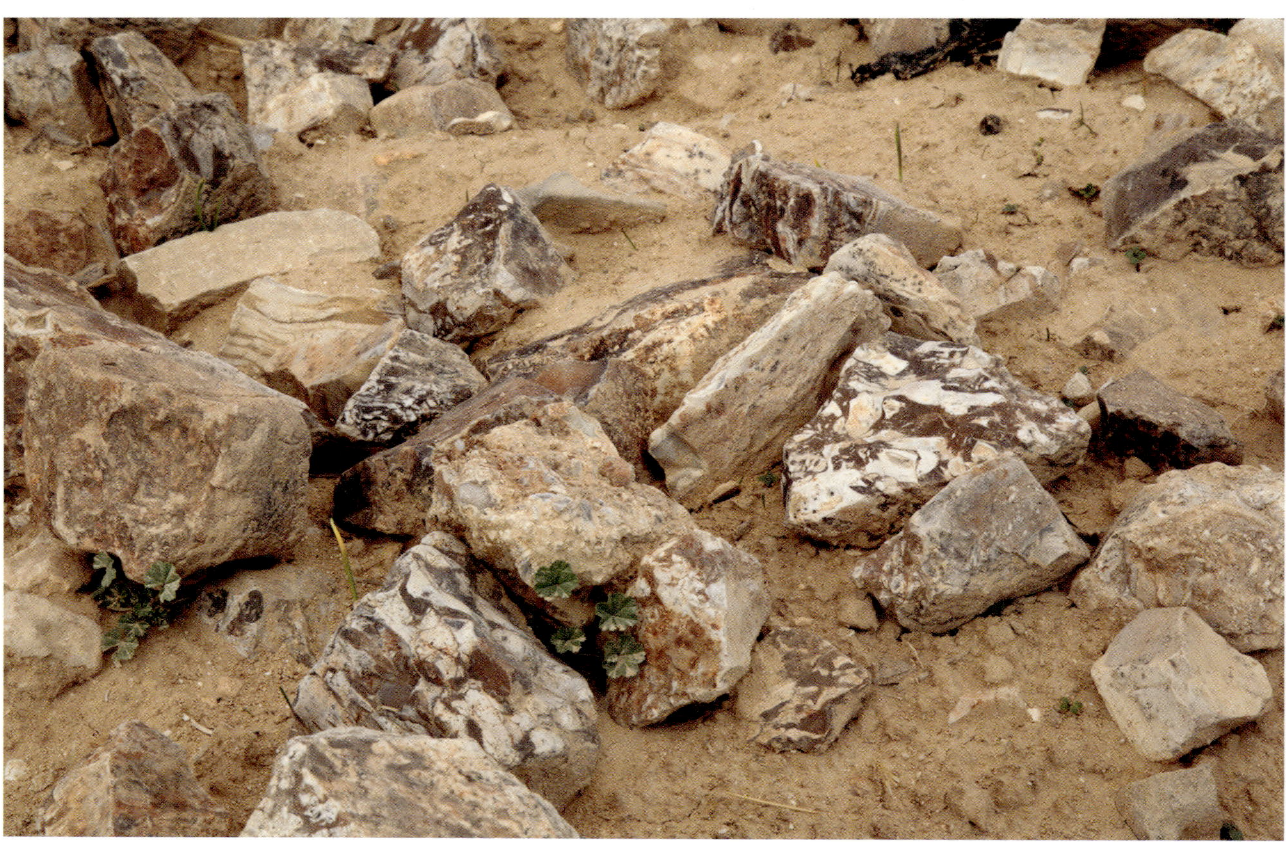

Some are jagged, with colorful veins, competing with one another like desert birds. Some emerge from the soil, and some seem to be sprinkled over it by an unseen hand.

1.4 Umm al-Ara'is, South Hebron Hills, March 2015.
1.5 (next) 'Auja, Jordan Valley, January 2022.

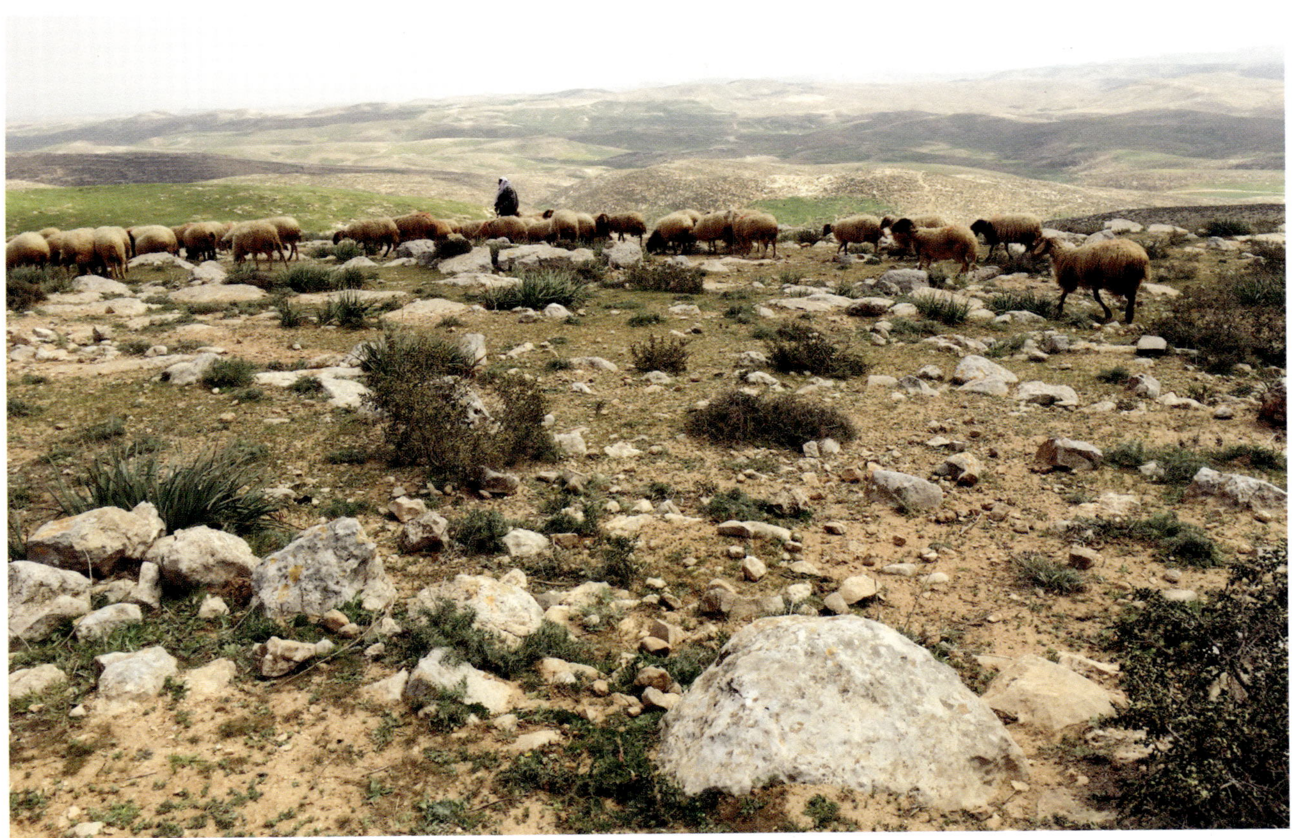

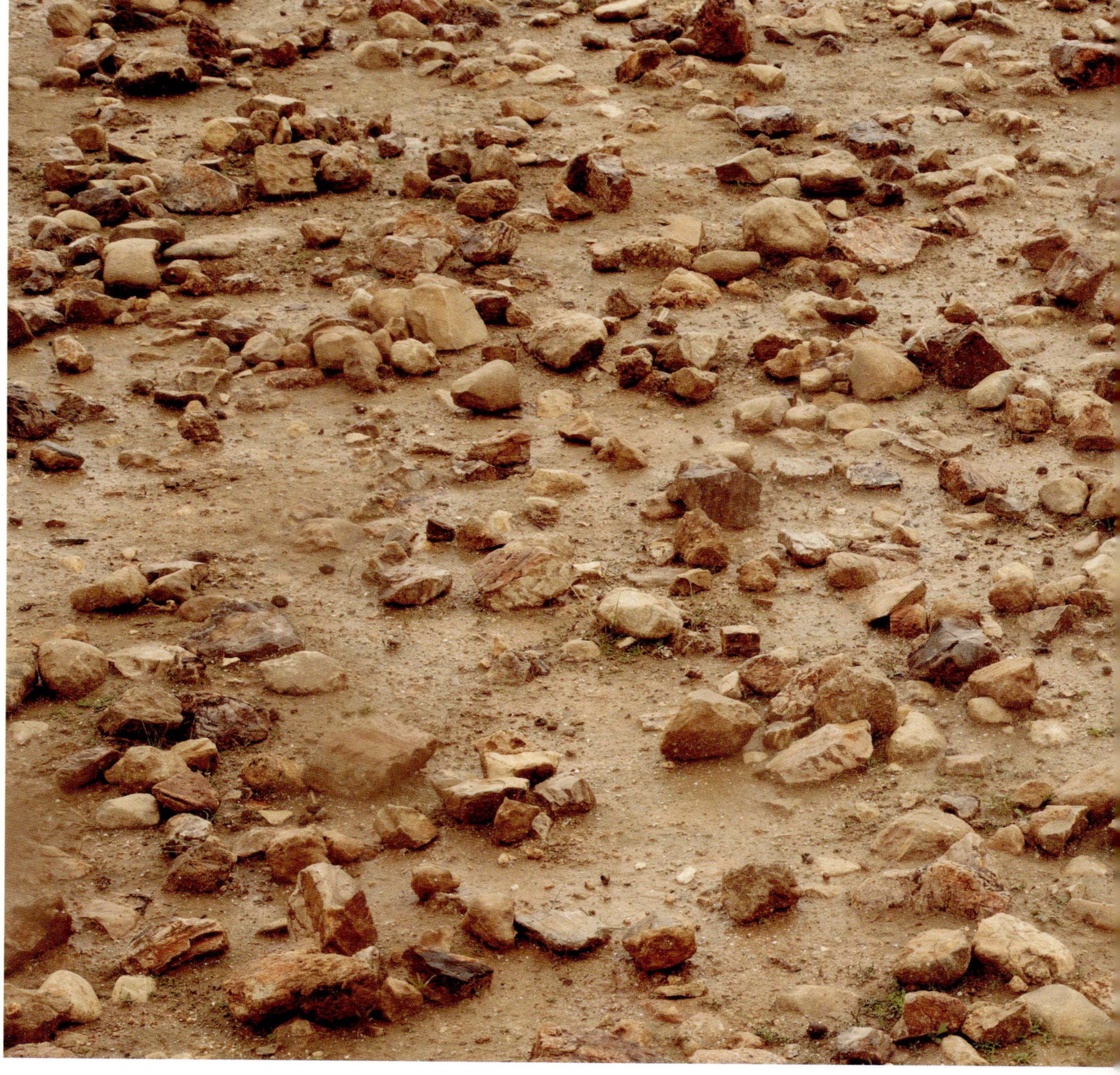

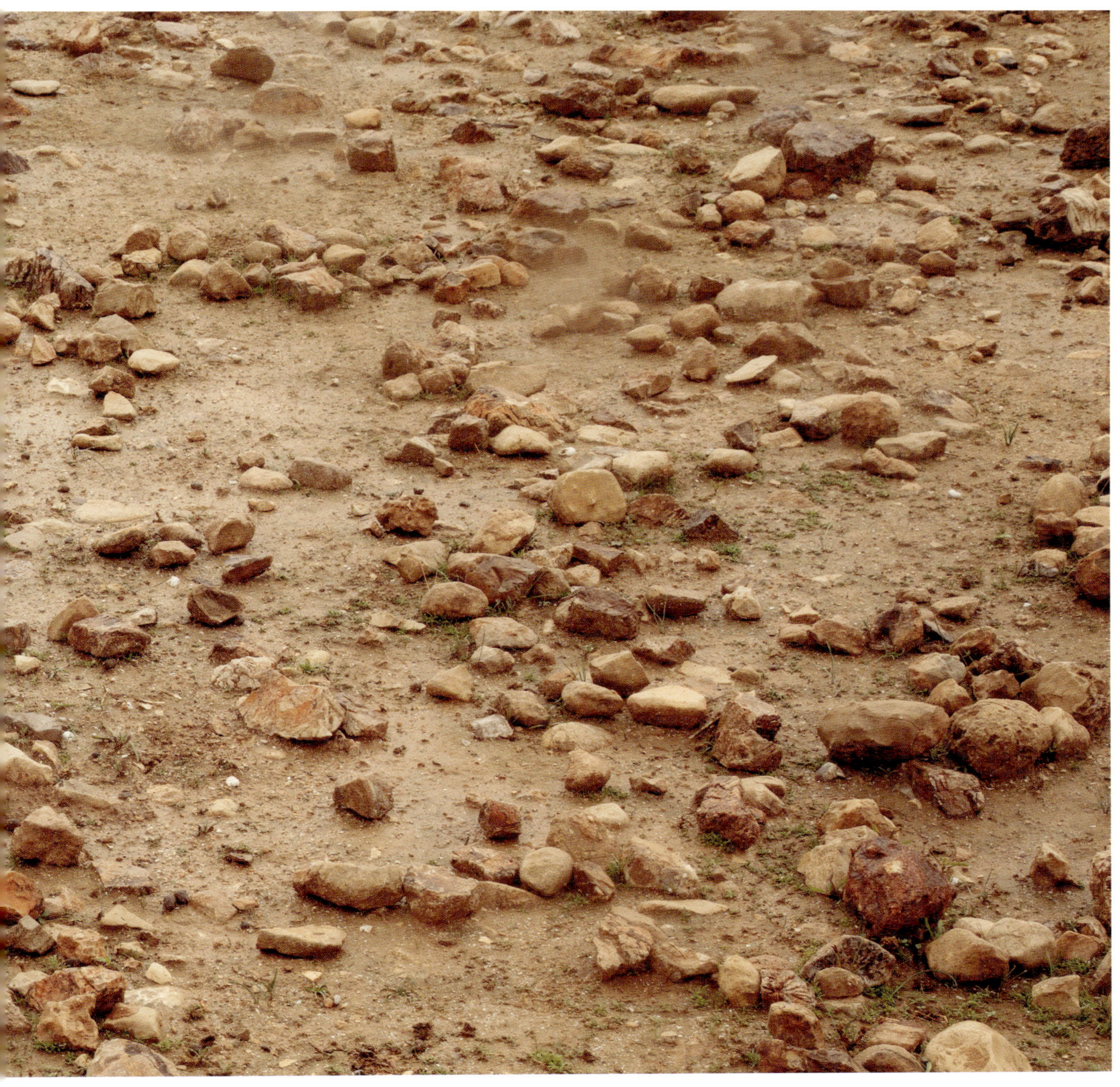

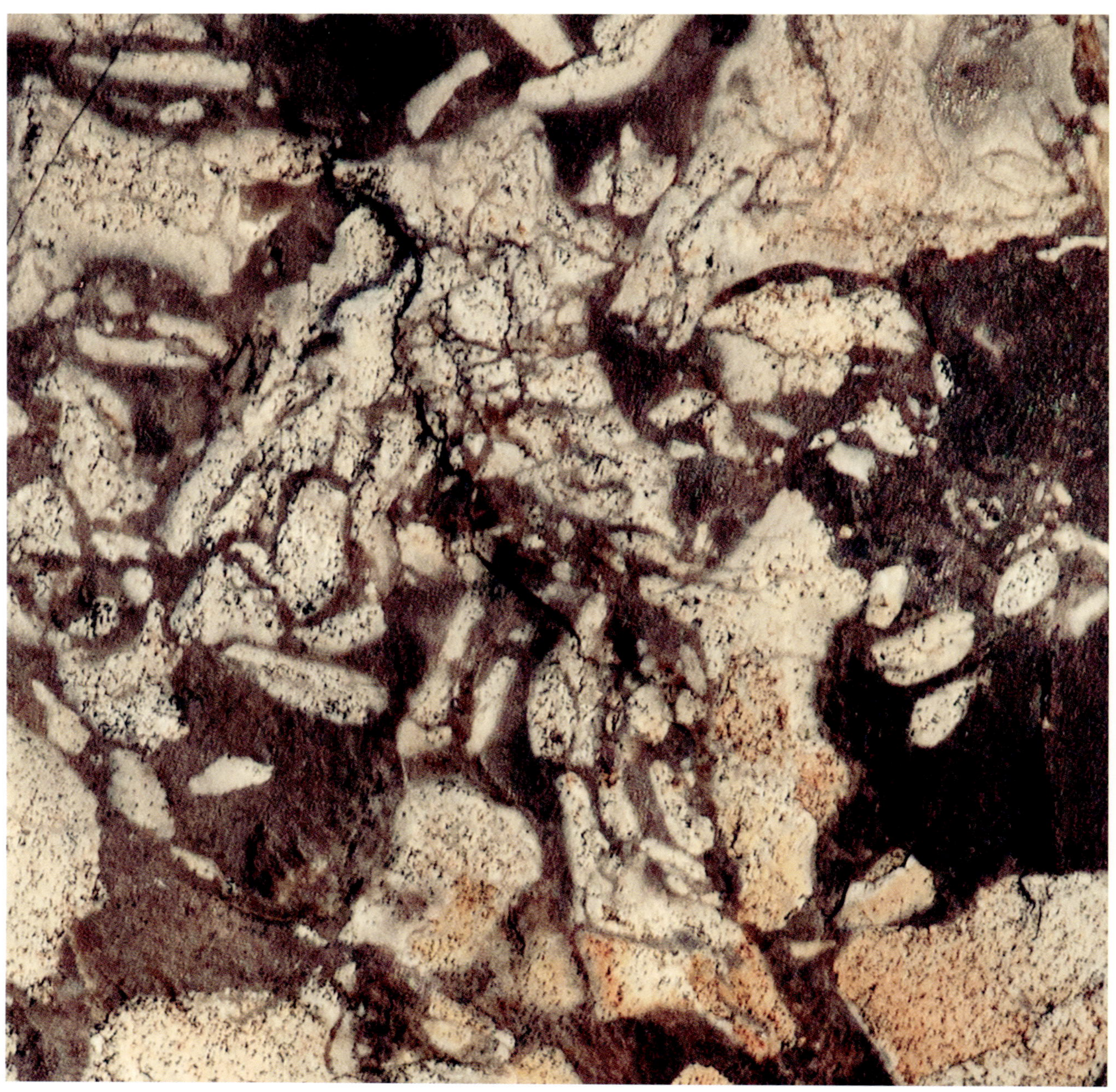

1. Thanks again to Stefan Nicolescu for the geology lesson.

The rocks that blanket the 918 firing zone in the South Hebron Hills have never moved much, but they are accustomed to cataclysmic changes.[1] Before we found them, long before the wheels of army jeeps tried to crush them, before people threw them at one another and before one group tried to confiscate the land on which they rest from the people already living there, these rocks were tested. It probably happened right where we found them.

The rocks are hydrothermal breccias of a variety of quartz called chalcedony (another is agate), its crystal size literally microscopic. They had once been country rocks: plain, homogeneous rocks that lay in this very spot. But the world around them had other plans. Hot liquid, loaded with minerals like a post-volcanic fluid containing dissolved silica infiltrated the country rocks and broke them up, dissolving their minerals like sugar dissolves in water. Because the rock was massively cooler than the fluid, which can be 200 degrees Celsius, the fluid temperature dropped and grabbed the wall of the conduit in which it flowed until it was unable to retain the minerals in solution anymore and silica crystals—quartz—precipitated out. It left a brown matrix, whitish, bluish angular "clasts," or fragments, and silica-loaded cement. The process lasted for minutes, maybe centuries, possibly thousands of years, depending on the speed of the flow. But in the end, the one-time country rocks bore the complex traces of the Earth-changing events that happened around and to them.

1.6 Masafer Yatta, South Hebron Hills, May 2018.

We're on the path to Susiya, we pass the tents and animal pens of Gawawis Foq.[1] They seem to have grown straight out of the rocks. A few scraggly trees, in bloom, are struggling to survive behind a wire fence. On the crest of the hill, two casuarina trees, mother and child, are standing guard, marking a boundary. Just beneath them is the entrance to a home, with its maze of ropes and loose wires and a wall of unmatched stones; also a satellite dish hopefully facing the stony wilderness.

1. In this book, we distinguish Palestinian Susiya from the Israeli settlement of Susya.

1.7 Gawawis Foq, South Hebron Hills, March 2015.

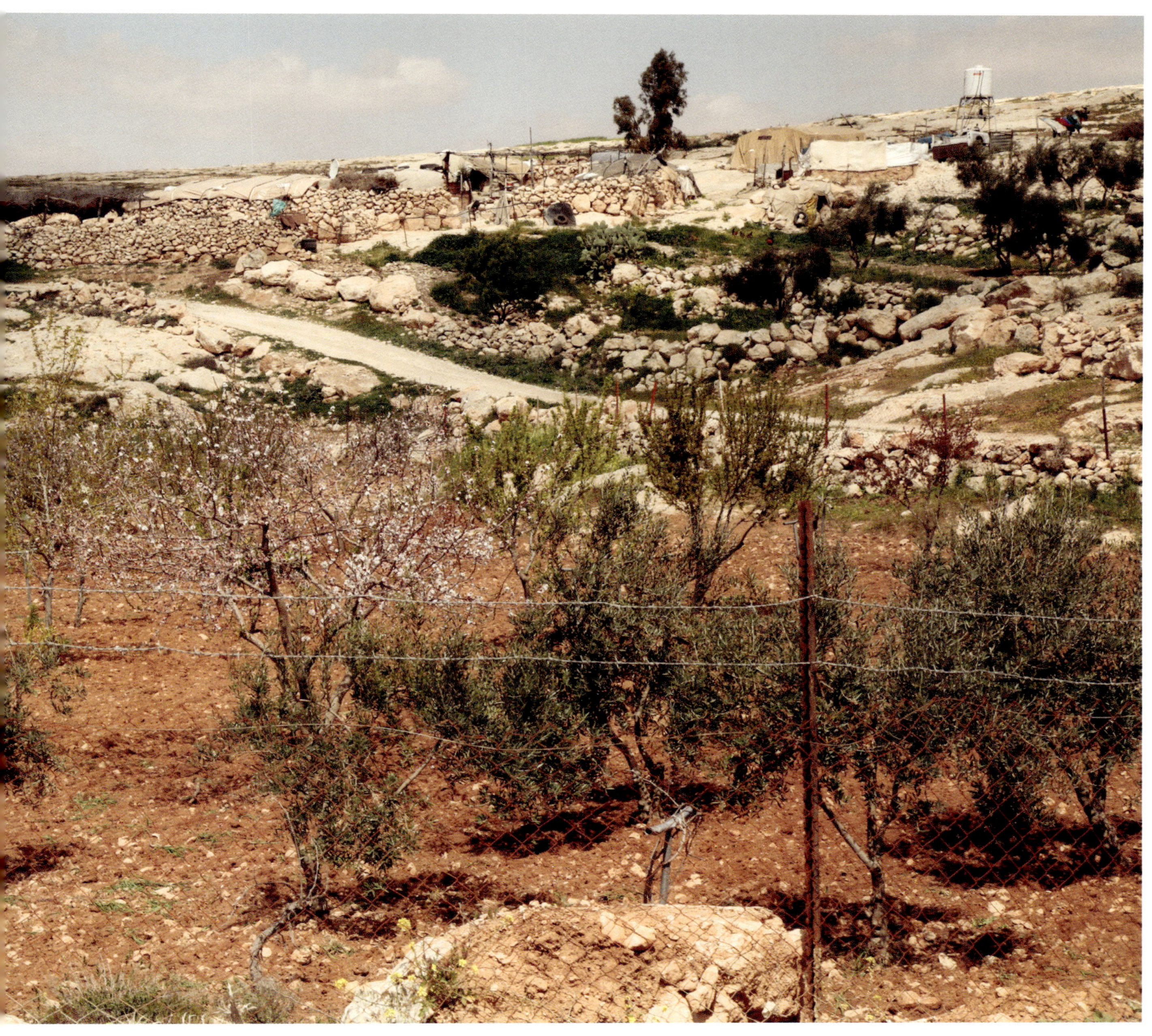

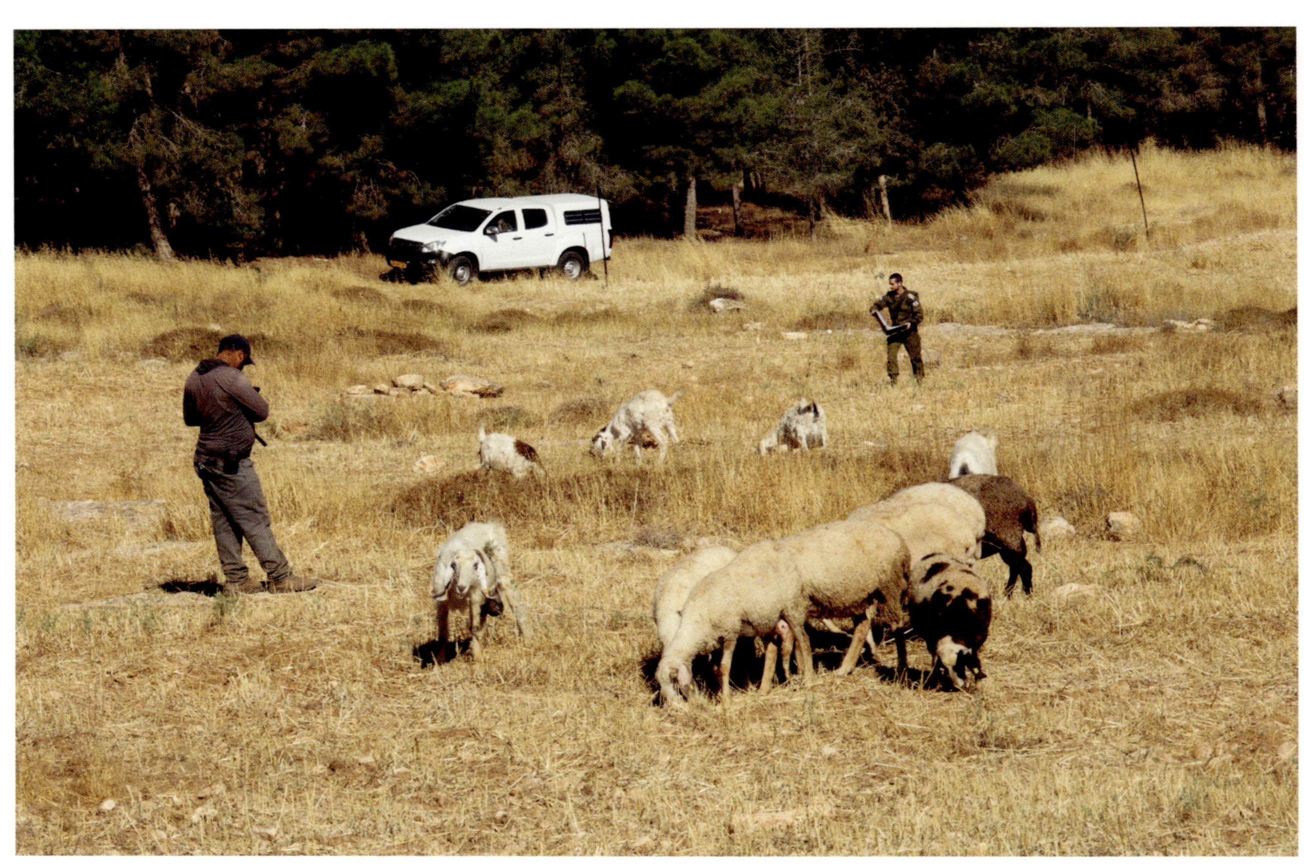

1.8 Wadi Sweid, South Hebron
Hills, July 2019.

After half an hour or so, we turn left to Wadi Sweid, which, like everywhere else, has its own story. It's privately owned Palestinian land that an Israeli settler tried to steal in order to plant a vineyard. That was in 2007–08. After long deliberations in the courts, the Palestinian claim to a fertile piece of the wadi was recognized, on condition that no Israelis, including activists, ever set foot in it. When the Palestinian farmers come to plow the field and sow it with seed, or to harvest, we watch over them from a slight distance. The Civil Administration destroyed the encroaching vineyard in 2011. From time to time, settlers have uprooted the hundreds of olive trees that the Palestinian owner planted; they have also burned the harvested stacks of barley in the field.

Suddenly there is wild grass, a flat meadow, good for grazing. Ahmad, from Gawawis, is there with his flock, like on most days. His world is made up mostly of sheep, grass, milk, and thorns, which is fine except when the soldiers come by to harass him, or when the settlers attack. The meadow tapers off into a small copse of trees where settlers lurk. They've put up a new, illegal outpost on the hill, now growing apace. The Susya settlers have their cemetery just past the good grazing ground, and there is a large plant nursery owned by the Israeli Hishtil company at the far end of the wadi.

Susiya is just a kilometer or two away, on a side road off the highway. First, we pass the Israeli settlement of Susya: stucco houses with red slanting roofs, crammed together, solar panels on some of them; water tanks on the flatter roofs; plenty of green; groves of trees; more rocks; a swimming pool.

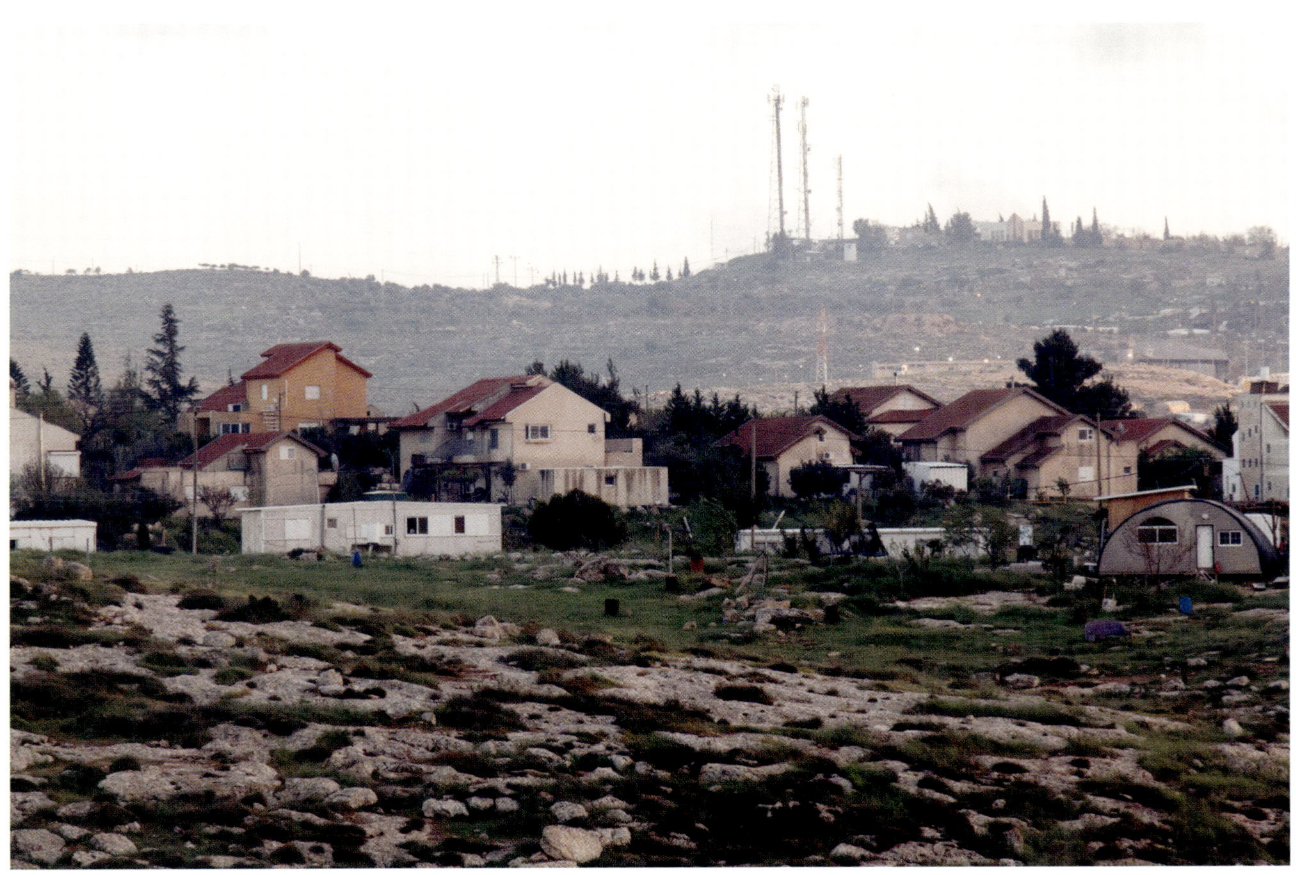

1.9 Susya, Israeli settlement, South Hebron Hills, March 2016.

Across the wadi, a few hundred yards away, is what is left of Palestinian Susiya. Tents, shacks, a few still usable caves, thorny bushes, lonely olive trees, improvised roofs made of old tires, a water tower, some solar panels, twined tubes and pipes, a few terraced gardens with potted plants, the big meeting tent, a couple of outhouses, a Palestinian flag, all on top of the silent symphony of stone. We are walking on stone. Inscribed on a wall: *Susya Will Not Die*. On another wall, in English: *Susya 4Ever*. Recently, they've upgraded the children's playground with slides and swings, thereby inviting a vicious attack by the Israeli Susya settlers, which was not long in coming.

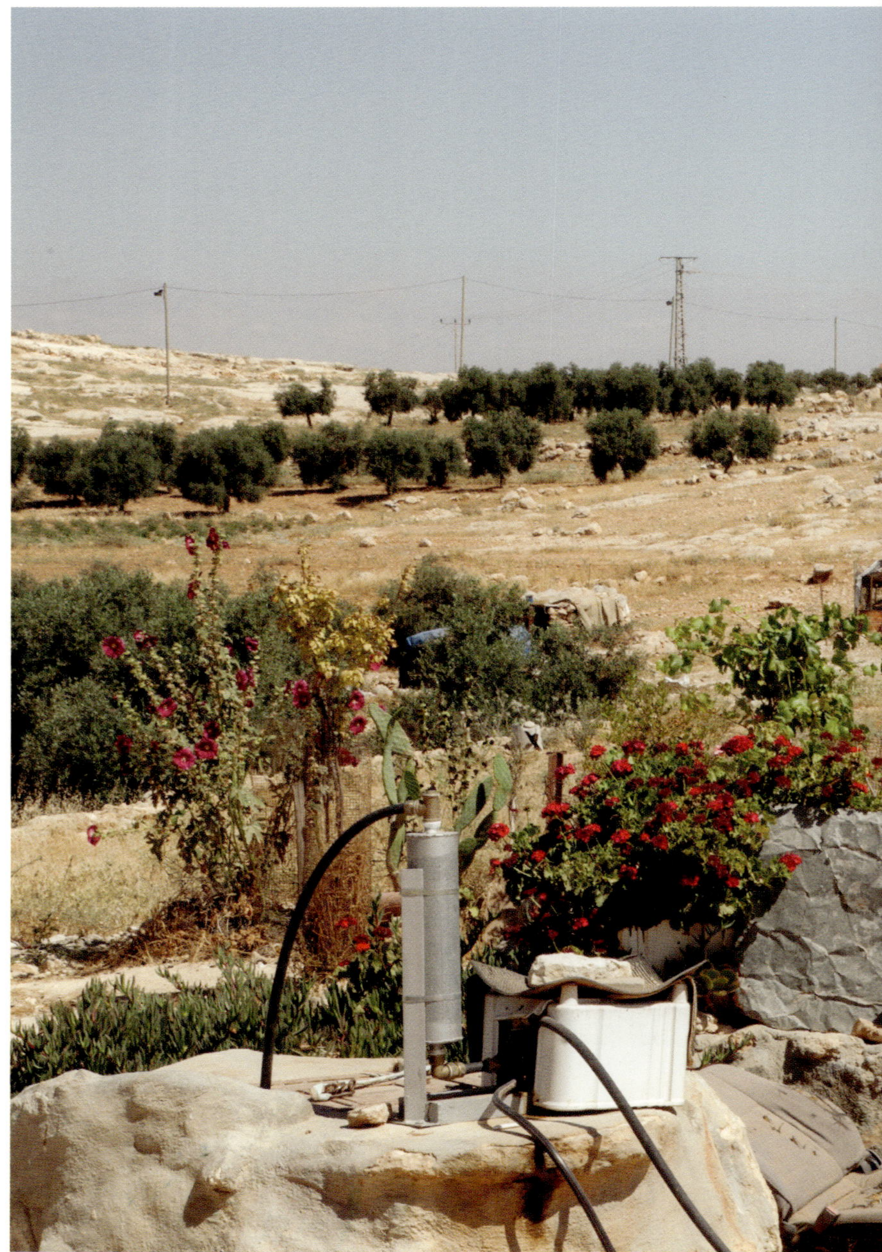

1.10 Palestinian Susiya, South Hebron Hills, June 2015.

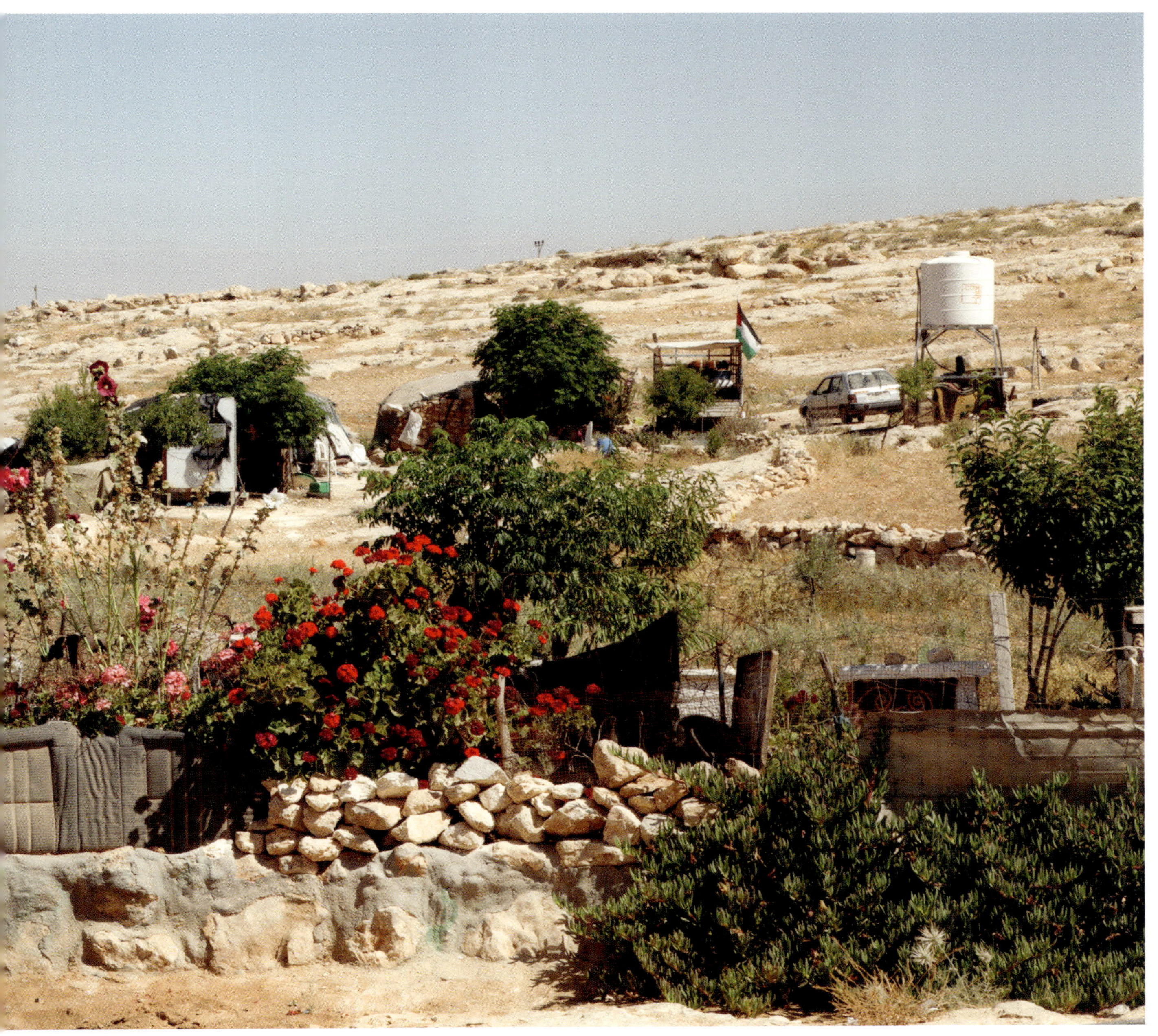

The grazing grounds have nearly all been stolen. Some 400 souls are hanging on after repeated demolitions and expulsions. Their original homes were just down the road on the archaeological site now known as ancient Susiya, with its Second-Temple synagogue and other remains. The State drove the Palestinians from those homes; they could, in theory, visit them today if they were prepared to buy an entrance ticket, like other tourists.

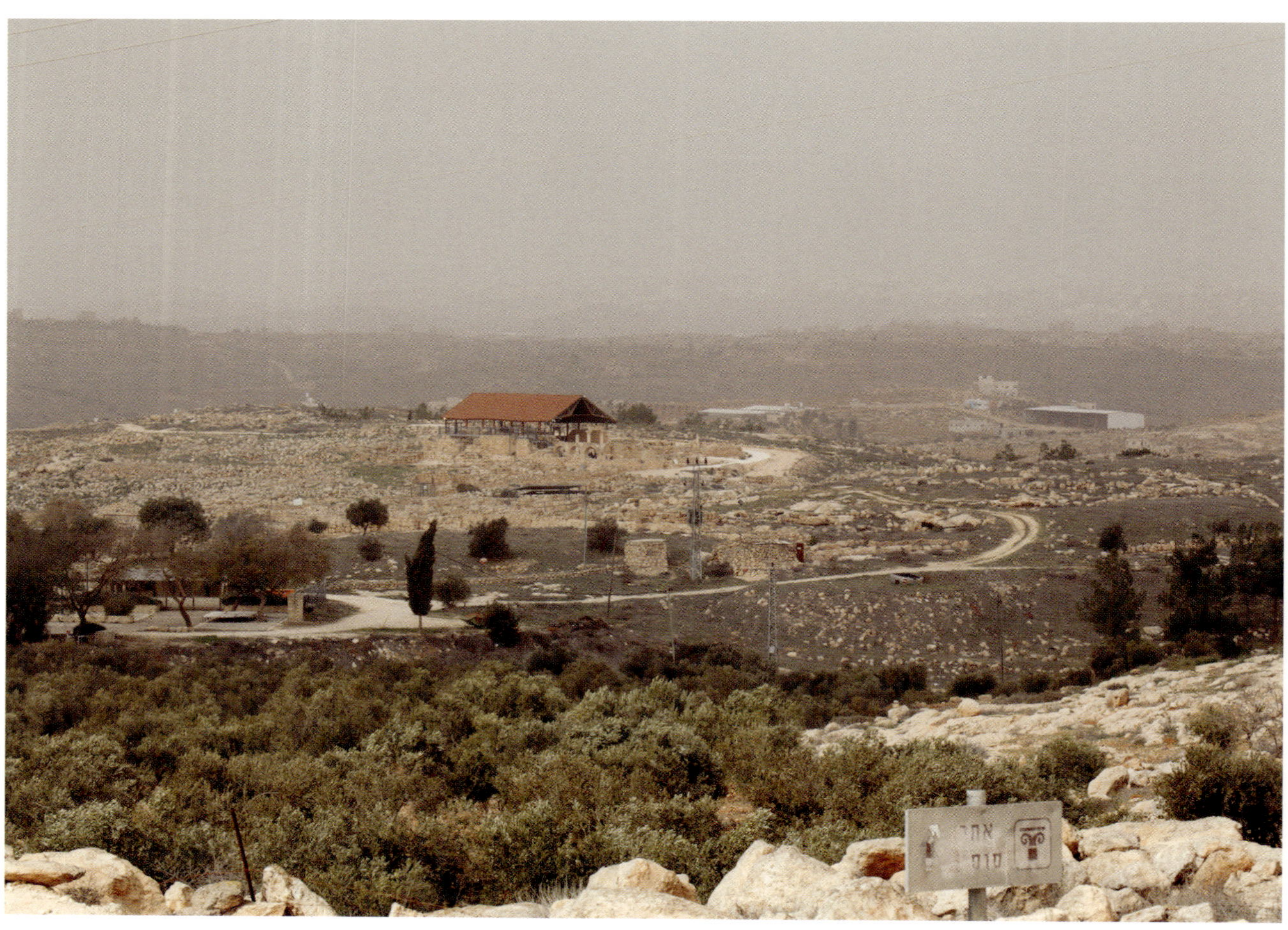

1.11 Ancient Susiya, South Hebron Hills, February 2022.

1.12 Susiya, March 2016.

1.13 (next) Susiya, February 2022.

All around the village are the wide open spaces of hills and sky and rock, the dusty, golden slopes merging with one another in the distance, the heavens reaching down to touch them.

Home.

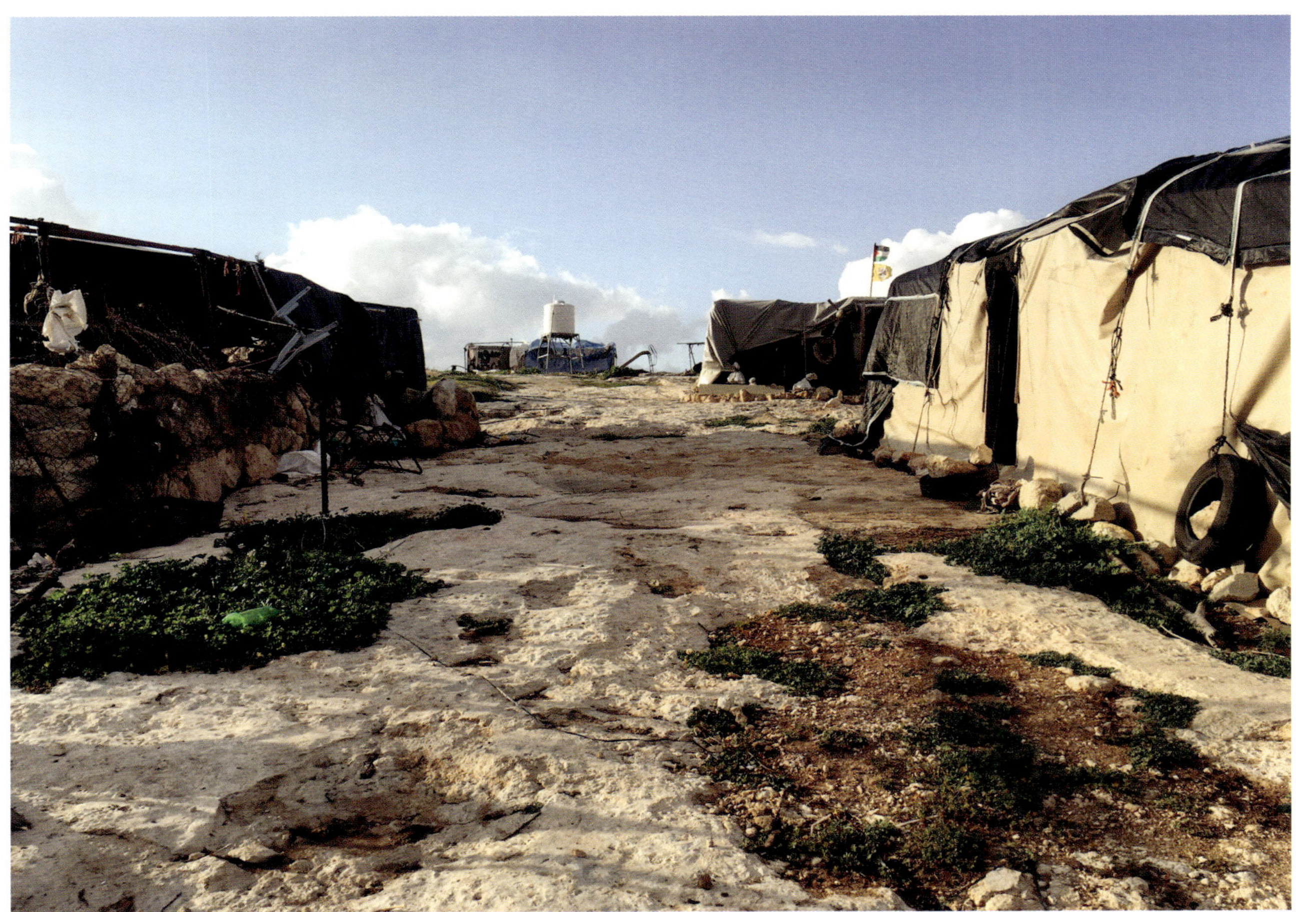

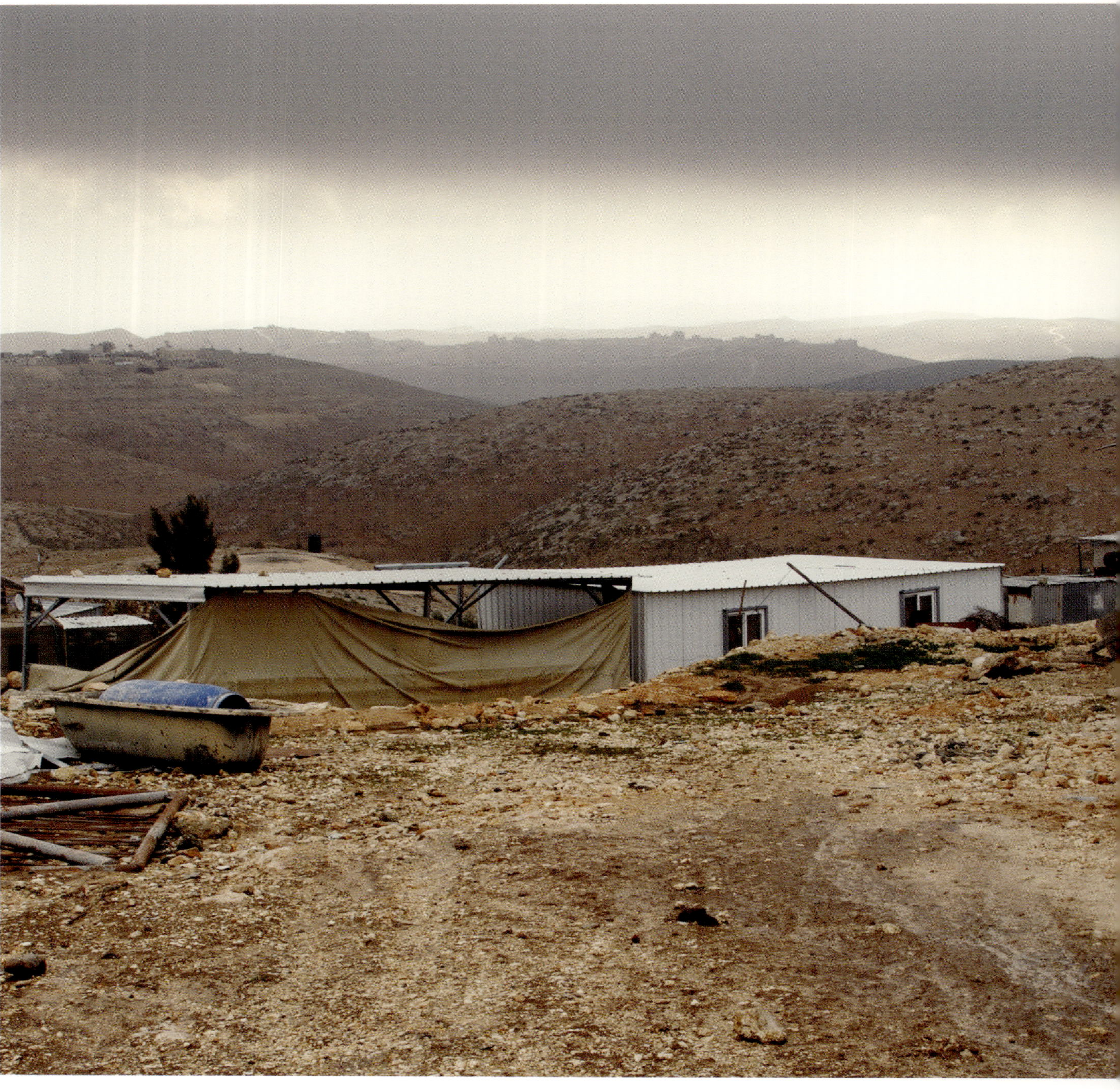

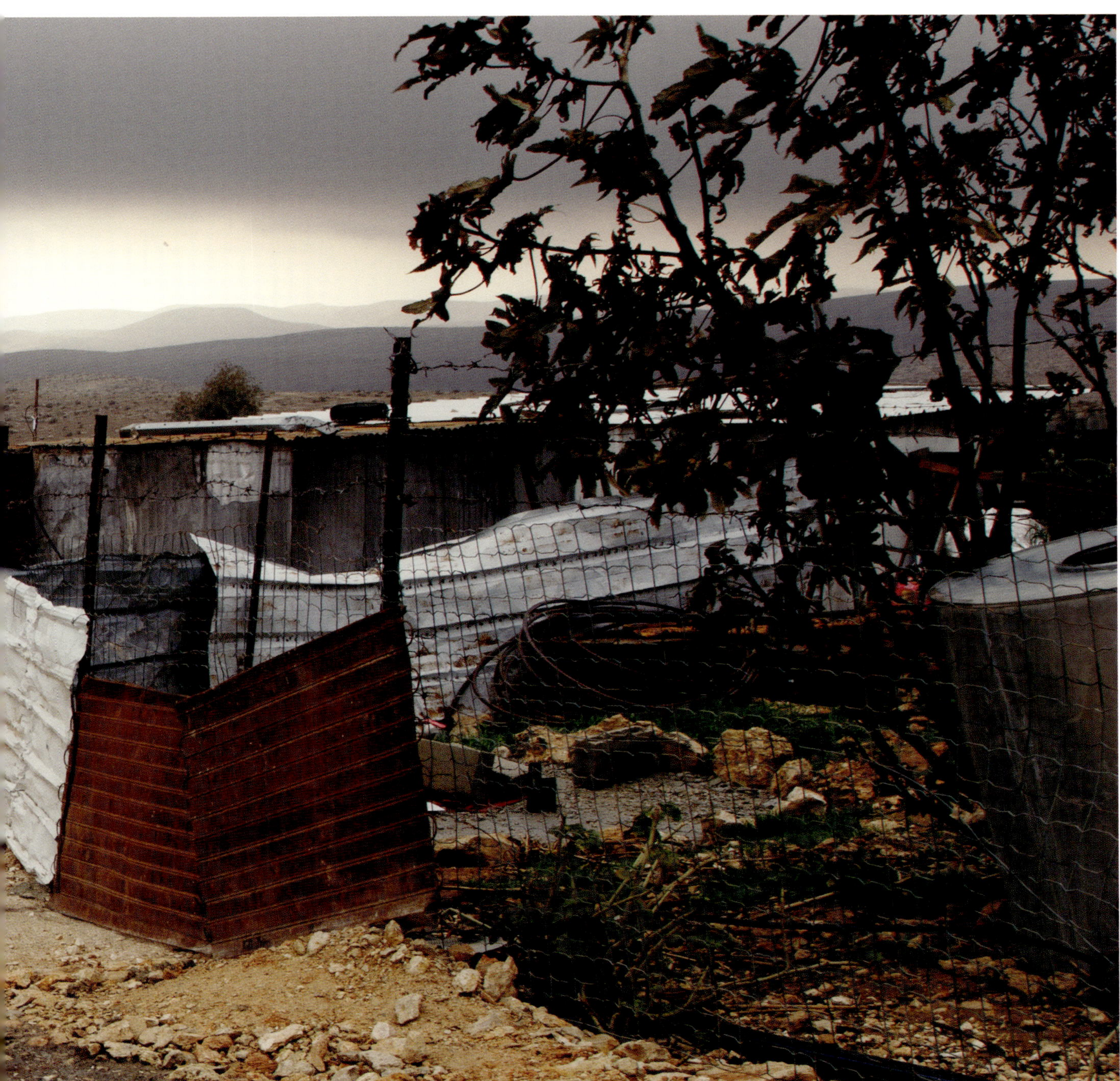

Laḥza: Al-ʻAuja

There is always the moment before.
The moment the soldiers emerge on the hilltop.
Before: our friend, the red sheep, searching for thorns.
Two activists guarding the herd. ʻAuja: where, in theory,
there was an agreement with the army that the shepherds
could graze on their land.

Then the moment after: the soldiers have announced
a Closed Military Zone. The lieutenant says: "I'm new
down here, just a month and a half. I heard about the
agreement, but I'm not much interested in that. I'm a
field soldier. I deal with reality. My job is to carry out
my orders."

Arik says to all of them: "I know you have your orders.
I'm not yet asking you to disobey them. But think about
what you are doing. Just think for yourselves, for a
minute or two. Remember that you are also citizens, and
sometimes you go home. Whatever you do is between you
and yourself or between you and your god."

Then a surprise. One of the privates says, "Maybe when I
get home I'll think about it."

But for now, shepherds, herds, activists are driven out.

Again.

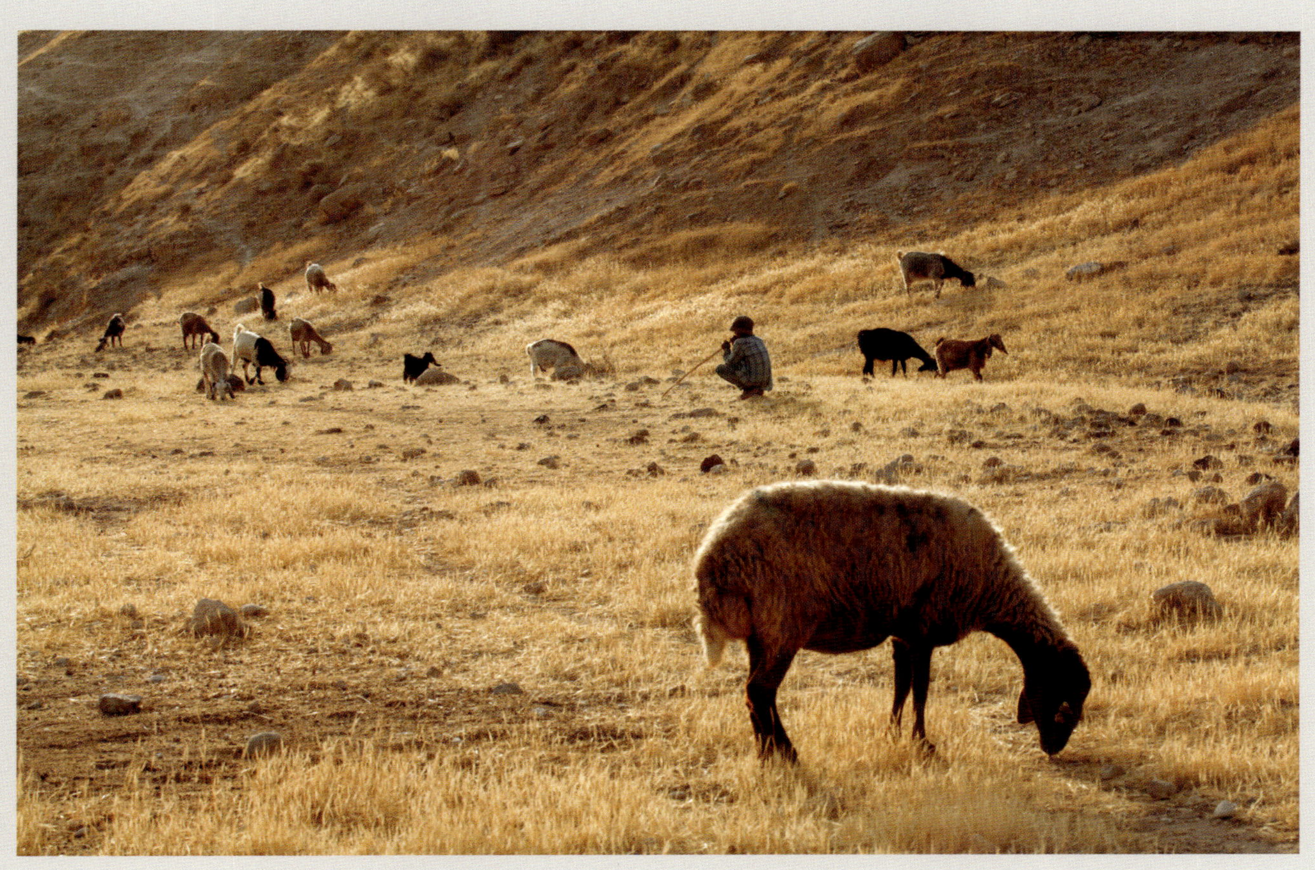

L.1 ‘Auja, July 2017.

2.1 ‘Ein ar-Rashash,
December 2018.

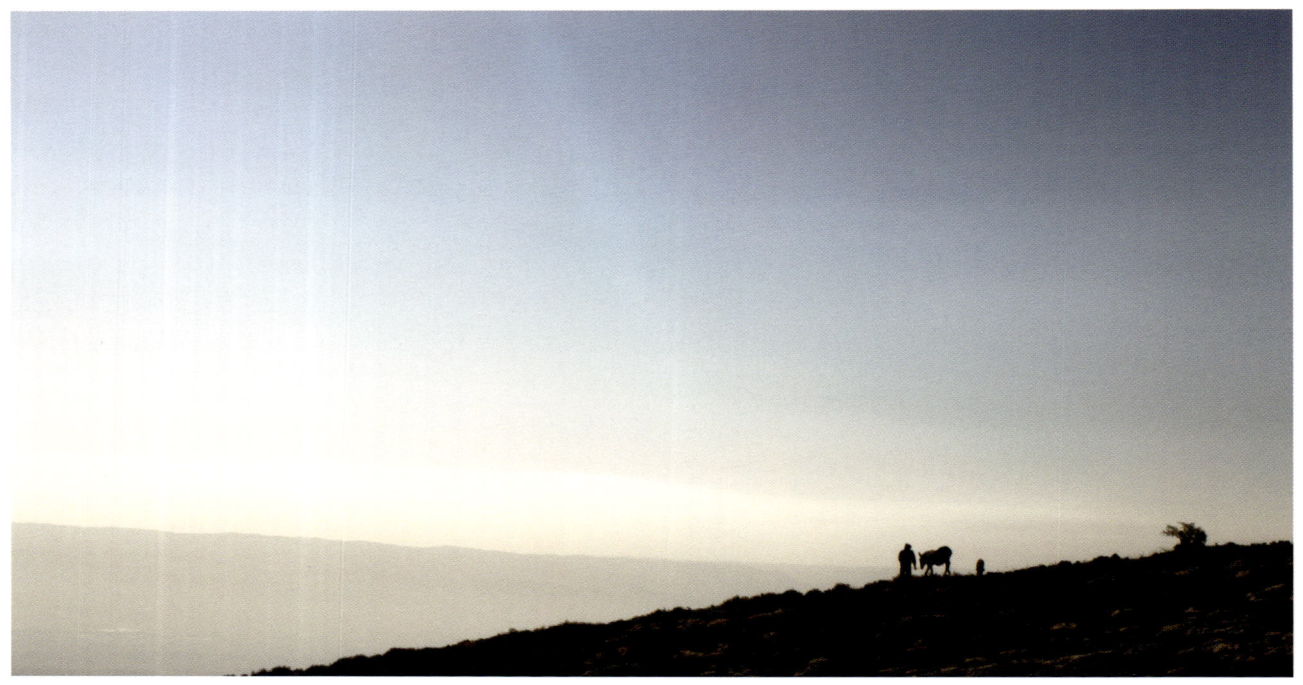

2.

Attack

There was the white gossamer light swirling upward from the valley and the liquid radiance pouring down from above. Early morning, white and blue. “And God said, Let there be a partition within the water, and let it divide water from water. So he made the partition and divided the lower from the upper waters, and he called it heaven.” We were watching the mingling of the lower and the upper lights and wondering at what point any particular photon might find itself either above or below, and know it, which seemed to be something confusing and playful that I know from inside.

And then they came.

"They" might be soldiers, trudging down from the hills in their boots with guns,

2.2 Umm al-Amad, March 2018.

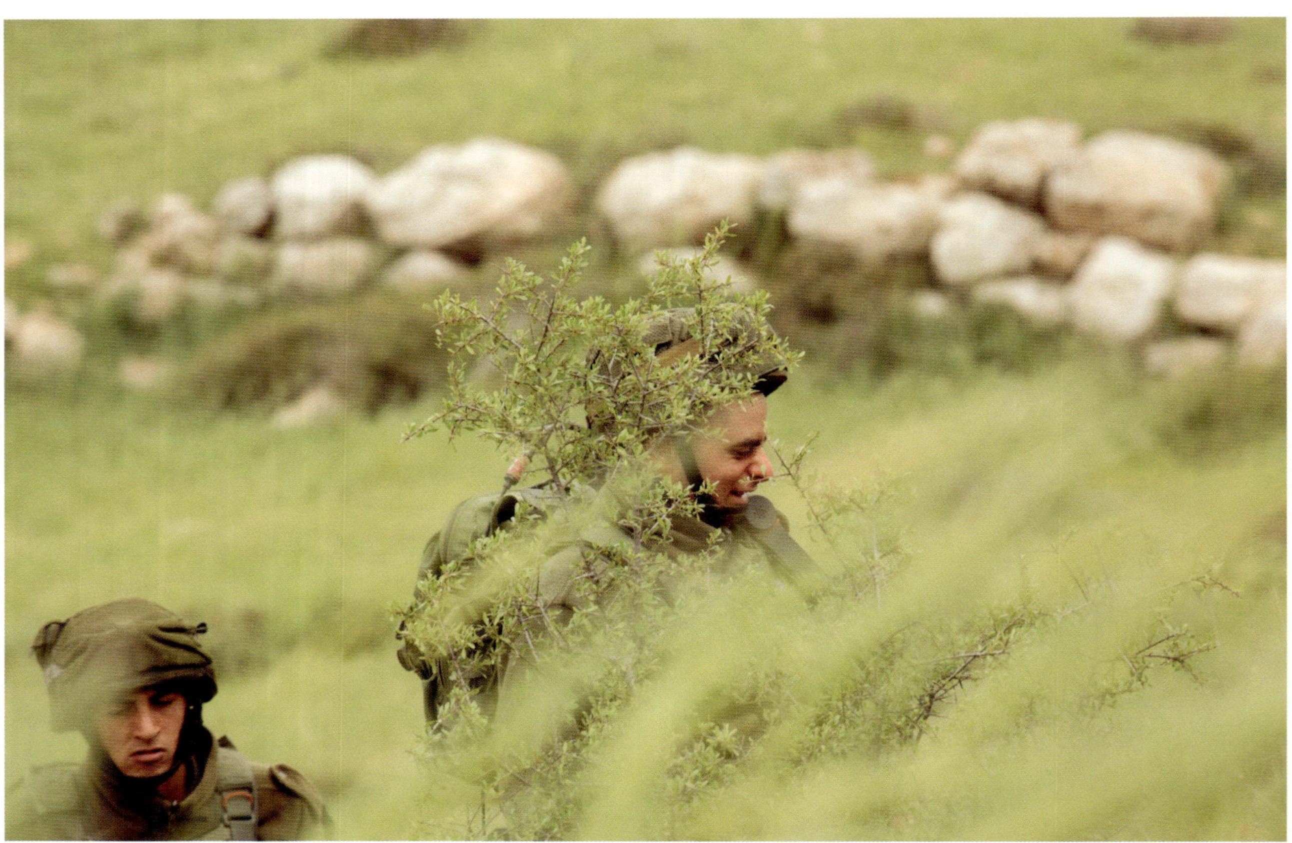

a settler bringing his own flock of troubled teenagers and the herd of sheep he cobbled together to help him expel Palestinian flocks,

2.3 ‘Ein ar-Rashash, December 2018.

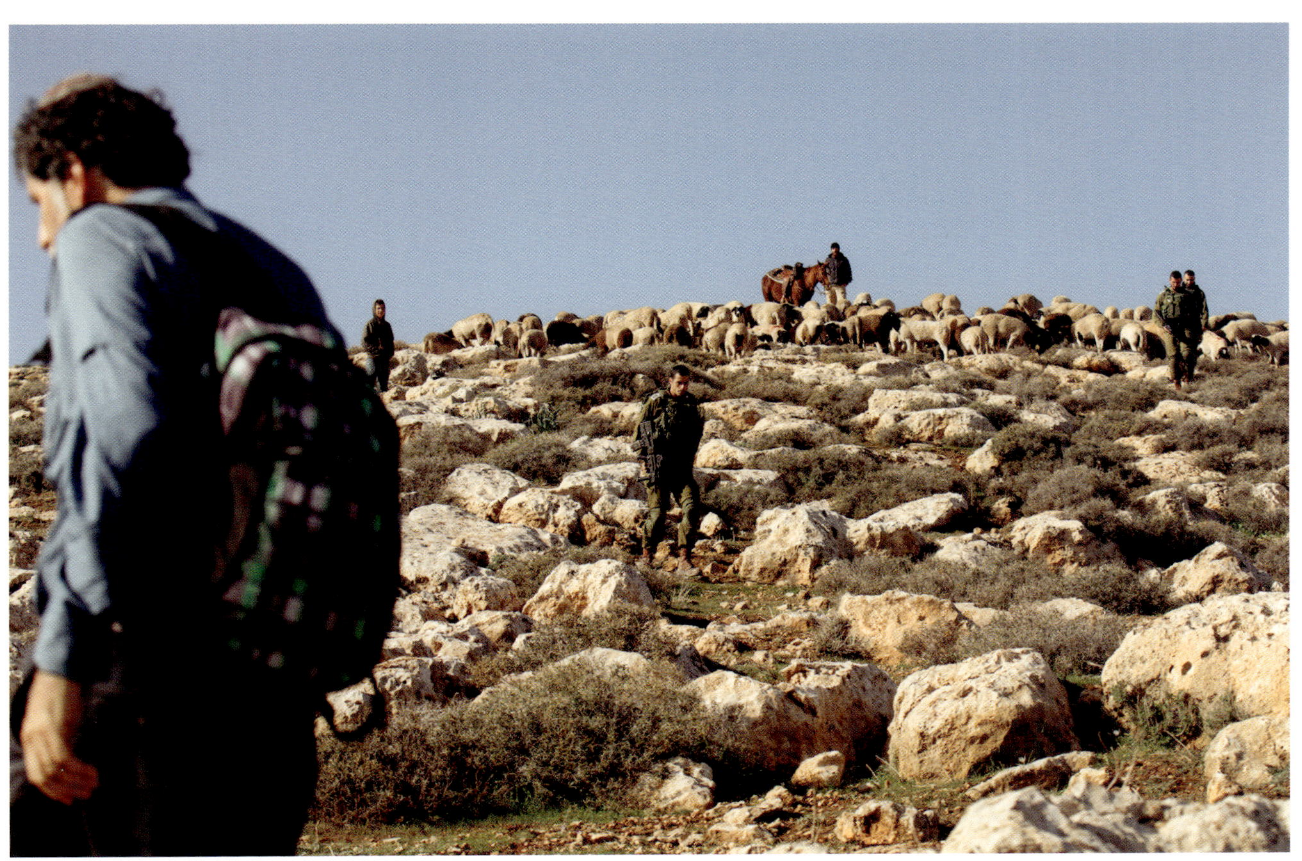

a settler or two throwing stones or running into the herd, scaring the animals,

2.4 ‘Ein ar-Rashash, December 2018.

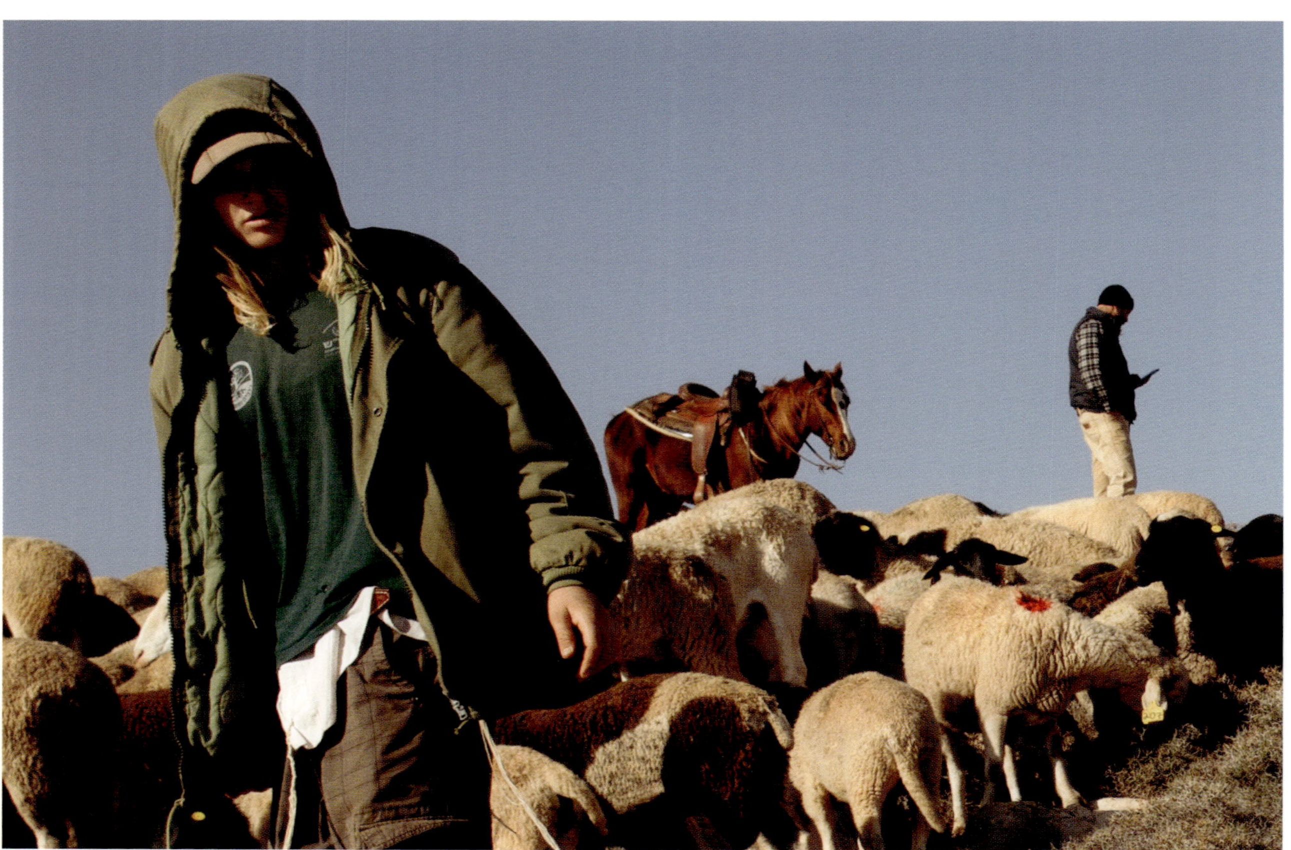

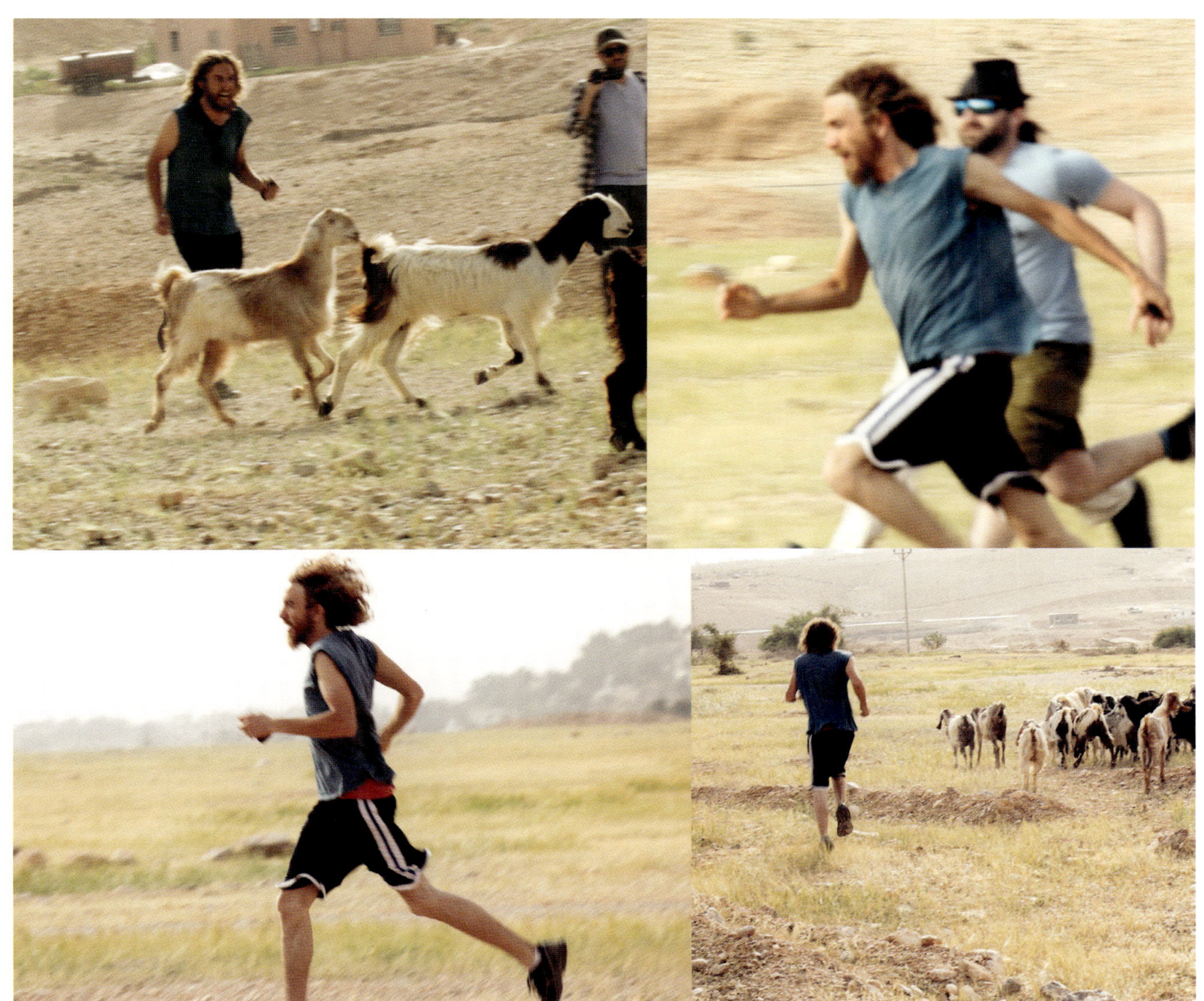

2.5 a–d Nu'eima, March 2018.

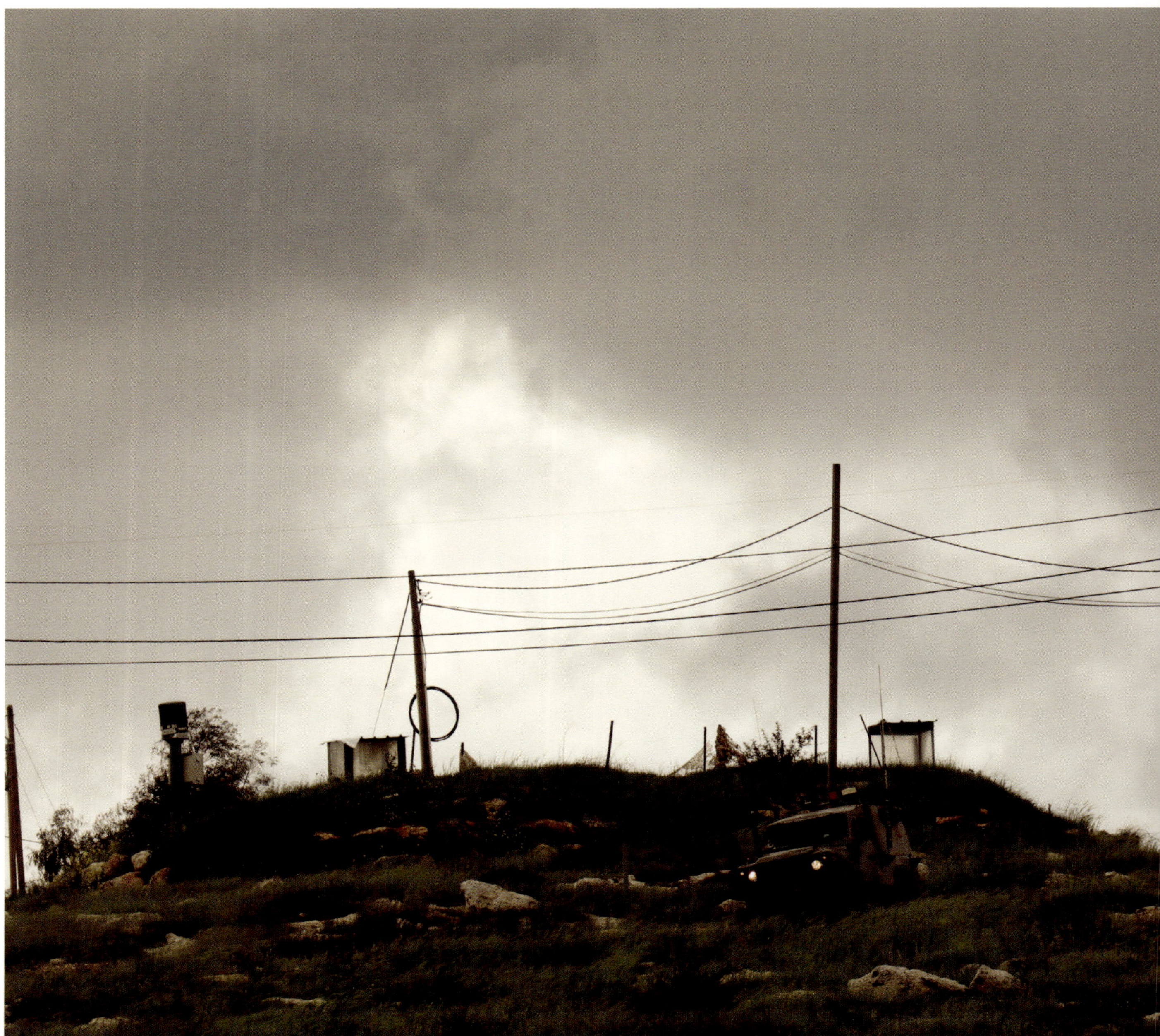

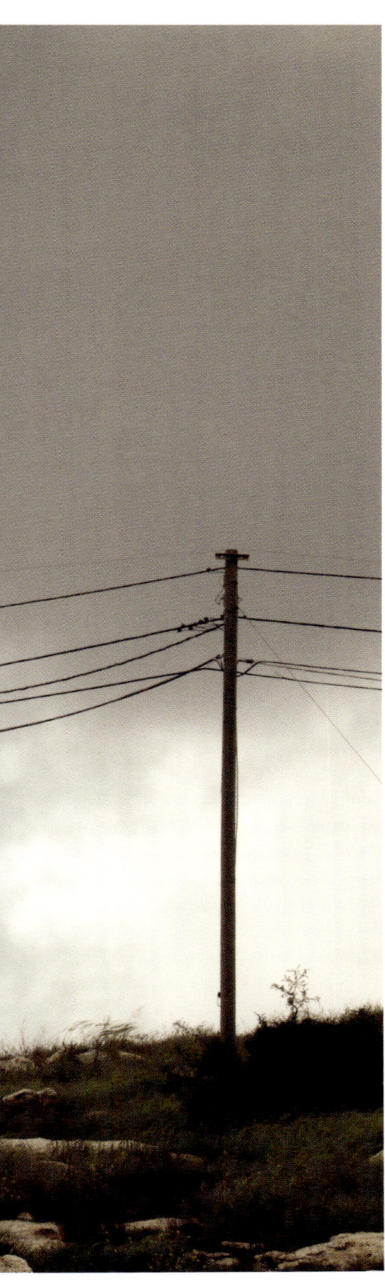

or an army jeep.

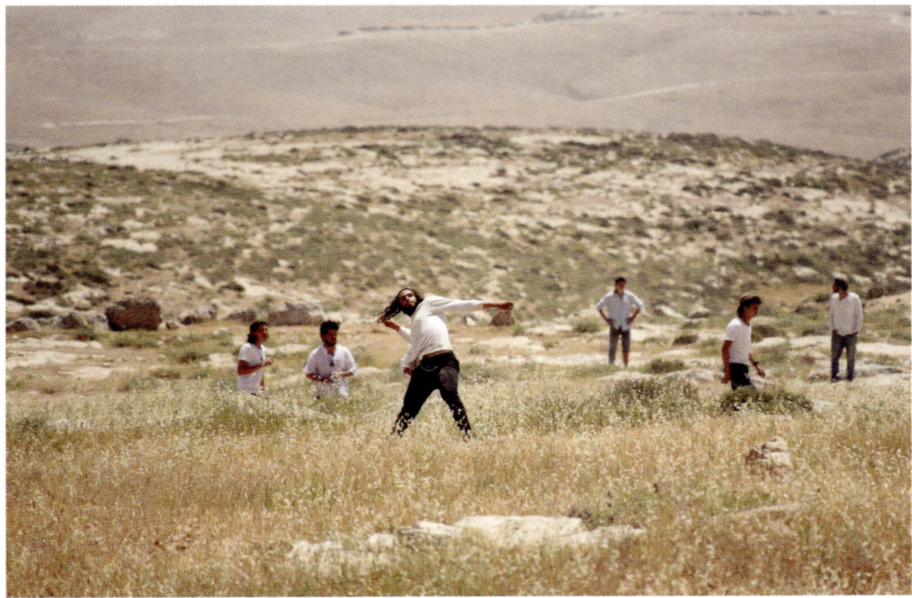

Then the rocks. And it tends to escalate. One lives with the dread of imminent attack. The fear of being hurt, or killed, and inevitably humiliated, reduced to impotence. There is almost never justice, or any form of punishment, for marauding settlers or violent soldiers.

2.6 Umm al-Amad, March 2019.

2.7 Homra, South Hebron Hills, April 2021.
Photograph: Michal Hai.

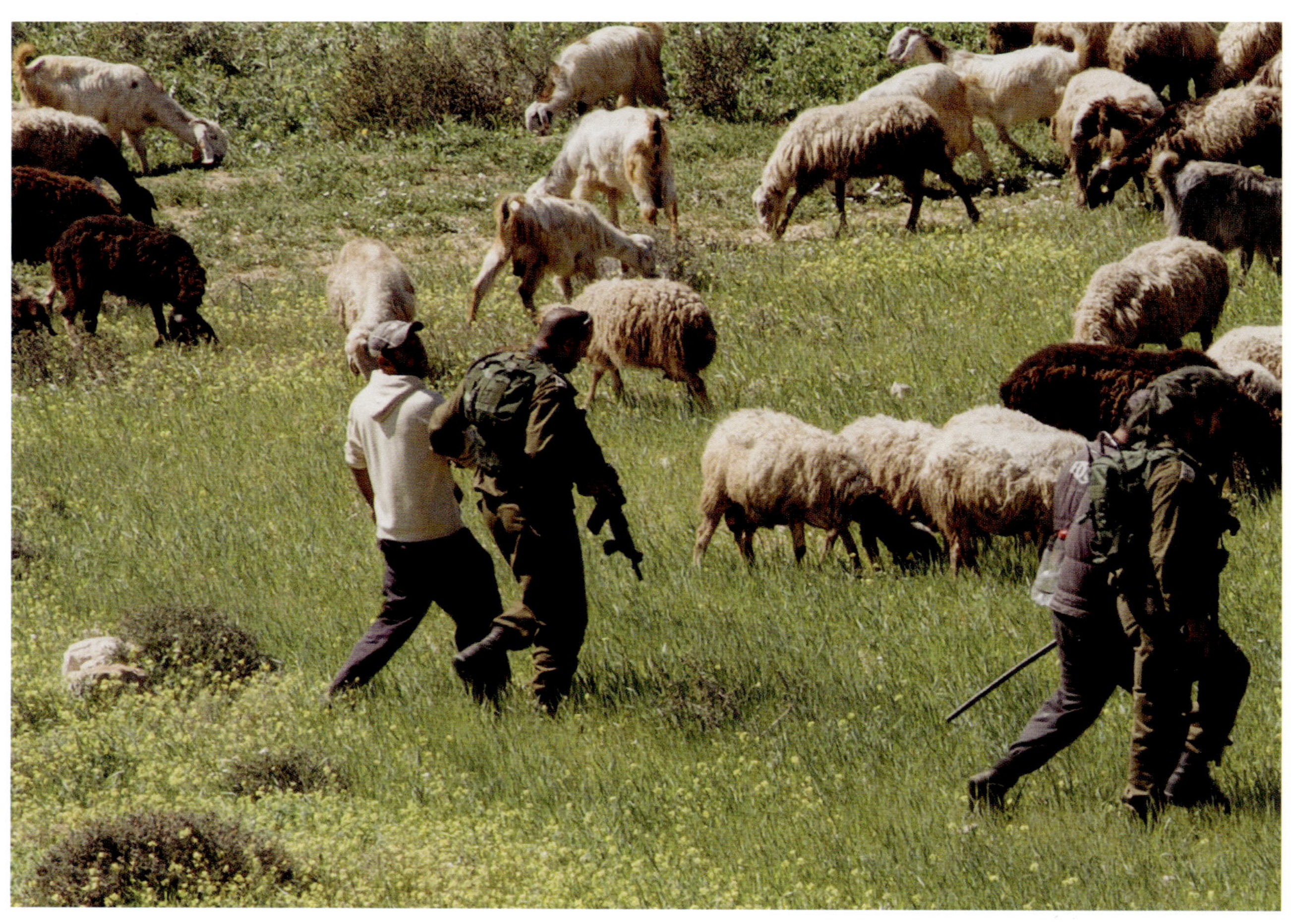

2.8 Zanuta, South Hebron Hills,
March 2015.

Zanuta, March 20, 2021. Nabil asks us if we will pay for bail if one of the shepherds gets arrested today.

It can happen at any moment. So they're always on edge, and too scared to go out alone with their flocks. Mhammed asks if we could also come on weekdays. Along with everything else, the settlers now harass them with drones, which drive the sheep crazy, scattering them over the hills.

These hills are still green after the winter rains, but the green won't last. Soon the world will turn yellow, and the sheep will have to make do with the silver-gray thorns. Today they ate their fill.

Five hours in the fragrant sunlight. That South Hebron kind of bitter-sweet happiness. Every moment of safety, of natural grace, every moment free from soldiers and settlers, is a miracle. The Muslims say that Allah creates the world anew literally second by second; time is made up of those always singular and fleeting flashes, *anat*, each one of them a wonder, *i'jaz*. If it were not for Allah's compassionate urge to create, our universe would vanish into emptiness even before I can finish this sentence. Today there was an infinity of *anat*. Perhaps it's something that sheep know.

2.9 (next) Zanuta, March 2015.

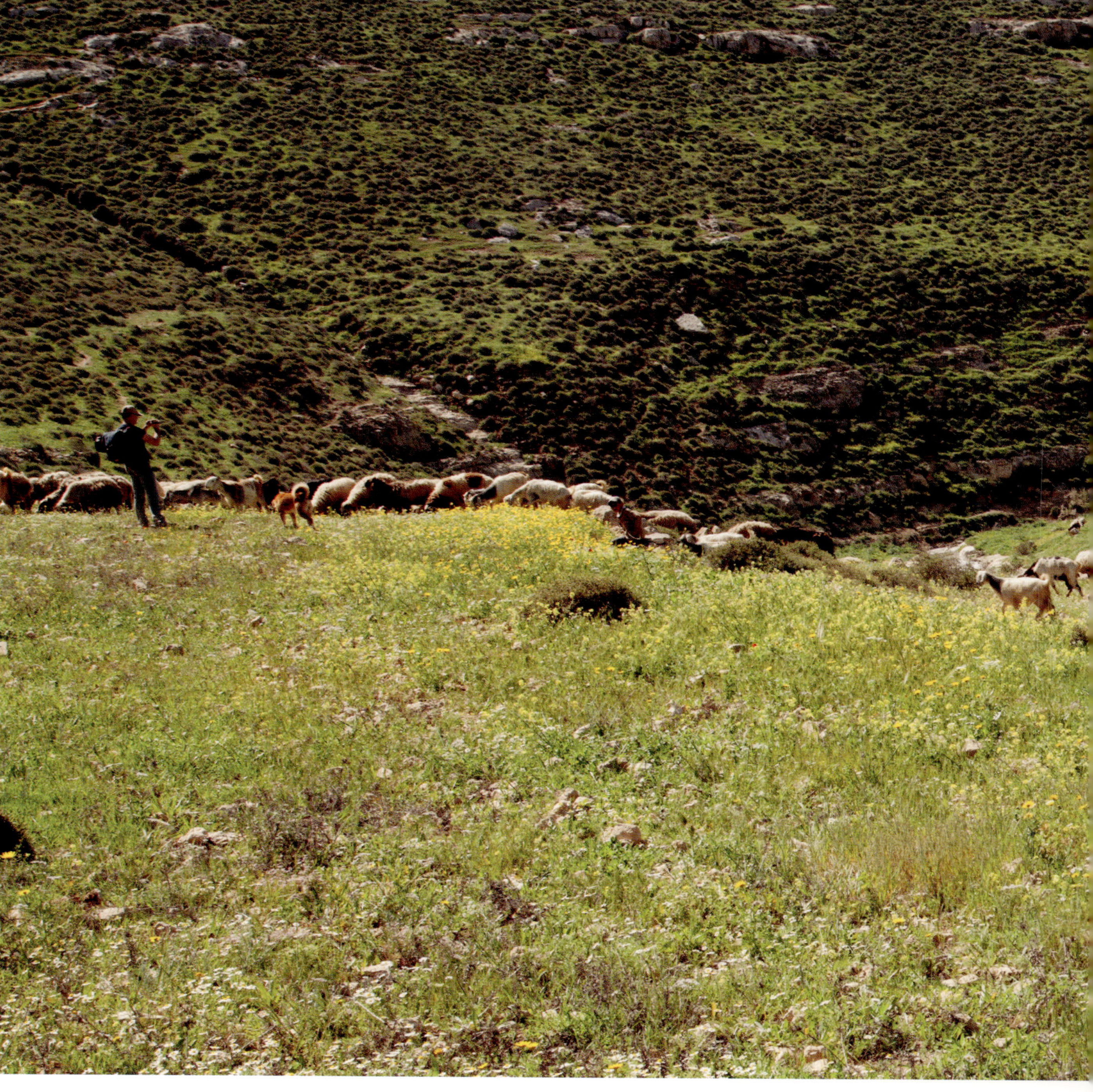

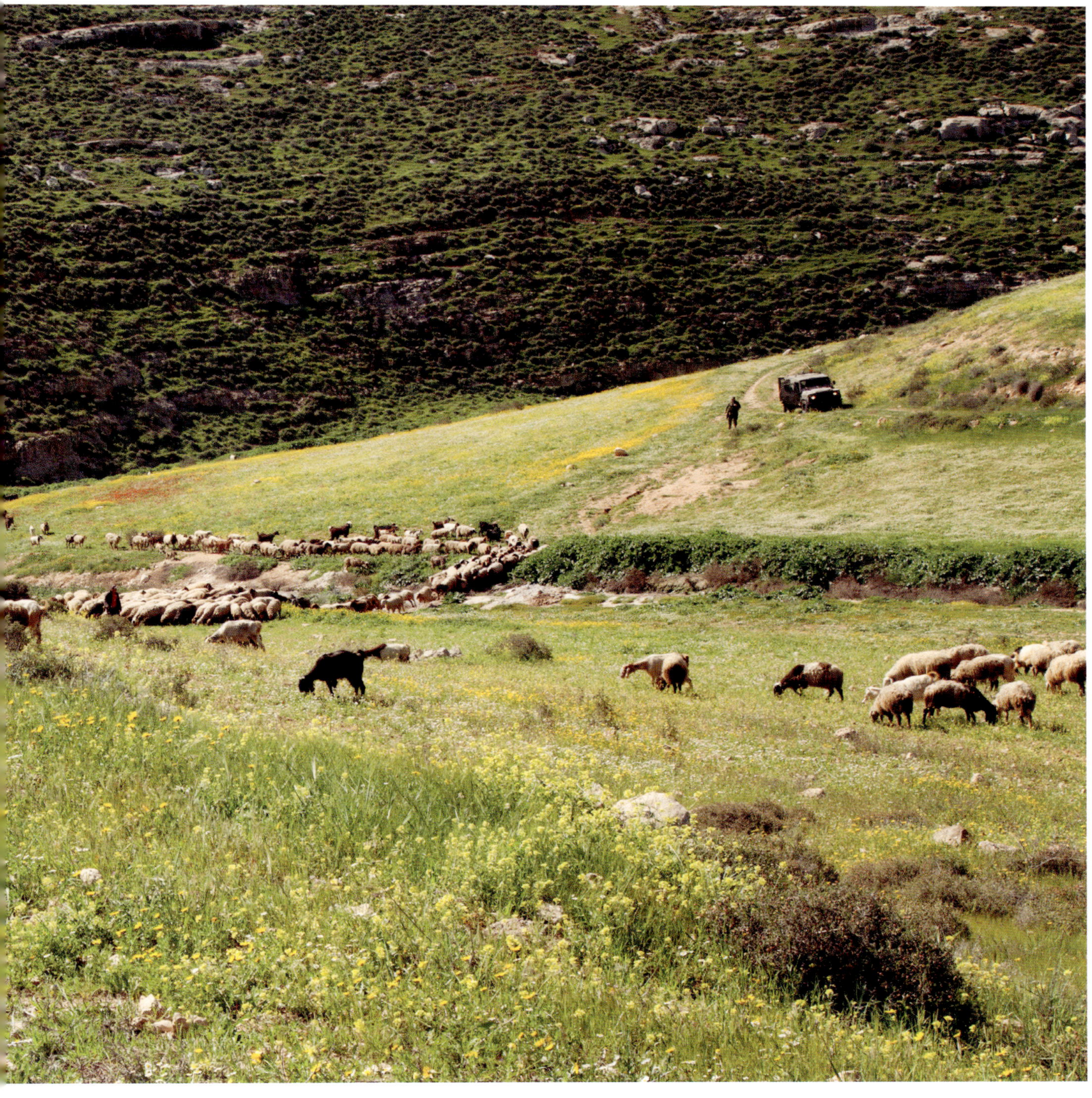

Laḥza: Morning Tea

Always surprised that pure light has taste.
It's not just any light. Never a single defined
color. A little dusty, like dawn
in the desert.

You pour this light out of a pot, usually one
blackened by a thousand fires. As it pours, you
can also hear the light speaking. It says
different things, depending on who is listening.

Some quite matter-of-fact, like Shob al-yom,
"it's hot today" (and therefore time for tea).
Others more practical, like Allah yihfazak,
"may God care for you", or a little sad, like Wen
hal ghebe, "Where (the hell) have you been?"

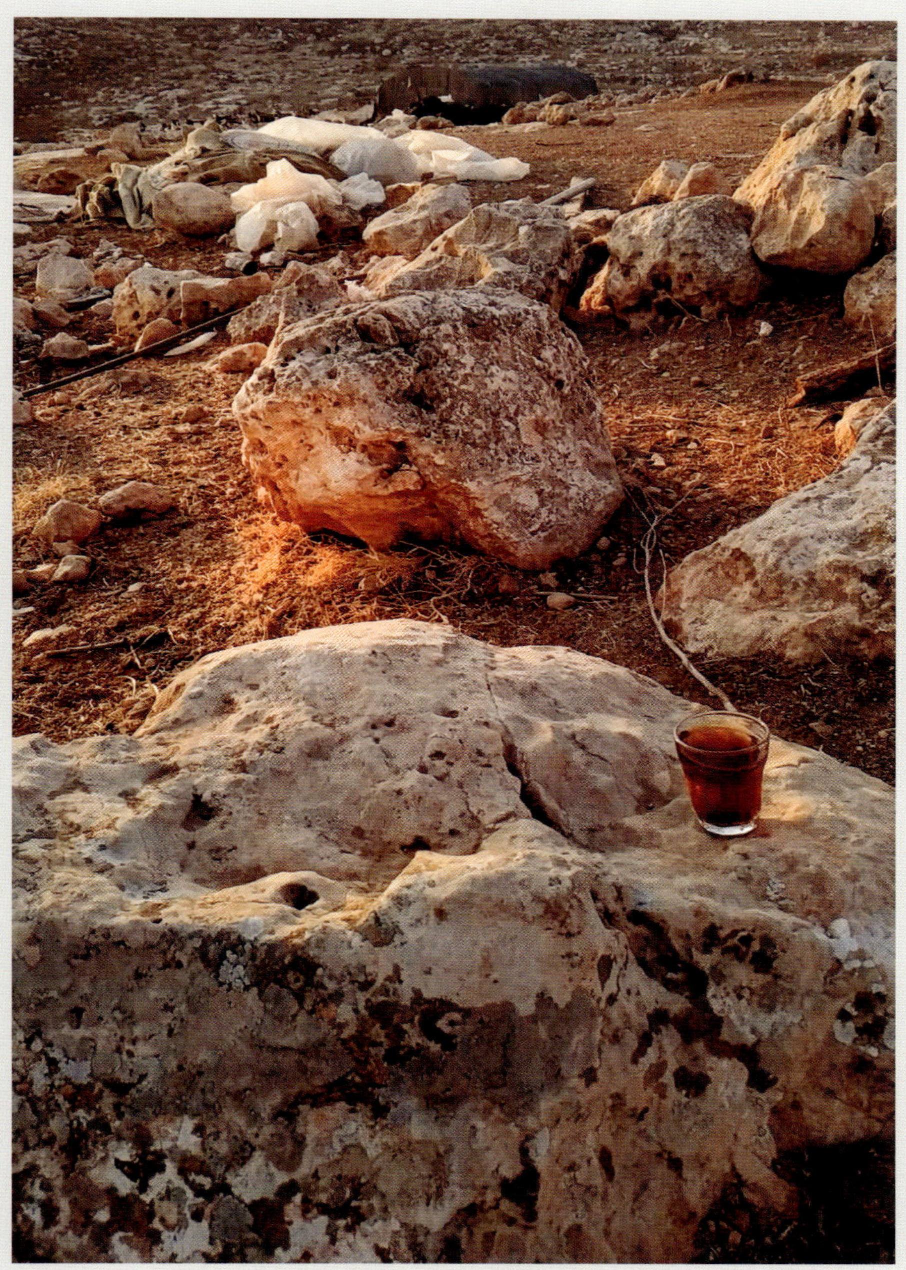

L.2 ‘Ein ar-Rashash,
November 2019.
Photograph: David Shulman

3.1 Susiya, July 2019.
3.2 Susiya, March 2016.

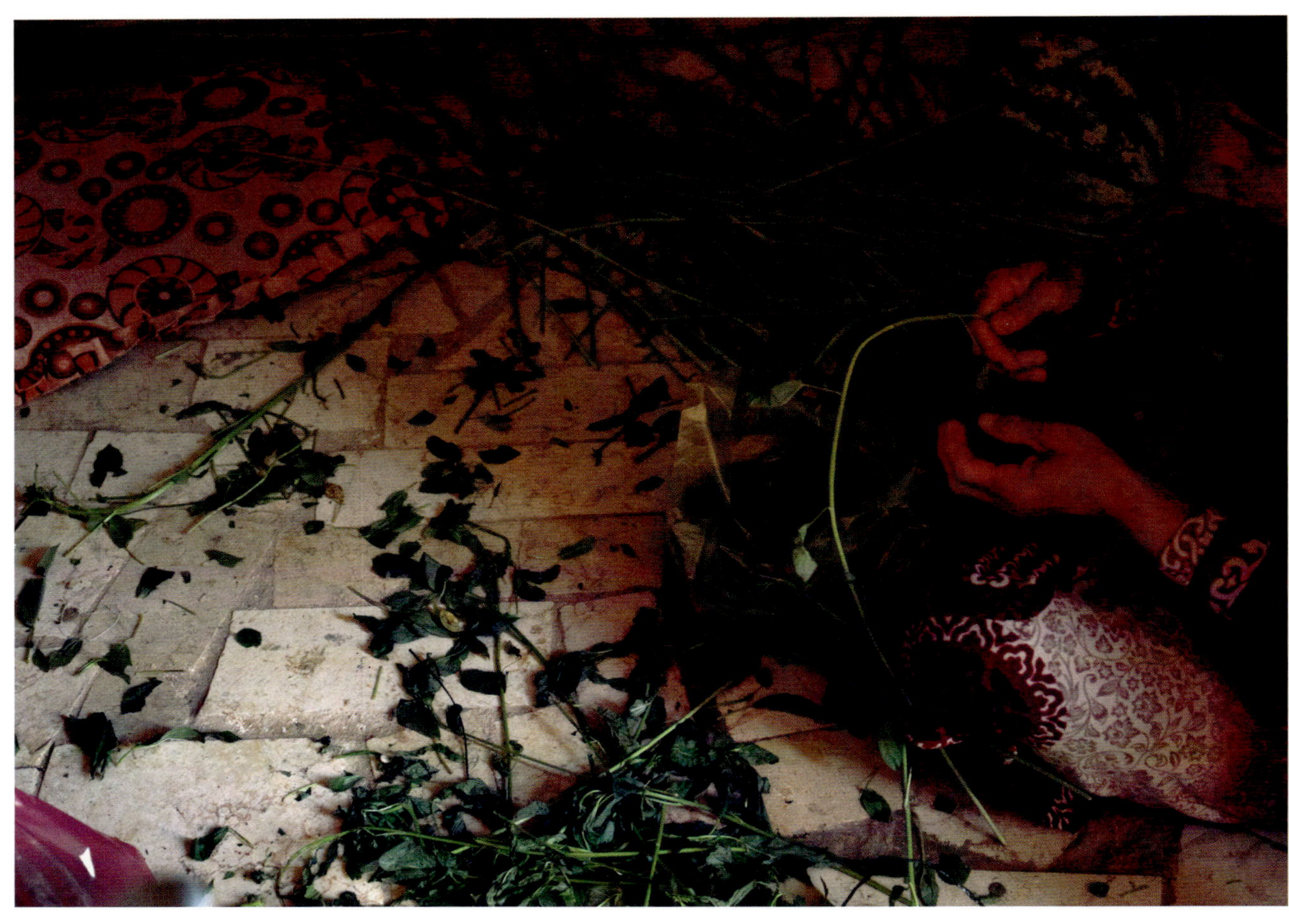

3.

Following Fatma

Do you teach about our lives here? Do you teach about this at your university?

I'm not qualified to teach about your lives, Fatma. I can make a few photographs, show you preparing molokhia, *or baking in a communal oven. I could photograph the pigeon roost where the children love to climb.*

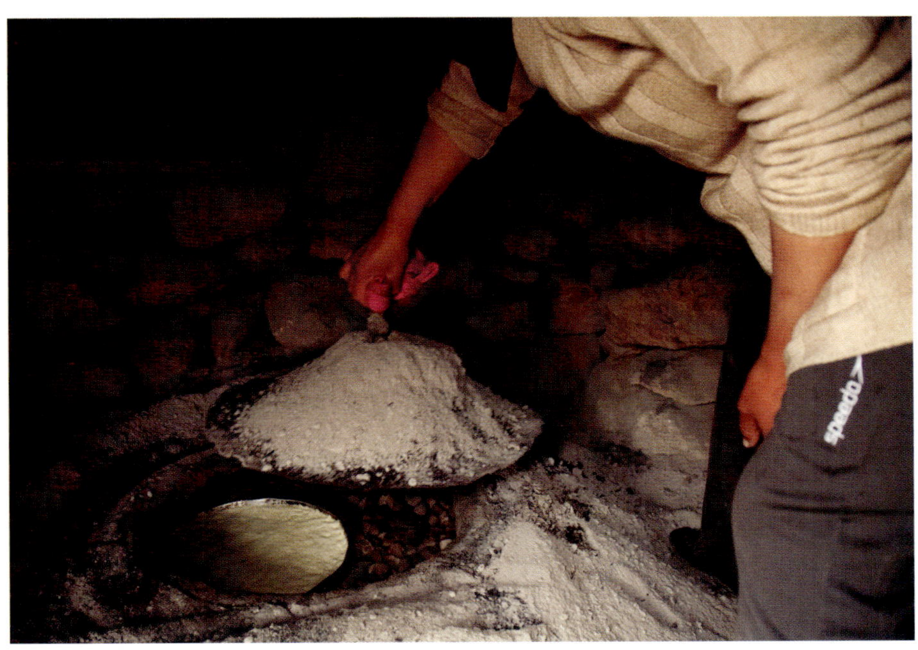

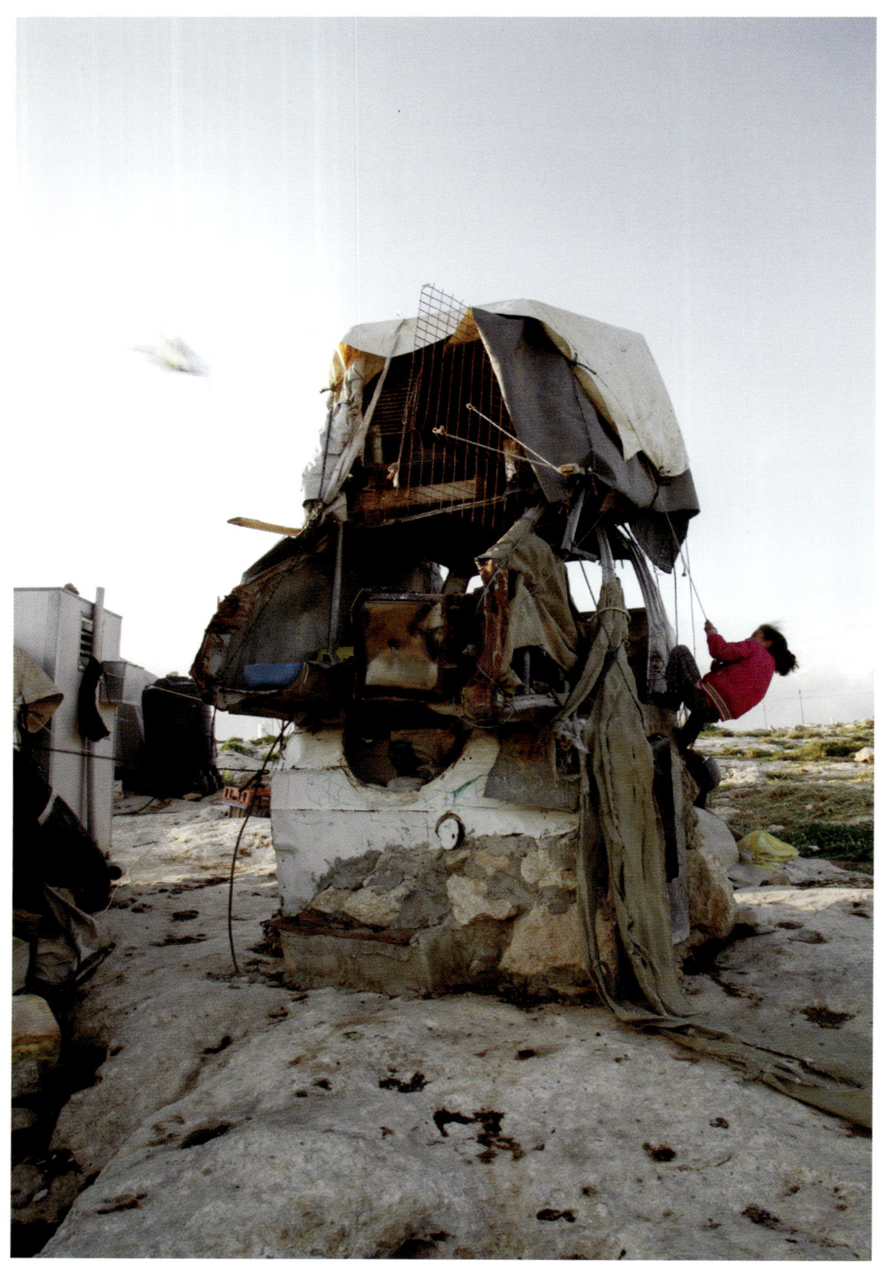

3.3 Susiya, March 2016.

A camera can't photograph the future, but it can show one in the making.

Follow Fatma to Susiya and Jubbet al-Dib.

3.4 Susiya, March 2016.

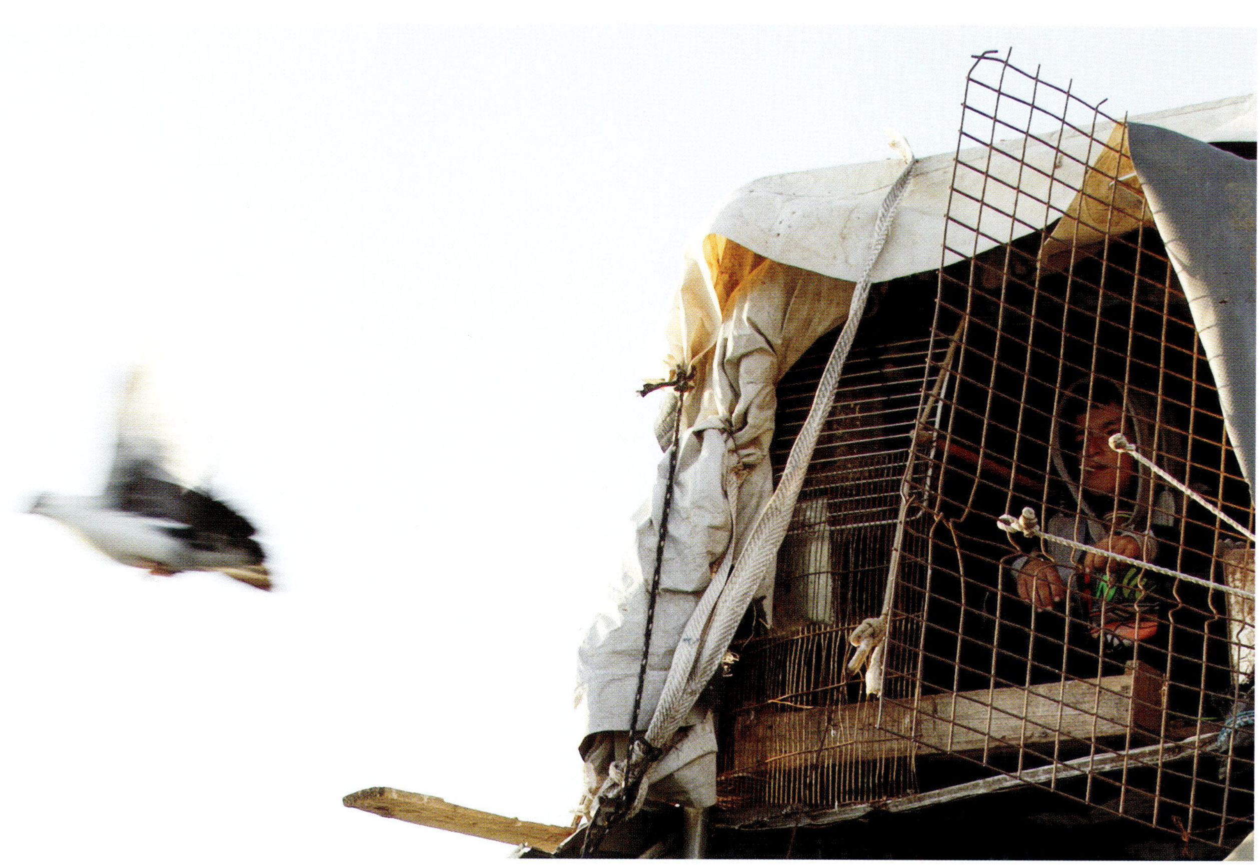

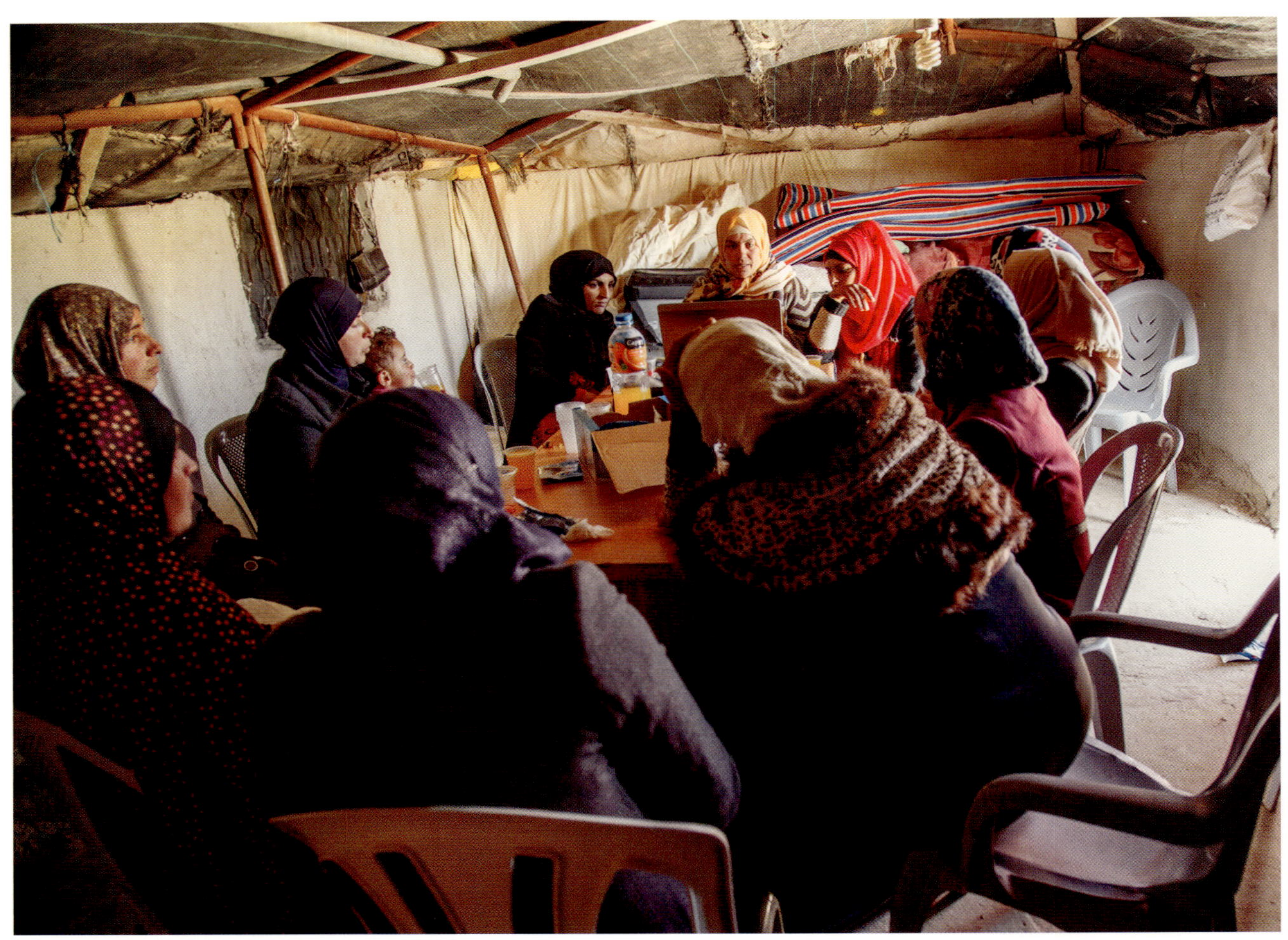

3.5 Susiya, March 2016.

3.6 Susiya, March 2016.

Susiya, 2016. The occupation sees to it that the Palestinian and Bedouin villages of the South Hebron Hills stay off the electric grid. It also forbids them to build houses. So the members of the Rural Women Association huddle around computers in a tent in Susiya under one bare lightbulb. They reach their meeting place on bumpy roads, in cars that need repairs and lack permits, that are subject to confiscation on any excuse. The small children are home with relatives, or they run about outside the tent with cousins and friends, or they interrupt the meeting. No one seems to mind.

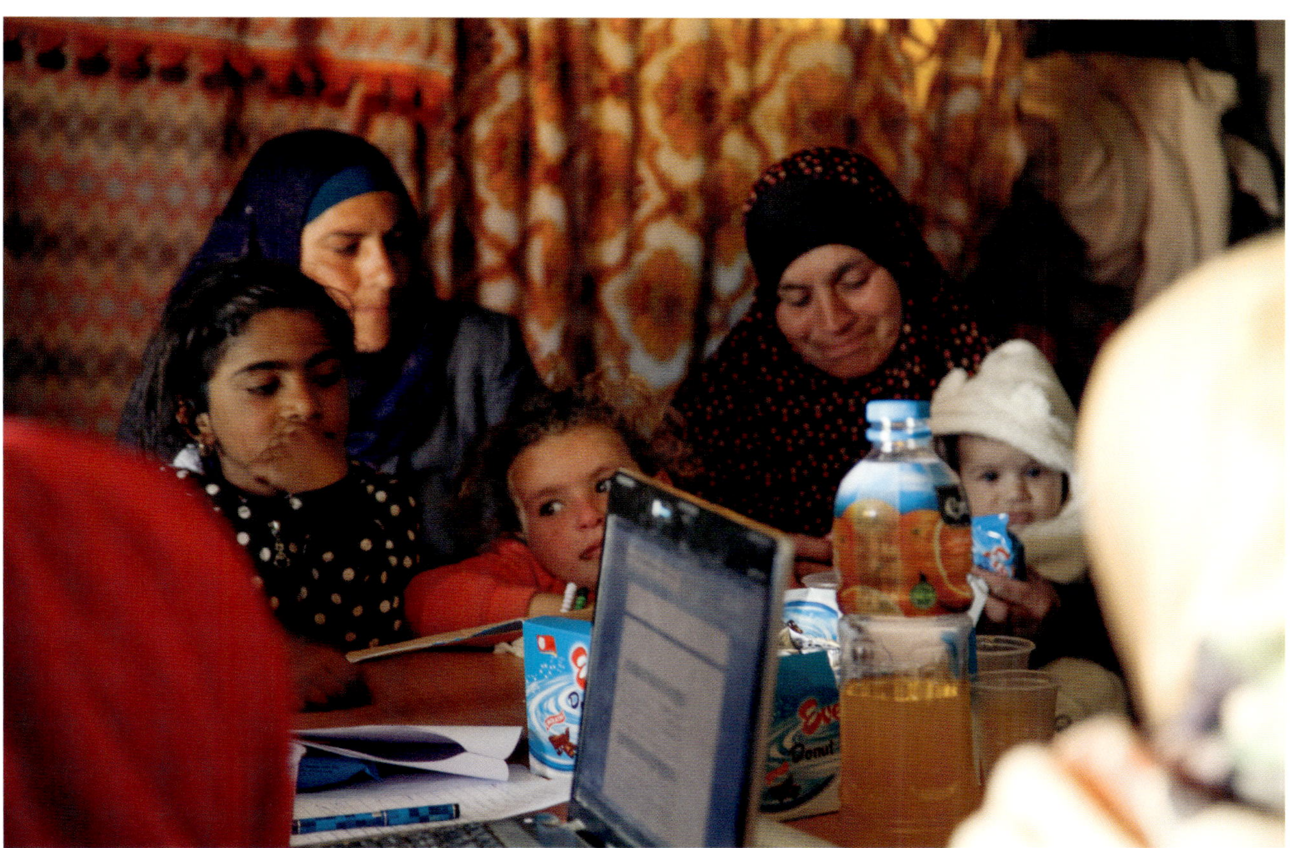

They discuss their website, which is filled with projects: spinning and weaving wool from the village's sheep; improving their embroidery; making yogurt. They want to provide women, and men, too (why not?), with lessons in reading and writing Arabic and speaking English; to train social workers and to establish community workshops in non-violence.

Some of their modest dreams are within reach. In Susiya's little shop, along with sodas and snacks, you can already buy locally made embroidered thobes and shoulderbags. When they have woven bags from the wool they spin themselves, they sell them there, too, as well as at fairs and to wholesalers.

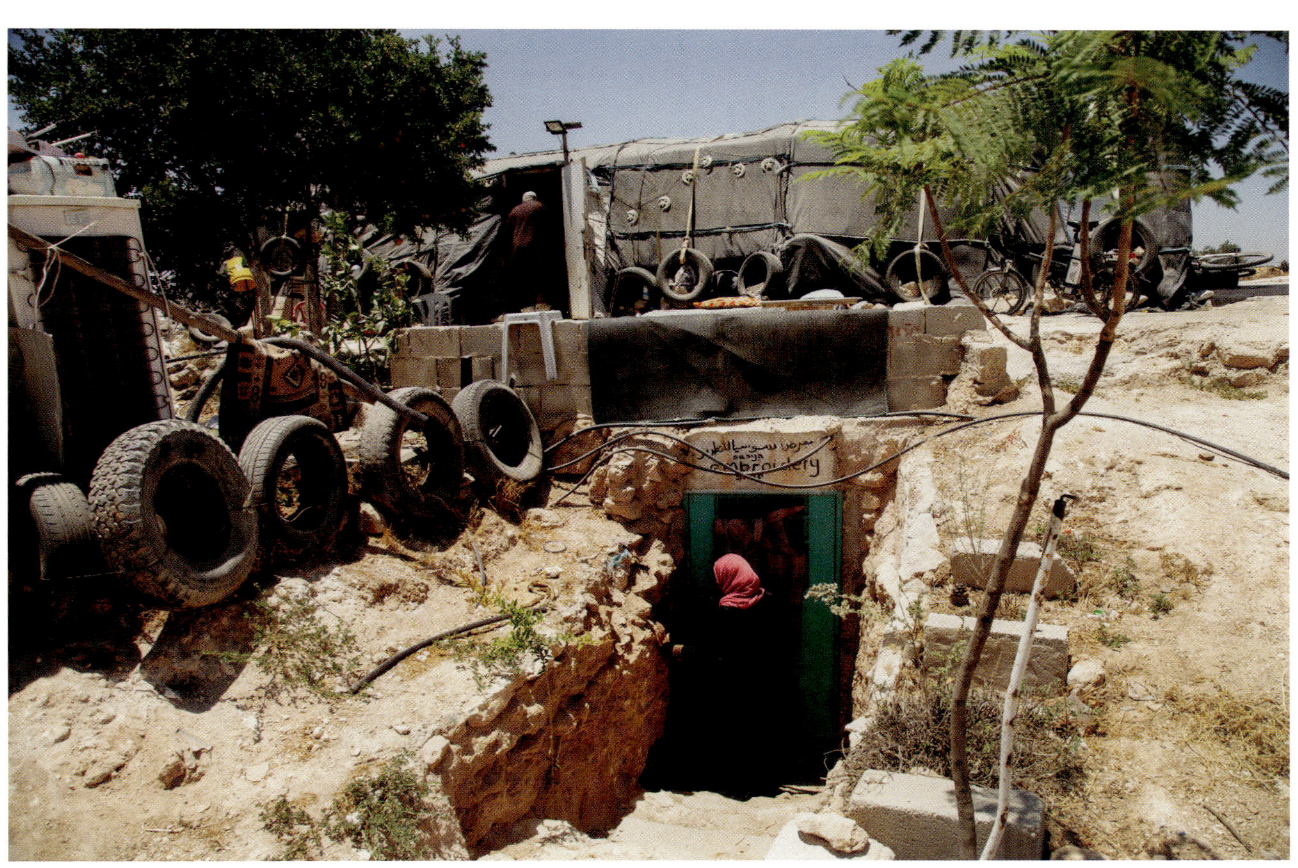

3.7 Susiya, July 2019.

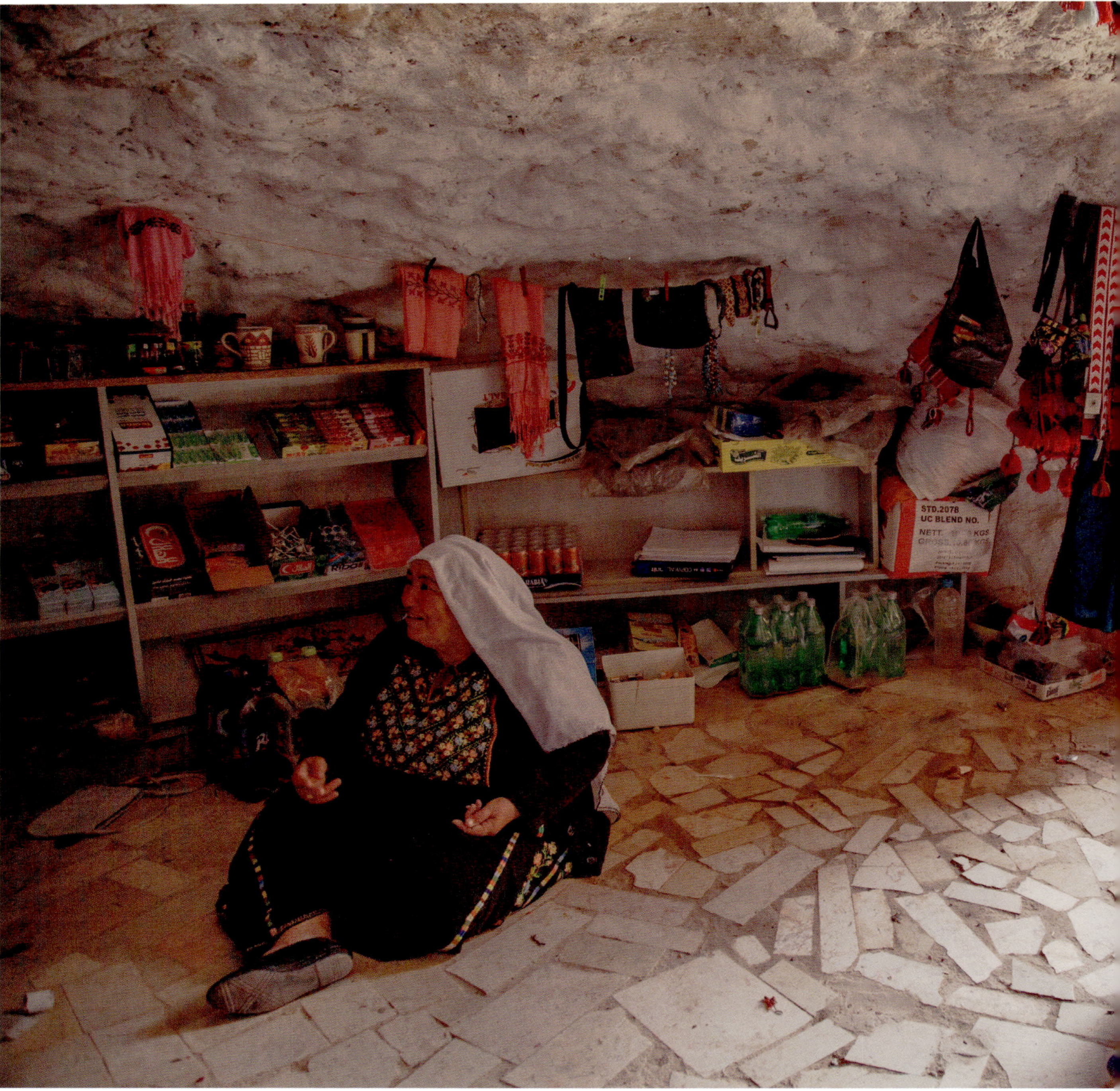
STD.2078
UC BLEND NO.

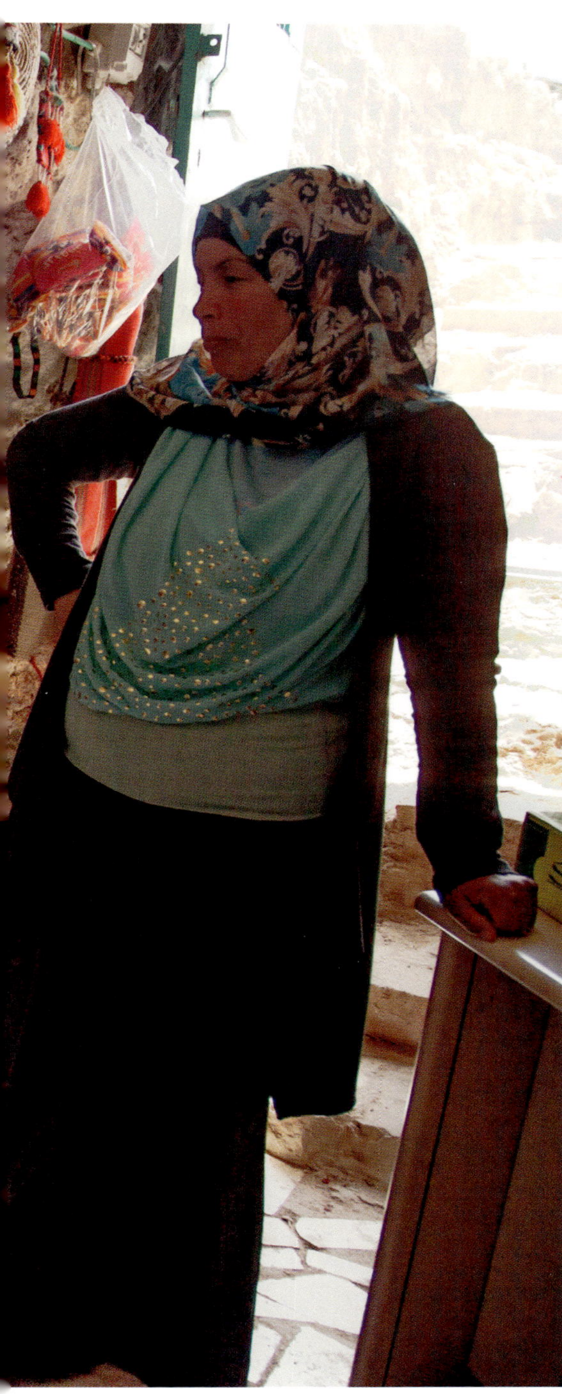

3.8 Susiya, June 2015.

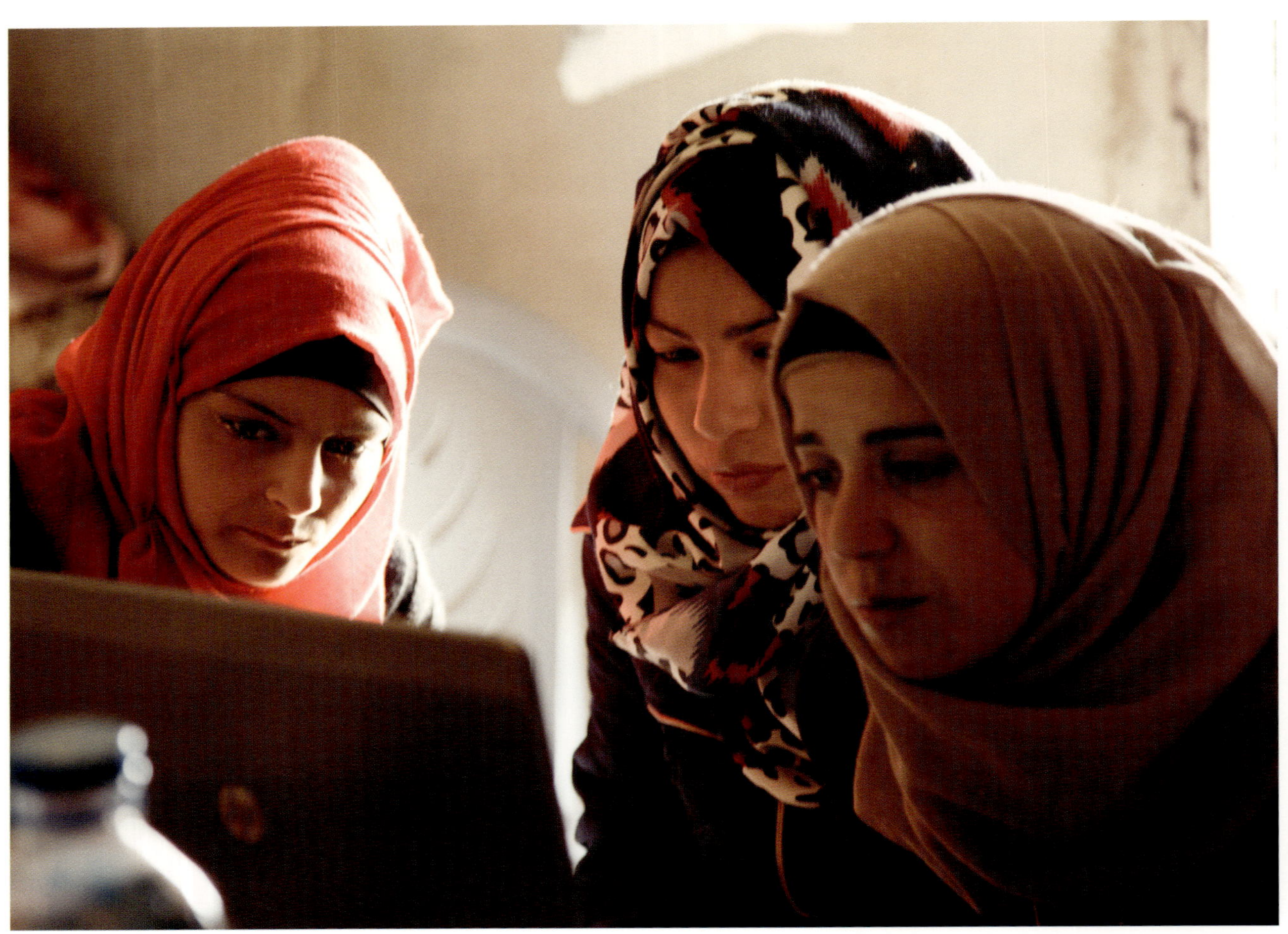

3.9 Susiya, March 2016.

All the little dreams spring from one big dream: autonomy, the kind of autonomy that comes from knowing you can contribute on your own to the community and your family's economic welfare. This kind of autonomy takes education. A grant from an NGO made it possible for Fatma to study for a degree in social work, and now she is focused on obtaining education, especially higher education, for others.

Certainly it would take money. The report of the treasurer, Naima, from the Beduin village Umm al-Khair, shows the group barely scraping by on its small annual dues and donations.

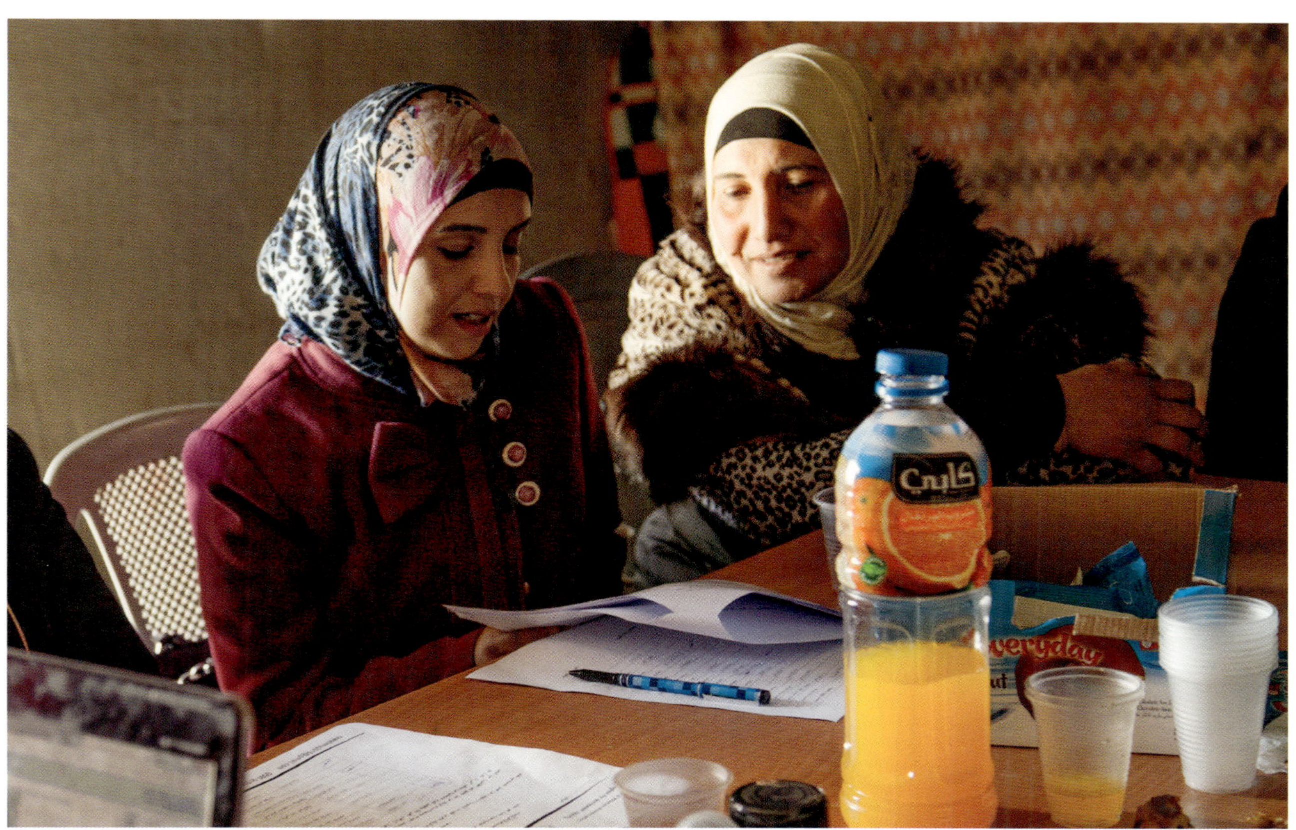

3.10 Susiya, March 2016.

But it takes more than money. To reach a school, children negotiate an obstacle course of paths that narrowly bypass settlements, where settlers block them or worse. And the children face other dangers. Recently one of the women offered a workshop to help children recognize explosives so that they will stop picking them up on the way to school.

Once they have completed their local primary schools, qualified boys and girls struggle to pay for secondary schools and find a way to commute to them. If they pass this hurdle, and some do, university education presents formidable challenges. Yet some students are able to attend university and the rare student can even study abroad.

Fatma: One of our goals is to be able to give more of our children an opportunity for higher education.

3.11 Susiya, March 2016.

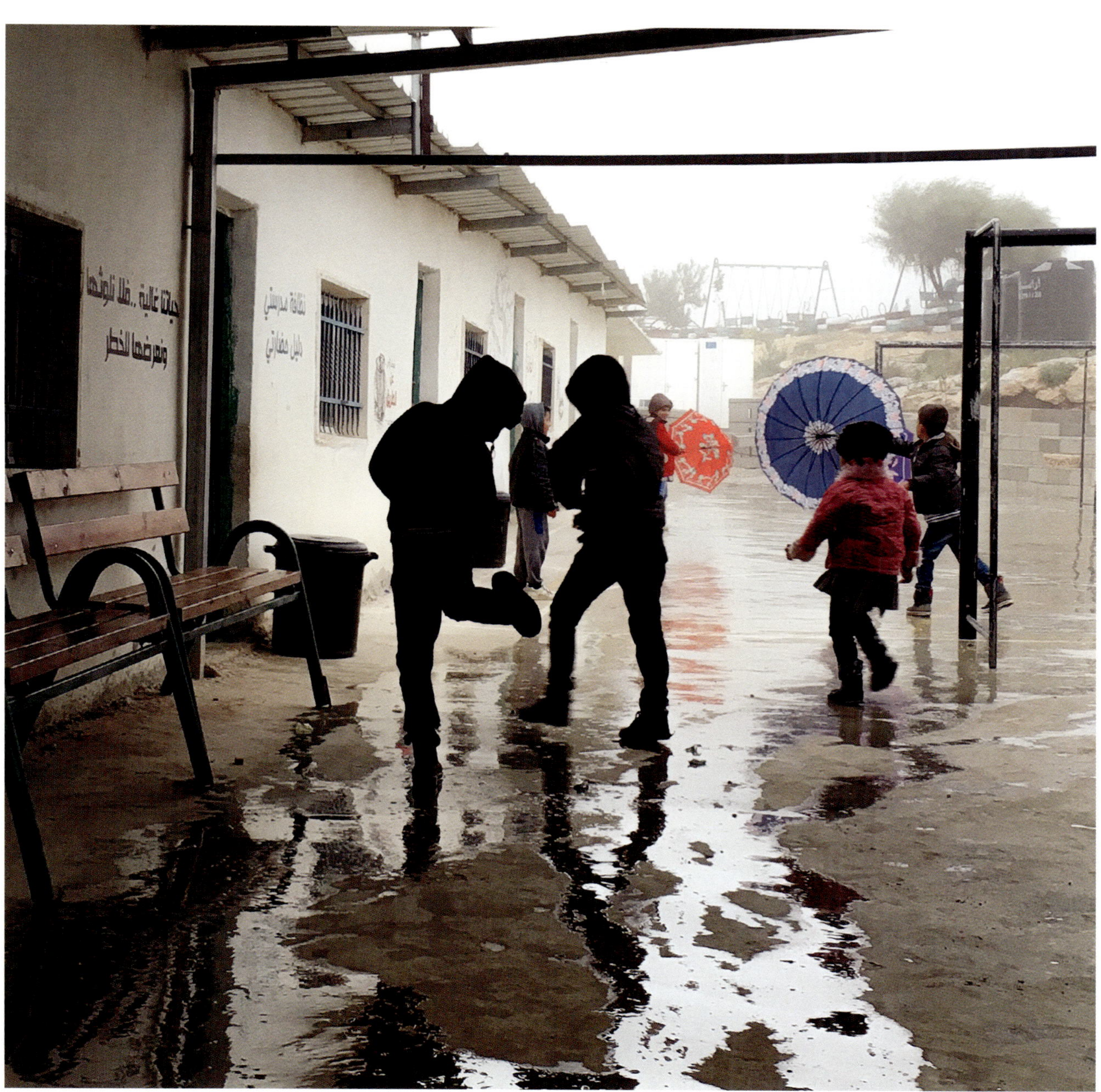

حياتنا غالية .. فلا نلوثها
ونعرضها للخطر
نظافة مدرستي
دليل حضارتي

Jubbet al-Dib, 2018. By 2018, the Rural Women Association has grown, and Fatma travels to other areas of occupied Palestine to support or help establish women's groups. The women in Jubbet al-Dib have had a head start. The village is a short, rocky drive from Bethlehem followed by an even bumpier ride, or better, a short walk. But it has real buildings. And the women here have already organized to acquire a battery of solar panels. Tanks for clean water line the rooftops.

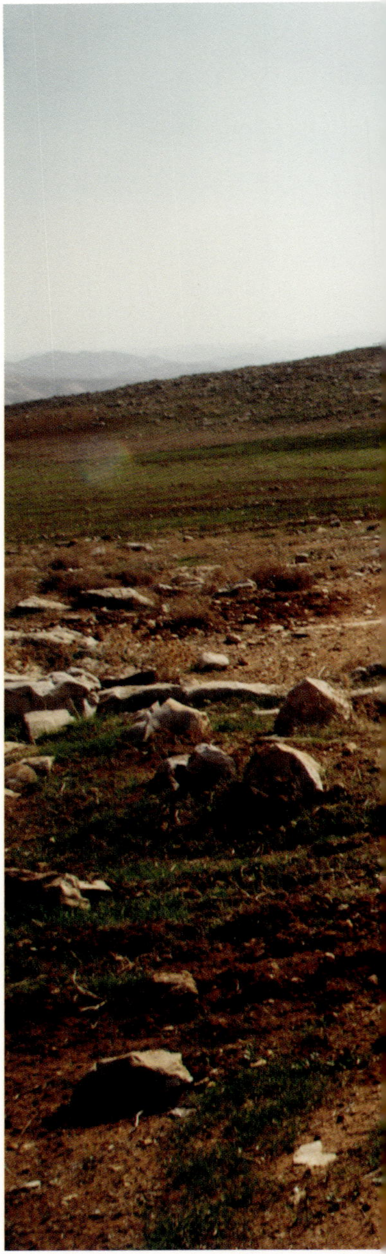

3.12 Jubbet al-Dib, Bethlehem district, December 2018.

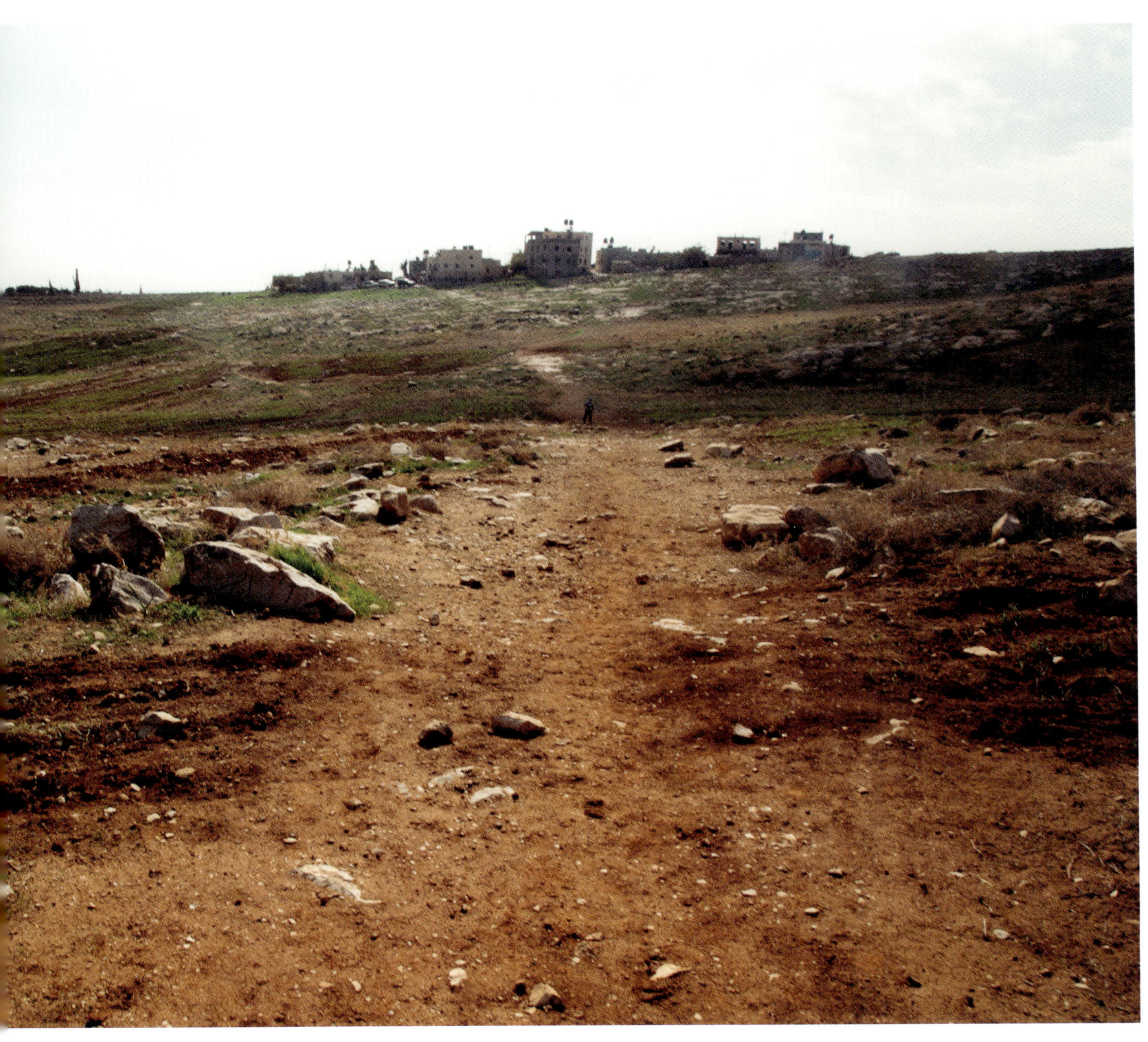

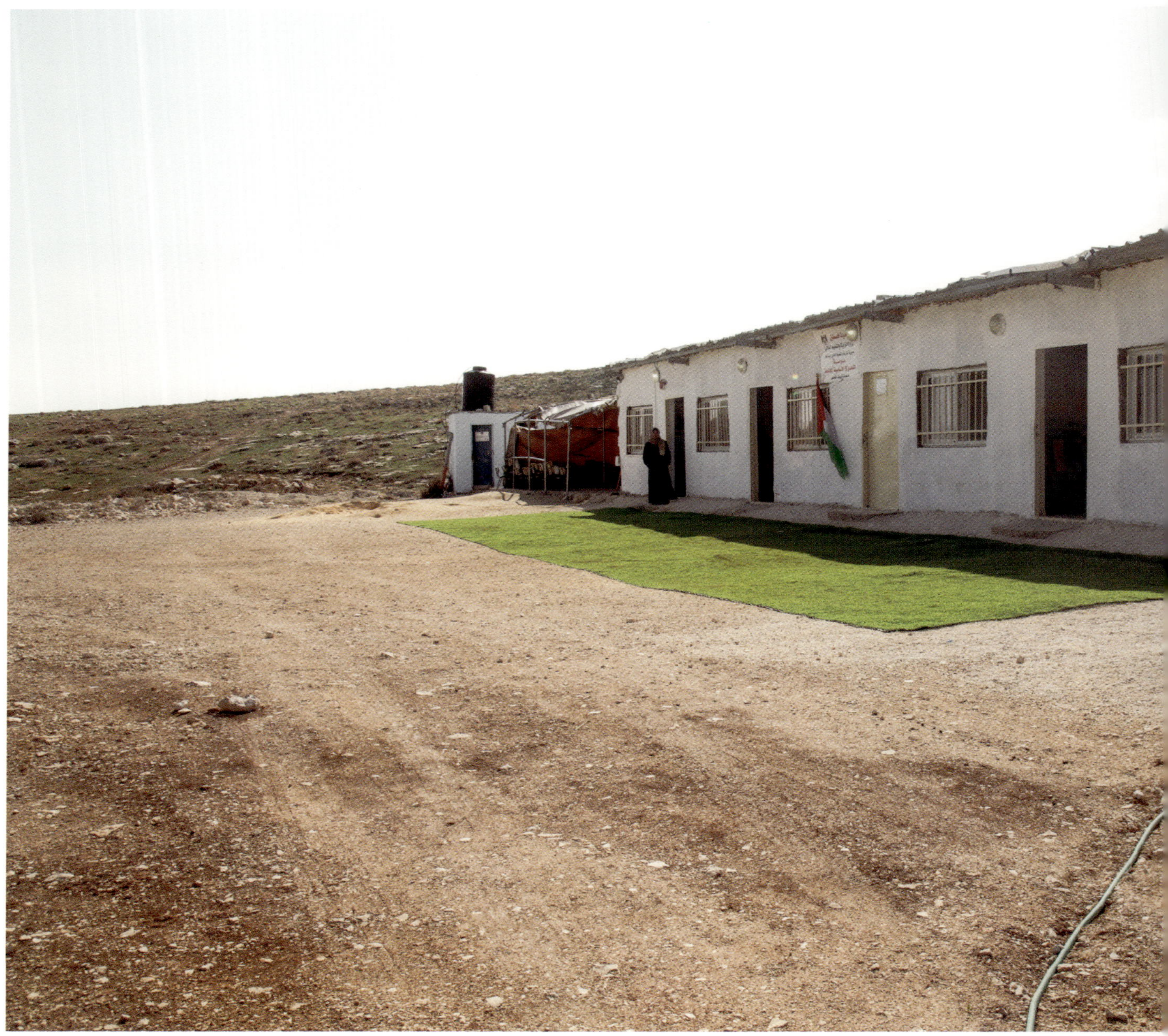

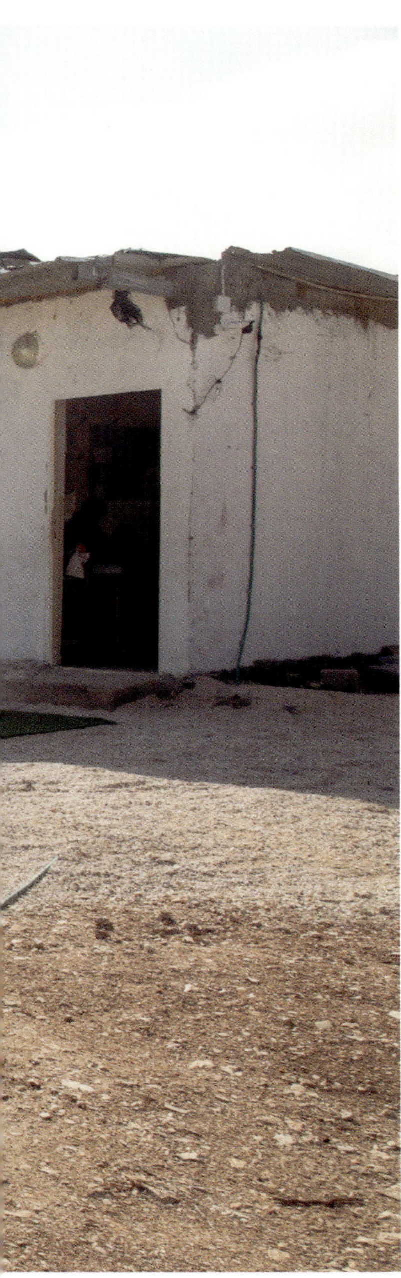

Most of the prefabricated buildings of its school, destroyed by Israeli occupation forces the night before classes began, were quickly rebuilt, and a tent was constructed to fill in for the rest.[1] Having tackled infrastructure issues, the women are eager to start on even more challenging projects.

The focus here is on medical and social needs. They have many.

1. On May 7, 2023, the school was demolished again.

3.13 Jubbet al-Dib, December 2018.

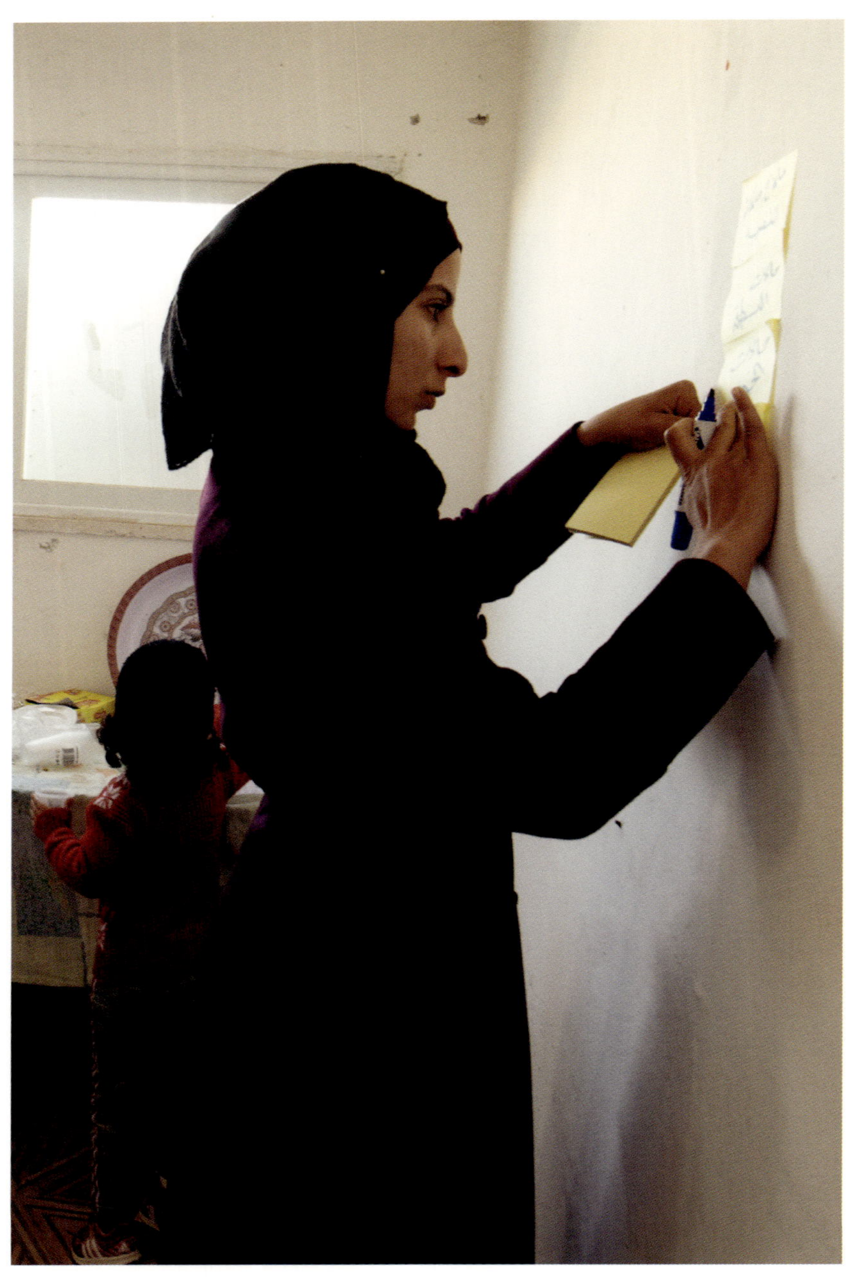

3.14 Jubbet al-Dib, December 2018.

Post-it notes accumulate on the wall listing more and more problems that the women want to tackle. Common ailments are not being treated: mental health workers are needed, and speech therapists. Someone needs to check and care for the children's eyes and ears. Slow students need remedial classes for math and English. Education for girls should be the same as for boys, but there's a problem. The girls are afraid of their teachers.

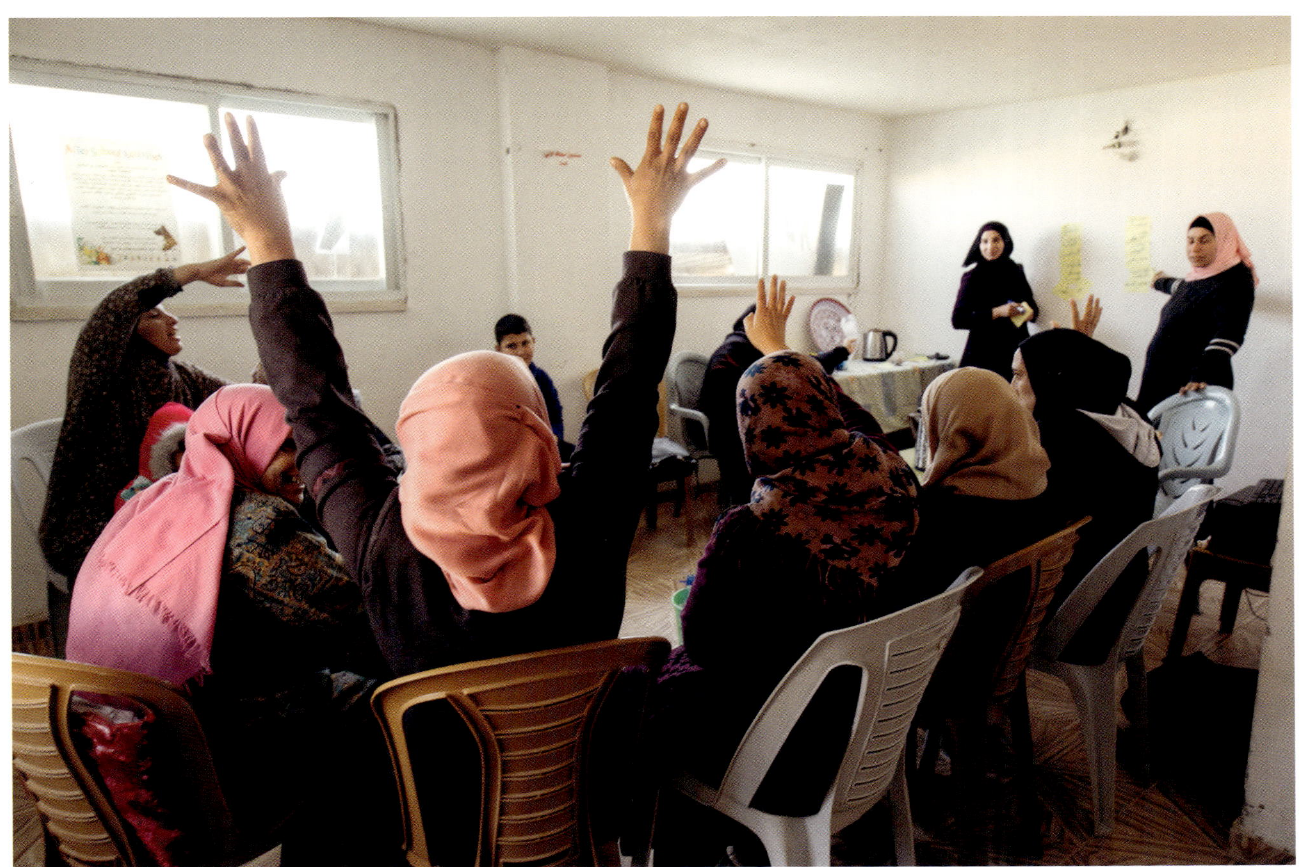

3.15 Jubbet al-Dib, December 2018.

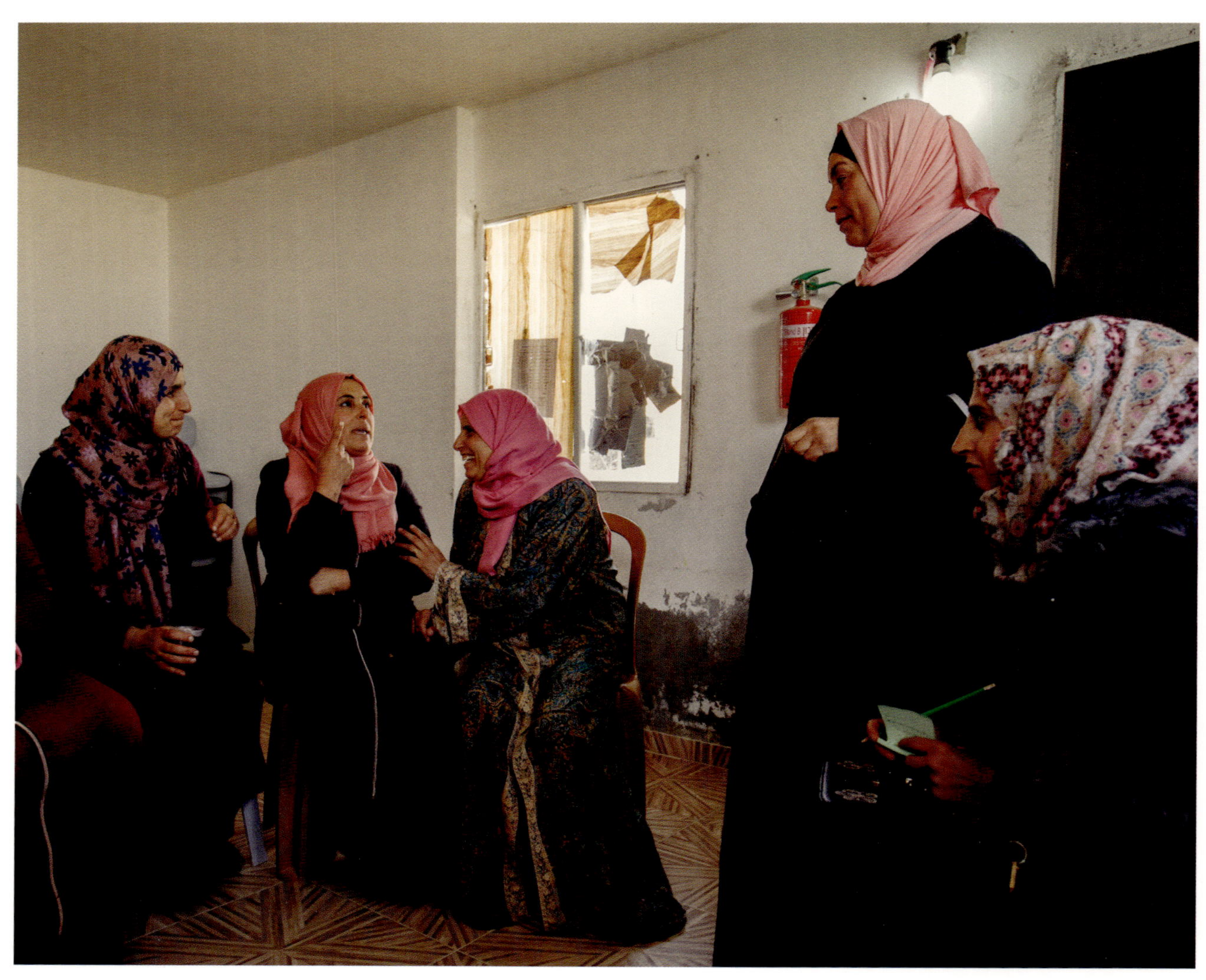

3.16 Jubbet al-Dib, December 2018.

And speaking of fear, the women are afraid, too. Nothing, not the culture, not the community, and certainly not the government, protects them from family violence or sexual harassment, psychological and physical. These serious worries color many of the comments; yet a boisterous, almost festive atmosphere prevails. Harmony and cacophony take turns.

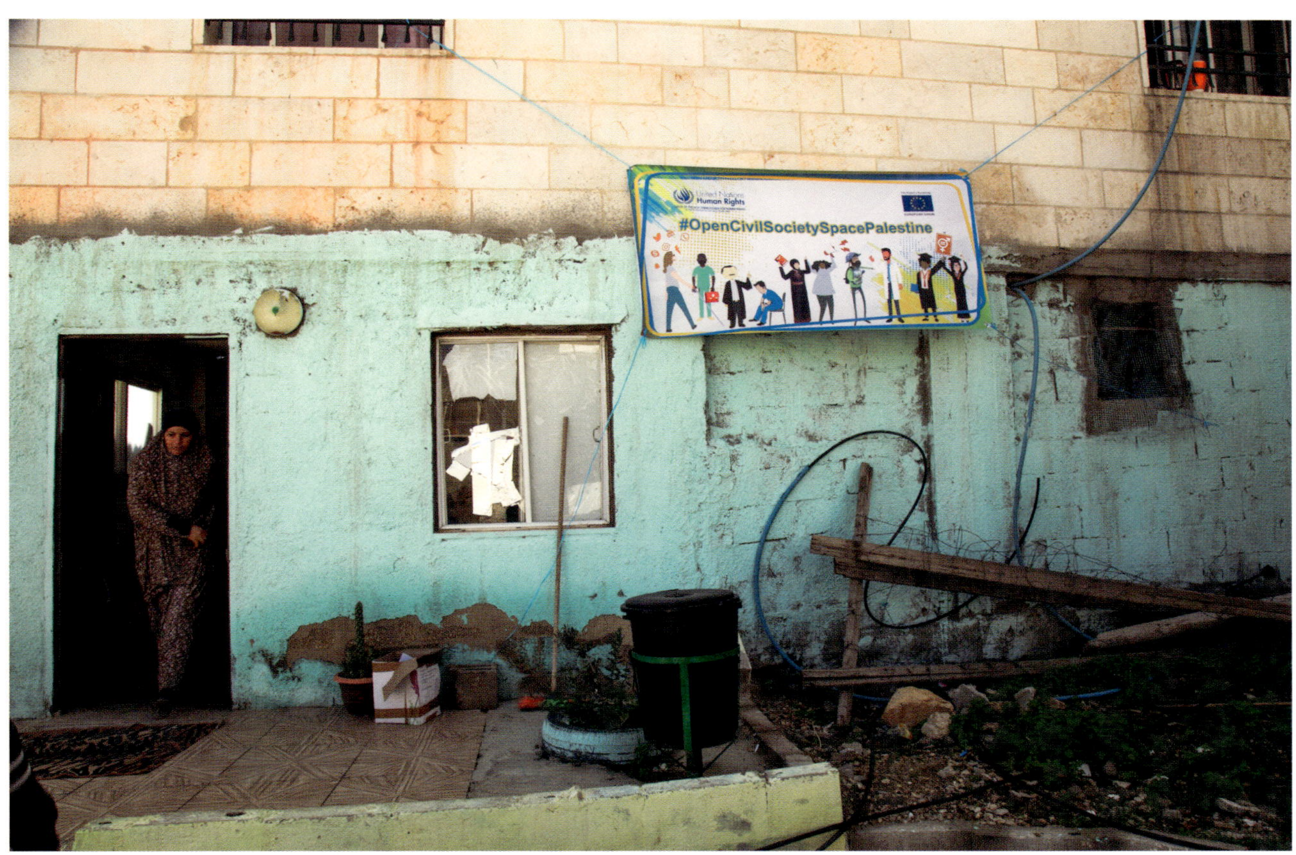

3.17 Jubbet al-Dib, December 2018.

Laḥza: Tea

Tea always happens now, free from time past or time future.

When soldiers intrude, usually in order to drive the tea-drinkers and their sheep away, they bring with them the bitterness of time—past and future insults, along with immediate, palpable fear. The very first thing an Israeli soldier is taught in basic training, under threat of dire punishment, is to be on time, although this almost never happens. Soldiers in Palestine tend to be anxious, arrogant, scared, and harassed by slow, remorseless time that is burdened with perpetual misery just as their bodies are burdened with guns, cartridges of bullets, helmets, boots, canteens, army knives, padded vests, and more. This conglomerate of metal and pain meets the airy simplicity of tea.

Sometimes the shepherds offer a glass of tea to the intruders, who almost always refuse.

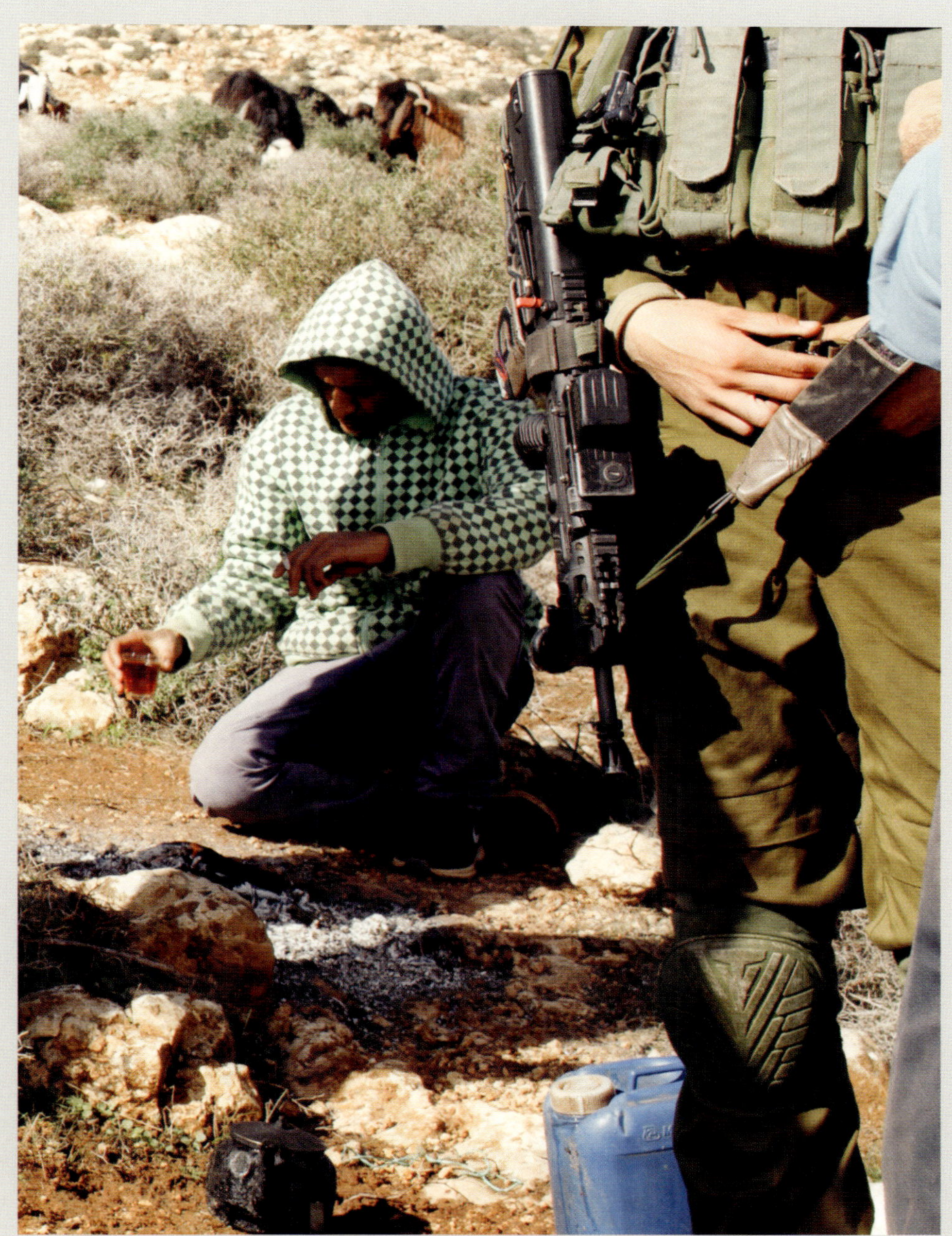

L.3 ‘Ein ar-Rashash,
December 2018.

4.1 ‘Ein ar-Rashash, December 2018.

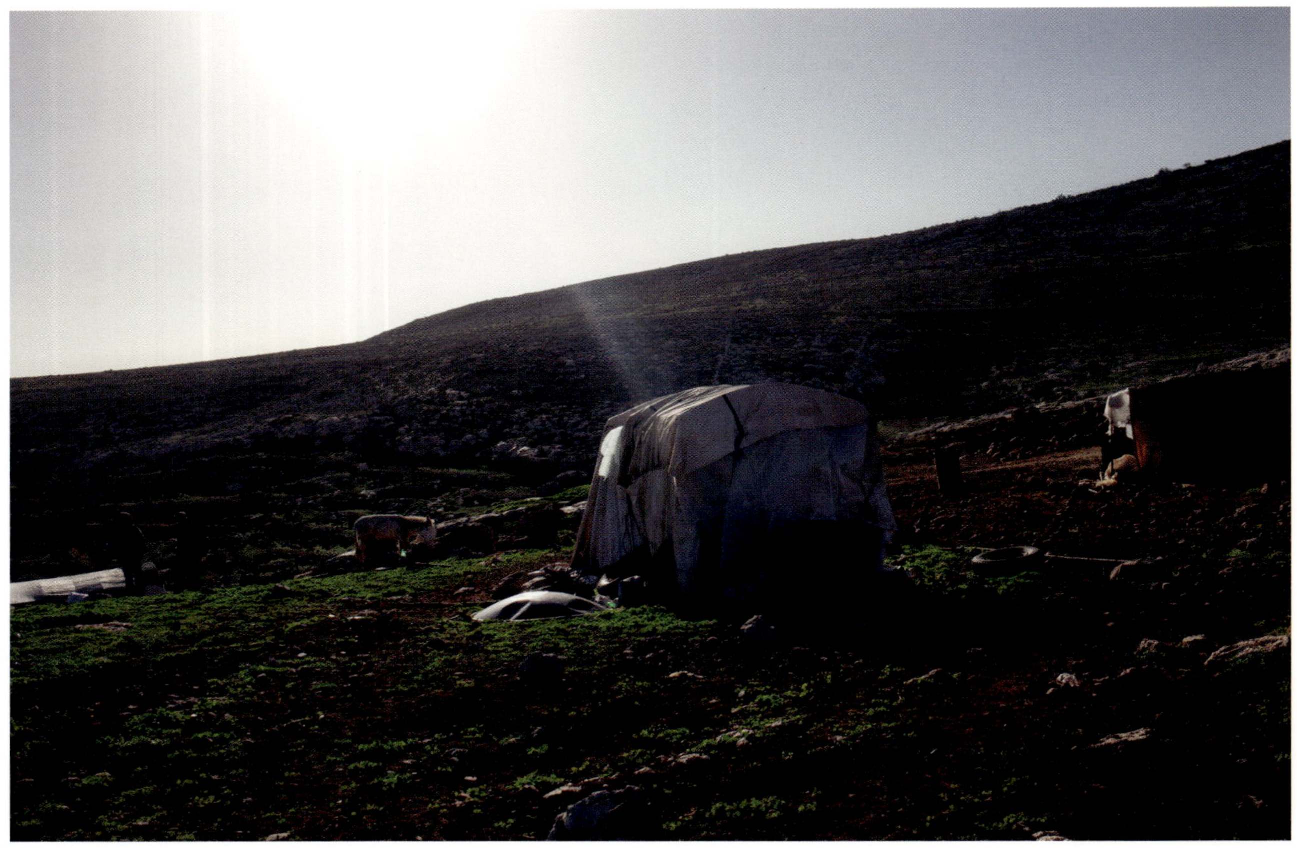

4.

Out of Sight: 'Ein ar-Rashash, December, 2018

'Ein ar-Rashash is a Bedouin community. Do not let the word "Bedouin" deceive you. Rashash is not a temporary encampment, and its shepherd community is there to stay. Some years ago, the civil administration, which controls "Area C" of Palestine for Israel, declared their grazing grounds a "firing zone." Even that made little difference in their lives. Demolitions seldom occurred, and during real military exercises—they, too were rare—soldiers would ask the shepherds to keep their flocks away from particular areas for a few days. But now the Israeli settlement outpost Malachei Ha-Shalom (Angels of Peace) sits next to an army base. For a while, the army supplied this outpost, illegal under both Israeli and international law, with water and utilities, but eventually someone exposed the practice. The settlement has remained, however, and the settlers do everything they can to keep the Bedouins out of the area. Like the Bedouins, they herd sheep; the idea that Israelis can capture more land by becoming shepherds has been proudly attributed to a current resident of the outpost.

The black tents and sheep-pens of ‘Ein ar-Rashash trickle down the hill toward the goat-paths. The dark Angels of Peace are just to the west of the village.

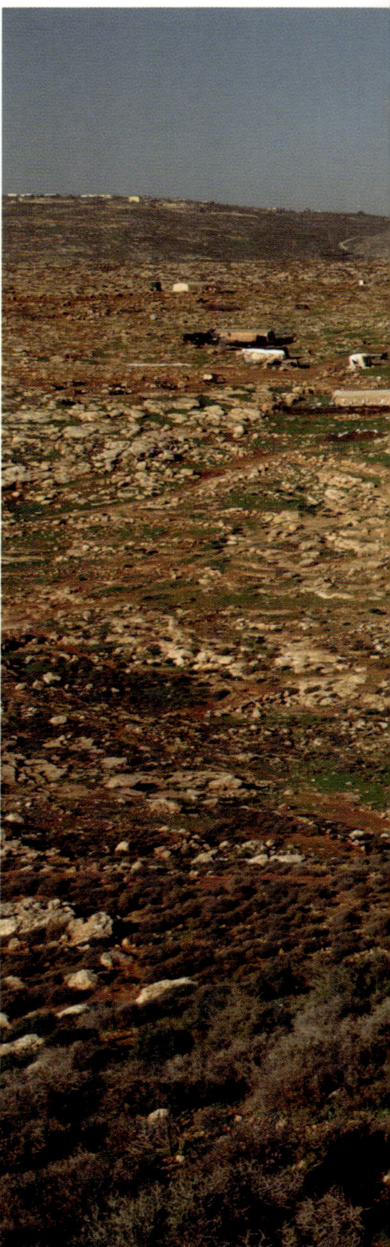

4.2 ‘Ein ar-Rashash, December 2018.

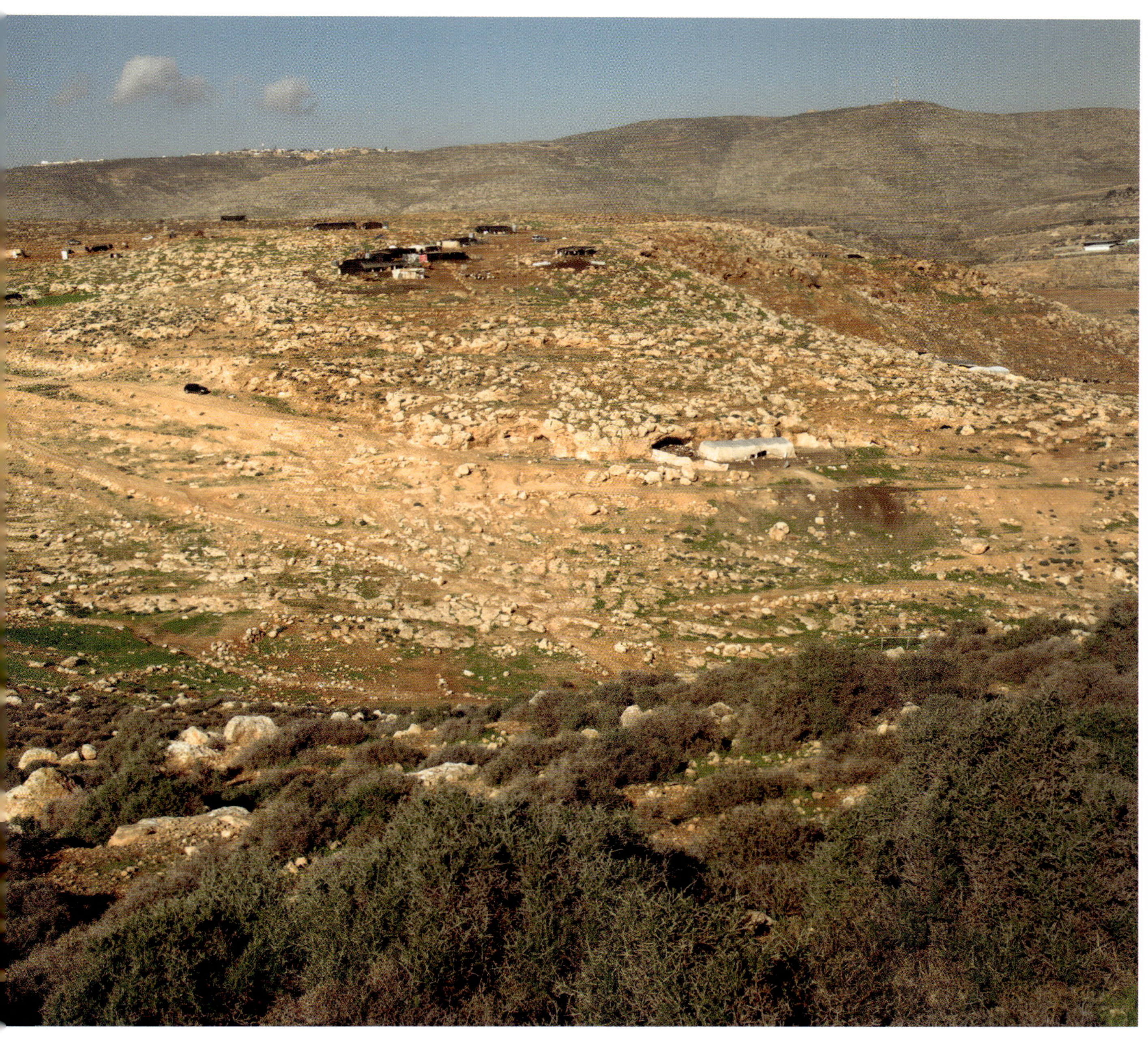

Ostensibly the army tries to be fair. A quiet road was briefly the focus of an attempt to divide the land between the settlers and the Bedouins. But the settlers weren't satisfied, and the army decided, in theory, to expel everyone equally from the firing zone. This means that if the two groups are grazing at the same time, the settler shepherds will move their own flocks just out of the zone and call the army. After the army expels the Palestinians, the settlers can return with their flocks undisturbed. Our mission for today is to help the Bedouins move safely past the one place where they can be seen by settlers. It worked yesterday. Today, not so much.

4.3 'Ein ar-Rashash, December 2018.

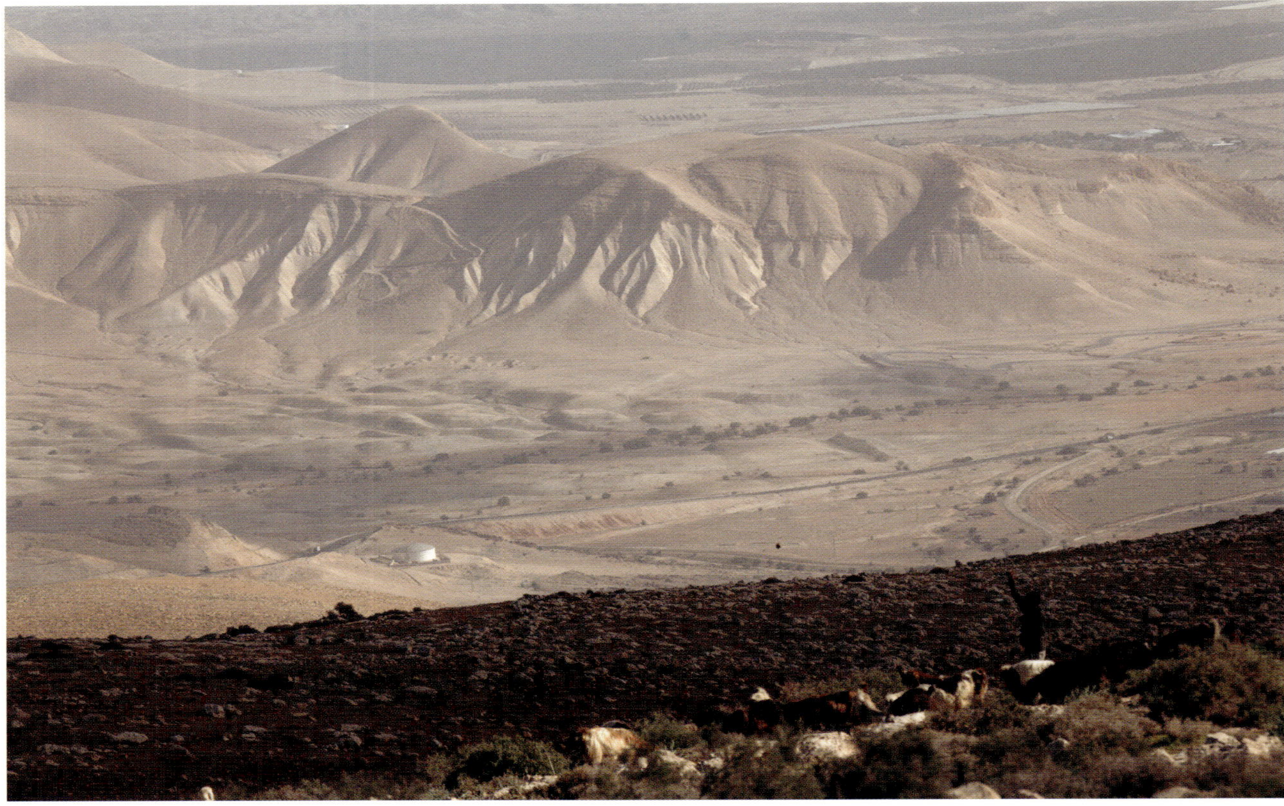

For a while, everything goes smoothly. We walk to meet the Palestinian sheep, who are nibbling happily, and their equally content minders. Eventually, settler shepherds and their flocks appear on a high ridge and watch the Bedouin shepherds below. From a distance, it is hard to distinguish one group of shepherds from another. At first, it seems that the settlers will be satisfied just to gaze down, knowing that they have the upper hand. Michal approaches them. She says that the settlers are annoyed because one of their sheep dogs has taken a liking to her. Imagine the dilemma of a sheep dog who can't tell the difference between settlers, Palestinians, Bedouins, or activists.

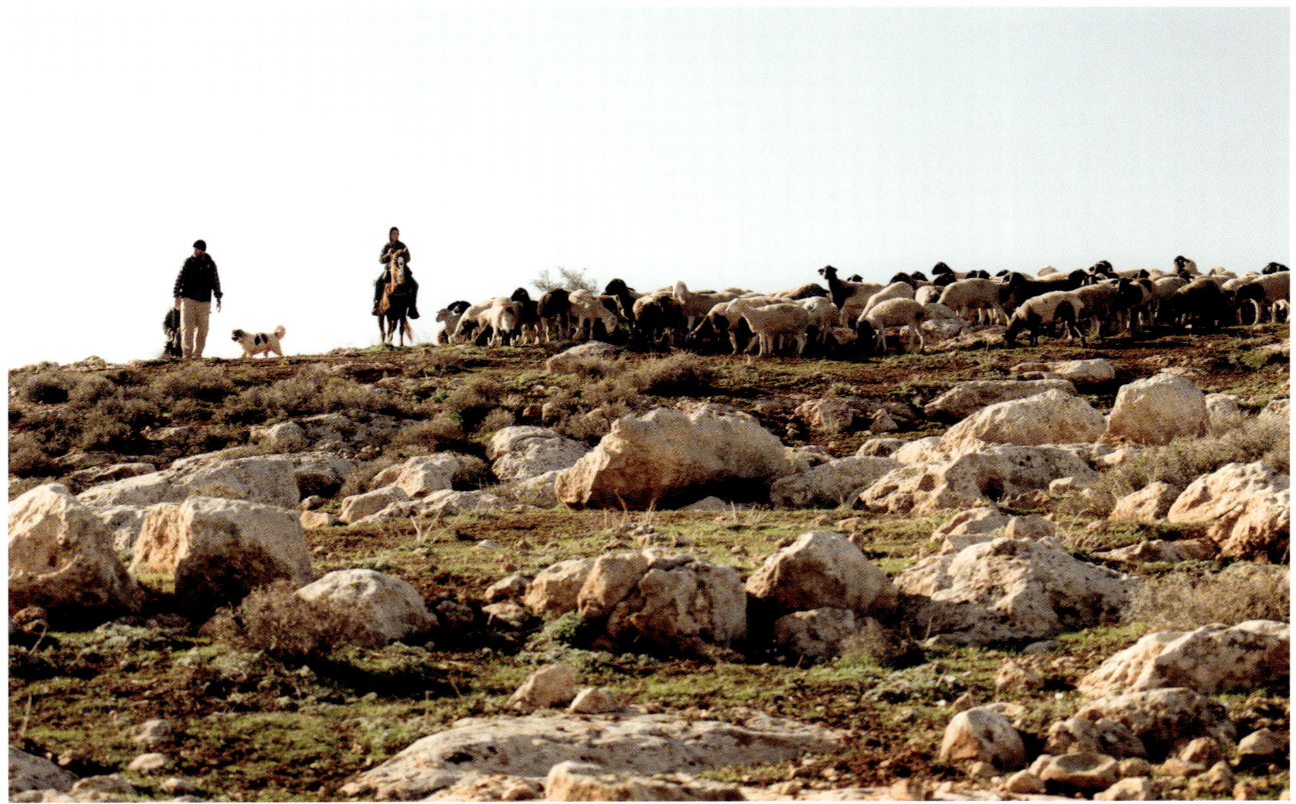

4.4 'Ein ar-Rashash, December 2018.

One of the settlers is on the telephone. Sure enough, a little while later, an army jeep appears on the hilltop.

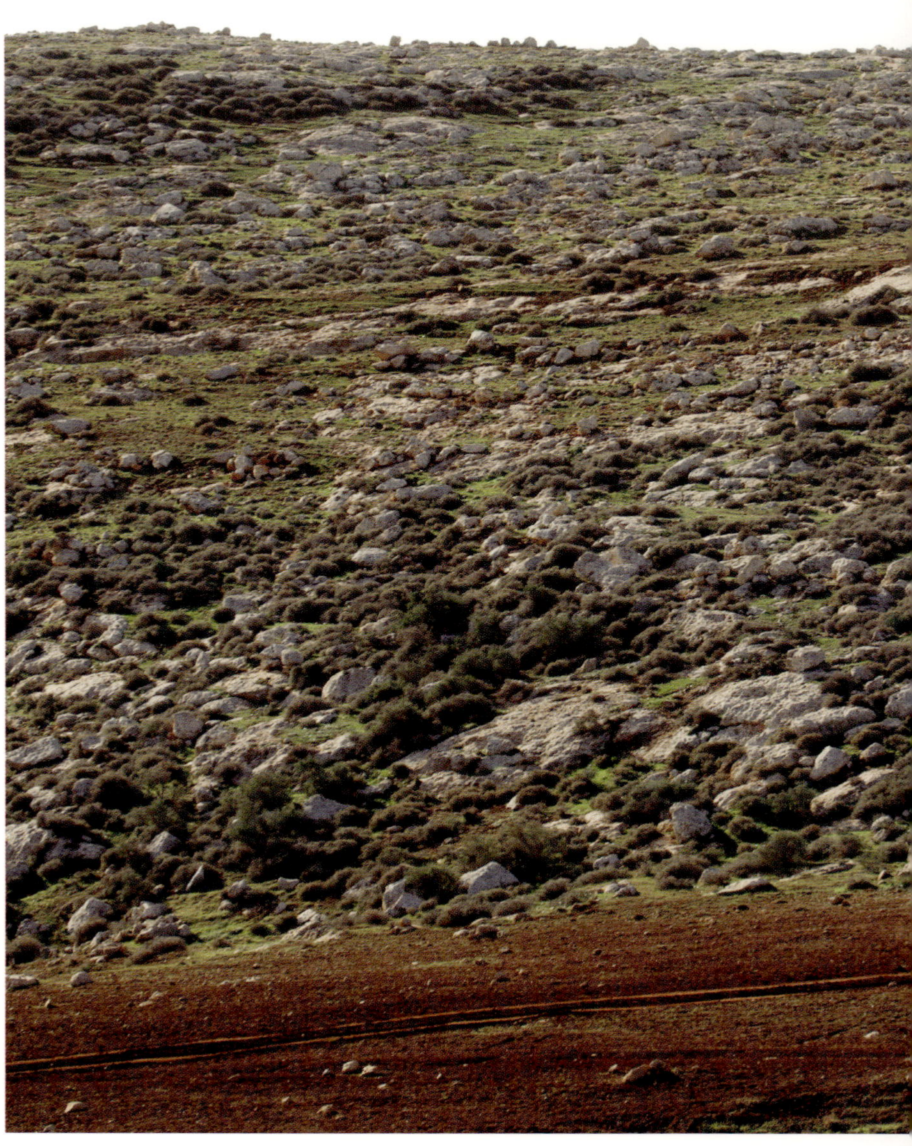

4.5 ‘Ein ar-Rashash, December 2018.

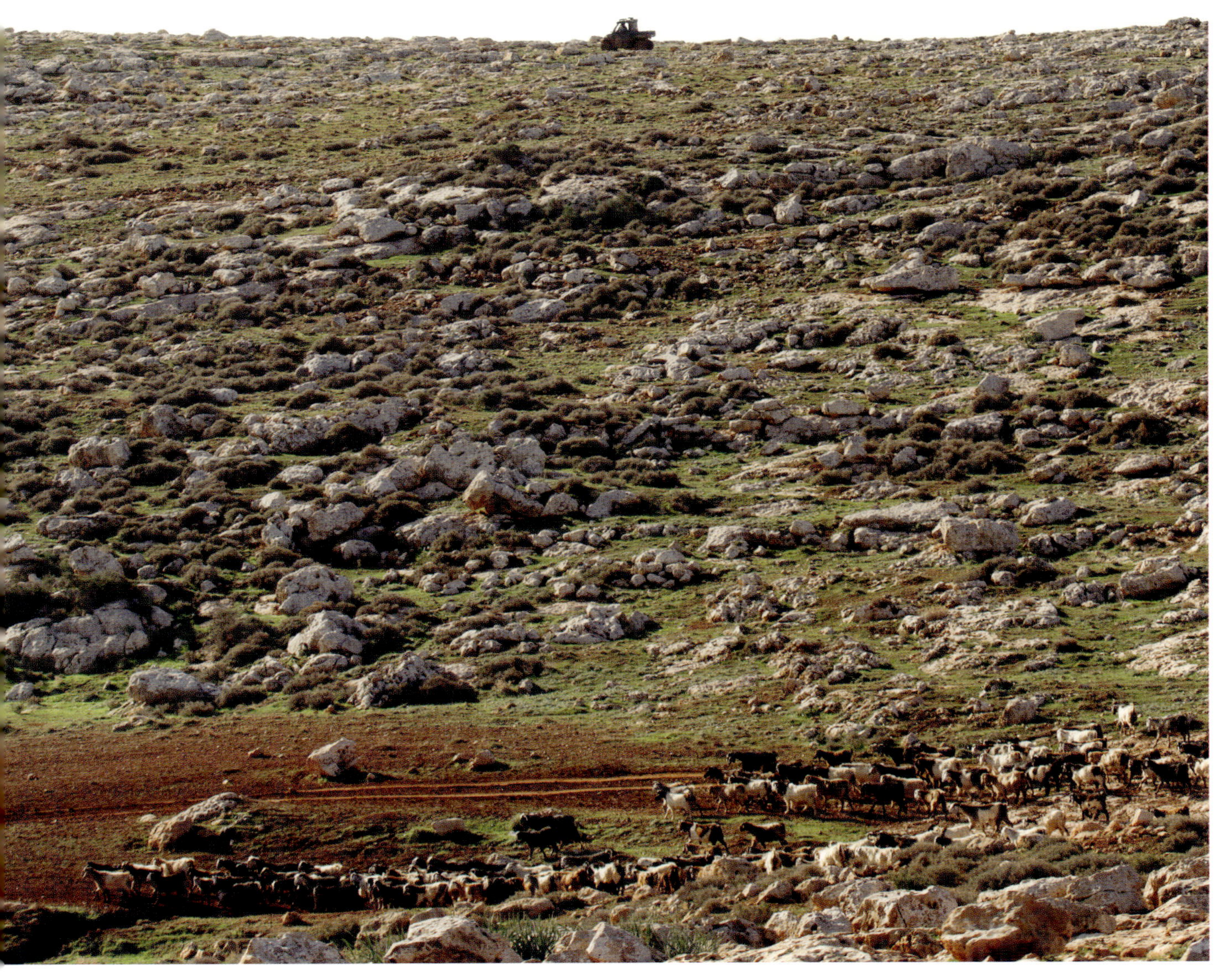

The soldiers are bored and aggravated. When they are prevented from doing their job in the simplest and most literal way, involving the fewest steps, they lose patience.

4.6 'Ein ar-Rashash, December 2018.

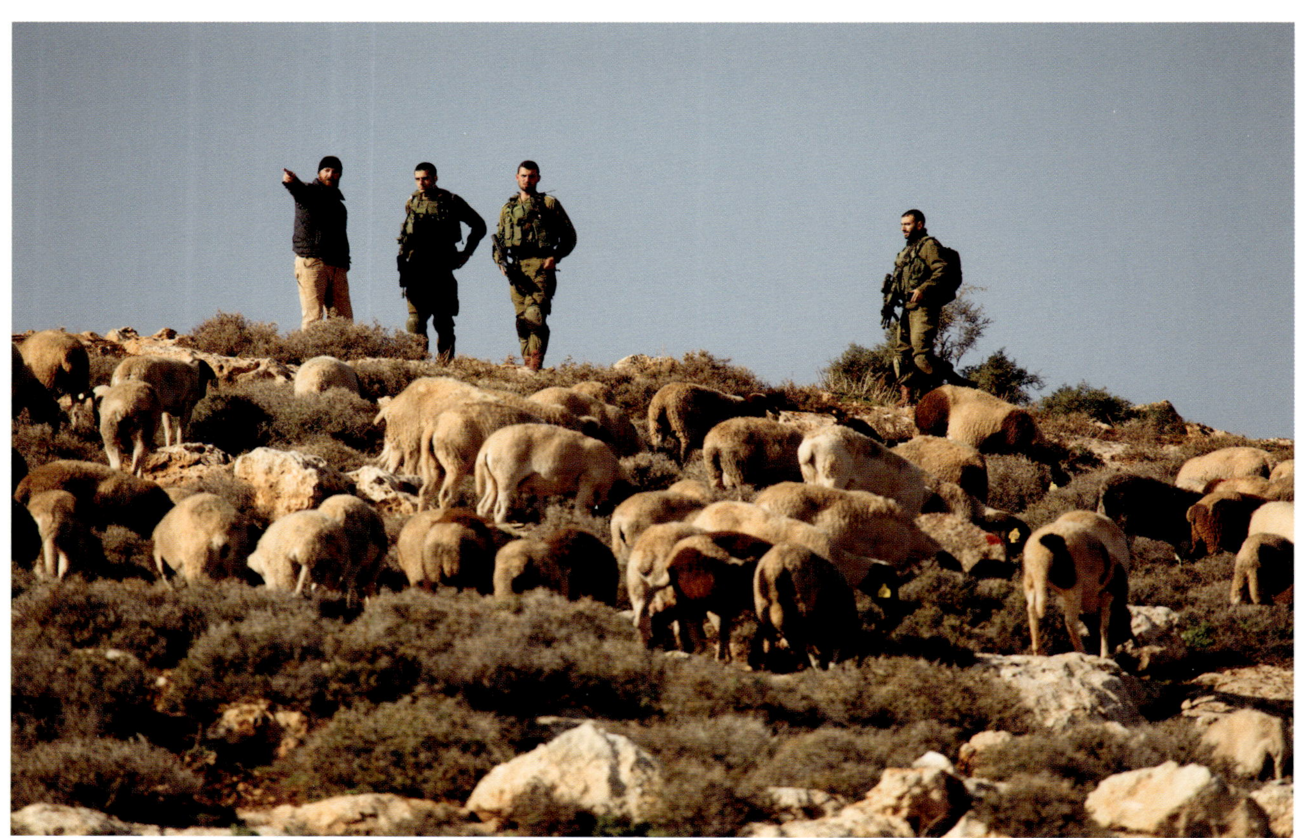

The Palestinians must leave the area, explains the officer.

4.7 'Ein ar-Rashash, December 2018.

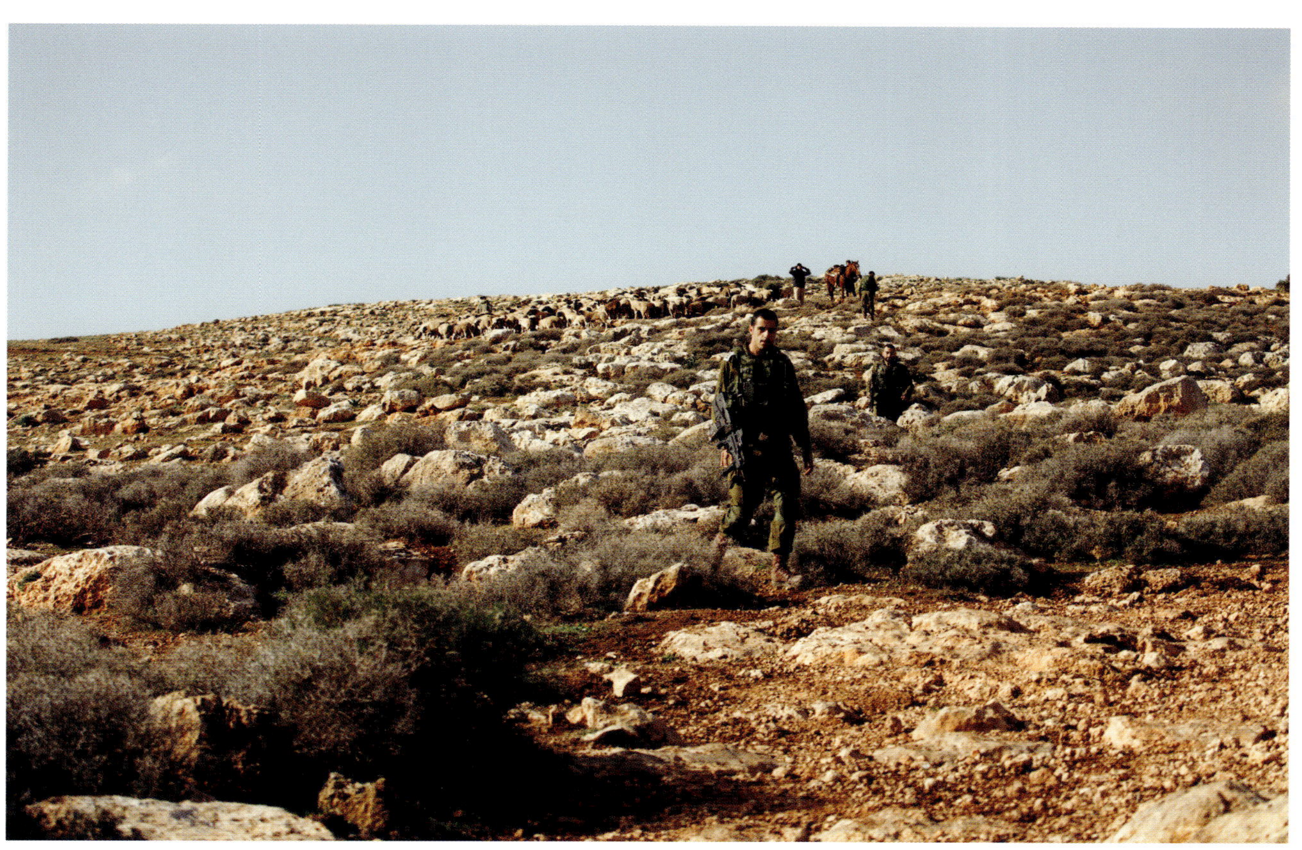

And yes, he says, the settlers will also have to leave. Except that they don't. The officer climbs back up the hill; the Palestinians disappear; but the settlers of course stay put. We point this out to the officer.

By now he is really cranky. He recognizes that for the sake of appearances, it would be nice, if the settlers would take a few steps back

4.8 'Ein ar-Rashash, December 2018.

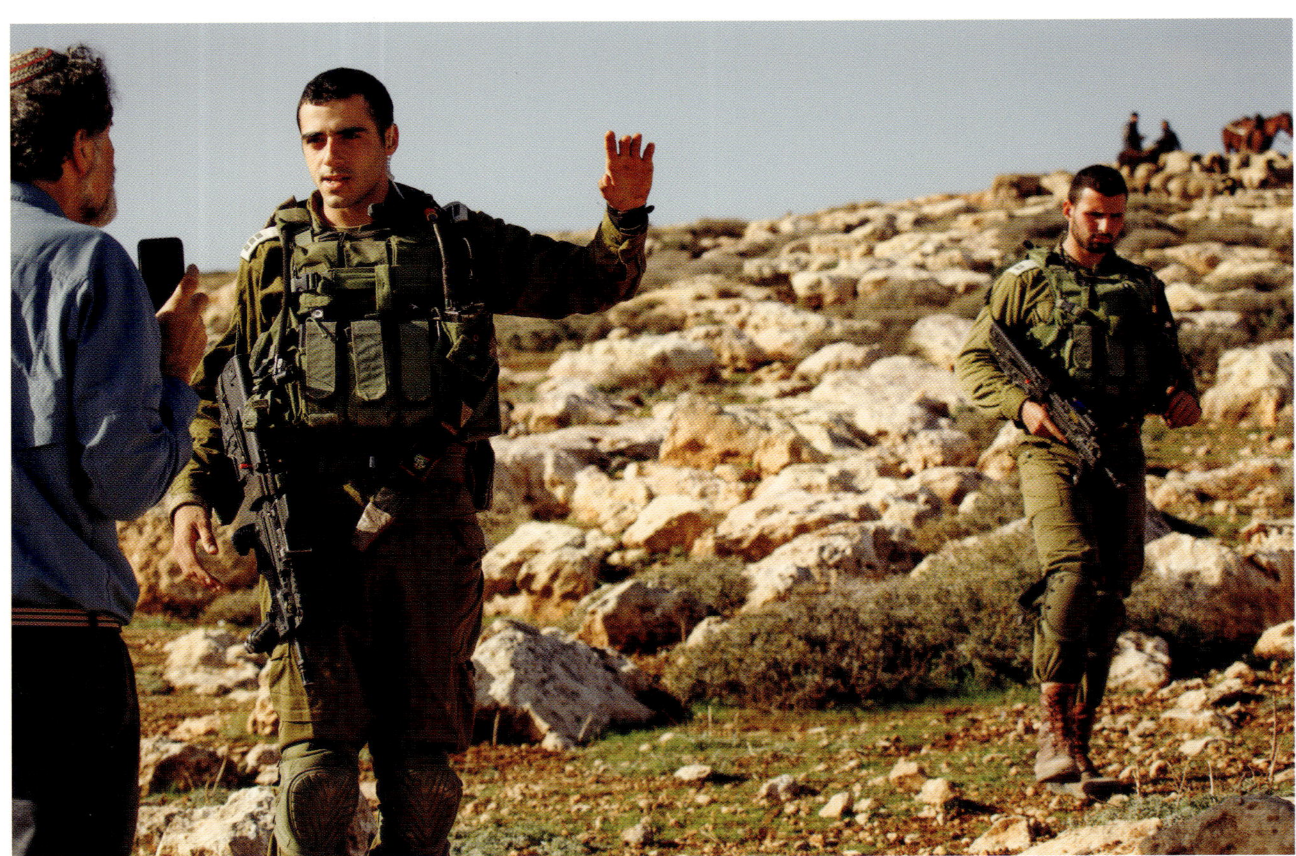

behind the hilltop where they could not be seen, even though they would still be in the firing zone. But the Bedouins, he adds, are playing the same game. Except that it isn't a game.

He threatens to up the ante. I can call the police, he says.

Below the ridge, the Bedouins have decided not to return home right away.

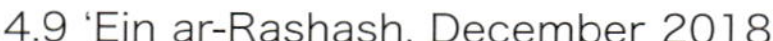

4.9 'Ein ar-Rashash, December 2018.

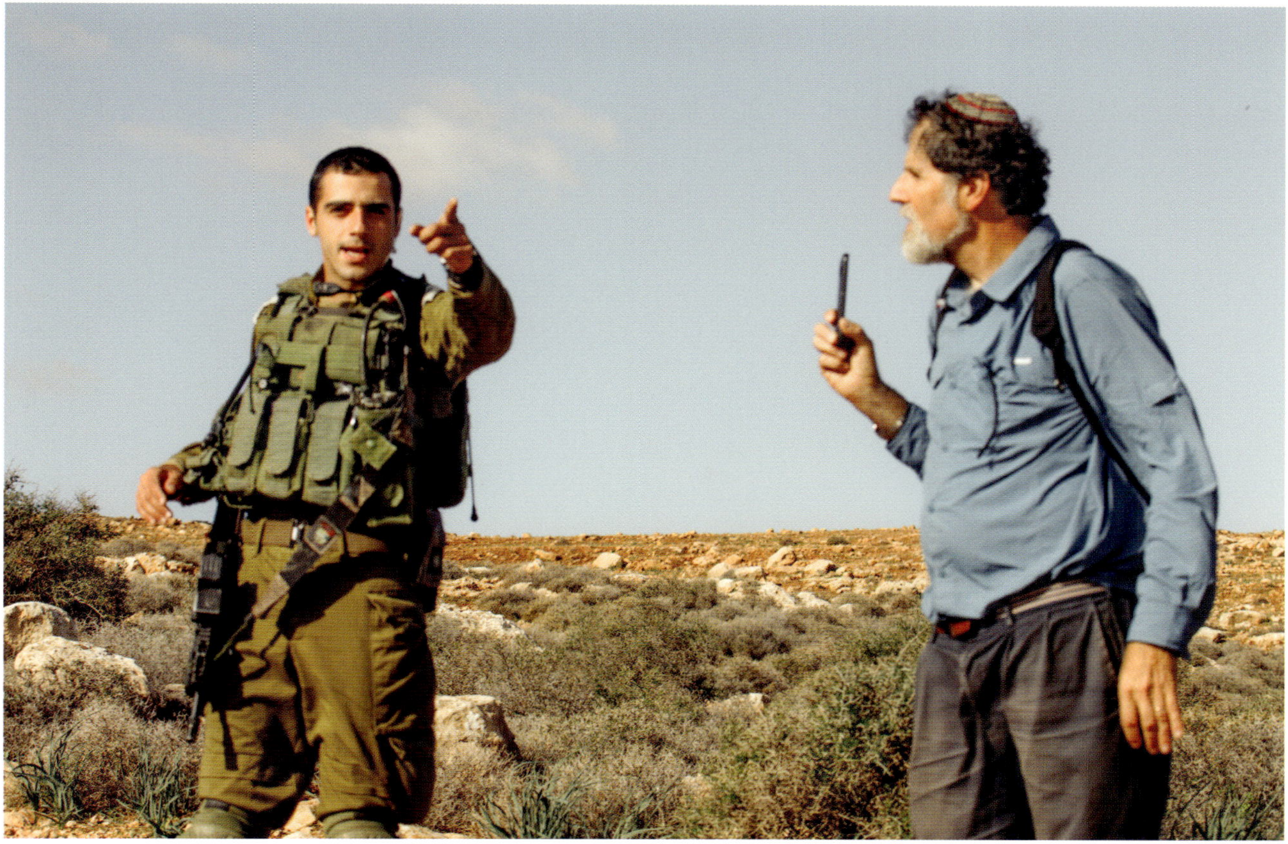

Arik speculates that they make the tea (which they offer to us) in order to claim their land. And also, we say, so that they can live their lives. Arik adds that they want to hold on to their dignity.

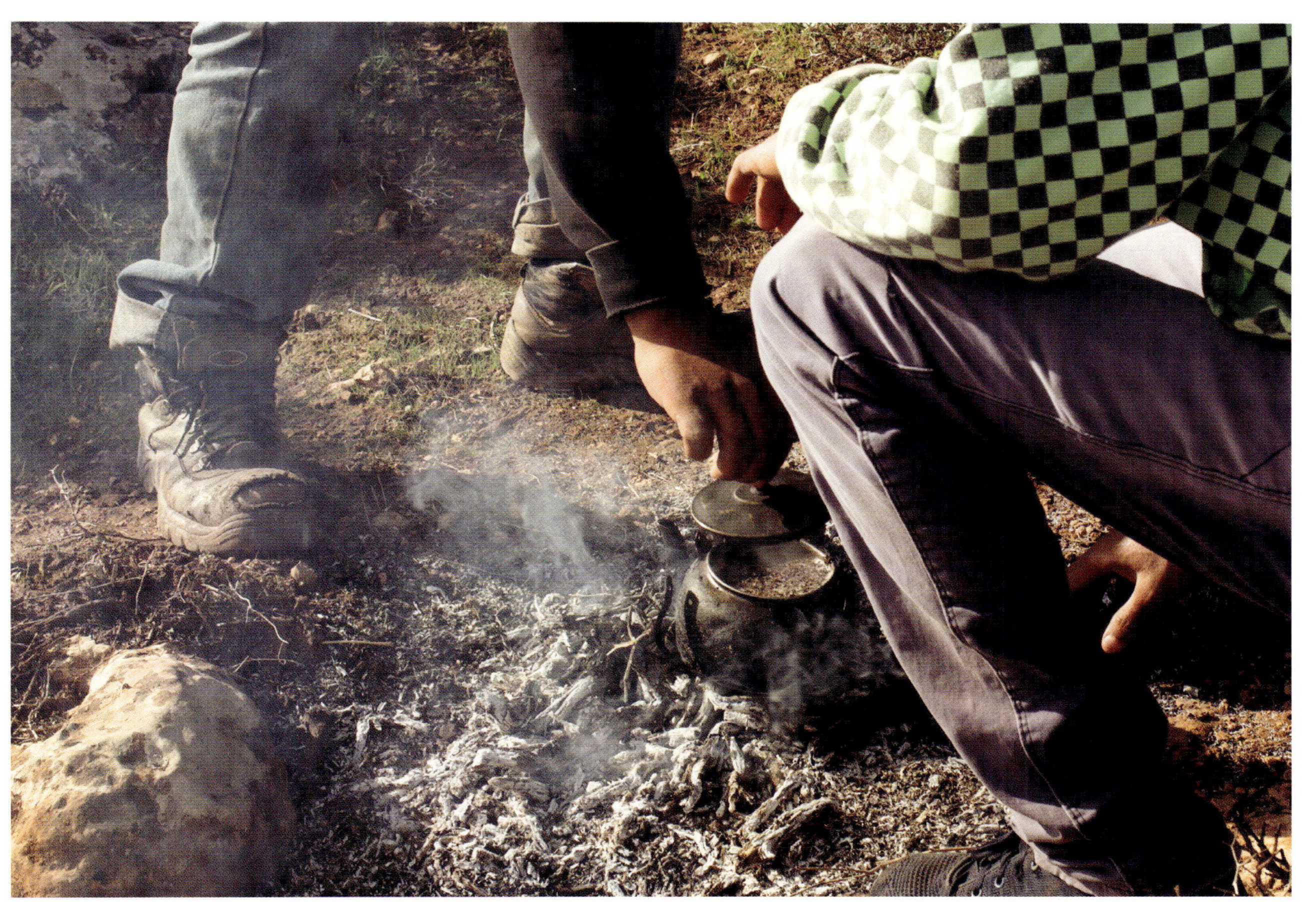

4.10 ʻEin ar-Rashash, December 2018.

Whatever their reason, none of us are allowed to enjoy the respite. By the time we have gulped down our tea, a new contingent of soldiers and police has arrived.

4.11 ‘Ein ar-Rashash, December 2018.

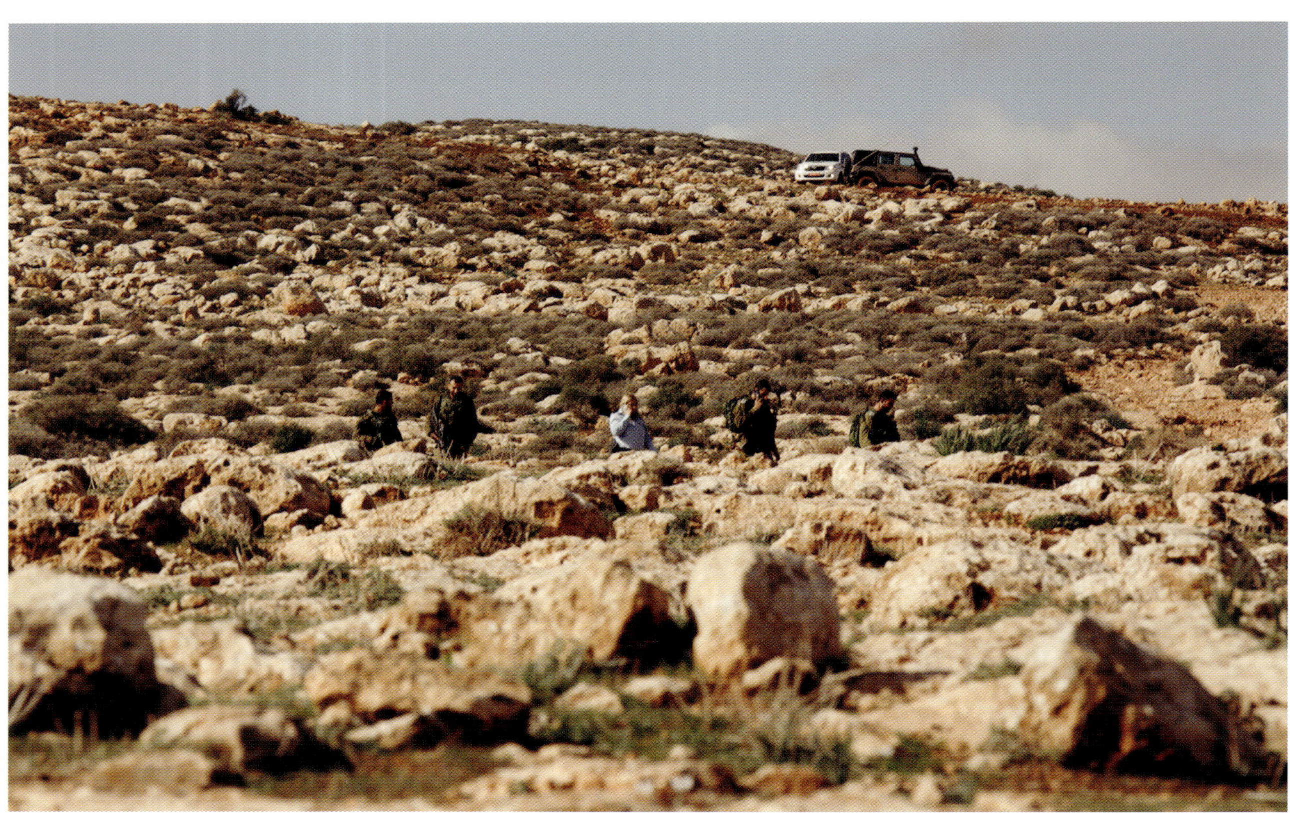

They are angry. Having to shuttle back and forth between us and the settlers (still high up on their ridge in the firing zone) has tested their endurance.

4.12 'Ein ar-Rashash, December 2018.

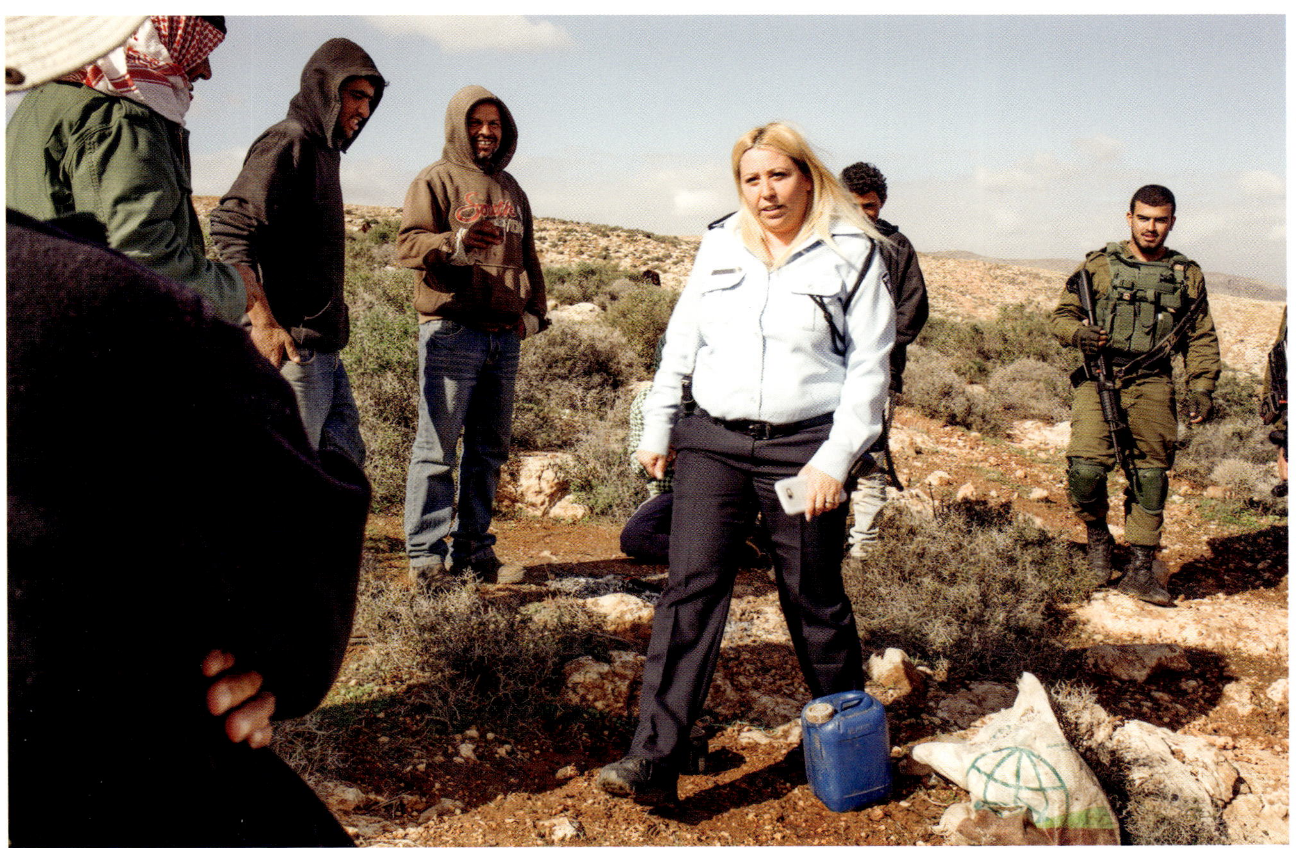

Or perhaps they are just tired of being surrounded by so much beauty.

October, 2023: The people of 'Ein ar-Rashash were expelled from their homes because of constant, fierce harassment by Israeli settlers. The village no longer exists.

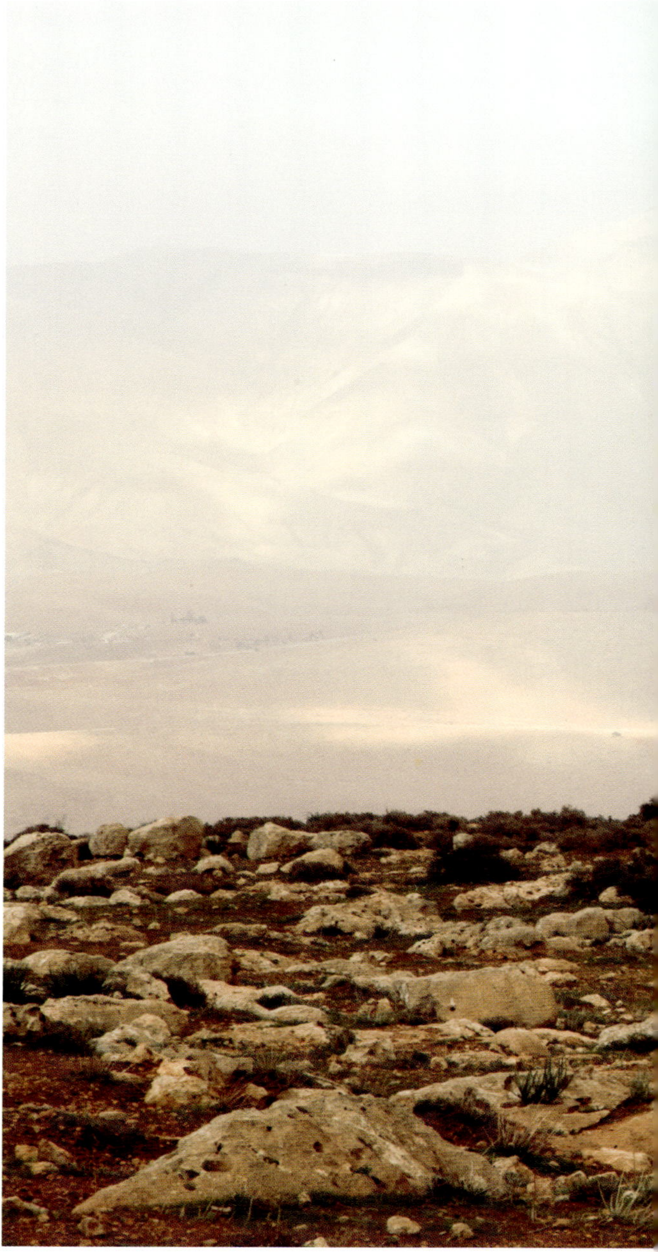

4.13 'Ein ar-Rashash, December 2018.

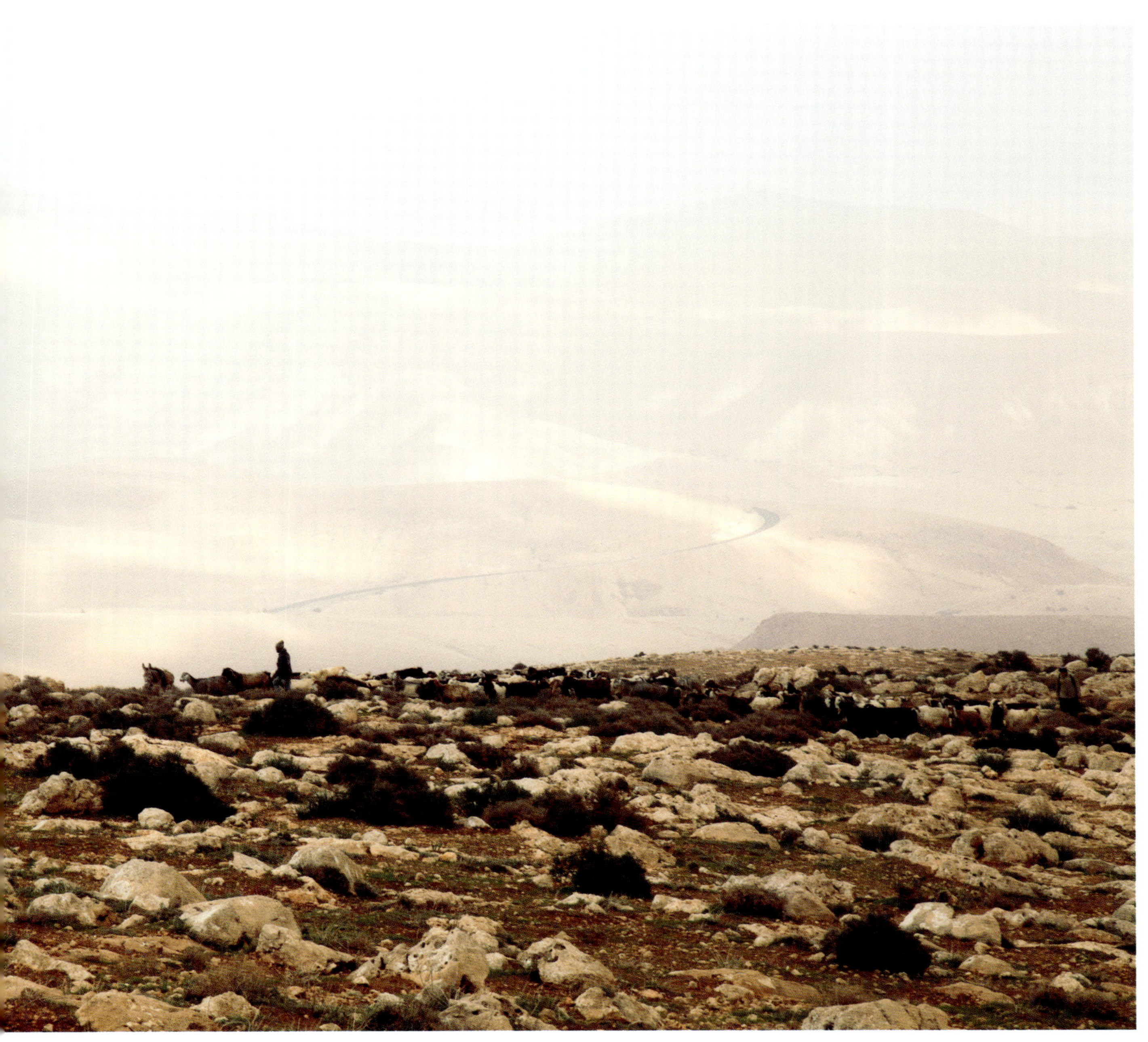

Laḥza: Abu Jibril

Abu Jibril remembers every day of the fifty years the community has been here—also the period of unrest that drove them here in the first place. Can he explain any of it to the officer, new to these parts?

What the soldier knows is the heaviness of gun and pouches. They don't share a language. The officer is fed up.

These people are a nuisance.
I can't believe I'm here.

For Abu Jibril: an urgency, also certainty, in his eloquent fingers that the officer cannot, will not, doesn't want to read.

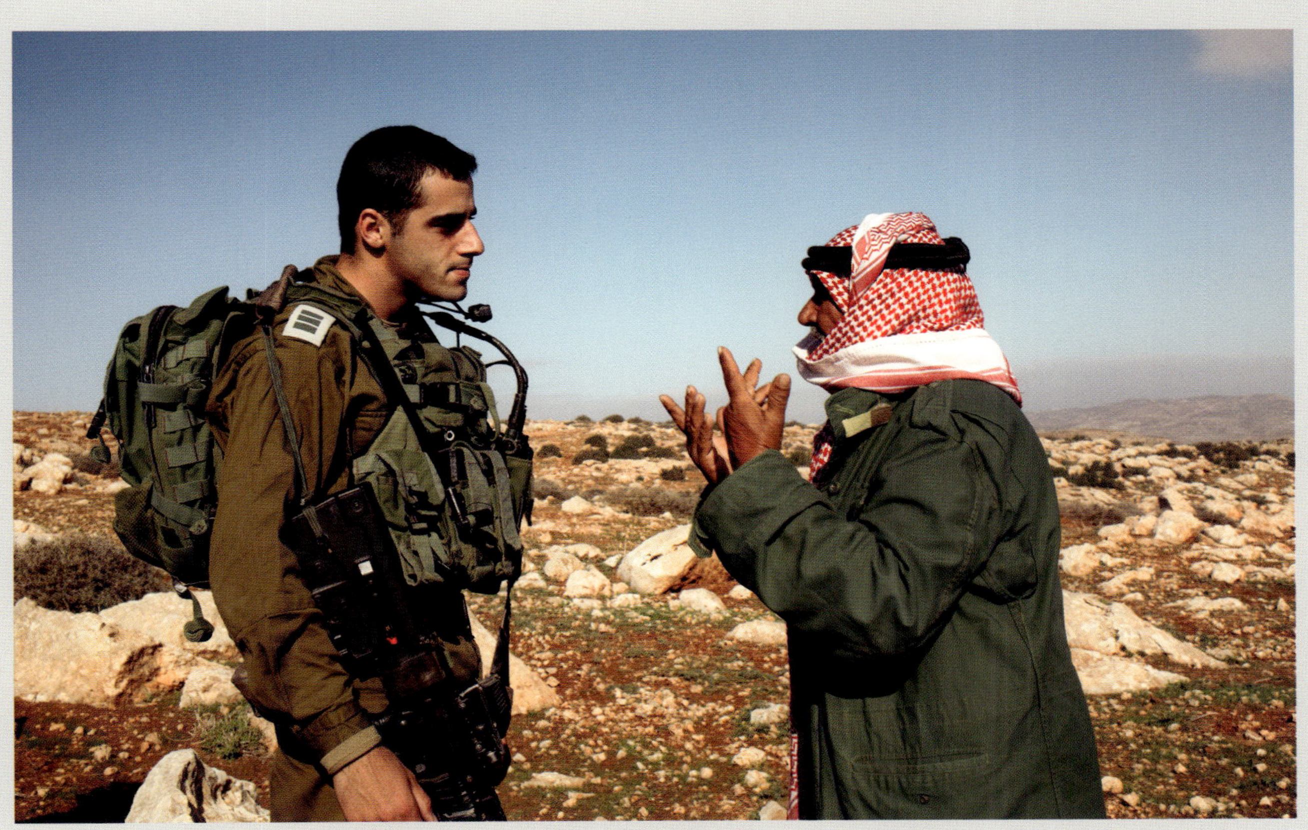

L.4 ‘Ein ar-Rashash, December 2018.

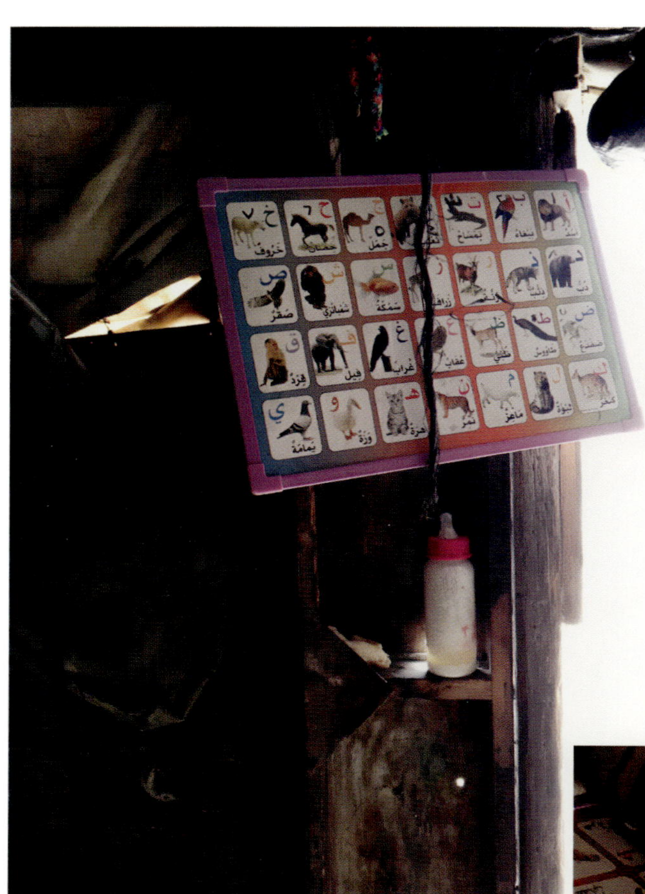

5.1 Susiya, March 2016.
5.2 Susiya, March 2016.

5. Arabic

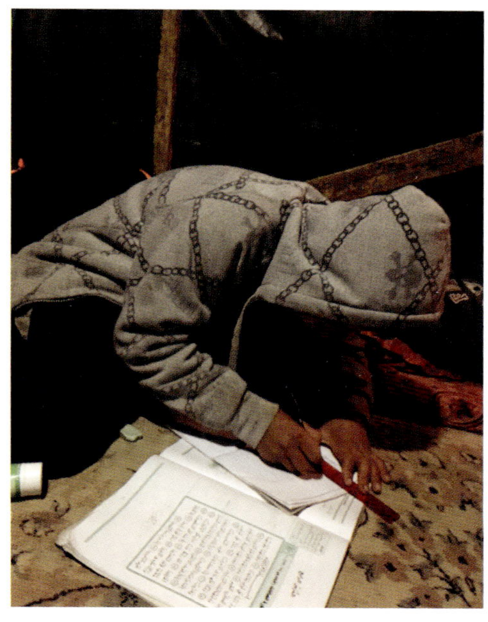

First, the music. It changes from place to place. The city Arabic of Jerusalem and Ramallah becomes gruffer, rougher, in the desert, where the guttural "q"—often pronounced only as a glottal stop, that is, a quick catching of the breath in the throat—turns into a "g." The shepherds' language flows seamlessly into the cries and whistles and grunts they use to speak to the sheep. At the same time, they sprinkle their sentences with the astonishing formulas of courtesy that come so naturally to the tongue: May Allah heal you, give you peace, bless your hands. We thank you, you have honored us. Welcome, you are our guests. Go in peace.

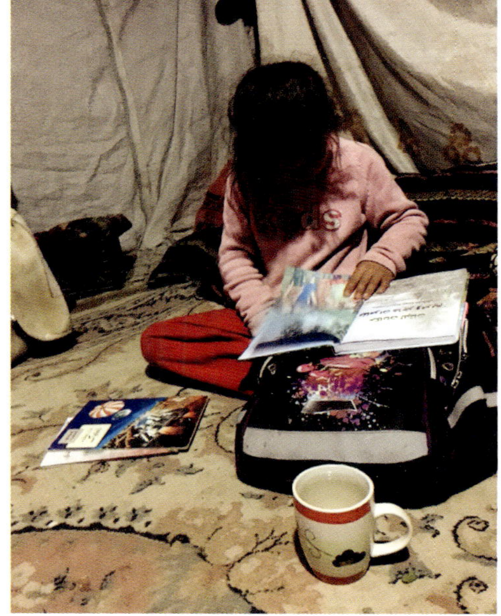

5.3 Susiya, March 2016.
5.4 Susiya, March 2016.

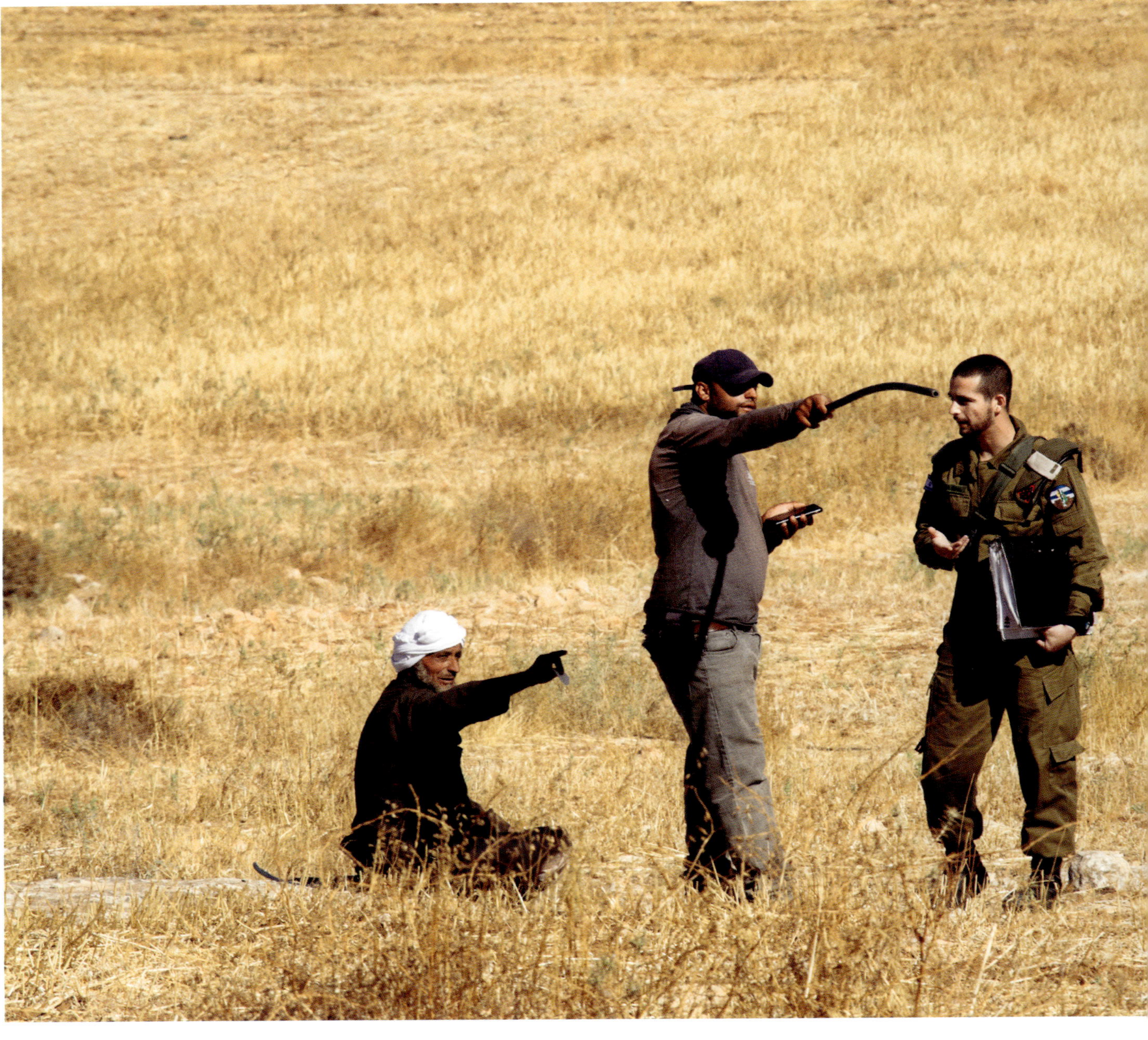

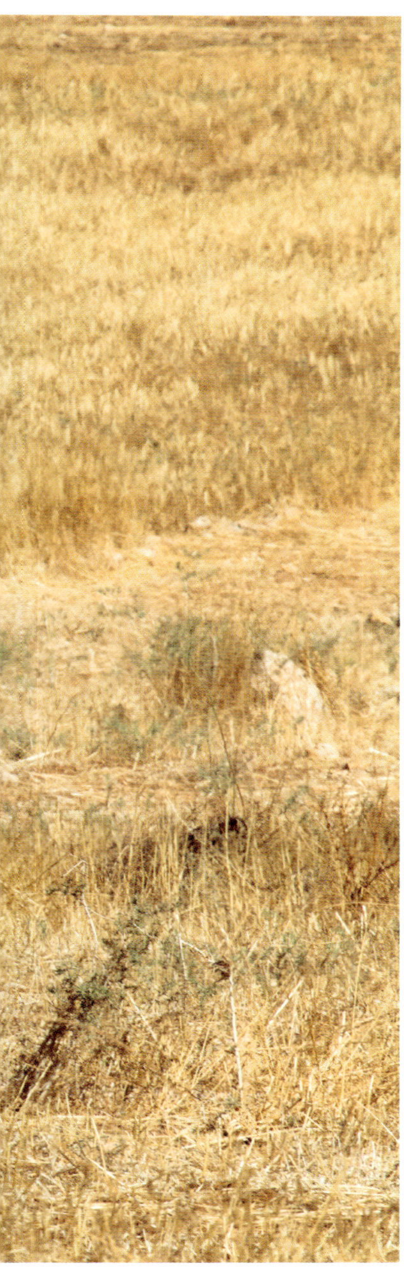

If one lives inside that language, some things become clear and necessary in a way that no translation can convey. Take, for example, the verb *zalam*—to wrong someone, to treat unfairly, to oppress—and its noun form, *zulem*, injustice. "*ayishin fi hayaah kullayaat-ha zulem eb-zulem*," "We are living a life of oppression within oppression" (J. Elihay, *The Olive Tree Dictionary*, s.v.). It's not only the Occupation that produces such sentences, though it's a fertile ground for them. Deep in the fiber of the language is a notion of malicious hurt—often linked to other words, such as pride or honor, *sharaf*, or what is right, *haqq*. *Zulem* (the noun form) happens all the time; it is almost as if one were waiting for it, with an exquisite sensitivity to potential pain that radiates outward from the core being of the person. Seen from the other end, this is the unthinkable grief that comes when that inner self, so deeply hidden, is violated, ravaged, disregarded. At the heart of *zulem* is an unfairness that no human creature can understand or withstand.

5.5 Wadi Sweid, July 2019.

It can happen any time, in everyday interactions, in love or friendship. It is something entirely tangible or sensual, felt not in the mind but in the pores of the skin and the invisible folds of the gut. But: The Occupation is a machine for manufacturing mass quantities of *zulem*. In a way, that is its true purpose. The settler or the soldier, carrying a gun, drives you off the land your father and grandfather and great-grandfather plowed and harvested, the land where they grazed their flocks. You feel the *zulem*-driven cry of that land inside you—the land that is a living part of yourself—and the violation can drive you mad. A thousand horses pulling your heart from your body with knives and ropes would hurt less than what the settler or the soldier is doing with words, a scrap of paper signed by the battalion officer, and a gun. All human beings may know this feeling, but in Arabic, it has an irreducible aspect of sacrality. Life itself is being abused, misused for the sake of cruelty, against the natural order of desert and rocks and trees and rain and sheep and the bread one bakes and the sun that rises and sets as an unerring witness to *zulem*.

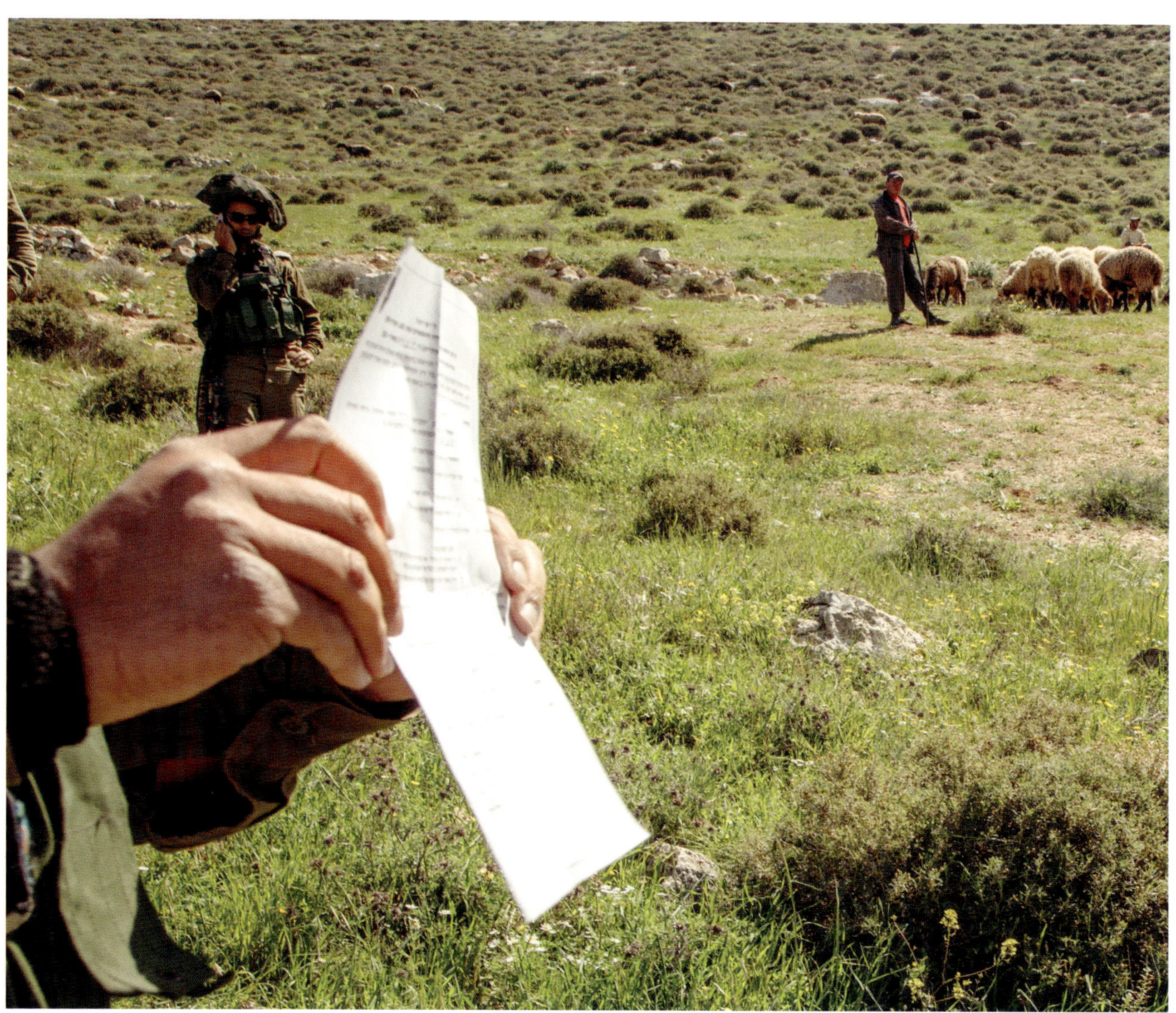

5.6 Zanuta, March 2015.

It's different from political injustice or unfairness, it's not a legal abstraction, it's not even something in the mind, a mentalistic configuration made with words. *Zulem* can be healed with words and deeds, if they are truthfully felt and uttered, but the Occupation regularly, hourly, compounds *zulem* within *zulem*.

There are other, more innocent words that carry that same tangible force and texture: "Show me the breadth of your shoulders" (from behind—in other words, "Get lost.") "Excuse me for mentioning it" (literally: "May Allah honor you"—*ajallak.*) Or the omnipresent *ma'alesh*, "I hope I haven't hurt you too much." There is the everyday politesse and the simplicity of wonder: "I like that a lot," *'ajabni ktir.* And always the appeal to the God who is very close, though sometimes not close enough; the God who lives in the throat or on the tongue and, dependably, in the density of sound.

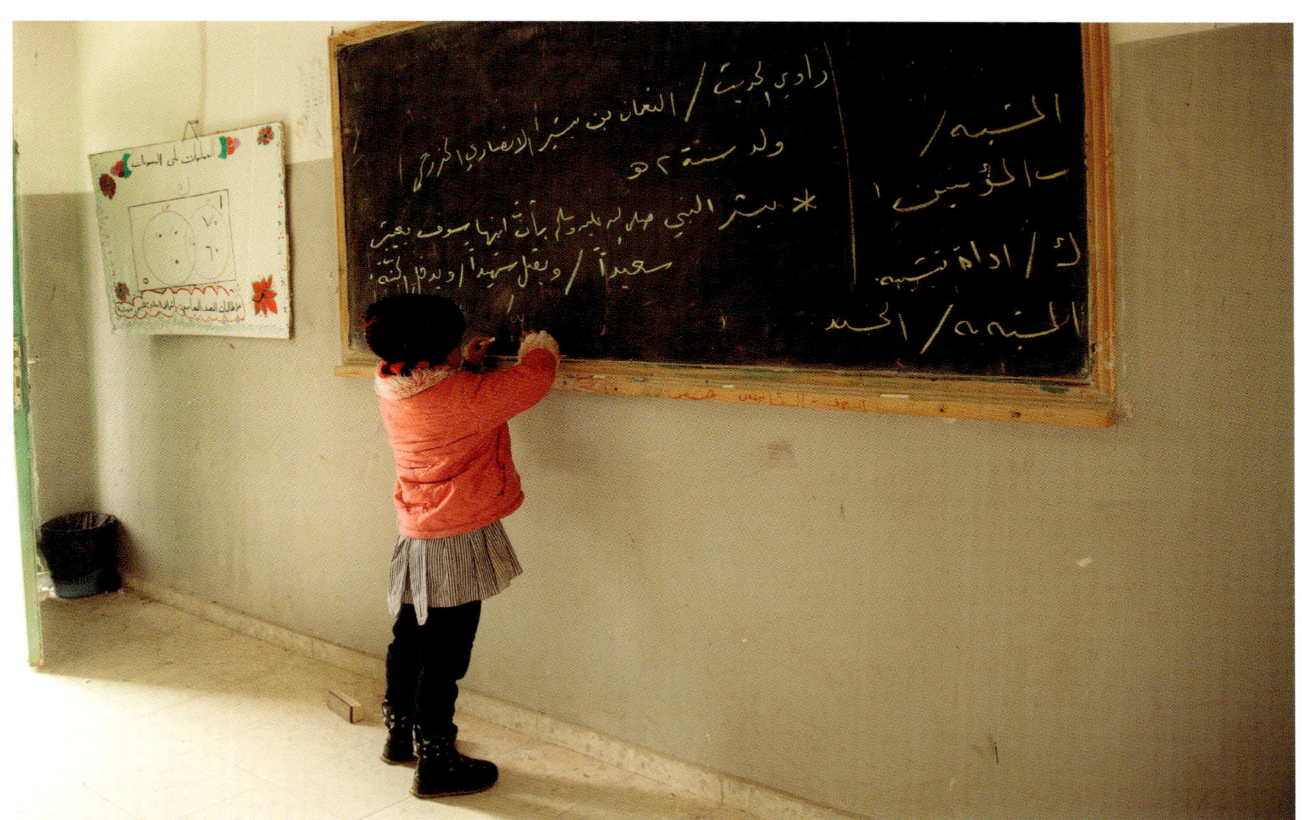

5.7 Susiya, March 2016.

Laḥza: Umm al-Khair

The name means "Mother of Goodness."

Whenever you go there, there will be new ruins. The Civil Administration loves to target Umm al-Khair. Like all Palestinians in Area C, the people of this village cannot get building permits, not even to add a rickety outhouse to their tent or shack. The committee that nominally issues permits sits in an army camp and is dominated by settlers. The birds in the sky would have a better chance of getting a permit than the Palestinians. So the army bulldozers come and go, as if they belonged there.

Rocks and more rocks. The sheep can't eat them, and the grazing grounds were mostly stolen long ago by the settlers of Carmel, who like to throw rocks at the shacks of Umm al-Khair in the middle of the night. They make a huge racket when they hit the tin-and-aluminum roofs. The children wake and cry. On many nights Ta'ayush activists sleep in the village.

Demolitions are particularly frequent in the winter months, when it is wet and freezing in the hills. A mother stands, barefoot, in the ruins of her home, a baby in her arms, kids hovering around her feet. An old man, Salim 'Eid al-Hathalin, waves a demolition order the soldiers have brought him. "Why do they want to destroy my house? Where can I go? Can I go to America? I have nothing, and they want to take that nothing from me."

Deep desert begins at the edge of the village. On a clear day, you can see across the Jordan River. The villagers bring water in tankers; it's expensive. In summer they have to buy fodder in Yatta. No water pipes, no heating, no school. Milk is churned into butter and hard cheese the old way, in animal skins, over many hours. The birds, black ones, white ones, seem always to be there, looking for goodness.

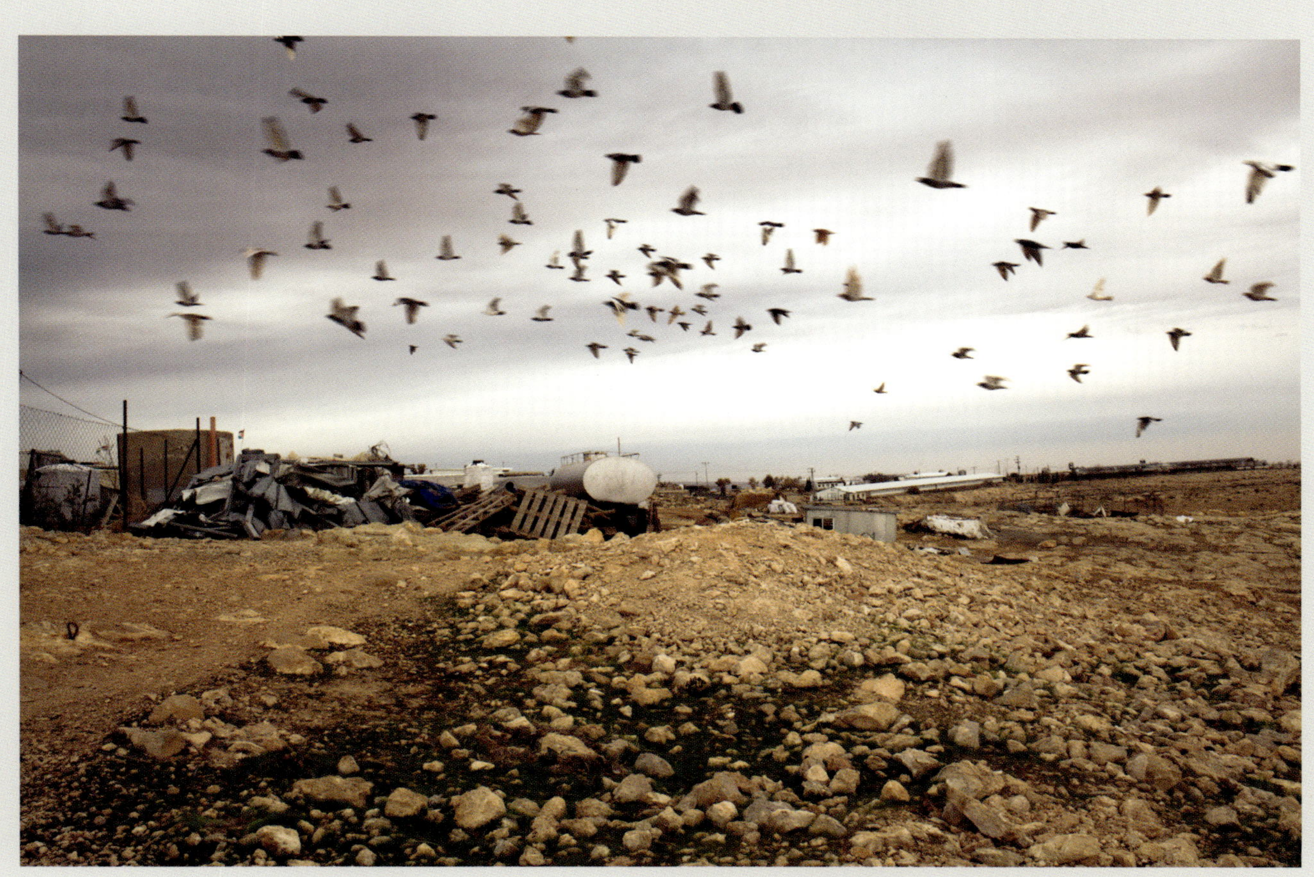

L.5 Umm al-Khair, January 2017.

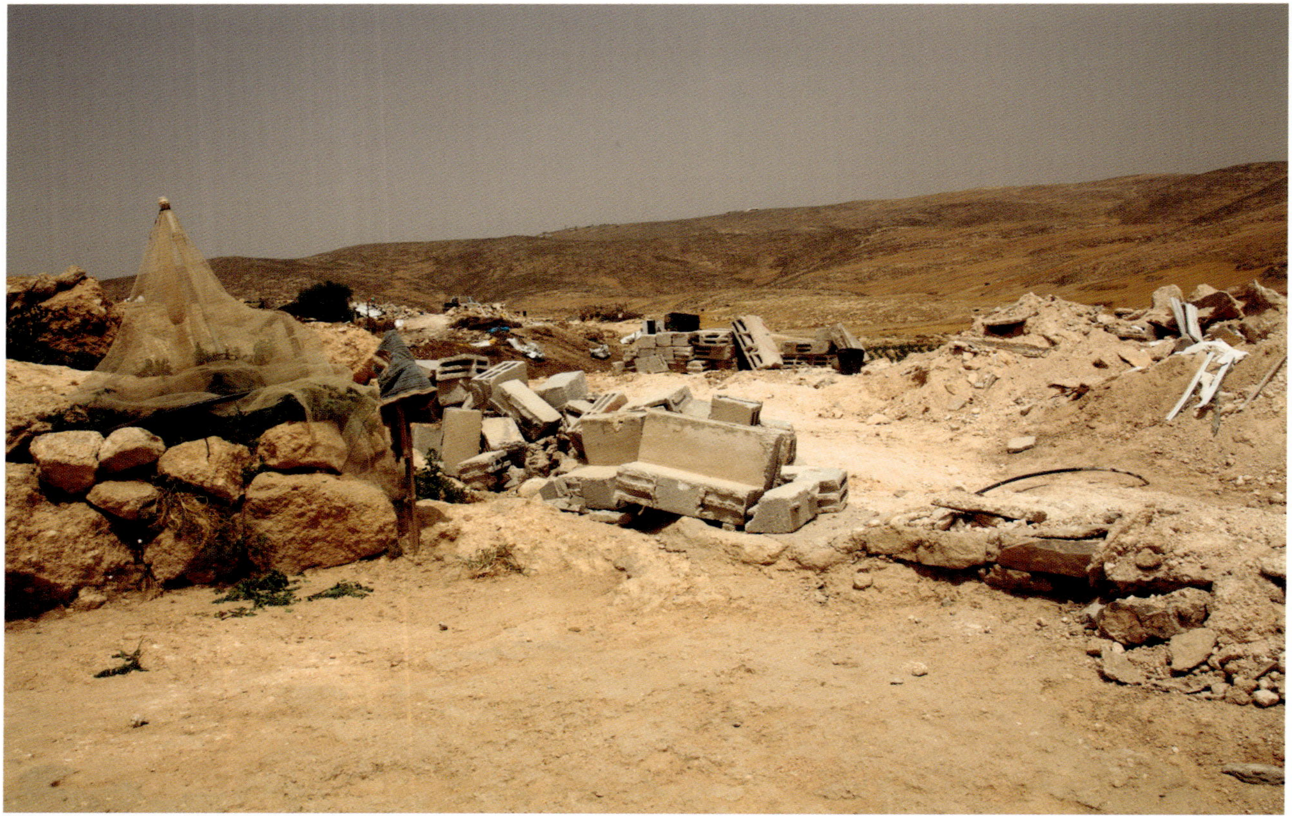

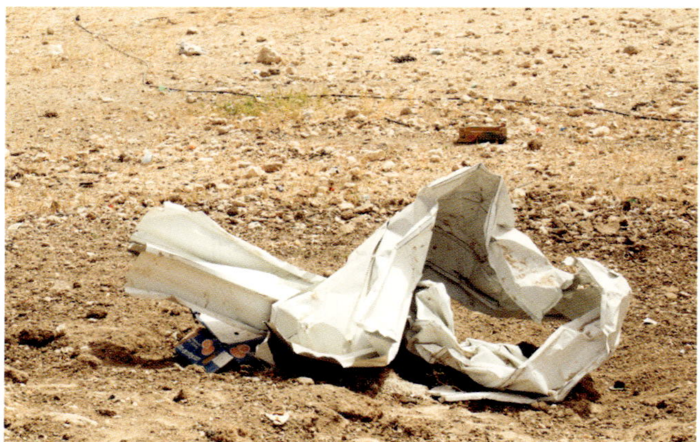

6.1 Mirkez, Masafer Yatta, South Hebron Hills, May 2018.

6.2 Mirkez, Masafer Yatta, South Hebron Hills, May 2018.

6.

Demolitions

It takes the bulldozers only a few minutes to kill a house. Things take their course: the soldiers come, usually at dawn; they give the owners a minute or two to salvage some prized possession—a chair, a coffee pot, a blanket—and then the execution takes place. The owners stand and watch. Sometimes they weep and scream and tear their hair and curse the killers.

A house is a living being—actually a person, unique in self, like everyone else; often, with its own name. Like the olive trees, who are seen by Palestinians as children in the family. When settlers or soldiers cut down a grove of olive trees, the owners may sit in mourning for a week, as they would for a brother or child. Think of a home as a somewhat extended olive grove.

House executions are entirely legal under Israeli law. Palestinians in Area C have no hope whatsoever of getting a building permit. They then build without one: no choice. Then the Civil Administration sends its bulldozers to demolish the home, or the tabun oven, or the outhouse, or the baby's pigeonhole bedroom, or the tent where women churn butter. The army seems to take pleasure in doing this at the height of winter, leaving the family outside in the wind and rain, or in the summer, when it is 45 degrees in the sun and there is no shade.

A supreme court justice, in court, to a Palestinian family whose home was slotted for demolition: "Let it be clear. The law is clear.

Anything built without a permit is destined for destruction."

Like cats, like Hindus, Buddhists, Jains, and Druze, some houses have many lives. There was the Peace House, Beit ʿArabiyya, in ʿAnata, just north of Jerusalem. We rebuilt it seven or eight times—it's hard to count. Sometimes a rhythm is established: the family builds, the army kills, we rebuild with the owners. A new demolition order appears. The owners appeal to the court, which rules against them (this process can take some time). The army repeats its wanton act; we come back to rebuild. And so on, until the end of time. At Umm al-Khair, one of the villages regularly targeted for demolitions, life is routinely déjà vu, except that the moment of devastation gets worse each time it comes round. God, the Talmud says, continuously creates worlds and destroys them—that is his profession—but he practices on the homes of South Hebron.

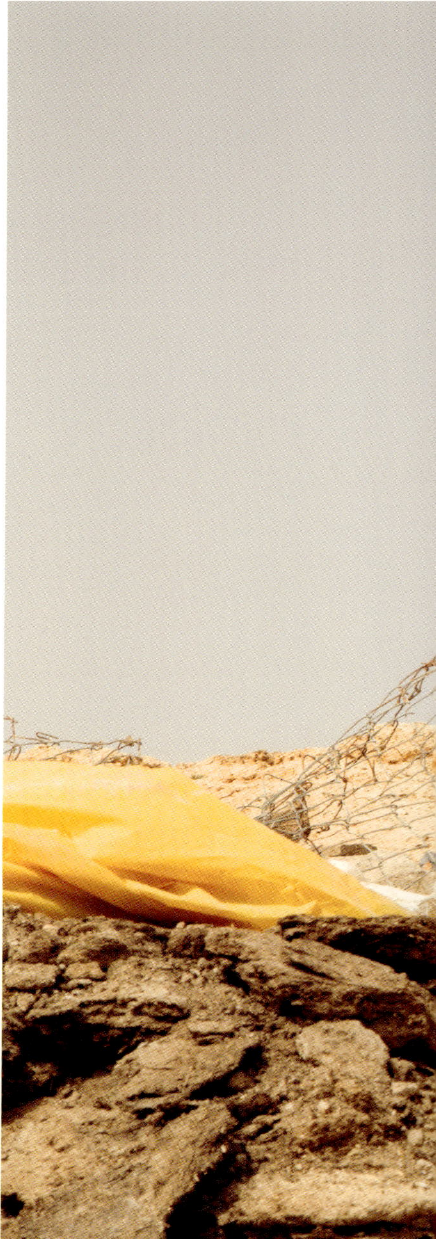

6.3 Mirkez, Masafer Yatta, South Hebron Hills, May 2018.

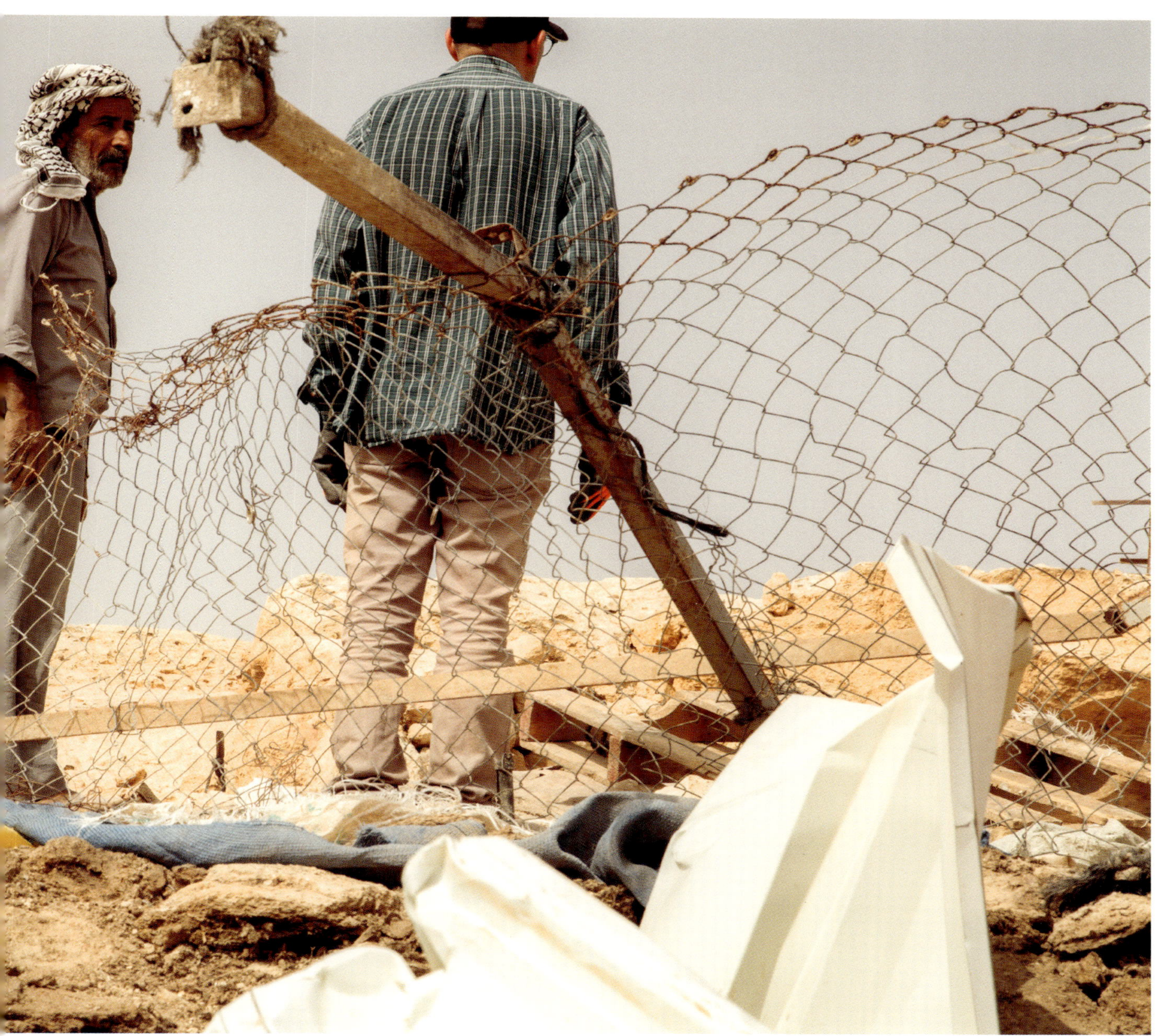

In the open desert, a broken house is a sculpture. Twisted white metal; a lonely door, hanging by its hinges, that once opened a wooden cabinet; lego blocks of cement, disarticulated, on a mound of rubble; a plastic chair; a colored curtain peeking from the dust; a satellite dish, no longer linked to the stars; electric wires, severed, blue, yellow, black; iron rods, once a grid and a scaffold; jagged hunks of stone. No one could produce so eloquent a witness just by trying to, by thinking. A mindless bulldozer can do it. Those who come to destroy are thus exquisite artisans of cruelty, leaving masterpieces behind them, each time, in the sand.

6.4 Mirkez, Masafer Yatta, South Hebron Hills, May 2018.

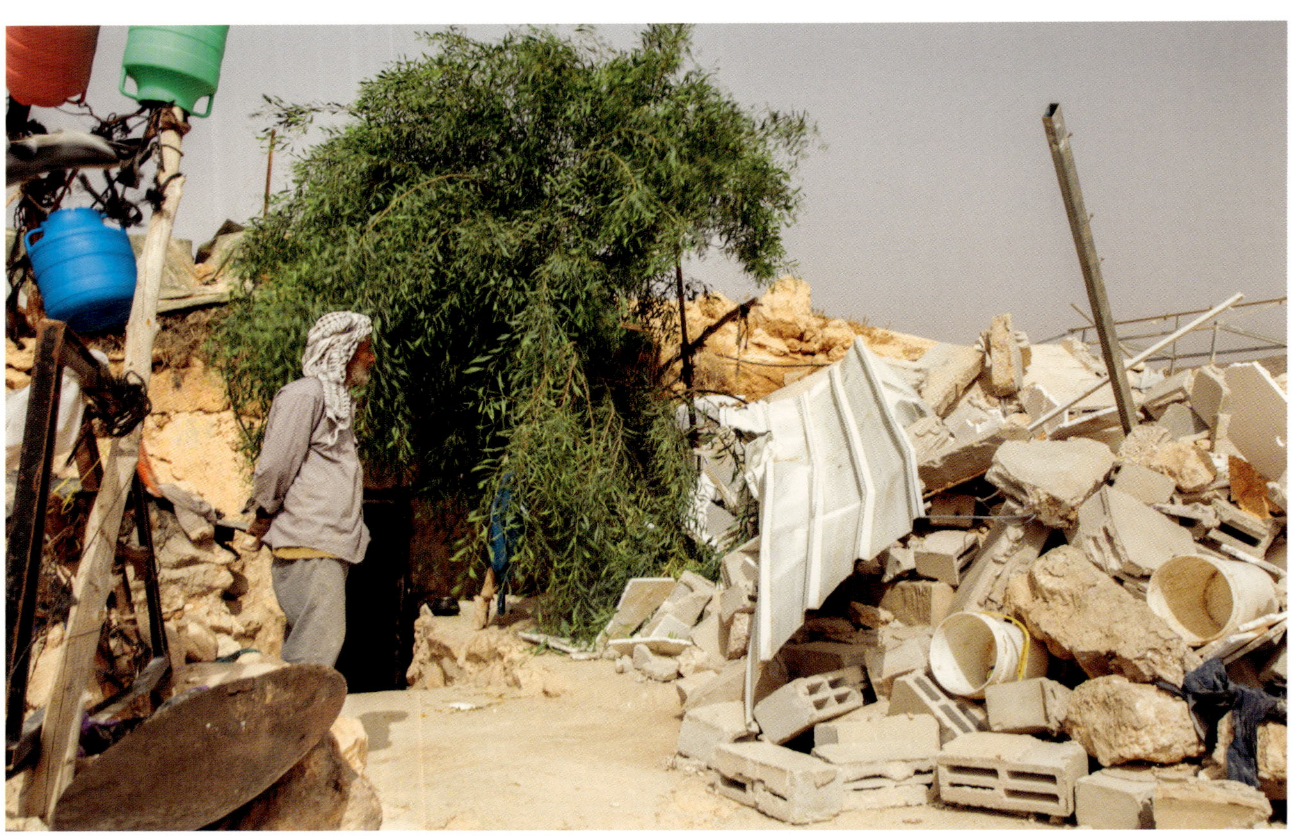

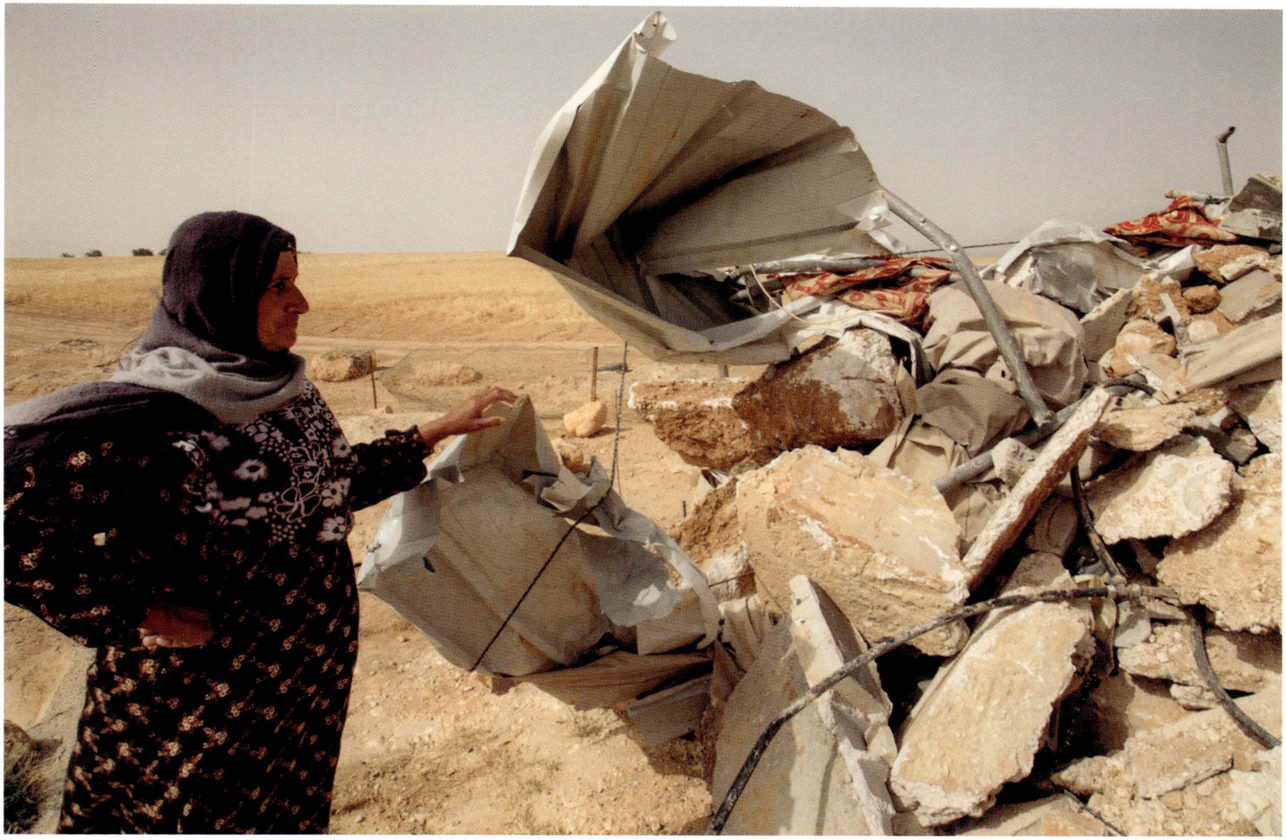

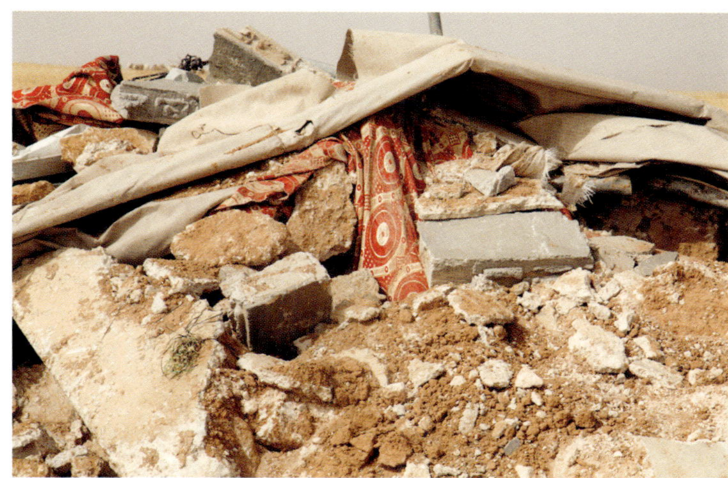

6.5 Mirkez, Masafer Yatta, South Hebron Hills, May 2018.

6.6 Mirkez, Masafer Yatta, South Hebron Hills, May 2018.

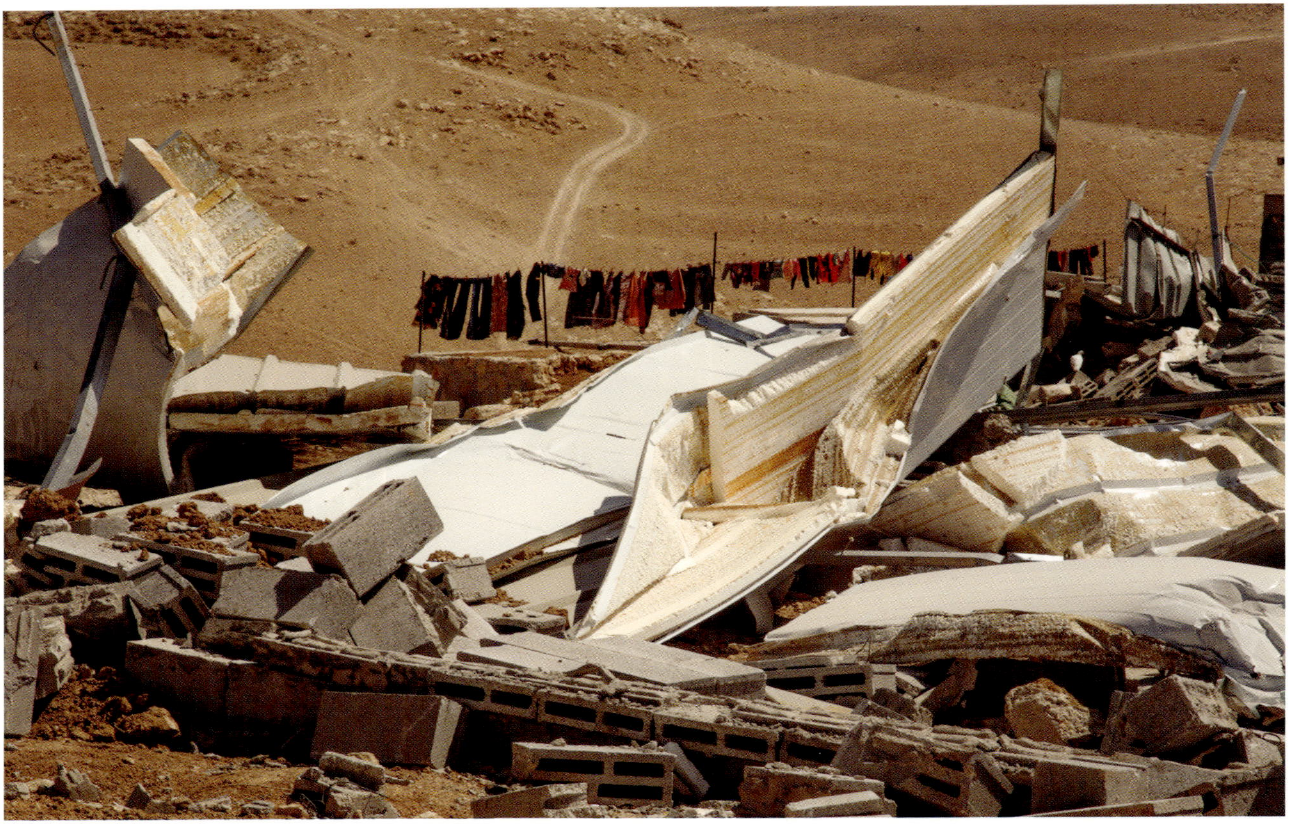

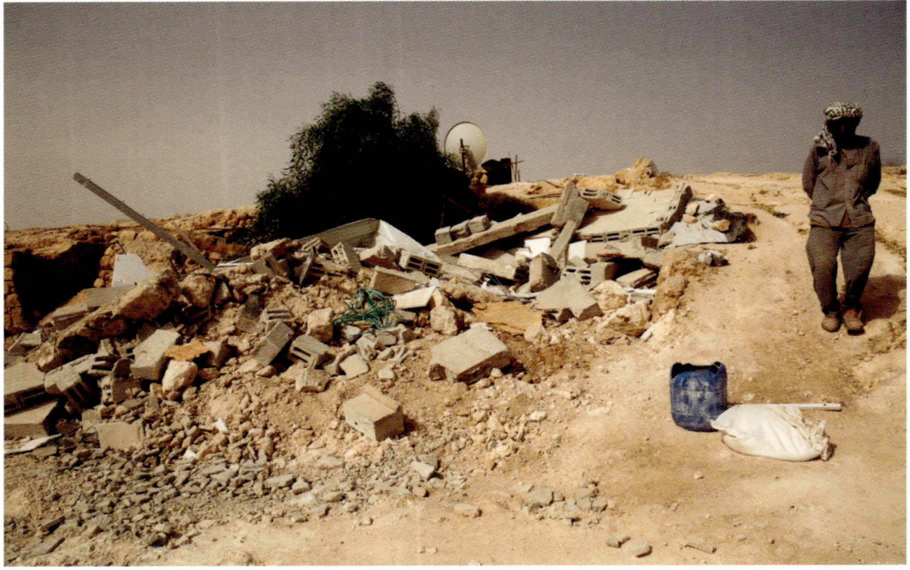

6.7 Fakheit, Masafer Yatta, South Hebron Hills, May 2022.

6.8 Mirkez, Masafer Yatta, South Hebron Hills, May 2018.

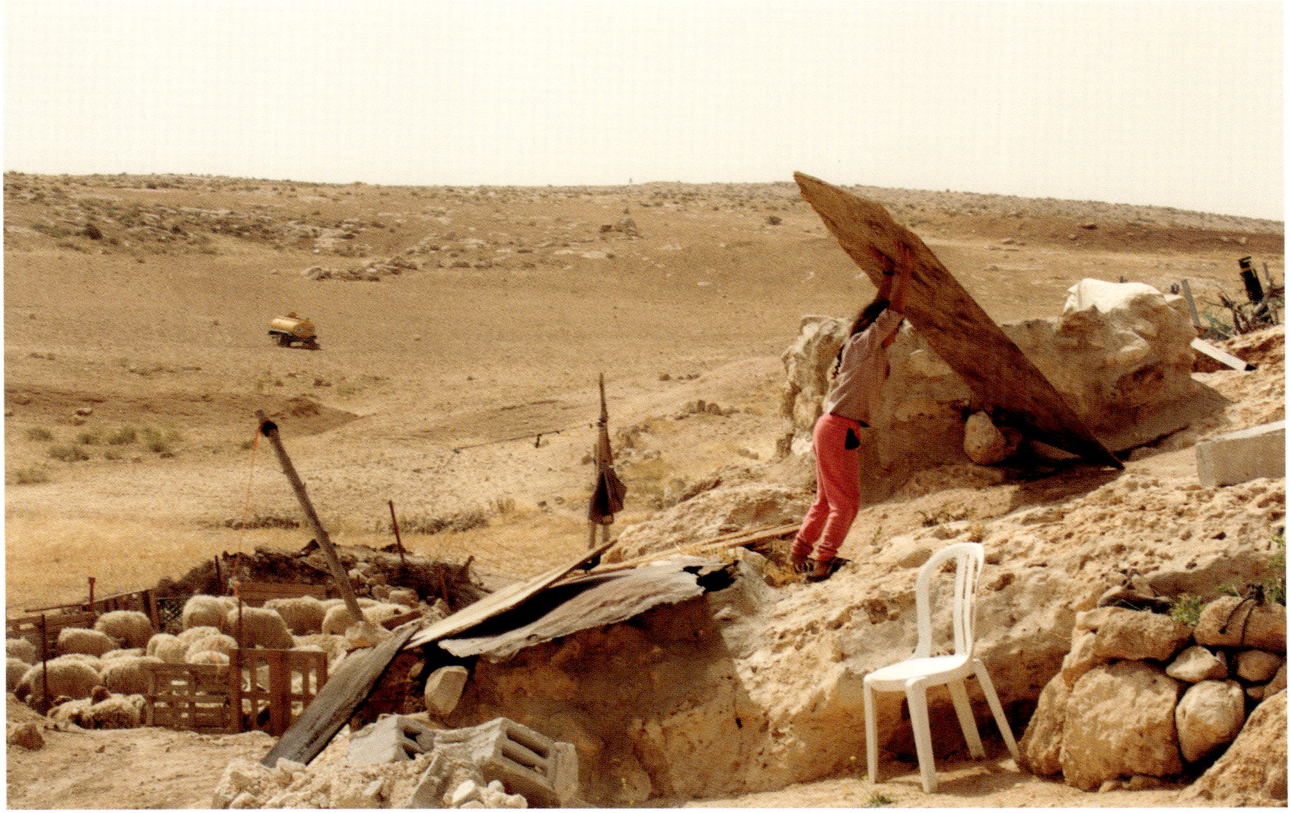

6.9 Mirkez, Masafer Yatta, South Hebron Hills, May 2018.

6.10 Mirkez, Masafer Yatta, South Hebron Hills, May 2018.

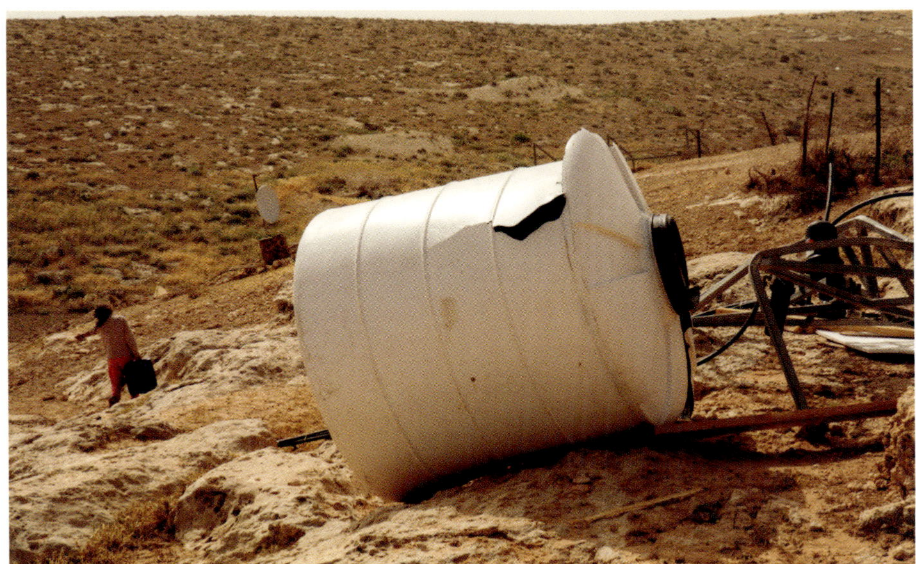

When the Occupation ends and the soldiers and settlers go away, someone should leave one or two of these visionary piles as a monument to our savagery, a solid heap of witness, *gal-'ed*, as the Bible calls it. The first one was built by Jacob and his father-in-law, Laban, as a boundary and a sign: "May God watch between me and you when we are hidden from each other" (Genesis 31:49).

6.11 Mirkez, May 2018.

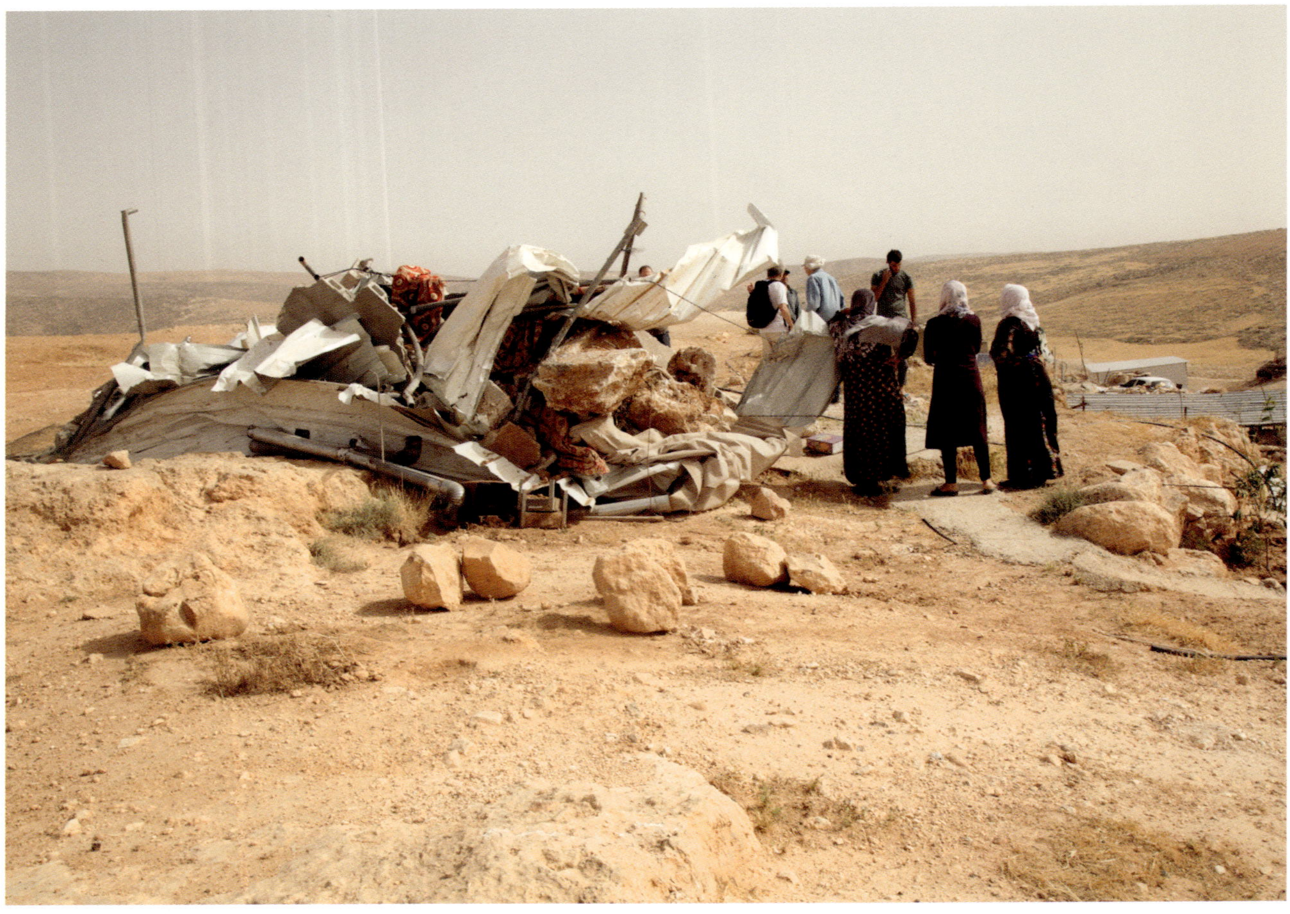

6.12 Umm al-Khair, July 2017.

Every pile of man-made rubble is one of His ten thousand eyes. But sometimes He forgets.

Killing a house is a kind of play, for the soldiers. Rebuilding, for whoever joins in, is a wordless poem, a prayer. Written on the wind. Inscribed on skin and fingers. It's heavy work.

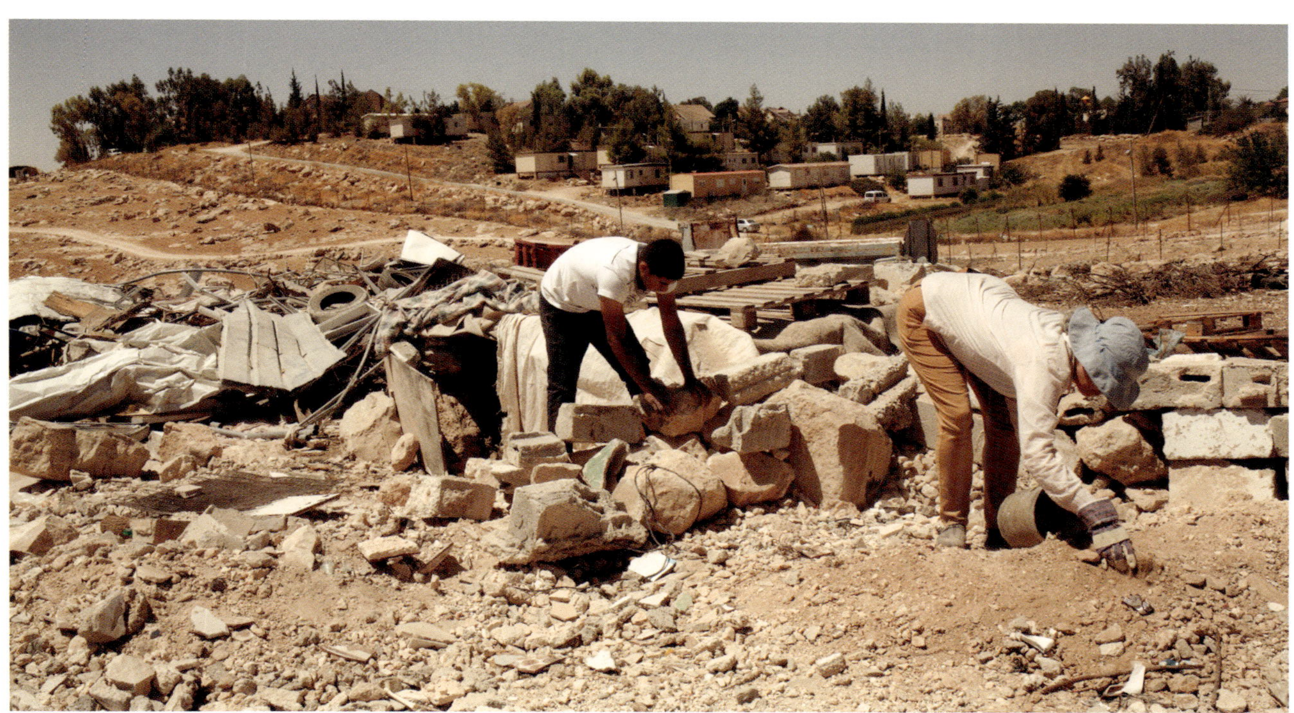

You can spend hours together just rolling one heavy stone back into place. The iron rods have to be extracted from the piles and carried to a new site, where they can be recycled. One runs a lot, up and down the hill.

6.13 a–i Mirkez, May 2018.

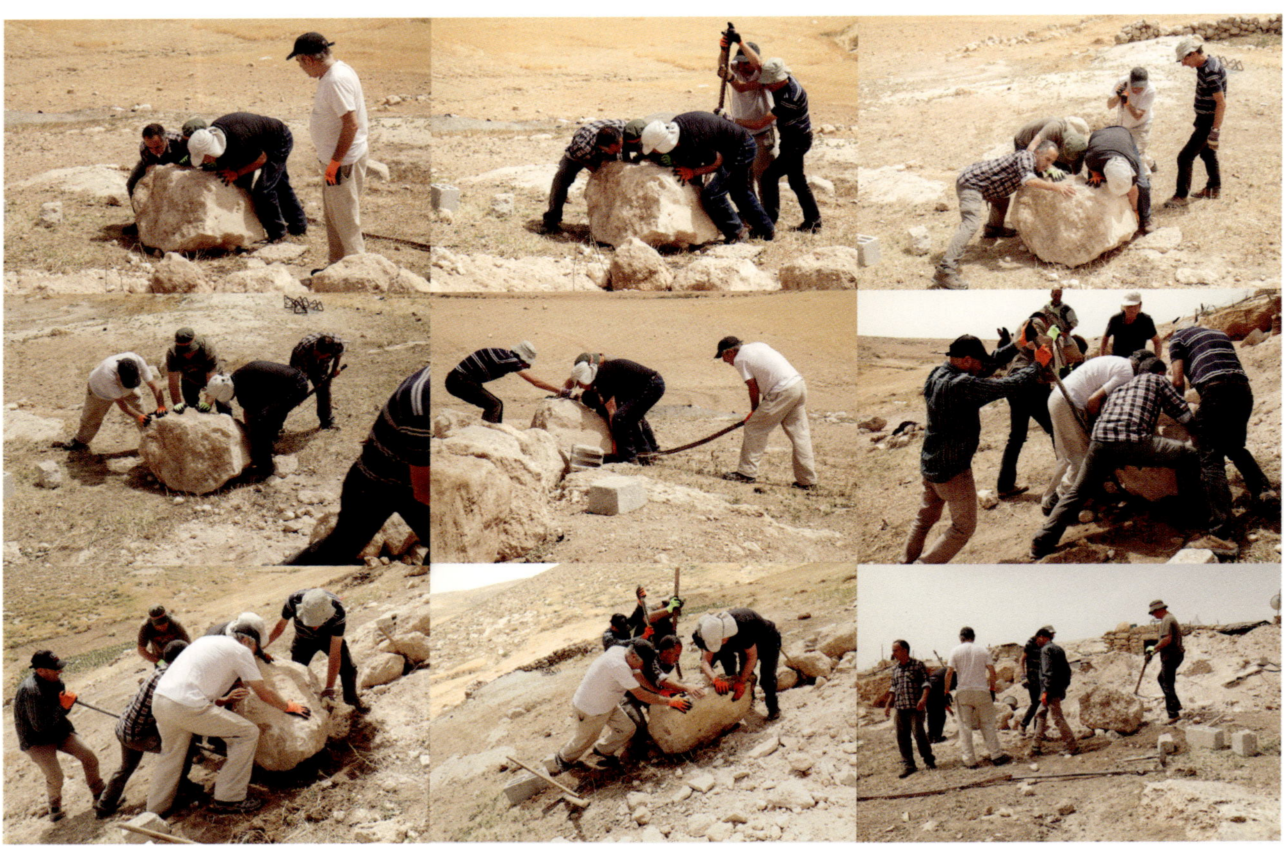

There is much shoveling and lifting and dumping, bucket by bucket. Heavy gloves help; so does tea. Every moment shimmers with the stark beauty of the evanescent.

6.14 Mirkez, May 2018.

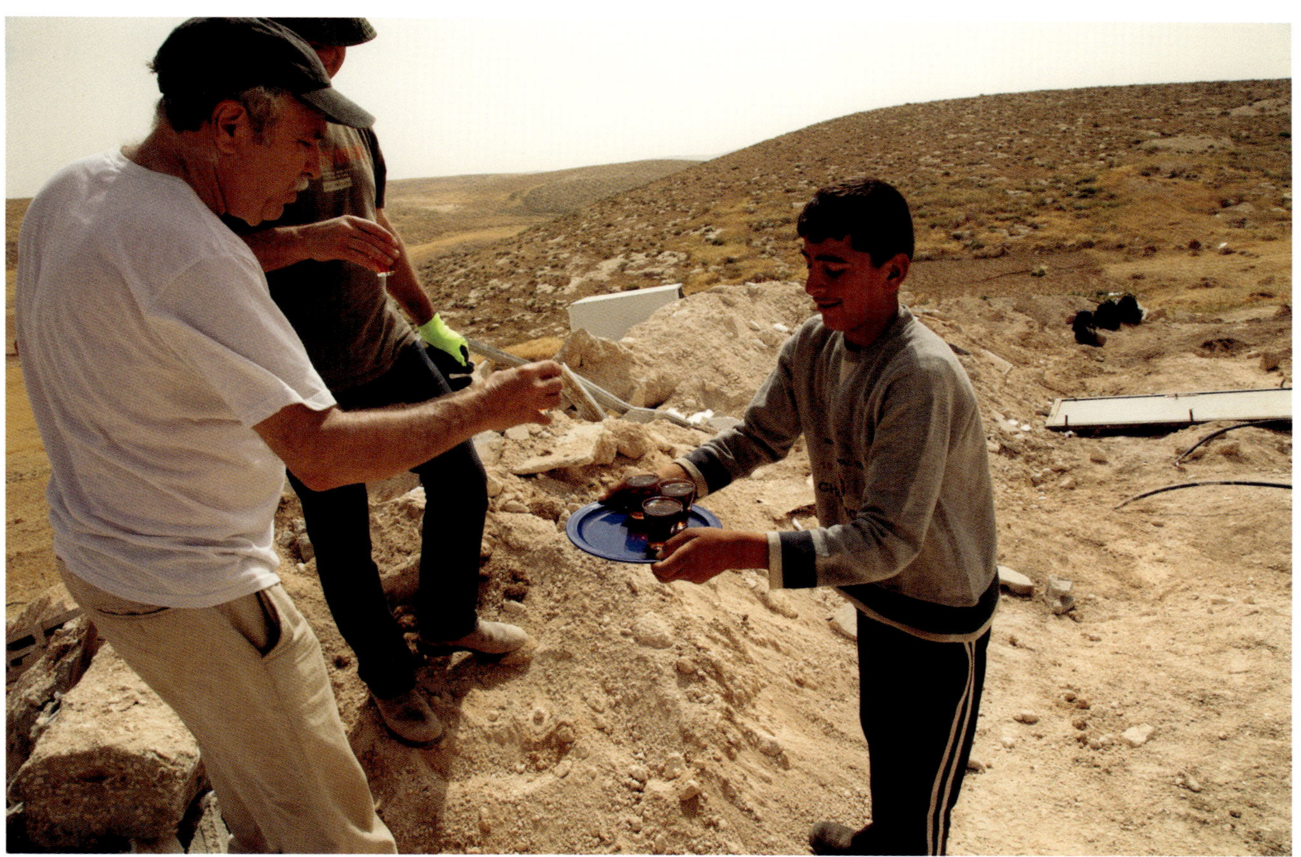

> God gives strength to good people, he enlarges their spirit, whoever they are. Muslims, Jews, international volunteers, it makes no difference, all of you are our guests today.
>
> You have come to do good. There will always be good people, and God turns away from the bad ones. That is what He tells us. We don't think of Arabs and Jews, and neither does He, we think of those who do good and those who seek to cause pain.
>
> . . . We will first clear away the ruins, and we will build again, close to the sheep-pens, so the sheep and the goats don't have to walk too far.

Shehada Salama Mkhamra, from Magha'ir al-'Abid, who lost his home; when we came to rebuild.

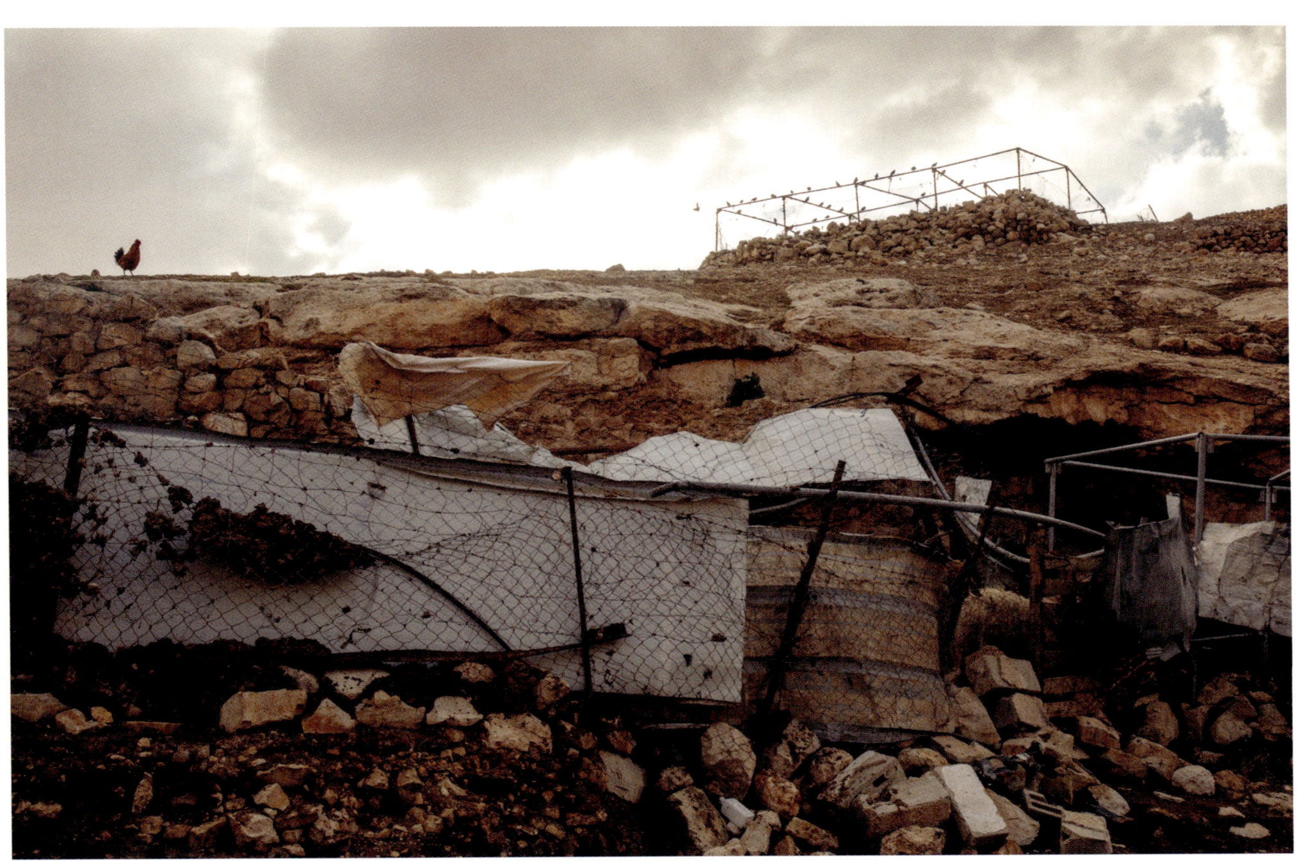

6.15 Magha'ir al-'Abid, January 2022.

Humsa al-Tahta, 2017. Rather than let bulldozers maraud through the whole compound on the way to his house, and then

6.16 Humsa al-Tahta, July 2017.

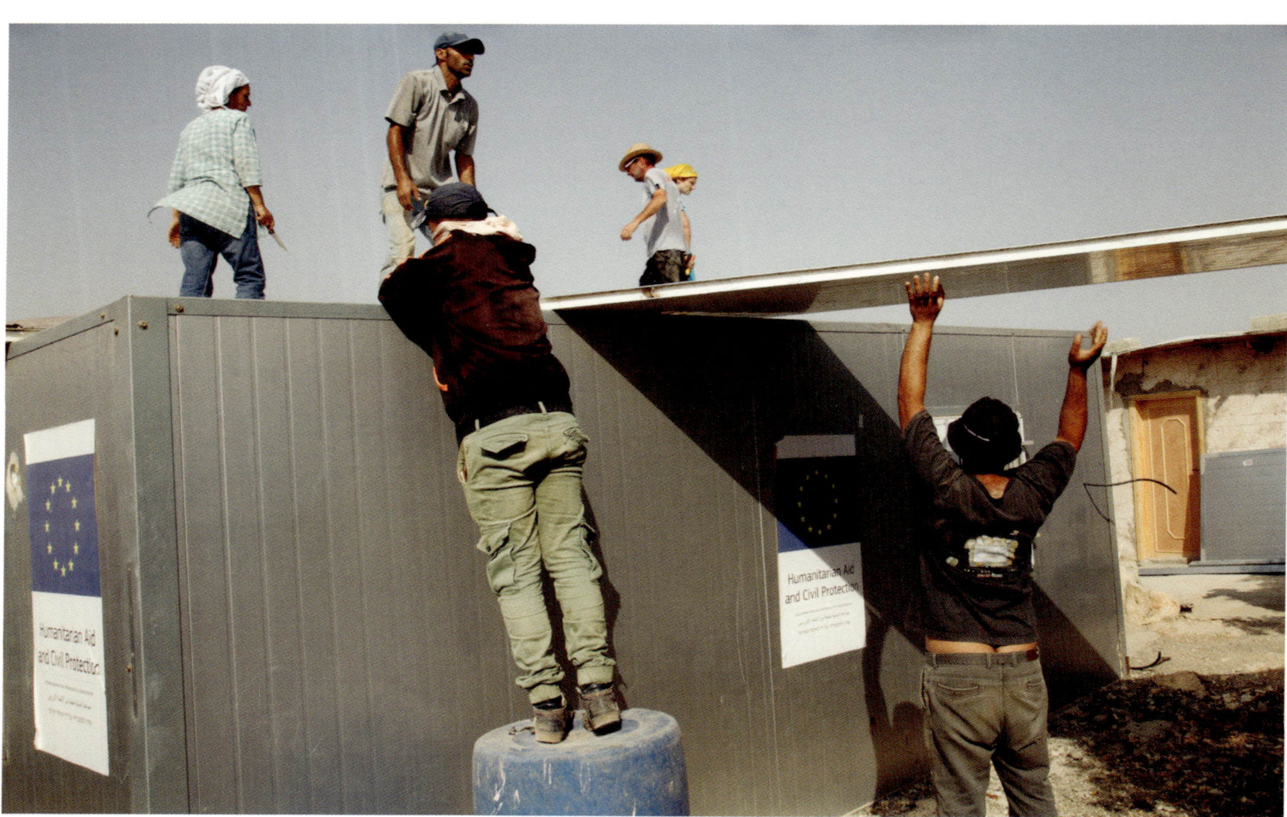

crush the structure into unusable debris, Mahmoud dismantles his own home with the help of friends, family, and activists.

6.17 Humsa al-Tahta, July 2017.

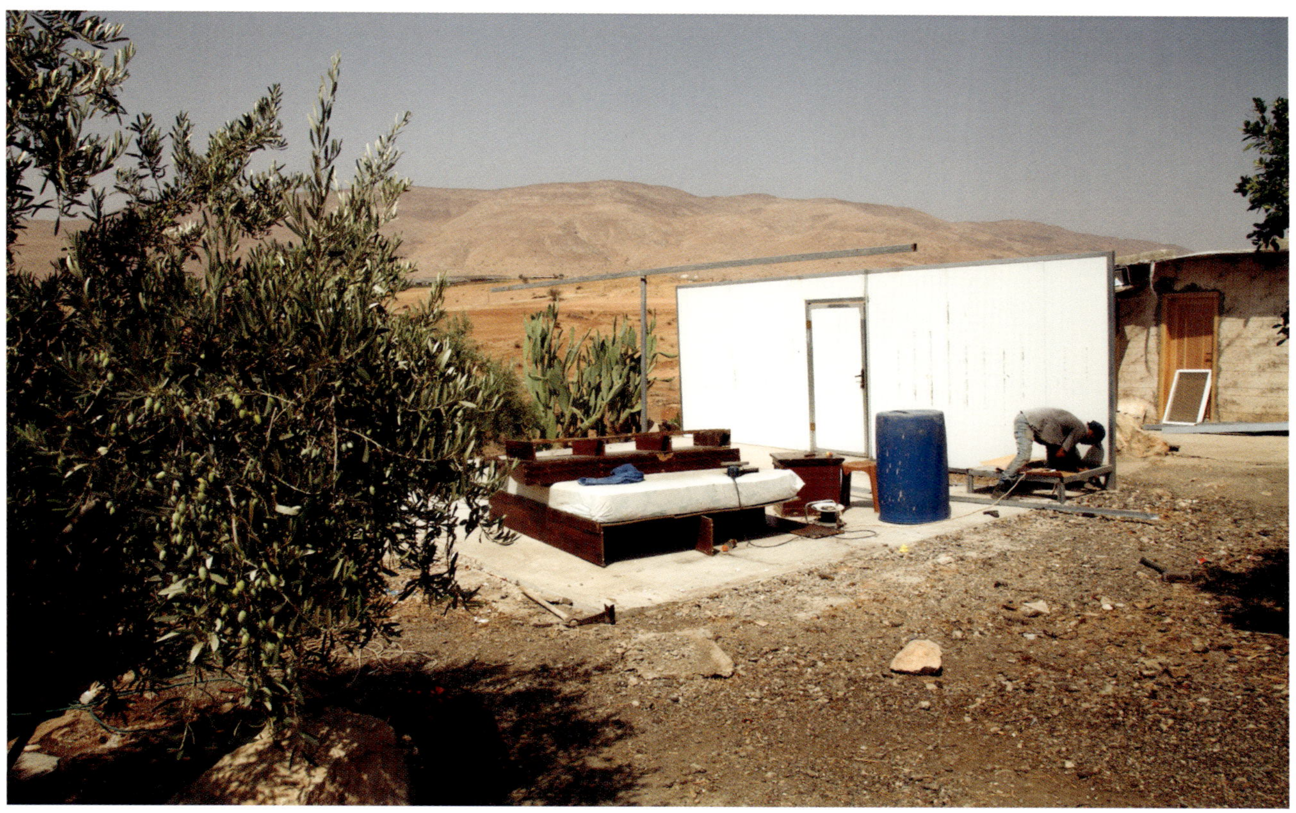

Mahmoud and his family will use the still intact pieces to rebuild.

6.18 Humsa al-Tahta, July 2017.

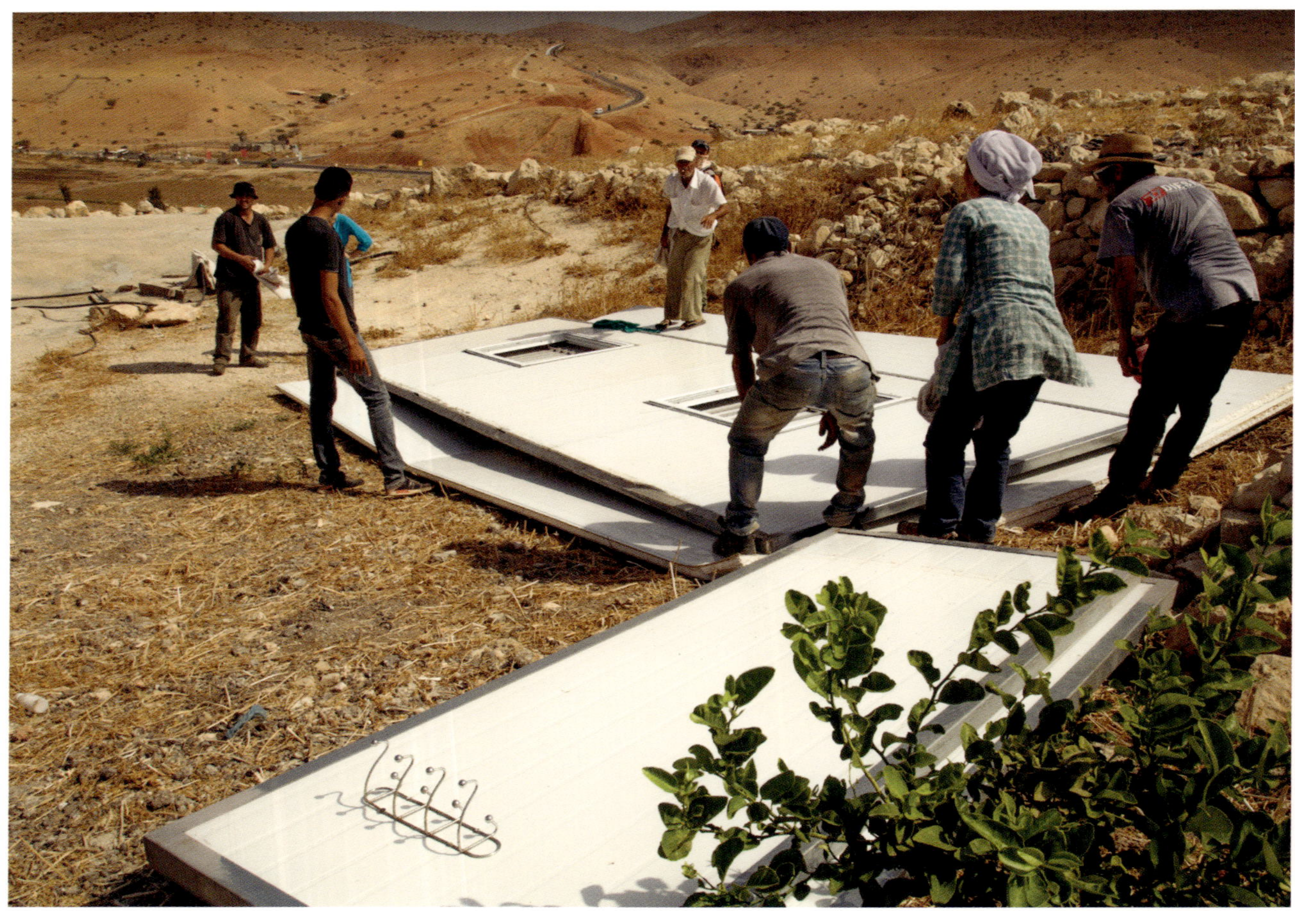

6.19 Humsa al-Tahta, July 2017.

His daughter looks on. It is only the first time she has seen her home demolished.

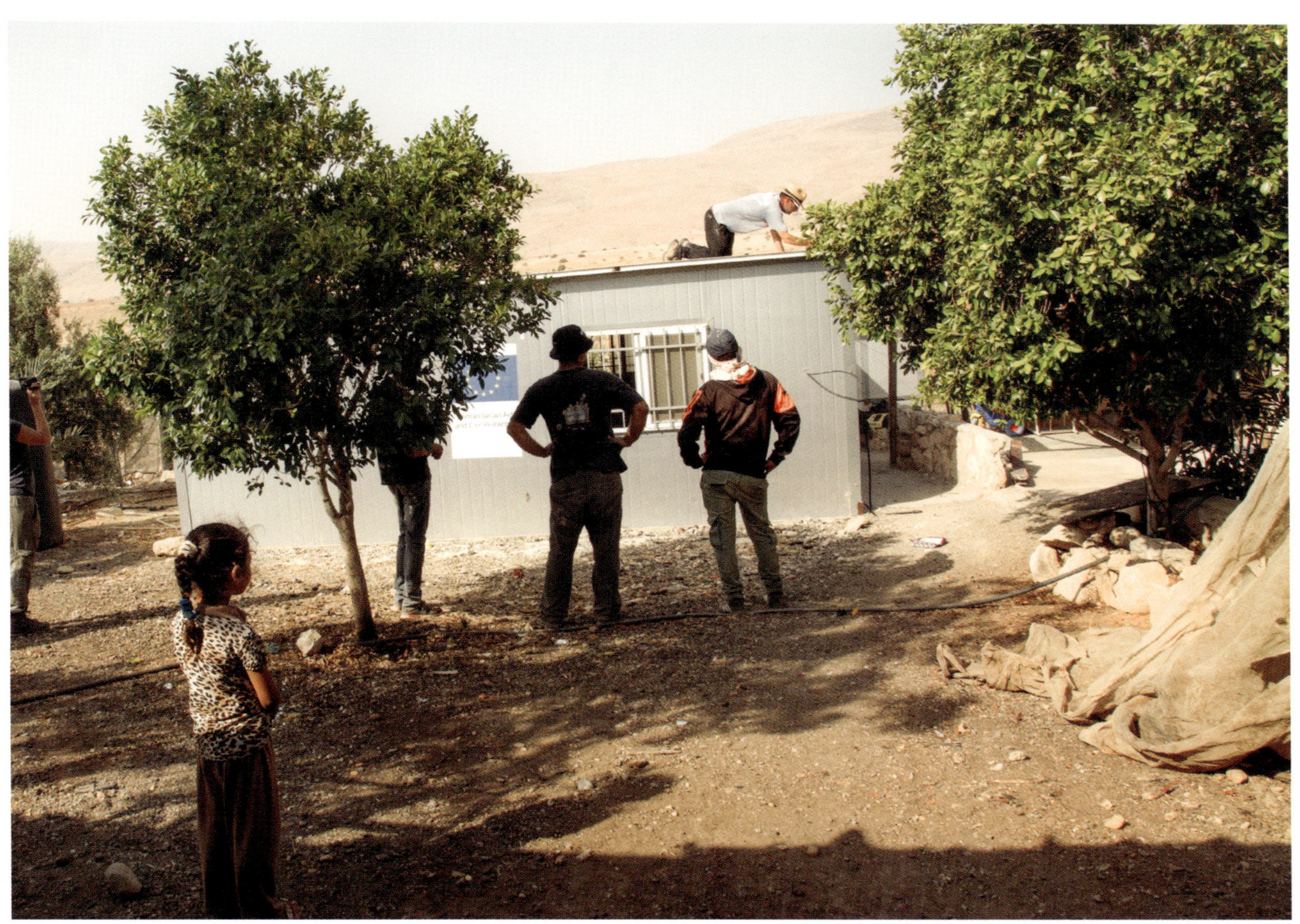

Laḥza: Tea in Protest

At Umm al-Ara'is, tea is an idiom of defiance. We arrive early—in summer before 7:00. The shepherds are already out on the hills. We pass the tiny encampment of Simri and continue over the hill and down to the wadi that the settlers have stolen. We might even get there before the first army jeep shows up. Soon Sa'id arrives, and his wife Rima, and three or four of his children, and other men from the Muhamre clans. Sa'id gives the sign. We march into the forbidden wadi, thick with thorns and yellowing grasses.

A remorseless sequence takes its course. Settlers may descend upon us, they may attack, sometimes the soldiers will join them in beating us, there may be arrests. Once they arrested ten of us, including a baby nursing at his mother's breast. The officer will definitely produce the order declaring this wadi a Closed Military Zone. For a long time, there was a standing order signed by some distant general, so the CMZ was a mere formality. We argue, we show the Supreme Court ruling from 2004 that says the CMZ is illegal.

Sa'id, invariably soft-spoken, lucid, repeats to the officer what he has said a thousand times before. The officer shrugs him off, or threatens him, or screams at him, or turns away. We are in no hurry to leave, we know our continuing presence in the wadi is a necessary, but not sufficient, condition for the hope that one day this land will be restored to its owners. It's been over ten years, and Sa'id hasn't given up.

The soldiers begin to push and poke at us from behind, we hold our ground, we wait for Sa'id's signal, we leave the wadi as slowly as we can and climb partway up the hill, over white rocks.

Twigs, thorns, a few dead branches are teased into flame. We nurse our wounds, our rage. Then: Tea. The children crowd around the fire. The soldiers stare at us from the jeep as we drink. We stare back, with contempt. There are the bitter words, ours and theirs, and there is the insouciant sweetness of tea. Liquid faith. A golden weapon, unlike theirs, and infinitely stronger. You will see. One day tea will win and the soldiers will leave.

L.6 Umm al-Ara'is, May 2022.

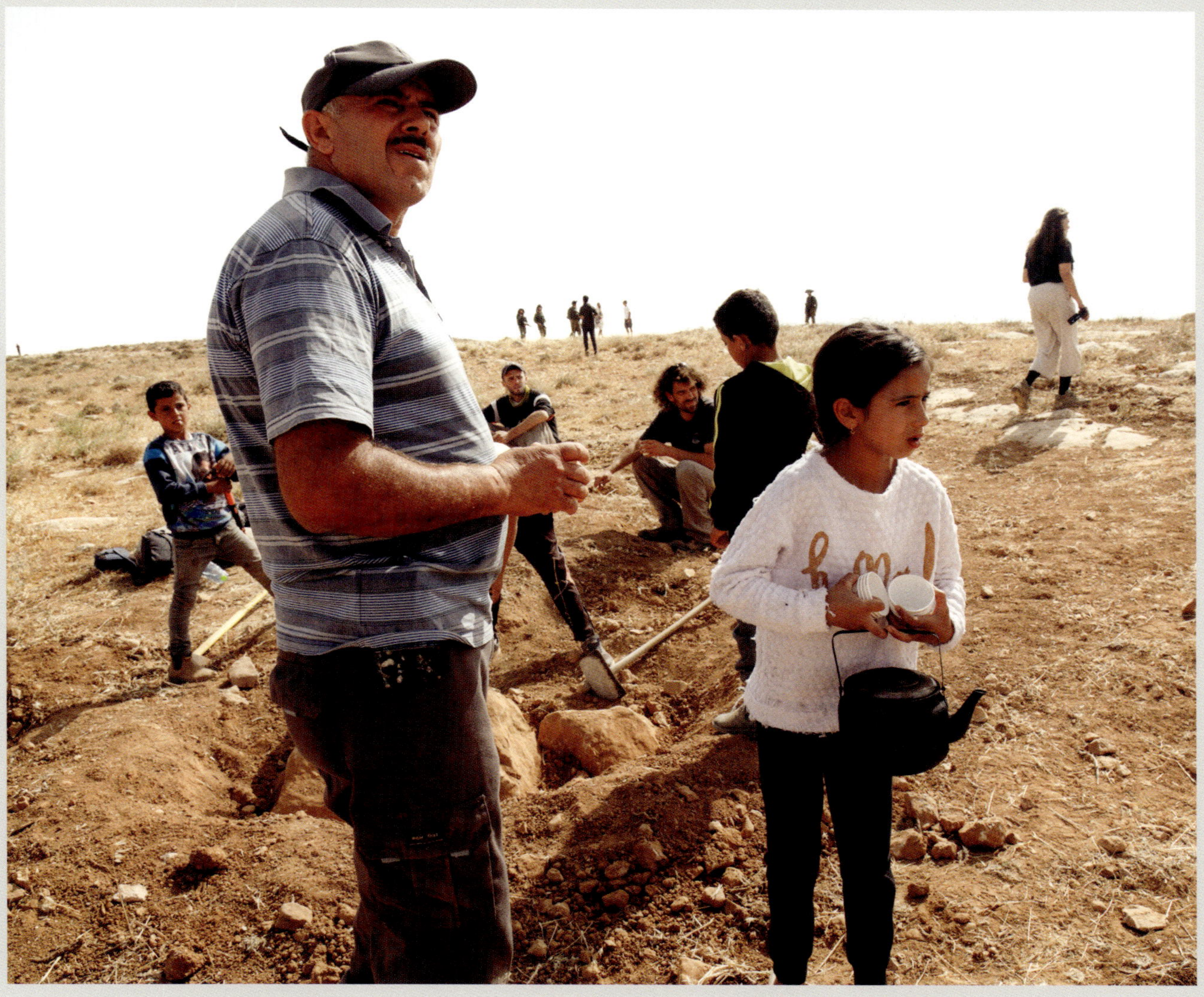

7.1 Asael, South Hebron Hills, January 2017.

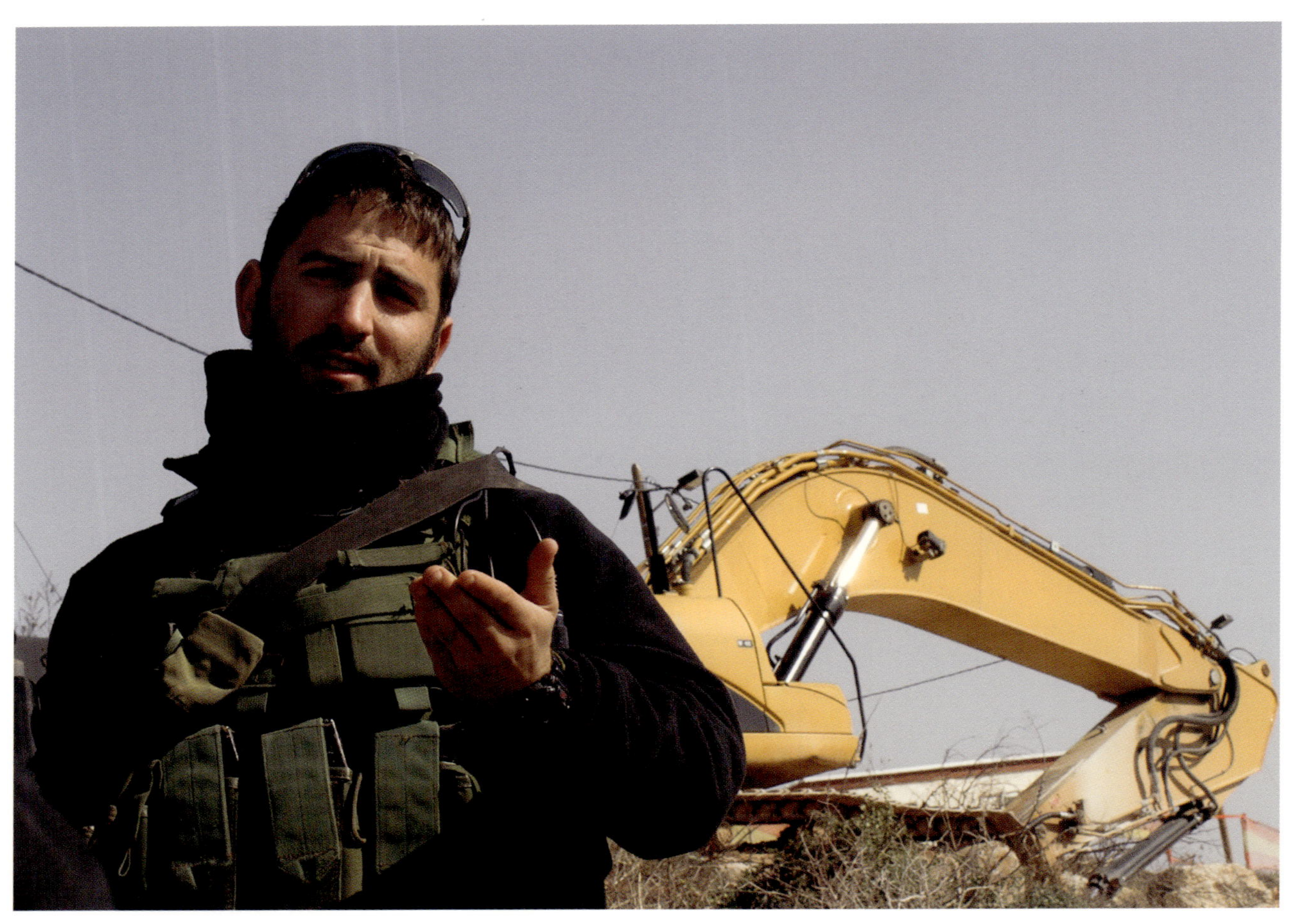

7. Asael, Twaneh, Umm al-Khair, January 7, 2017

1.

Asael, possibly the ugliest of all the illegal outposts in the southern West Bank—and the competition is fierce—is rapidly expanding. Yellow bulldozers, parked at the perimeter fence of the settlement, have carved out a huge swathe of intermeshed, crisscrossing gashes in the hill and valley just below. This wide, deep wound in the soil has been sliced, needless to say, through privately owned Palestinian land. We know the families. We've plowed here, on the edge of the outpost. There have been many bad moments with the Asael settlers, the ones we can see this Shabbat morning walking their dogs over the hill or praying to their rapacious god or swinging their children on the swings in the painted park just under their pre-fab caravans.

Winter morning, sunny, ice-cold. Guy is photographing the earthen gashes meter by meter. The families who own the land will submit a complaint to the police, not that it will do much good. The Civil Administration stopped the bulldozers earlier this week, but the fact that they're still parked here bodes ill. Each one of them costs a few thousands of shekels per day, and they're still here. Actually, everything bodes ill here at Asael on this sun-drenched day.

The soldiers appear on cue. Three of them clamber down the hill to put a stop to our intrusion. They're in winter uniforms,

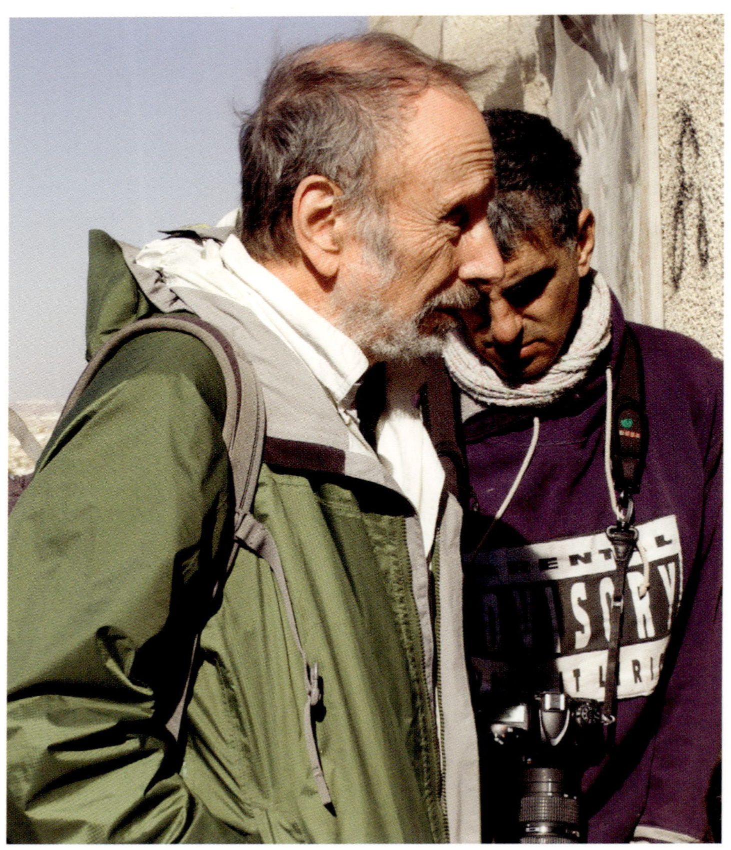

7.2 Twaneh, South Hebron Hills, January 2017.

black on top, with ski-masks and heavy weapons. Their officer, affable enough, asks for my identity card. I hand it over. He studies it. "You live near my grandmother's house. What are you doing here, and why are you photographing me? You're old enough to be my grandfather, aren't you ashamed?"

"Why should I be ashamed?"

"I don't like it when you photograph me. It's impolite."

I can see what's coming. Harmless chatter, nothing worse. I turn off the camera. Peg is still photographing, despite the officer's repeated demands that she stop. It seems this business of the cameras is all we have to talk about today. Over and over again he tells us that we're not being nice.

He consults his superiors on the phone. "There are four Israeli citizens here," he reports, "they have the right to come here and photograph the bulldozers and the digging, they haven't invaded the settlement, and they won't stop photographing me." By now this is becoming an obsession. I'm tired of it. Moreover, the cognitive dissonance is eating away at me, so wearily I say to him, "Look, forget this stupid thing about the cameras, I'm not photographing you now, just look around you at what is happening here. You know as well as I do that this outpost is illegal, and you can see that they're now stealing more Palestinian land."

"That's none of my business. If you have a problem with the settlers, work it out in the courts. I have my job to do."

Later, thinking back on it, I find the conversation insane, and I'm sorry I got into it. A crime is taking place, here and everywhere in the occupied territories. It's picking up speed. The soldiers are complicit in it, though it's coming from far above them, from the prime minister's office on down. And on this bright winter morning, the officer on the spot thinks we're being impolite.

2.

These are violent days in South Hebron, also in the Jordan Valley. We reach Twaneh around 2:00 and find a Ta'ayush detachment still shaken after being attacked by masked settlers from Chavat Maon. The Ta'ayush volunteers were there to protect Palestinian farmers who had come to plow. The plowing was successfully completed, and the volunteers were on their way back to Twaneh when fifteen settler thugs attacked, hurling big rocks, lots of them, and assaulting our people with their fists. Dudy was hit in the head by a rock. Danny was beaten. One of the Italian volunteers living in Twaneh was hit, and her (expensive) camera stolen. By sheer good fortune, no one was badly wounded or worse.

Guy calls the police, who eventually respond. We head uphill toward the site of the attack. The settlers are still flitting through the trees at the end of the path. We have good video footage, but it rapidly becomes apparent that there's little point in submitting a complaint. The police will do nothing, the settlers were masked, to fill out the police forms is hardly more than a ritual gesture. We move on. Fifteen years ago, almost to the day, I was attacked, beaten, stoned, and shot at by the settlers of Chavat Maon at this same point. I know what it feels like. I know for sure that they are celebrating their splendid raid and reveling in their spoils. Maybe I shouldn't care.

3.

Eid is waiting to welcome us to Umm al-Khair. He's become almost famous, with exhibitions of his sculptures and installations in Tel Aviv and most recently Berlin. We embrace. We run through the dismal litany of house demolitions from the past few months. For the moment—always only for the moment—the courts have put a freeze on further demolitions at Umm al-Khair. Eid says, "No matter what we do, the Israelis will never let us live here; sooner or later, they will take these lands too."

The settlement of Carmel abuts the shanties of Umm al-Khair, and recently the settlers have invented a new form of torment for their neighbors. Their sewage now flows through pipes that open onto the fertile fields in the wadi and the Palestinian grazing grounds. We pick our way over the rocks to study the large open pipe.

It's one of those crystal winter afternoons. Every thorn stands out on the hills. Sheep cluster around the well on the next ridge. Ruins from the last four demolition raids are neatly stacked beside what used to be tents and homes. We've rebuilt a little, for the umpteenth time. The hills across the Jordan River turn to limpid mauve. It's cold; one of the young girls, maybe four years old, in ponytail and a blue sweater, stands barefoot at the entrance to her home. Goats bleat; toward sunset, they get hungry. Tea appears. A wild parabola of pigeons swirls over the golden slope. Beauty is made from pain, great beauty from greater pain.

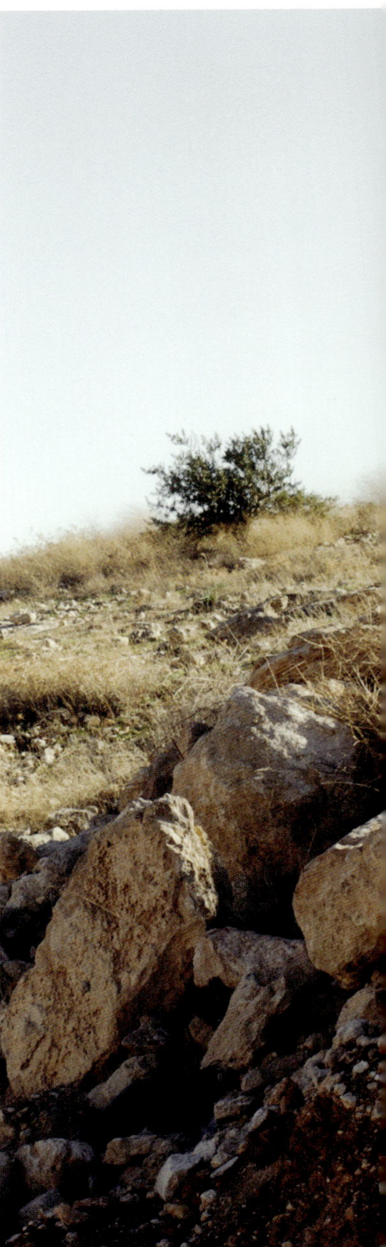

7.3 Umm al-Khair, January 2017.

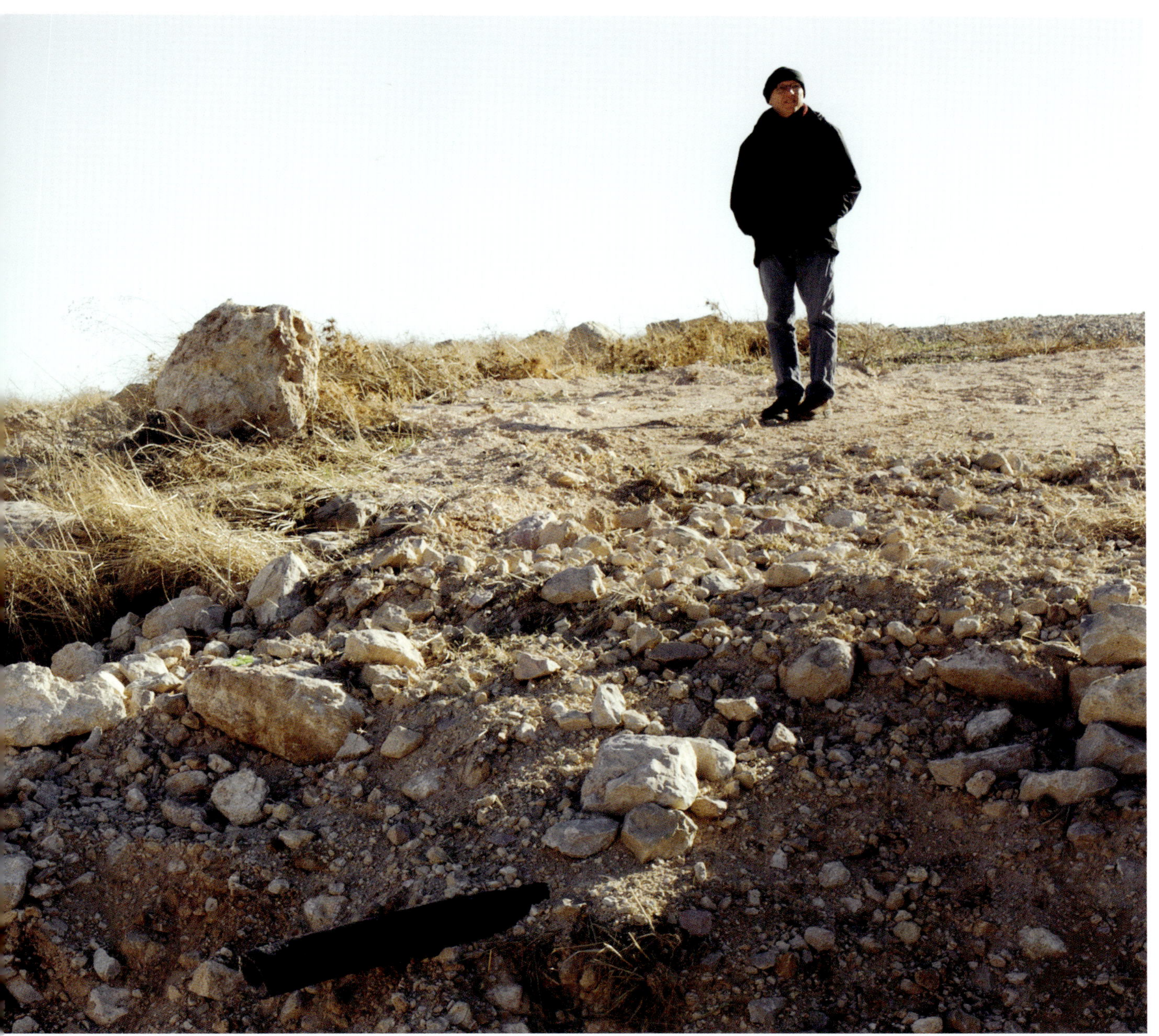

Laḥza: Tea Break

It's always strong, golden red, and very sweet,
but sometimes they add wild
zaatar *to it that gives it a bitter tang,*
to complement the sweetness.

A nonchalant solemnity pervades this ritual, as if
in the desert, tea and kindness and friendship could
protect you from the ravages of time and men.

Sometimes they look for a scraggly
juniper tree and make tea while sitting
in its semblance of shade.

Goats eat thorns, shepherds drink tea, rocks and bushes
and sand drink light and shadow in a thirsty world.

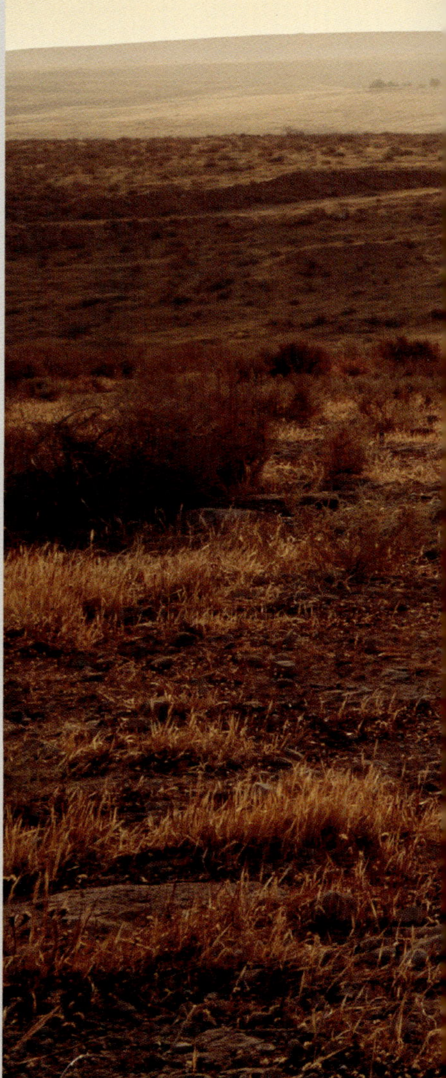

L.7 'Auja, July 2017.

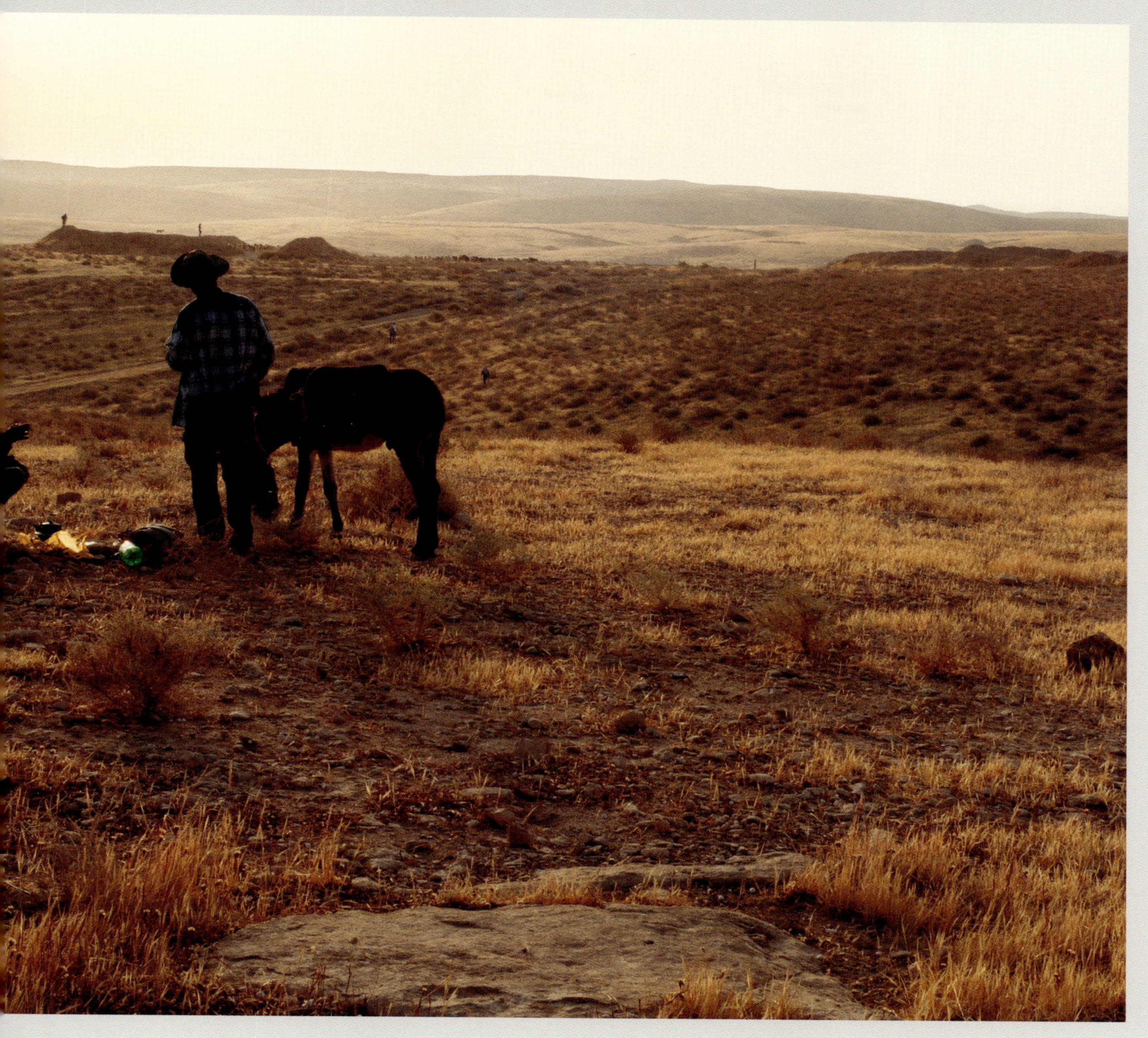

8.1 Susiya, March 2016.

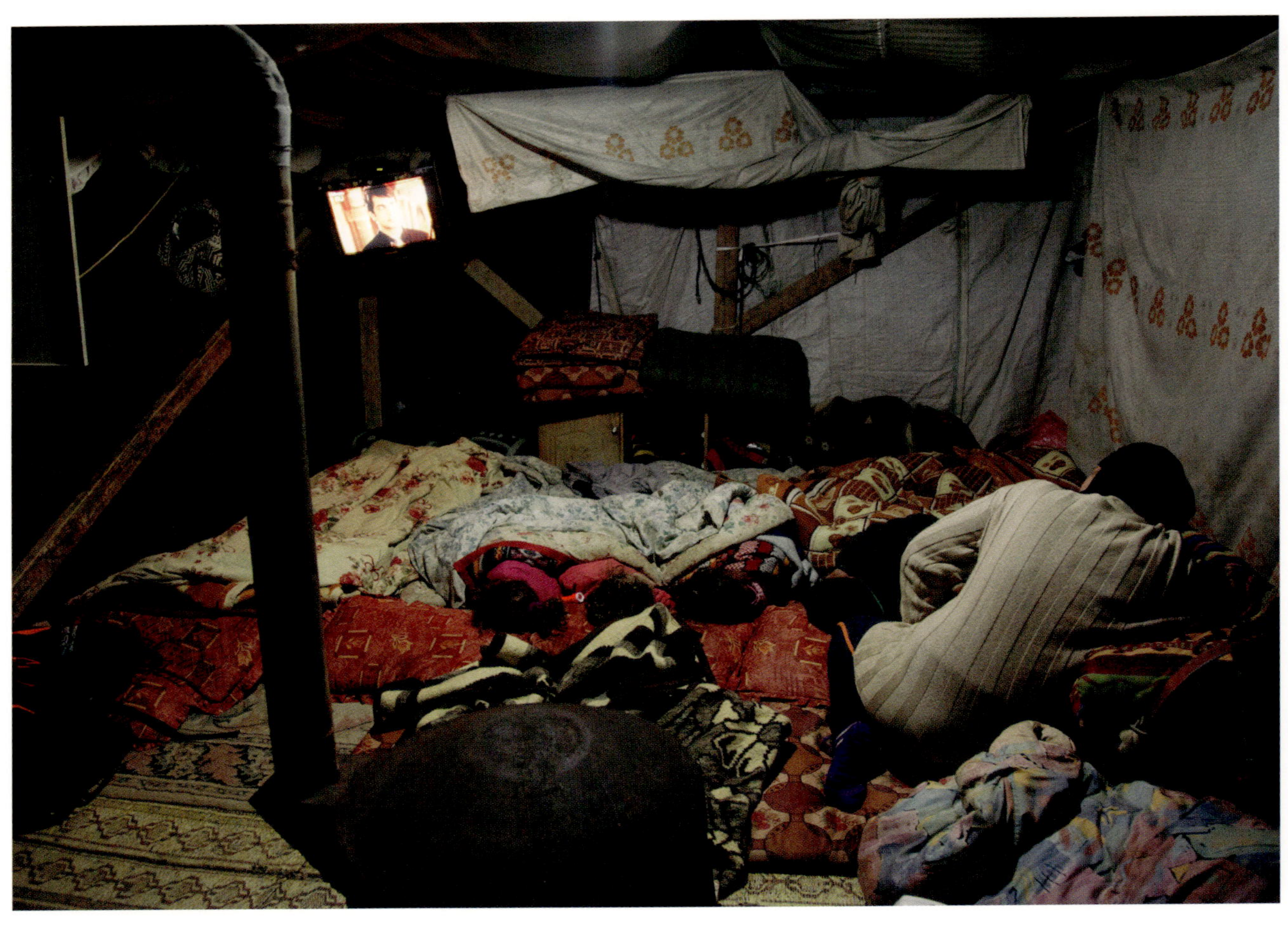

8.

Wind, Sun, Power

The NGO Comet-ME, focused on sustainable energy, meets many of South Hebron's needs with solar panels and wind turbines; it helps the Rural Women Association run computers; it powers the bare light bulb that lights their meetings; and it allows exhausted families to watch Bollywood movies in their tents at night.

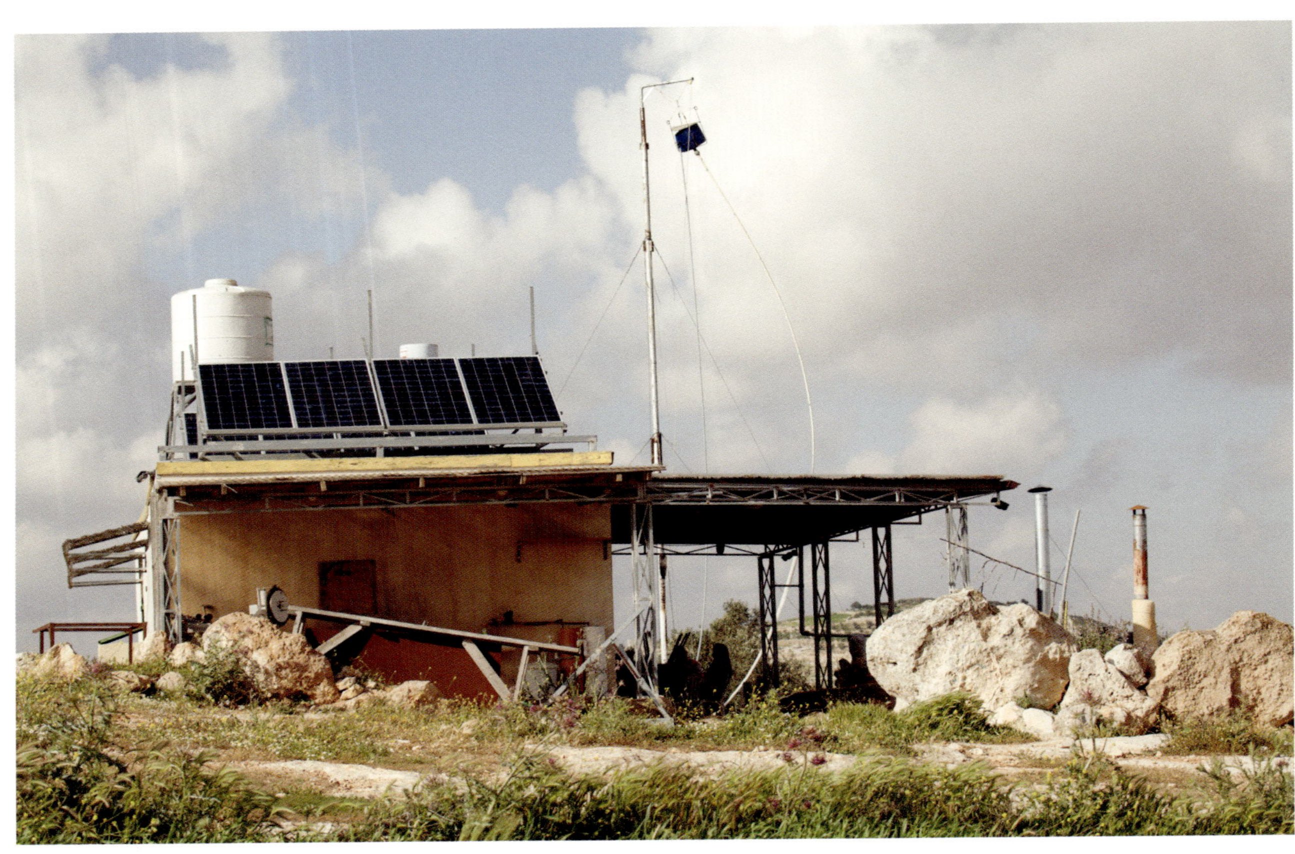

8.2 Comet-ME headquarters,
Gawawis, March 2016.

Comet-ME employs some local Palestinians who have managed to study and earn engineering degrees. But the organization has no better luck with building permits than the villages it serves. The awning on its repurposed building is under a demolition order,

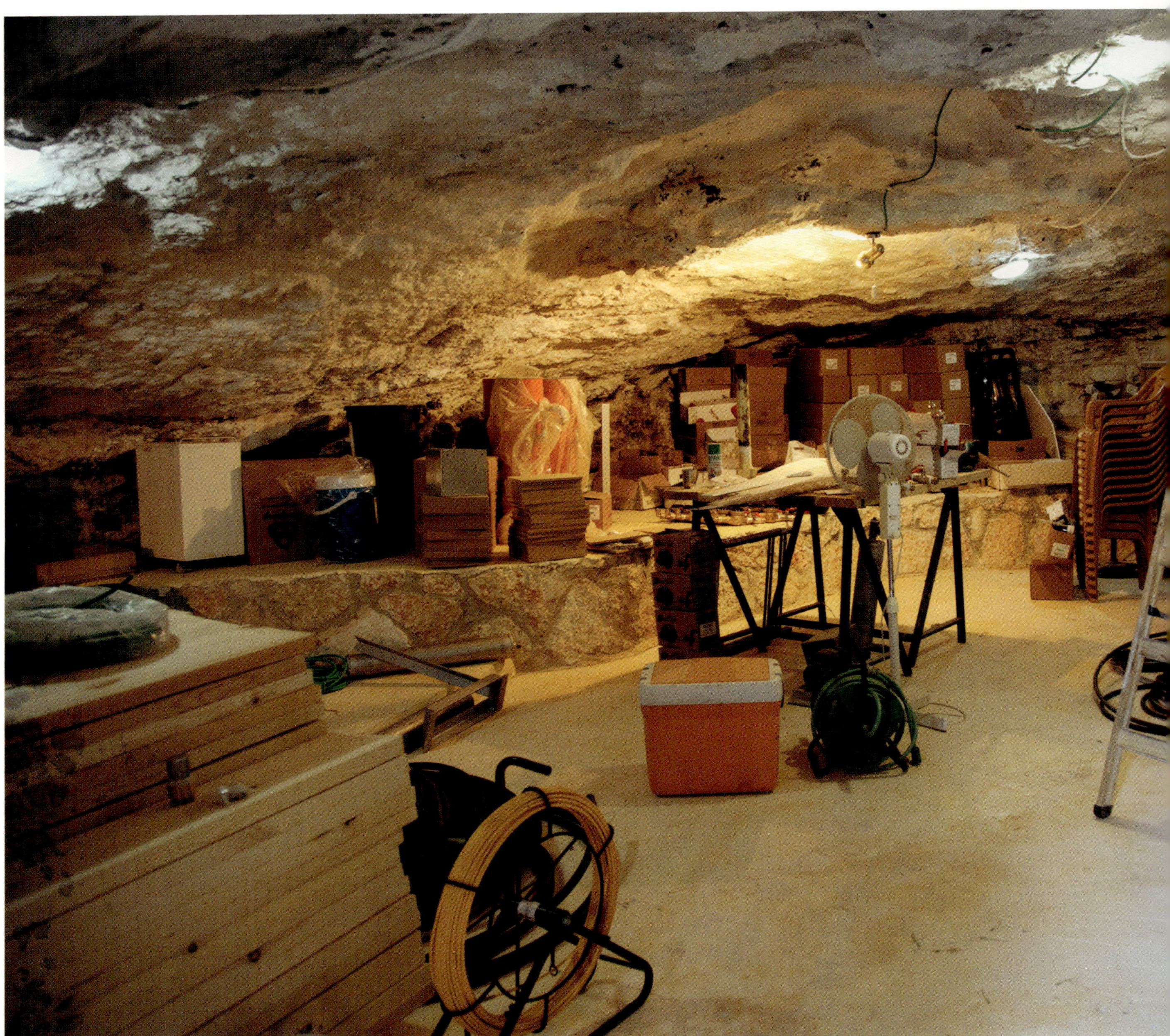

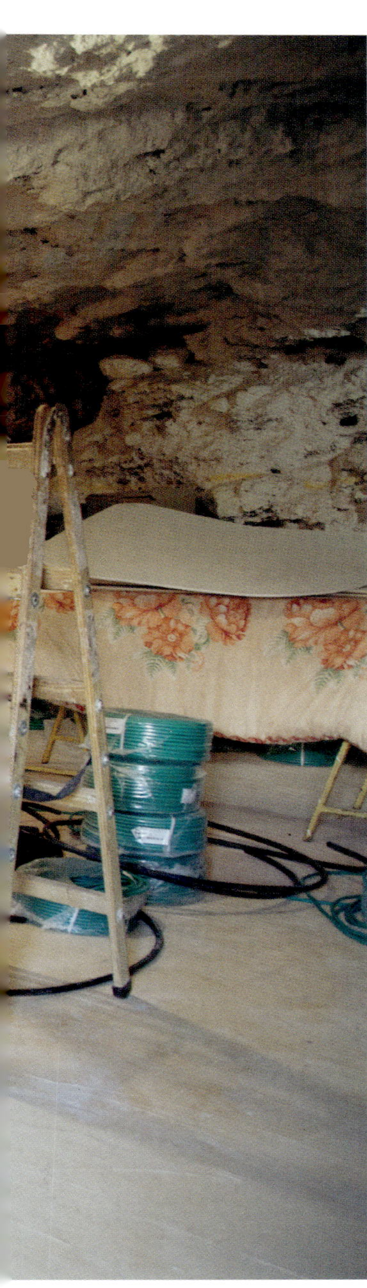

and its factories are in caves.

8.3 Comet-ME headquarters,
Gawawis, March 2016.

At first the Comet people worked in secret, fearing that the army, if it found out what they were doing, would immediately come to destroy it.

8.4 Bi'r al-'Id, June 2015.

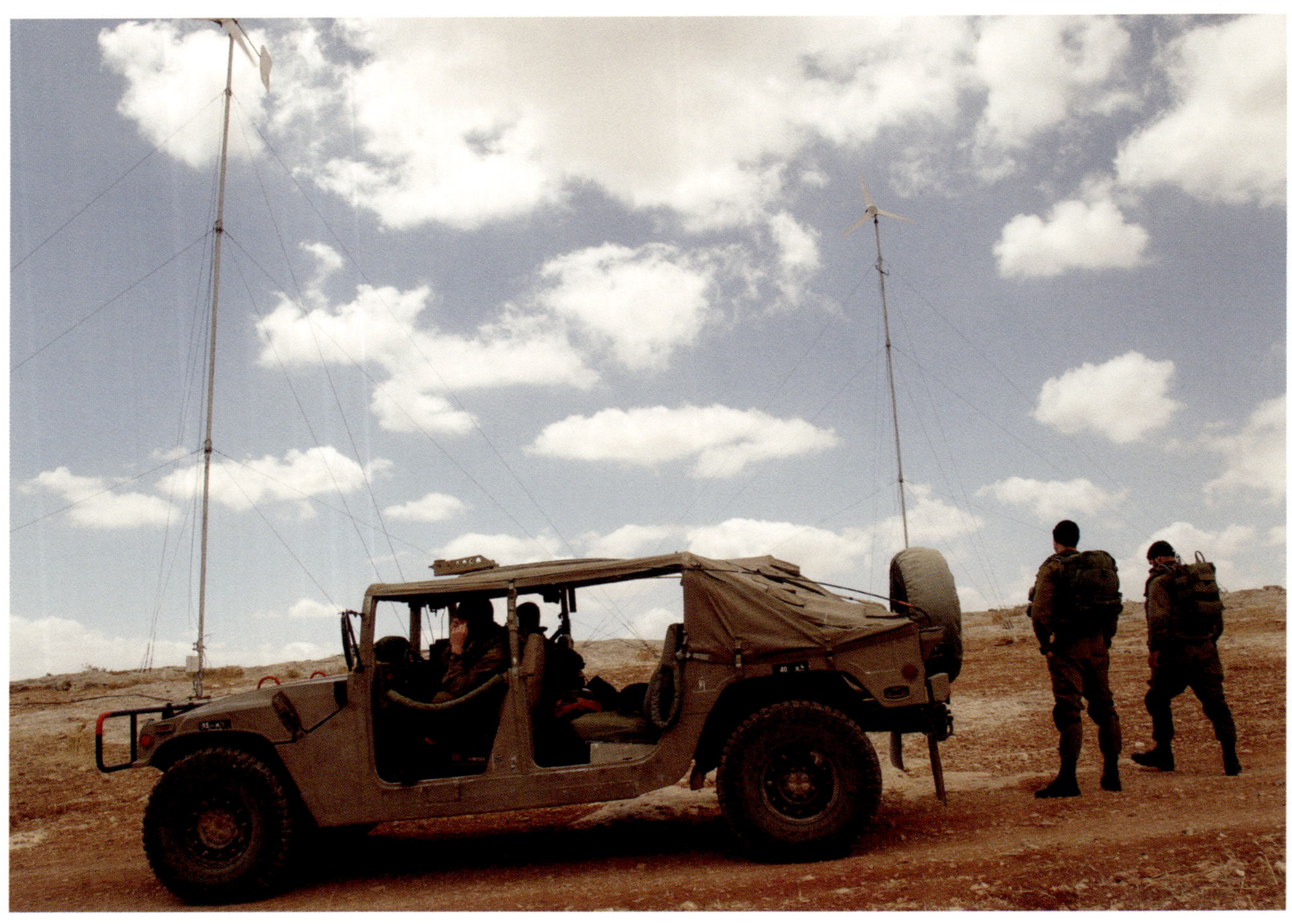

8.5 Tuba, South Hebron Hills, January 2017.

Once a wind turbine is firmly in place, a court order may be needed to eradicate it. But sometimes the soldiers kill it anyway.

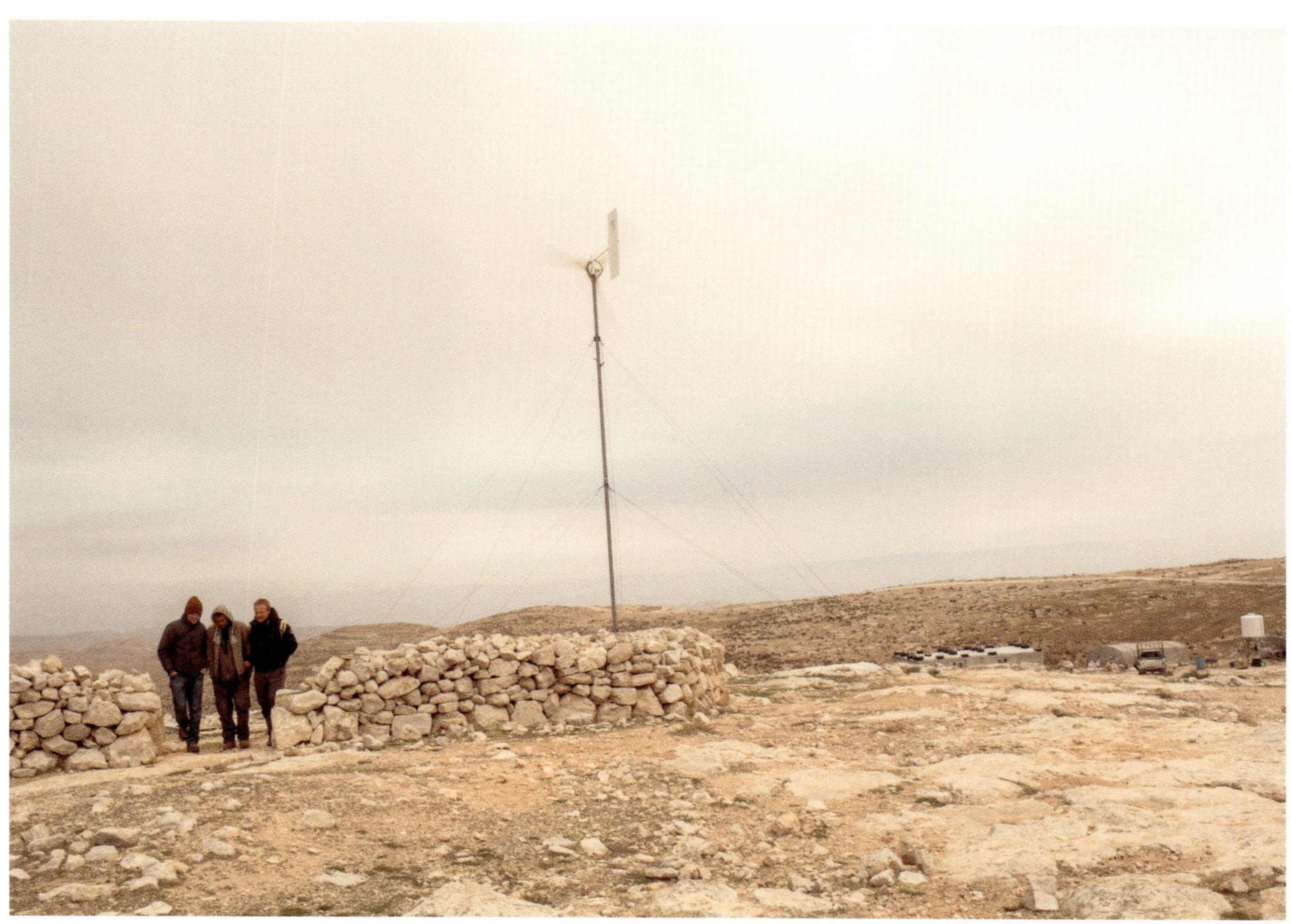

Laḥza: Harun Abu Aram

Meet Harun, from the village of Ar-Rakiz.

He was 25 years old. He was about to be married. His neighbor Ashraf was trying to fix a roof over his sheep-pen with the help of an electric generator, when soldiers arrived, sent by settlers. They tried to confiscate the generator, since Palestinians don't deserve to have one (or for that matter, to have a roof.) Harun's father Rasmi was also there, and the soldiers beat him; Harun ran to help. A scuffle broke out between the soldiers and four Palestinians, and the generator changed hands several times. Then a soldier standing on the side shot Harun at point-blank range. The bullet penetrated his spinal cord, leaving him paralyzed, probably for life, from the spine down. The soldiers then set up two roadblocks to prevent the car carrying the dying Harun from getting to the hospital.

They somehow made it. Harun survived, his life ruined.

We promised him that we would make his story known to people all over the world.

On February 14, 2023, two years after the attack, Harun died.

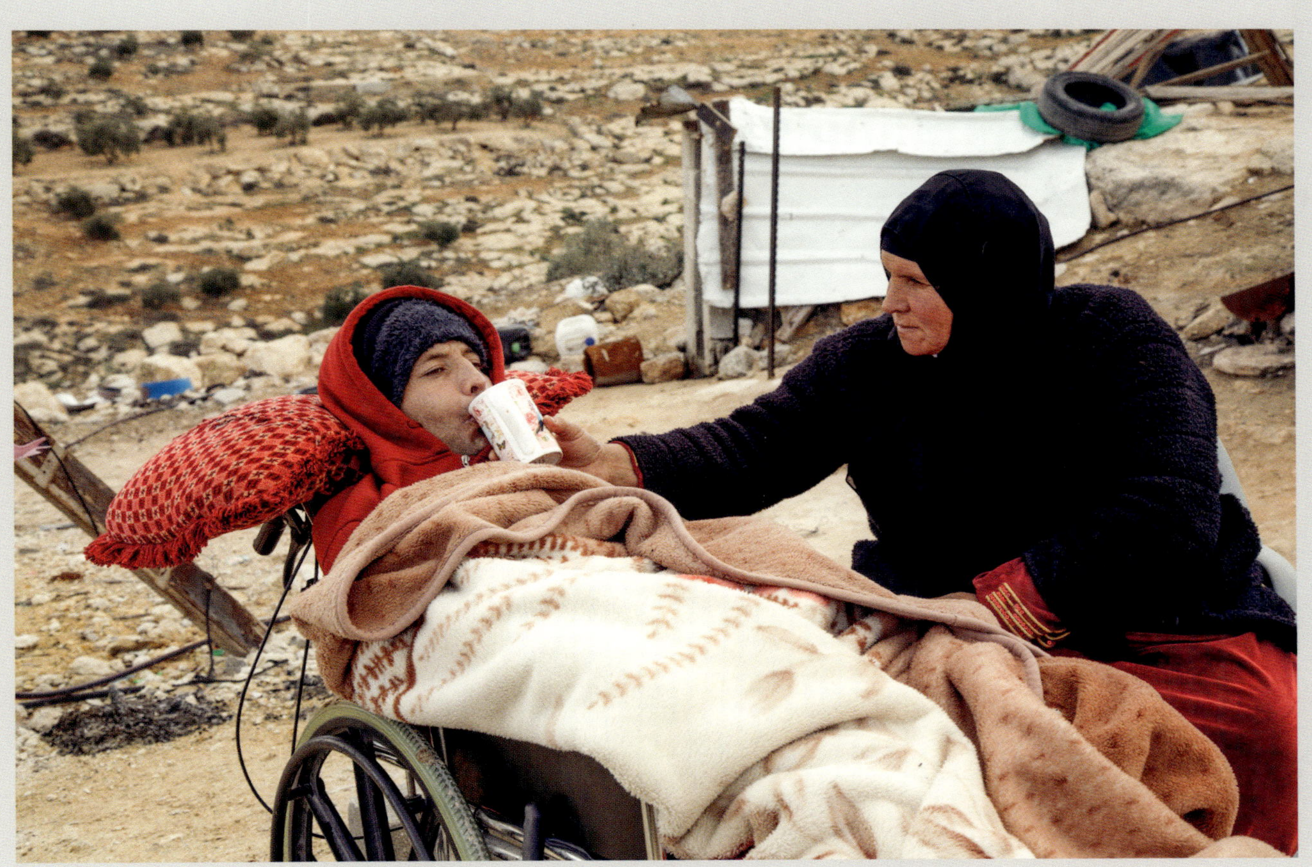

L.8 Ar-Rakiz, January 2022.

9.1 Al-Khan al-Ahmar, July 2019.

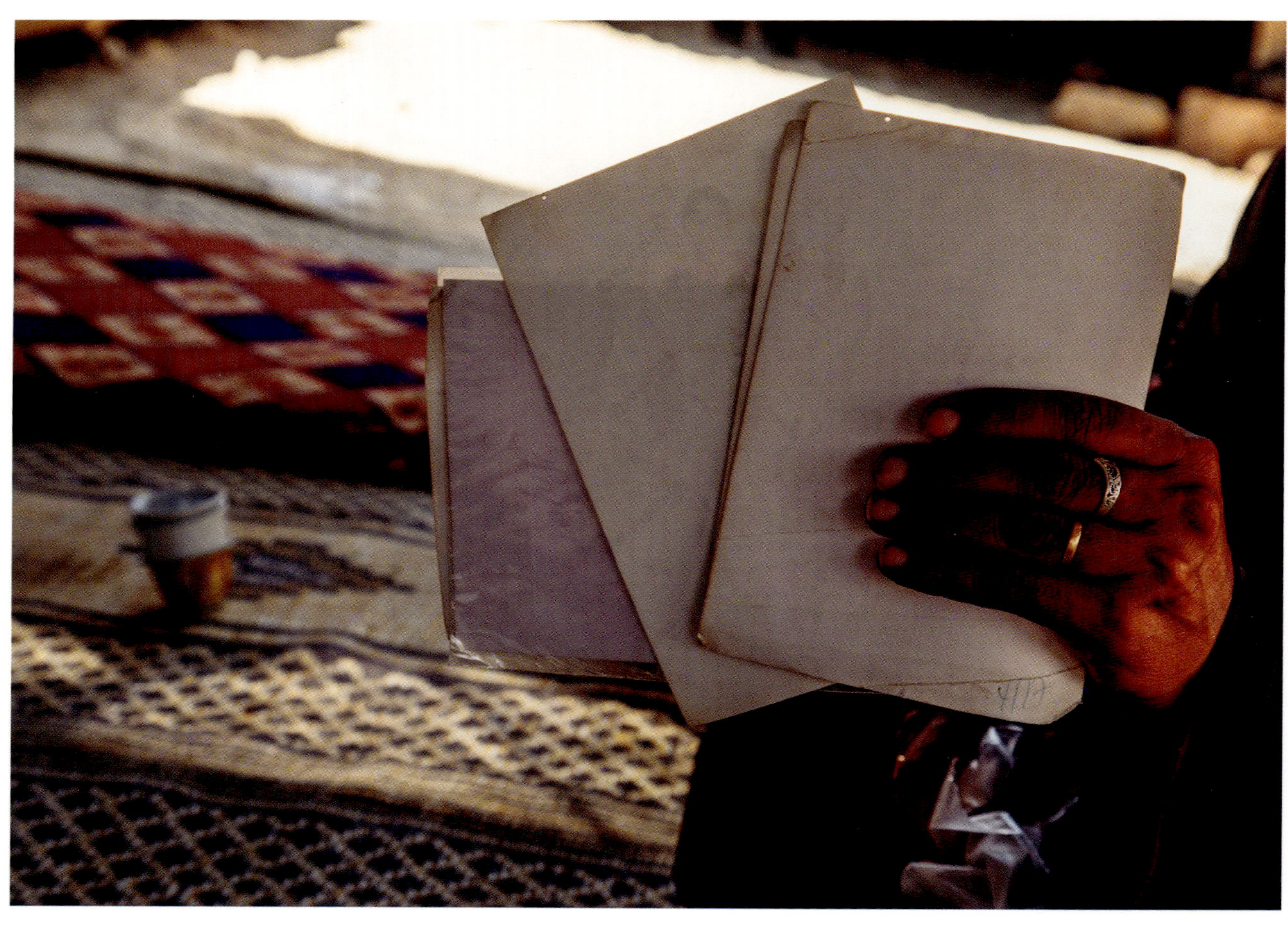

9. Al-Khan al-Ahmar, 2018–2019

Sheathed in plastic, the pictures that Jamila (Umm Isma'il) happily brings out to show must have been taken by professional photographers. In perhaps half a dozen she wears gracefully embroidered dresses, her rich black hair sometimes fully visible. There's even a picture of her as a "modern woman" in slacks.

To photograph these photographs of Jamila is forbidden, just as it is forbidden to photograph the face of Jamila herself, but she allows me to photograph her hands holding the photographs. Jamila was beautiful when these photos were taken and she remains beautiful, her hair still shiny and her smile intact after eleven children, three of whom died soon after birth.

I cannot photograph Maha's face, either.

9.2 Al-Khan al-Ahmar, July 2019.

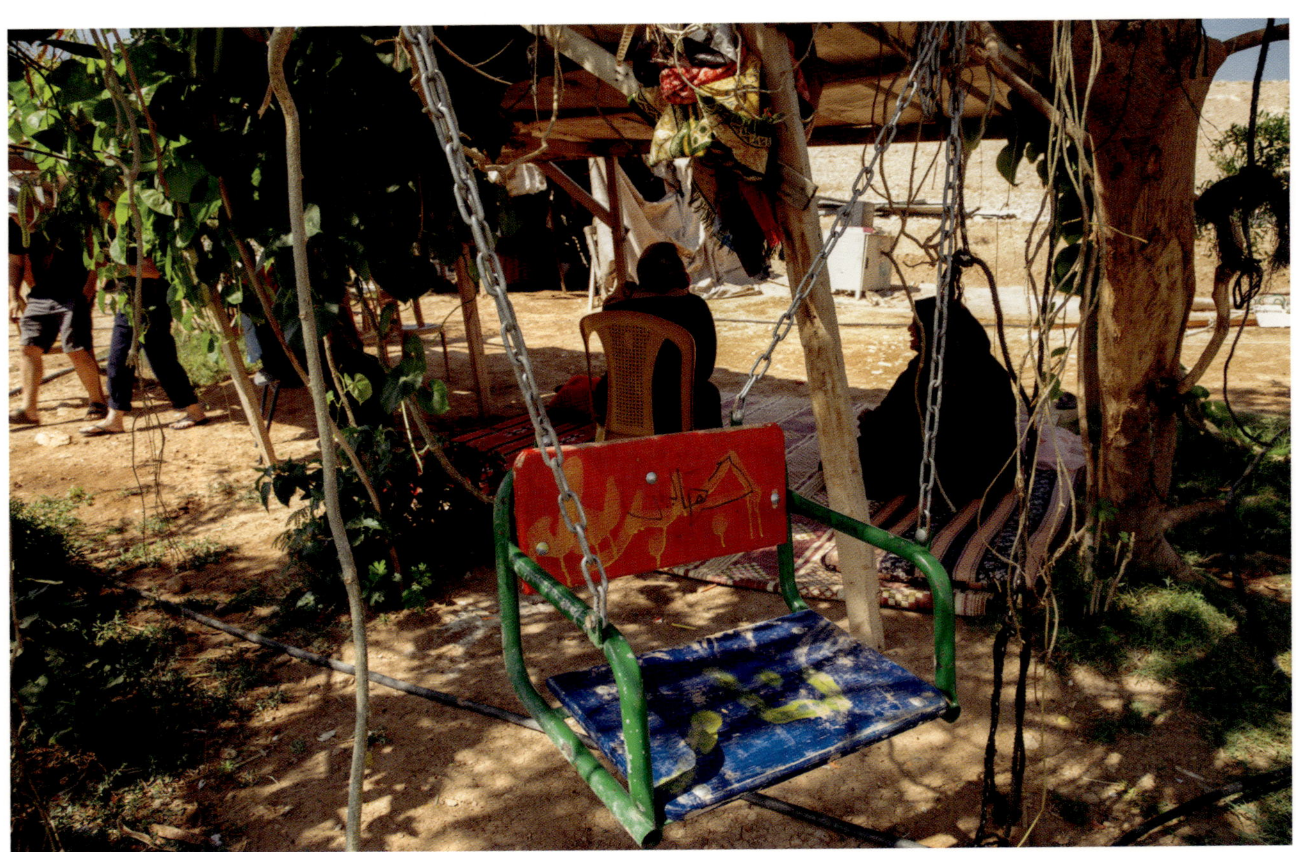

Maha's home blew down recently in a storm.
She will need 4000 shekels to rebuild it.

9.3 Al-Khan al-Ahmar, July 2019.

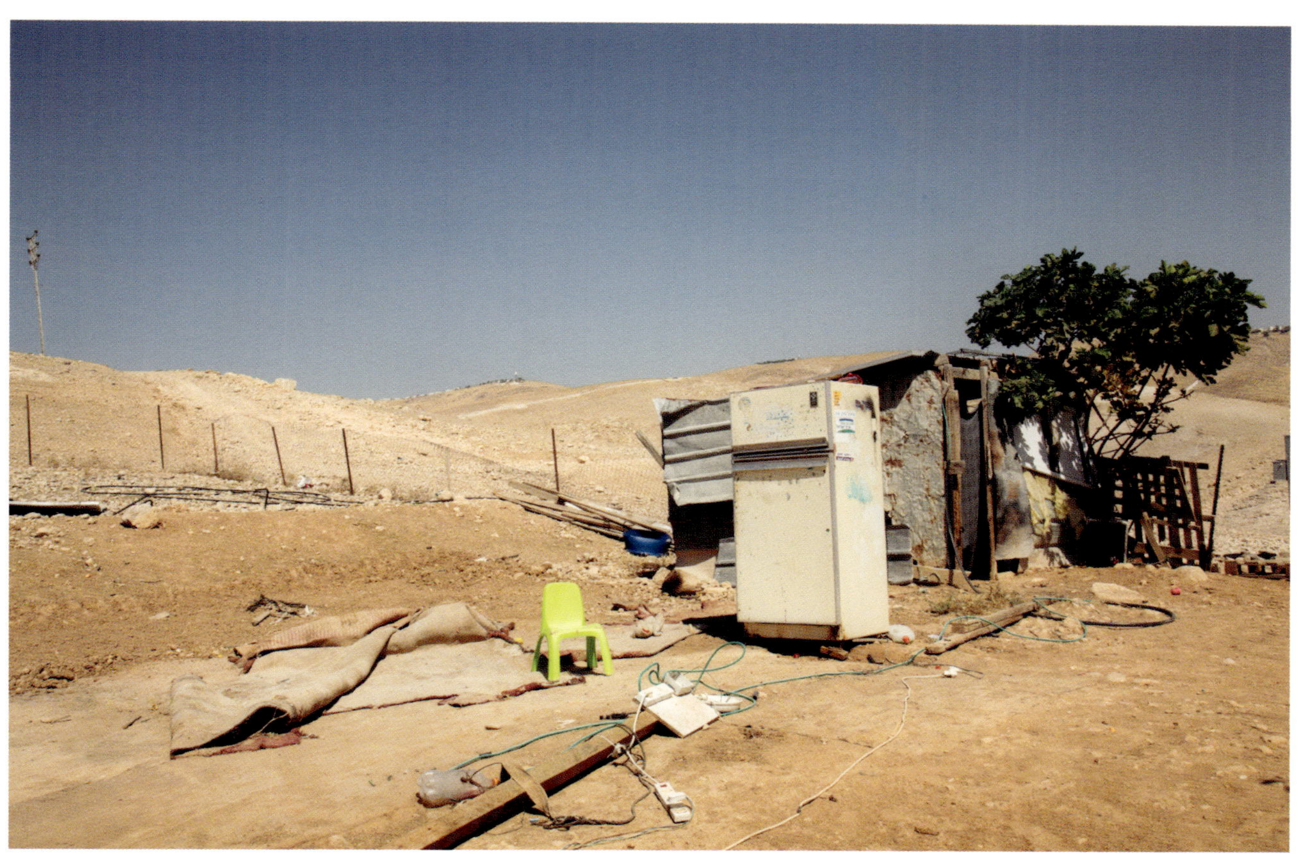

Al-Khan al-Ahmar is not very pastoral for a Bedouin shepherding community. The village nestles next to a freeway. Visitors drive through a tunnel beneath the freeway to reach the village, and sheep swarm through it with their shepherds to graze on the rocky hills just above.

The Israeli settlement of Maale Adumim looms above Al-Khan al-Ahmar. But the highway and the settlement are newcomers, while the village has been here since the current inhabitants were expelled from the northern Negev in 1953.

In 2018, in order to give the settlement more room, it seemed to the government best to schedule the village for demolition, and the Bedouins for forcible removal to a site by a garbage dump next to a larger town, Abu Dis. The chief prosecutor at the Hague was of a different opinion, and only her decree prevented the state of Israel from carrying out these plans.

For the moment.

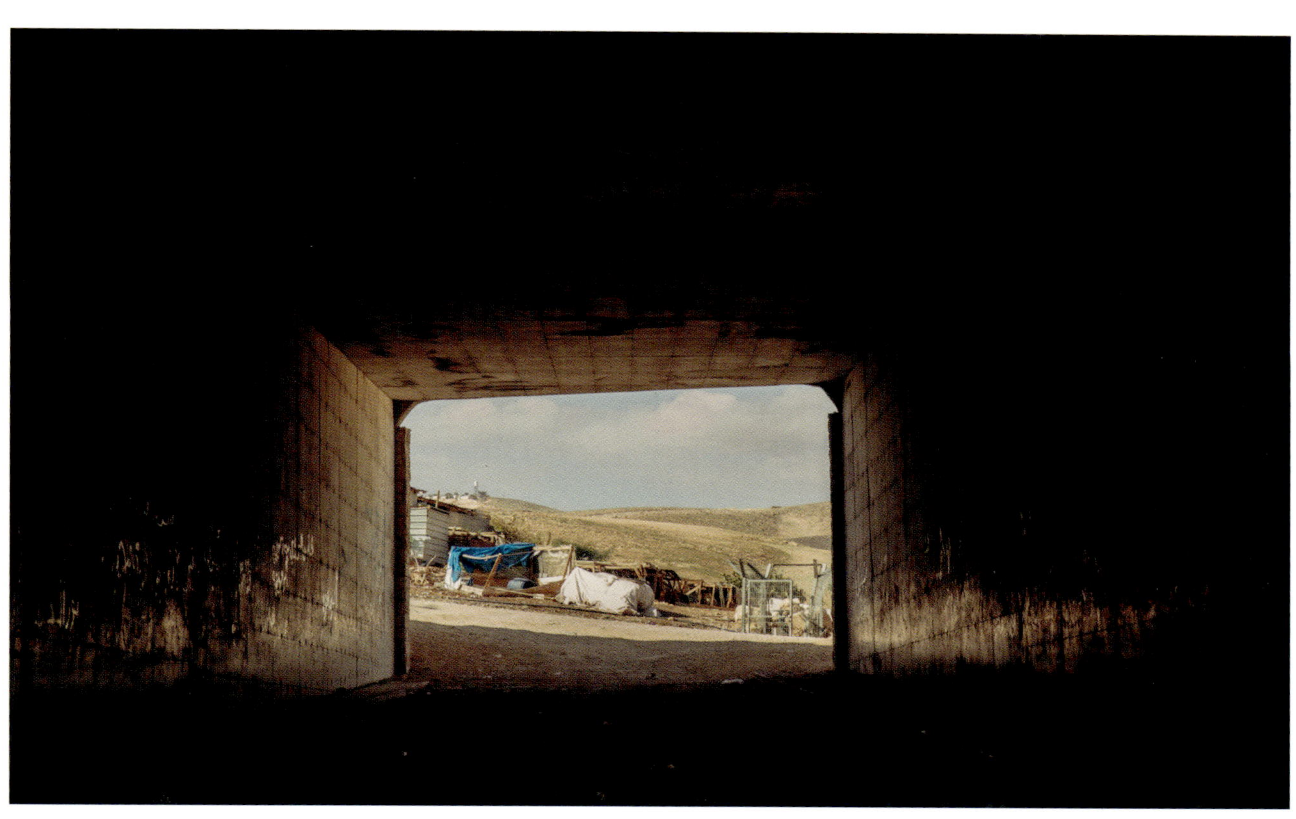

9.4 Al-Khan al-Ahmar, Wadi Og,
December 2018.

The moment continues. The village, in suspended animation, waits. Meanwhile the women continue to hide—behind the trees, behind the fences, and behind their beautiful embroidery.

9.5 Al-Khan al-Ahmar, July 2019.

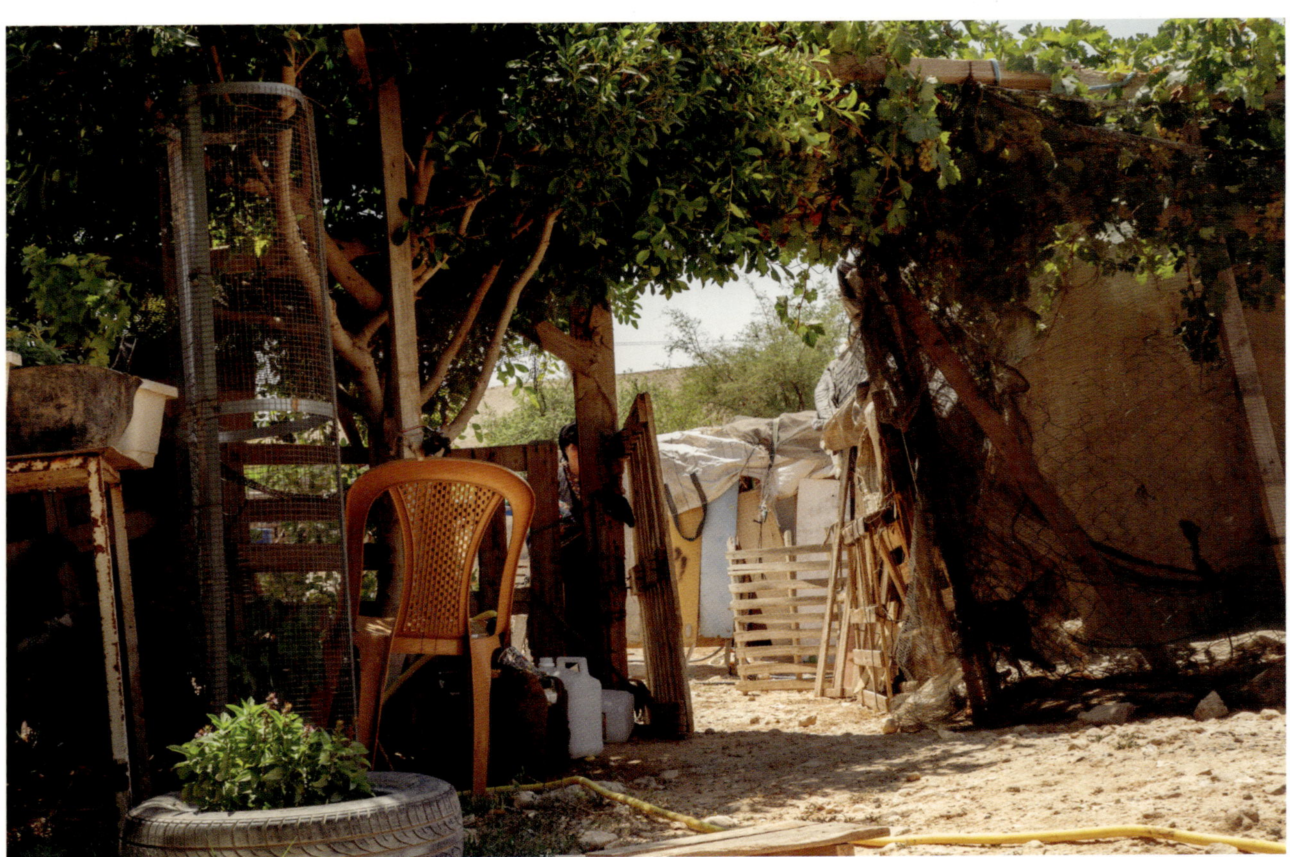

9.6 Al-Khan al-Ahmar, July 2019.

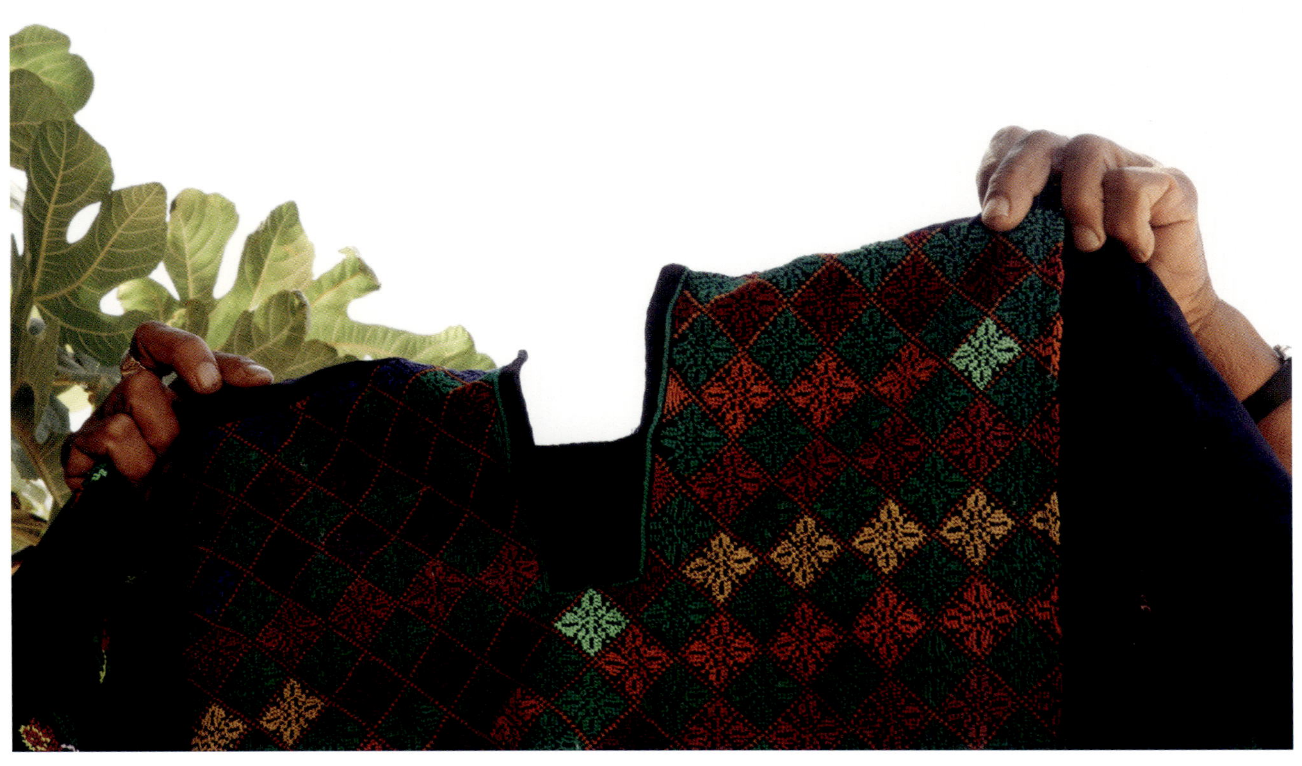

December, 2018. Fatma (remember her?) and another woman huddle over photographs of Susiya on Fatma's phone. The two women bond for a moment over the shared experience of living in villages kept forcibly in primitive conditions and under the constant threat of demolition. But when Fatma turns to issues of women's education, the other woman cuts off discussion flatly. Bedouin women, she says, are meant to stay at home.

At strategic moments, whenever the specter of demolition arises, so does the question: wouldn't the women be better off if the

9.7 Al-Khan al-Ahmar, December 2018.

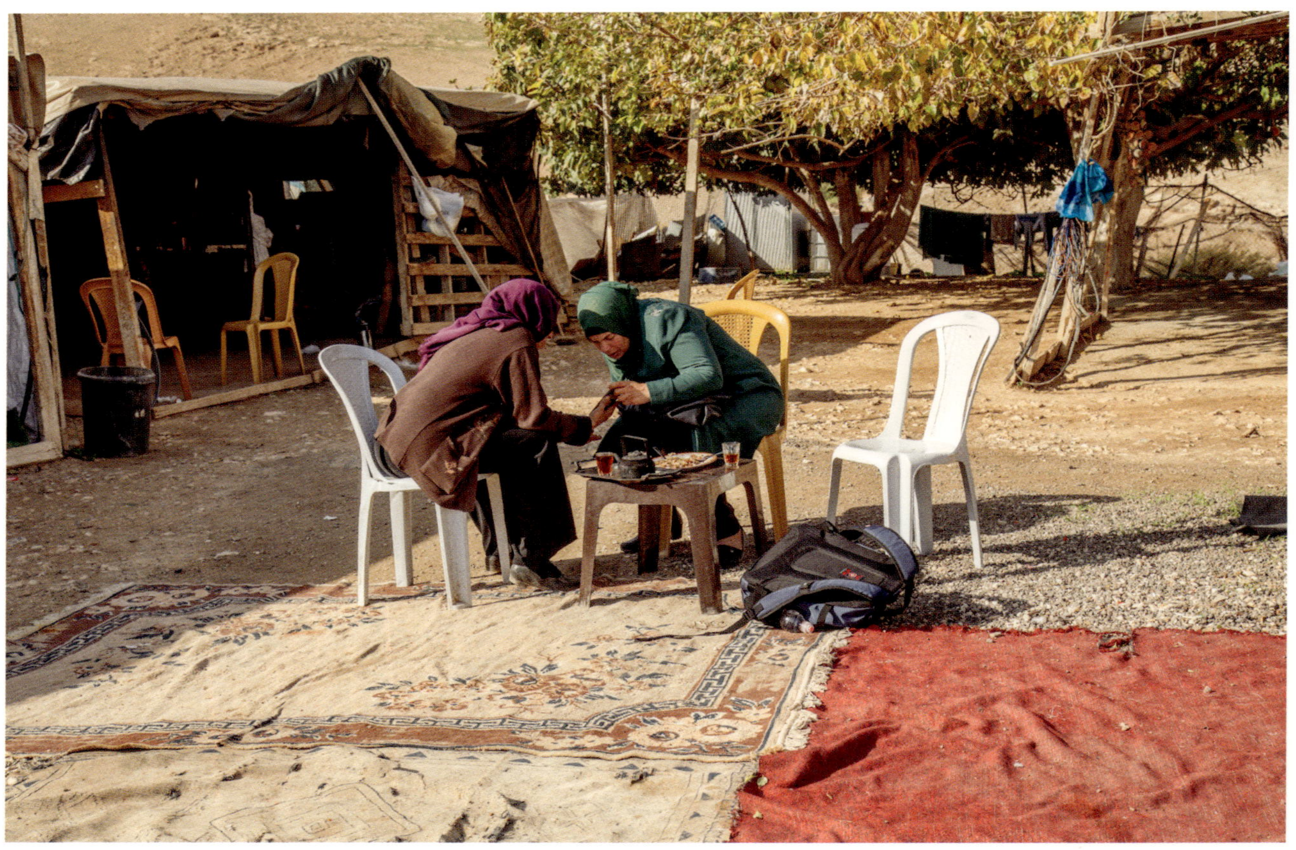

community moved, perhaps to an urban center with its economic and social advantages?

That is what the Civil Administration, that is, the occupation authority, earnestly recommends.

Yet the argument is deceptive, because the system of occupation has been intent for years on making life in Palestinian villages like this one so unlivable that everyone there—men, women and children—will see no other alternative than to leave.

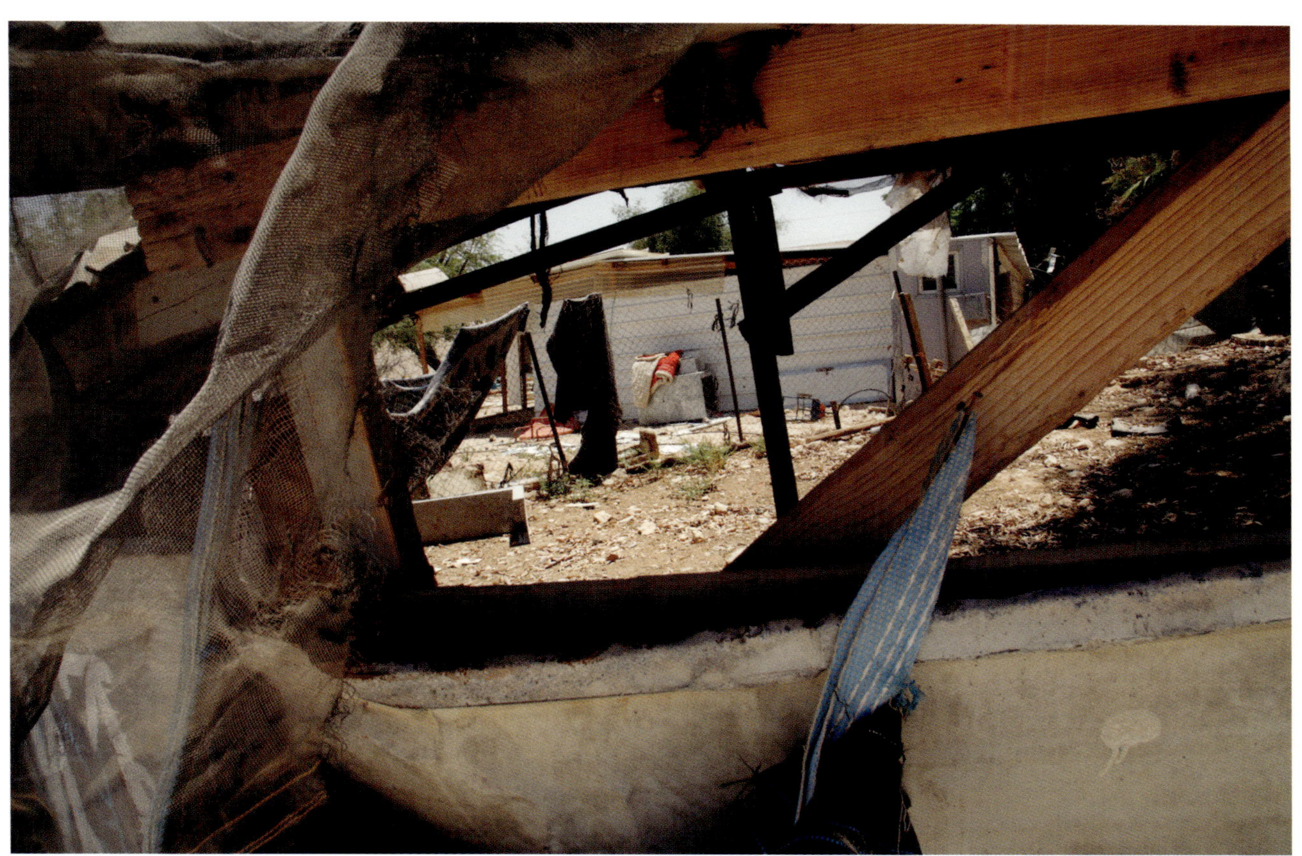

9.8 Al-Khan al-Ahmar, July 2019.

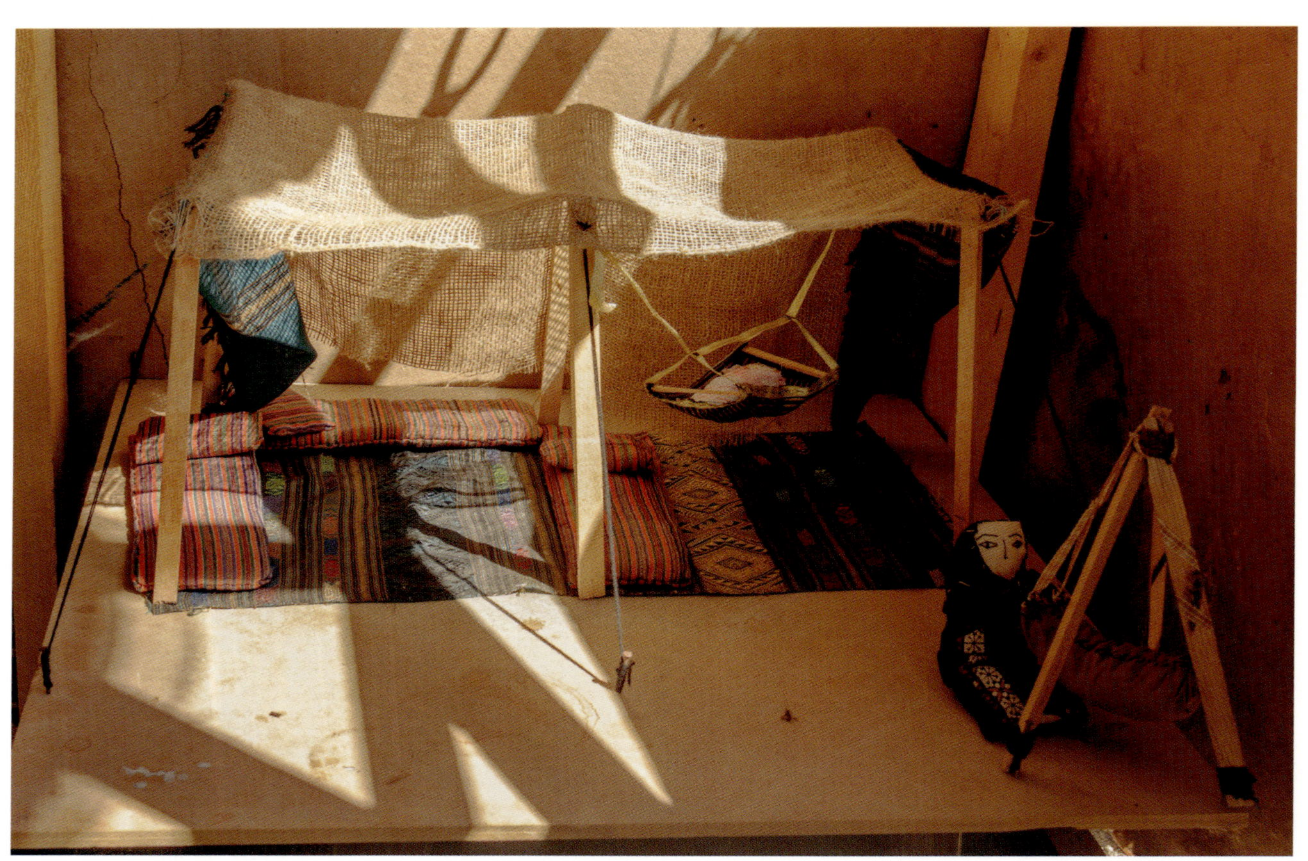

9.9 Al-Khan al-Ahmar, July 2019.

Yet there are some glimmers of hope, even in al-Khan al Ahmar. The Friends of the Jahalin (Bedouin), who include even some few brave souls in Maale Adumim, asked what they could do to help the community. 'Id, a leader of the protests against the threatened demolitions and expulsions, asked them to focus on women. He worried that they were at loose ends with no sense of purpose. The Friends supplied resources for the women to profit from their embroidery. They engaged a doll-maker to teach them and help expand their repertoire.

Some women made rag dolls; some specialized in clothing for the dolls. Doll making was not enough for one shy, retiring young woman. She began to make environments for the dolls, rather like doll-houses, to transform bits of cloth and sticks into a model of her world of tents and cradles, and she put the dolls themselves to work rocking the cradles.

She's become a lively and confident person. And she has even earned some money by selling some of these miniature houses.

Things may change even in Jamila's household. One granddaughter has just finished her education at the local school. On holiday now, the school's energy is still apparent in the eighth-grade classroom, where the children have built models; bright colors teeming with ideas hang from the ceiling and cover the walls. The granddaughter plans to continue her secondary education in Jericho next semester. This rather unusual step will cost money, and she will need transportation.

And perhaps after that she will be the first in her family, certainly the first woman, to attend university. It will be difficult: her father will have to let her go, and she will have to find the money. She may blaze a trail.

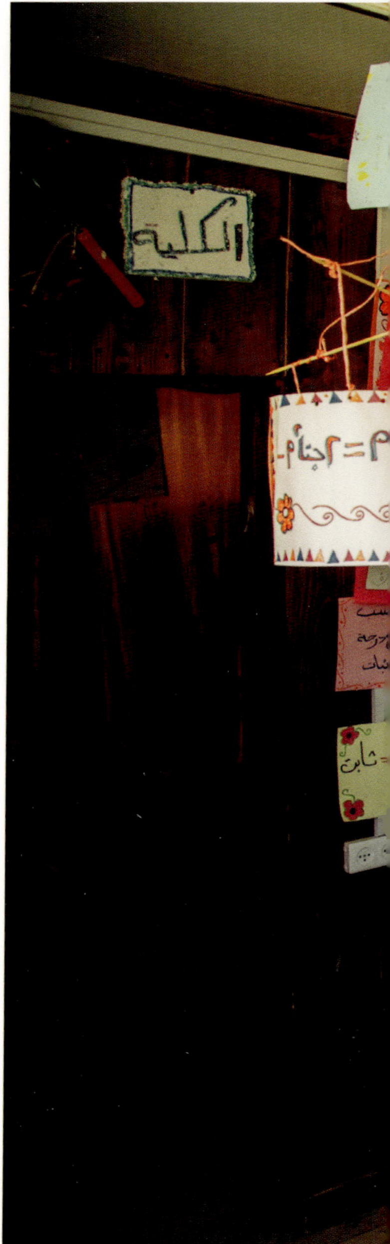

9.10 Al-Khan al-Ahmar, July 2019.

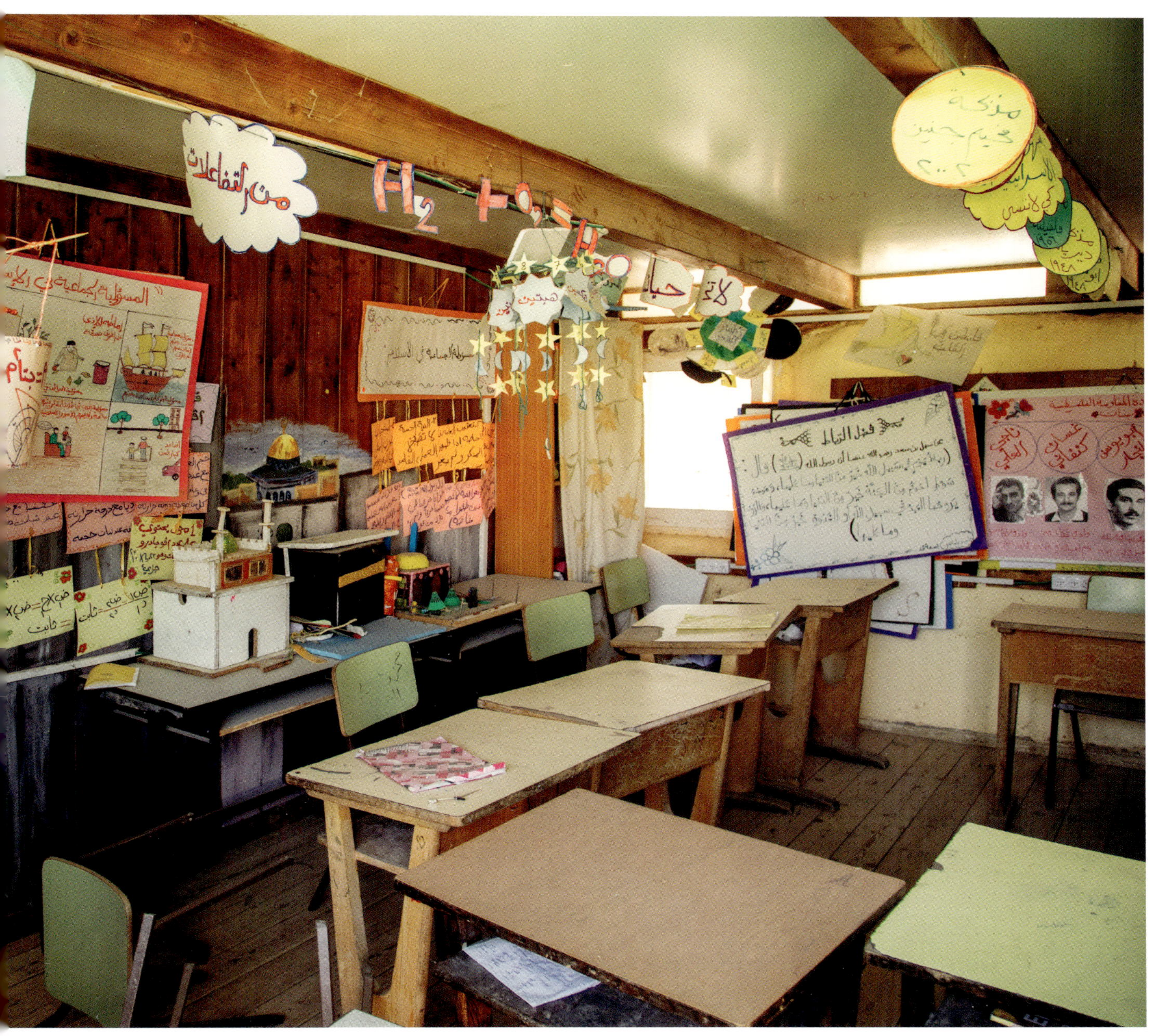
من التفاعلات
فضل الرباط
غسان كنفاني
ناجي العلي

The school that inspired these thoughts, like most Palestinian schools in the territories, is a prime target for demolition.

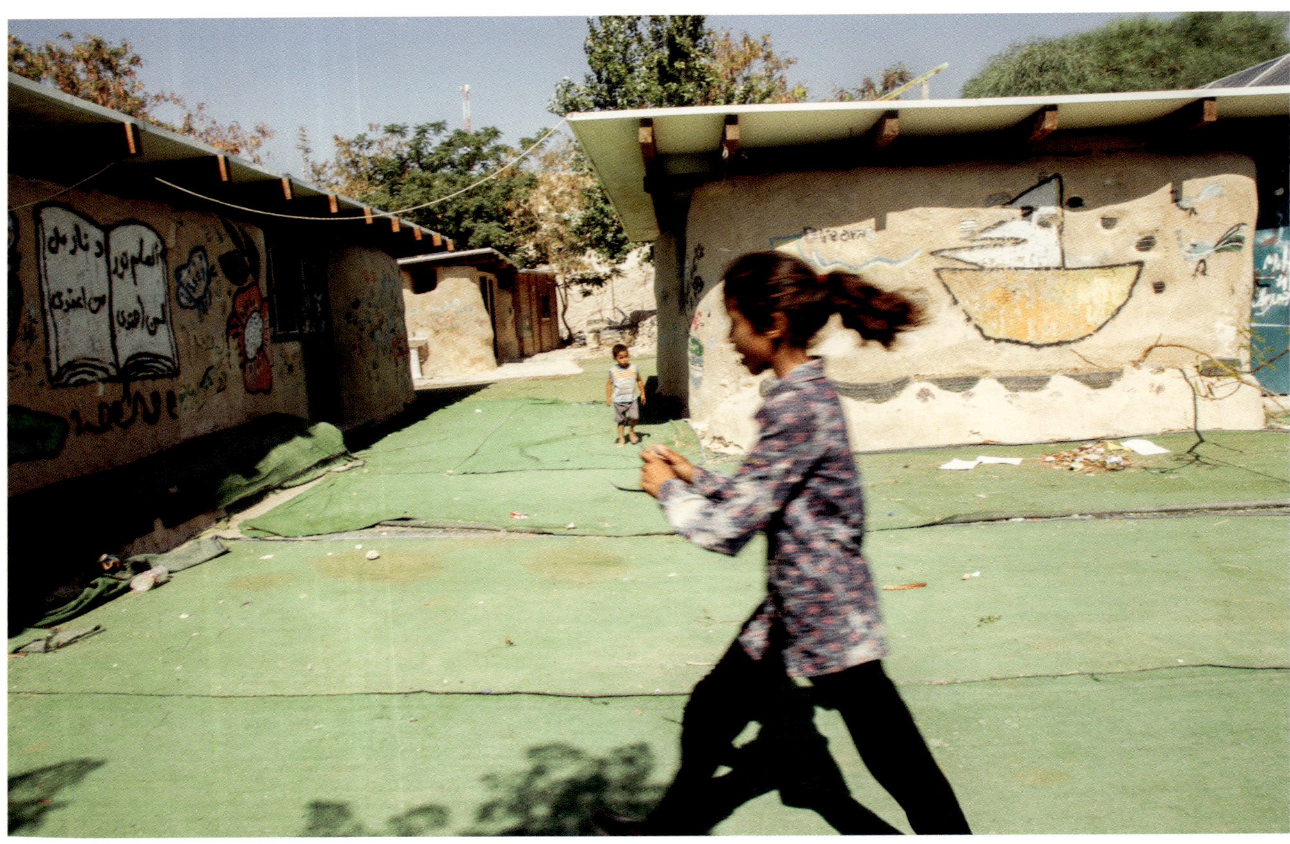

9.11 Al-Khan al-Ahmar, July 2019.

9.12 Al-Khan al-Ahmar, July 2019.

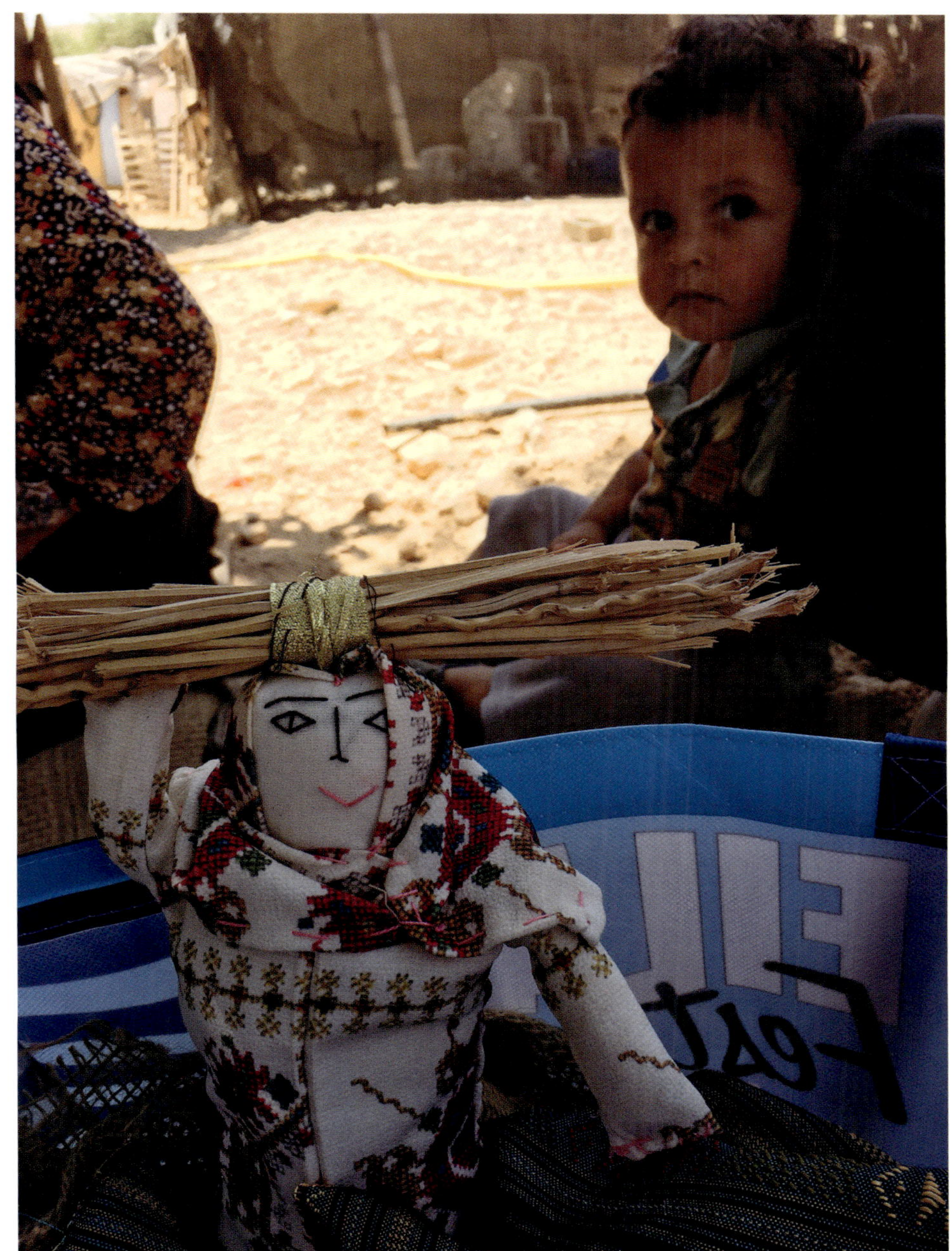

Laḥza: More Tea

Tea may arrive after a mid-morning or early-evening snack.

L.9 ‘Auja, July 2017.

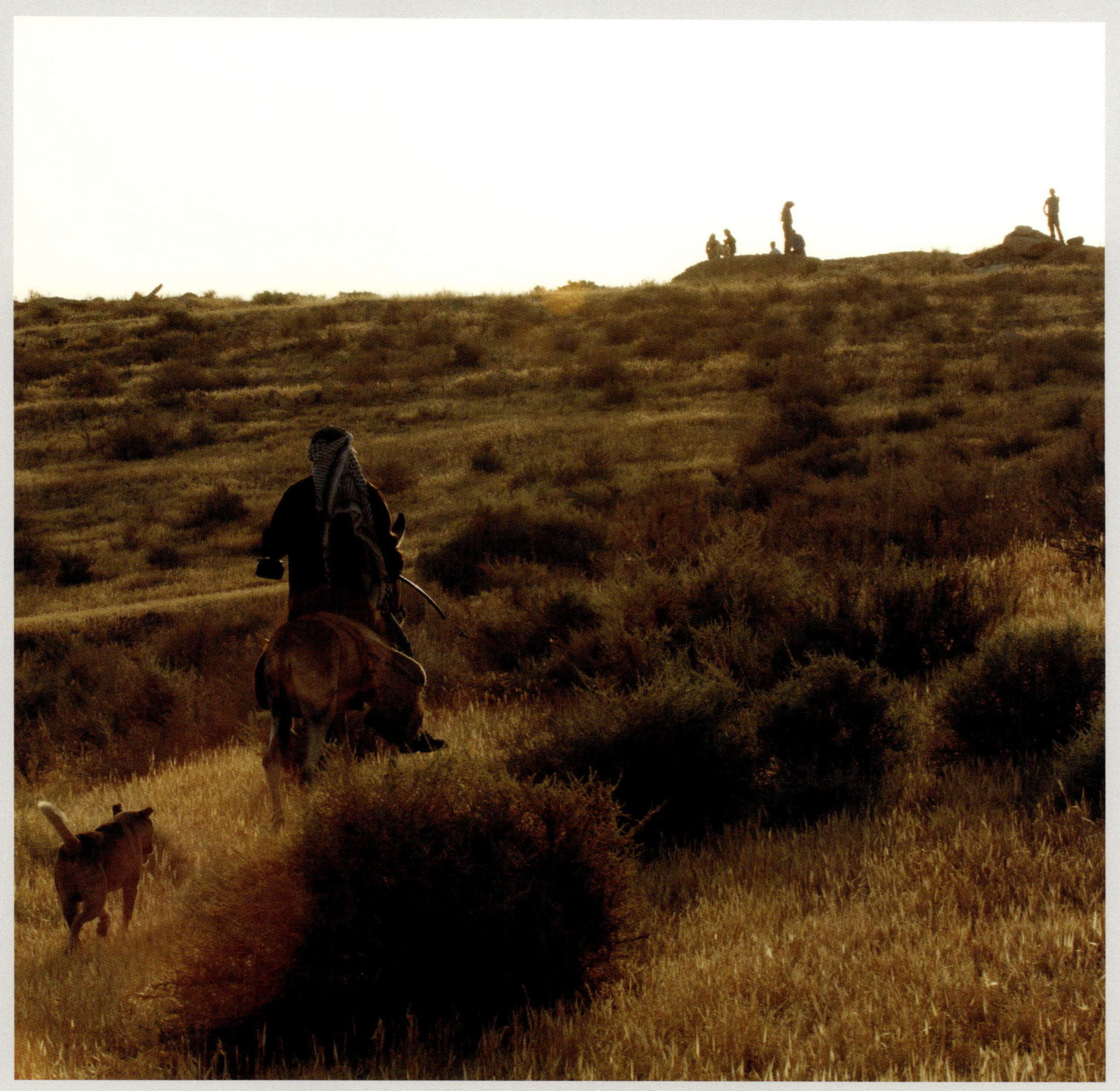

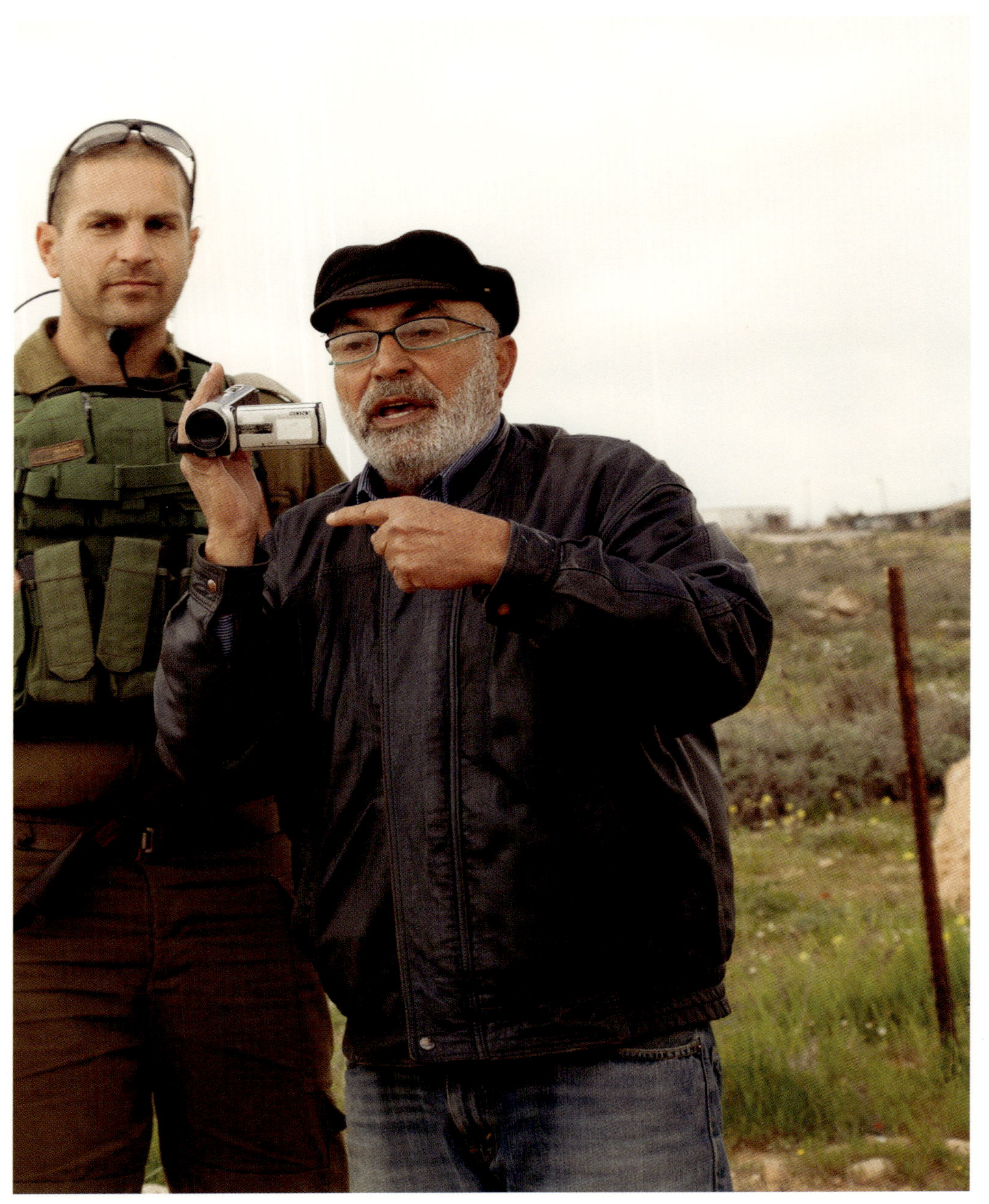

10.1 Umm al-Ara'is, March 2015.

10.

Ezra Nawi, 1952–2021

Ezra Nawi. A Baghdadi Jew, born in Israel, fluent in Arabic. A man like and unlike all others. He taught us non-violent resistance without reading about it in books.

Ezra might have invented the magical word "No," the word you use to defy soldiers, police, security goons, and similar creatures.

During the eighteen years that David knew him, he was usually under arrest, or on the verge of being arrested, or just released from jail. Unknowingly, he embodied the Gandhian principle, or rather its negation: the best way to maintain an unjust system, Gandhi said, is to obey its laws.

10.2 Wadi Sumsum, May 2014.

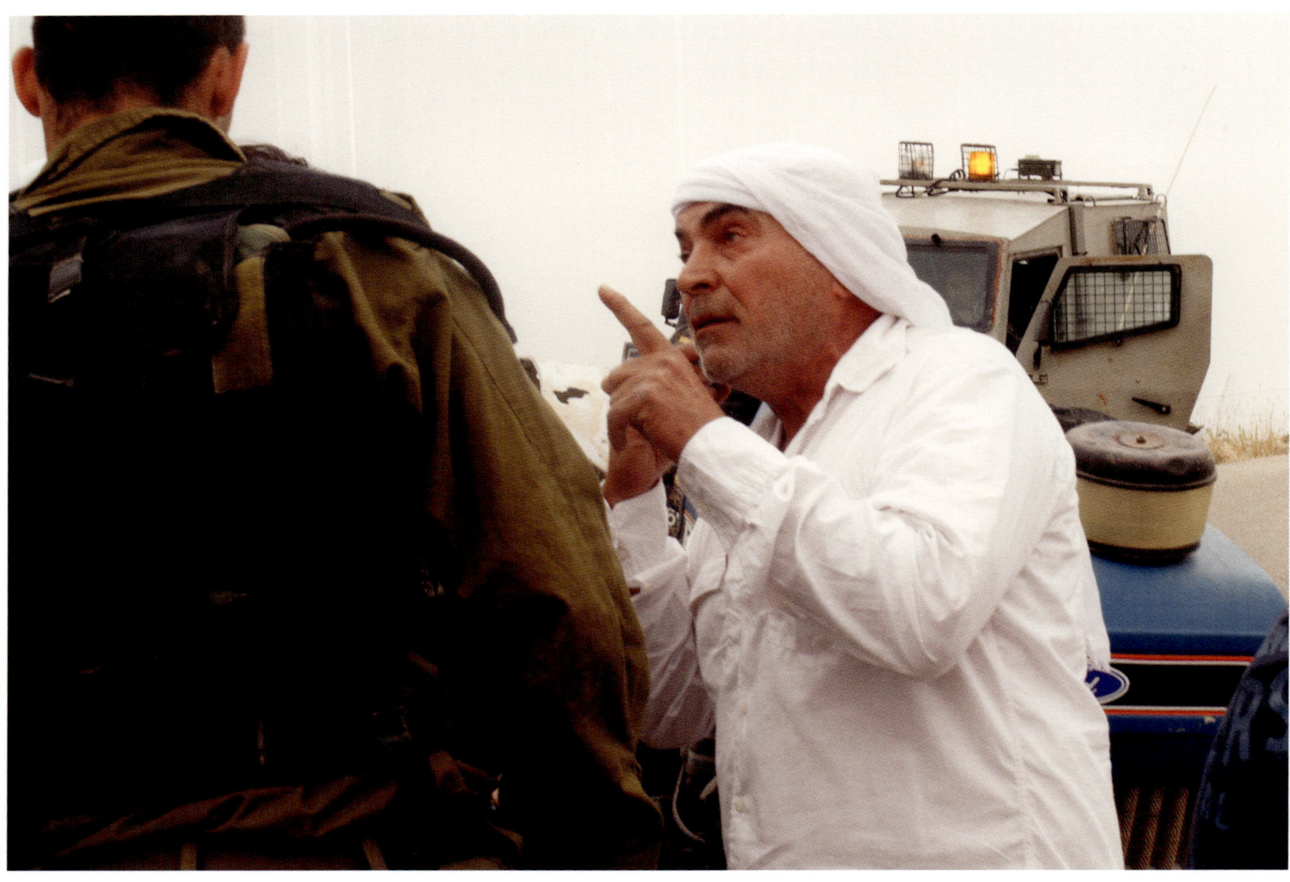

Settlers have blocked the path the schoolchildren take to school; soldiers and police turn up, numb at heart. We open the path. The standoff goes on for hours; we aren't prepared to give up. At the end someone says, "It's already hopeless, and it's getting worse." Ezra says: "No. It's like water dripping onto a rock. Speaking truth is like that. It takes time, but eventually the rock gives way."

10.3 Wadi Sweid, October 2010. Photograph: Michal Hai.

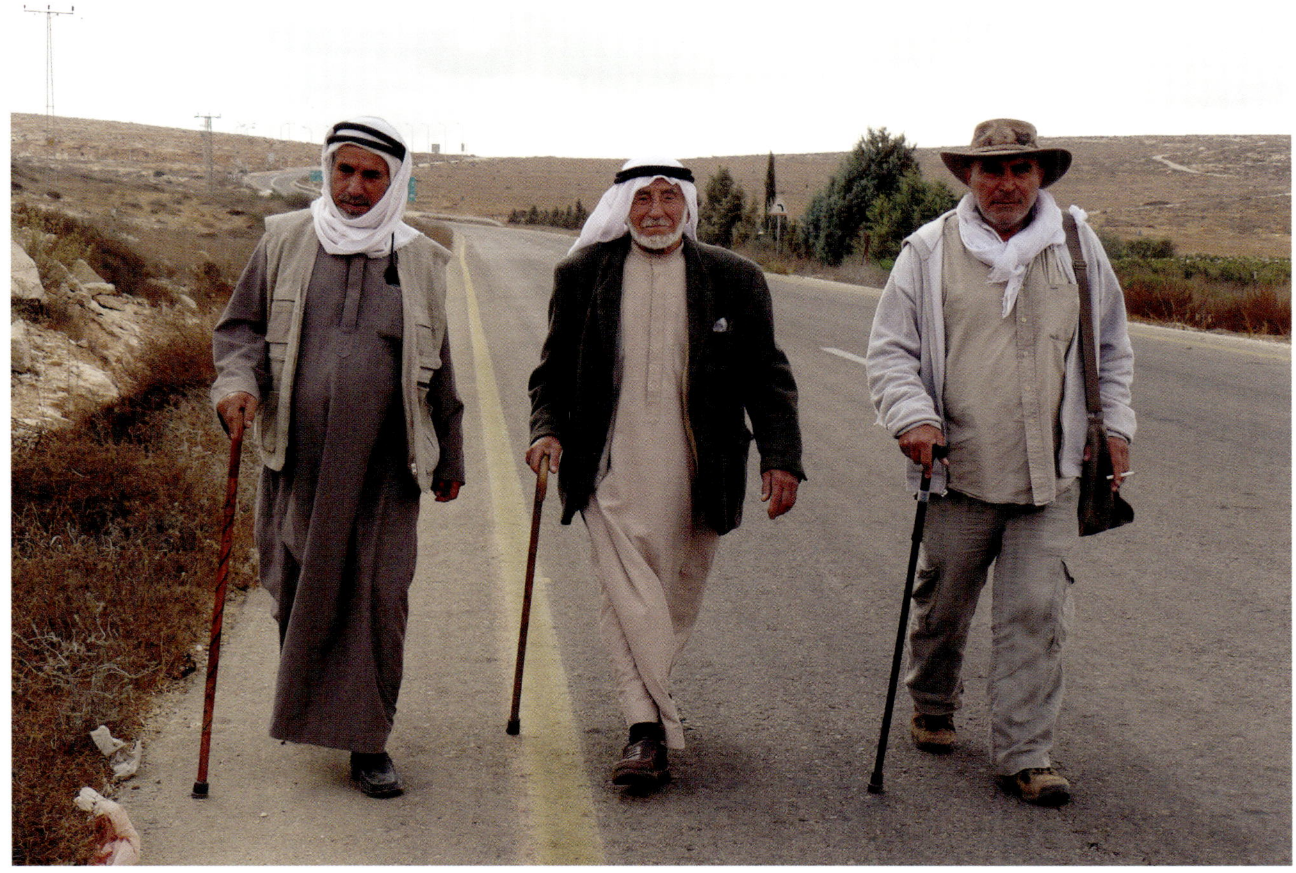

Jyotirmaya Sharma, University of Hyderabad: All of us were trying to clear the roadblock that the Israeli security forces had created on that dusty stretch in South Hebron. I was picking up mud and stones with my hands. I must have done this for just ten minutes when Ezra came up to me and said:

> You have done enough. You have shown your solidarity with us and our cause. Now you must just stand and watch. The soldiers are here already. There might be arrests. You are our guest. We don't want you to spend the night in a Jerusalem prison, or worse still, in a South Hebron prison.

Workdays, cleaning out a cave in Jinbah, the buried home of a family. The army filled in most of the caves in a series of devastating actions in the 1990s and again in 2000. We are inching downward, bucket by bucket. Ezra watches us, amused. Loses patience. "Let me show you

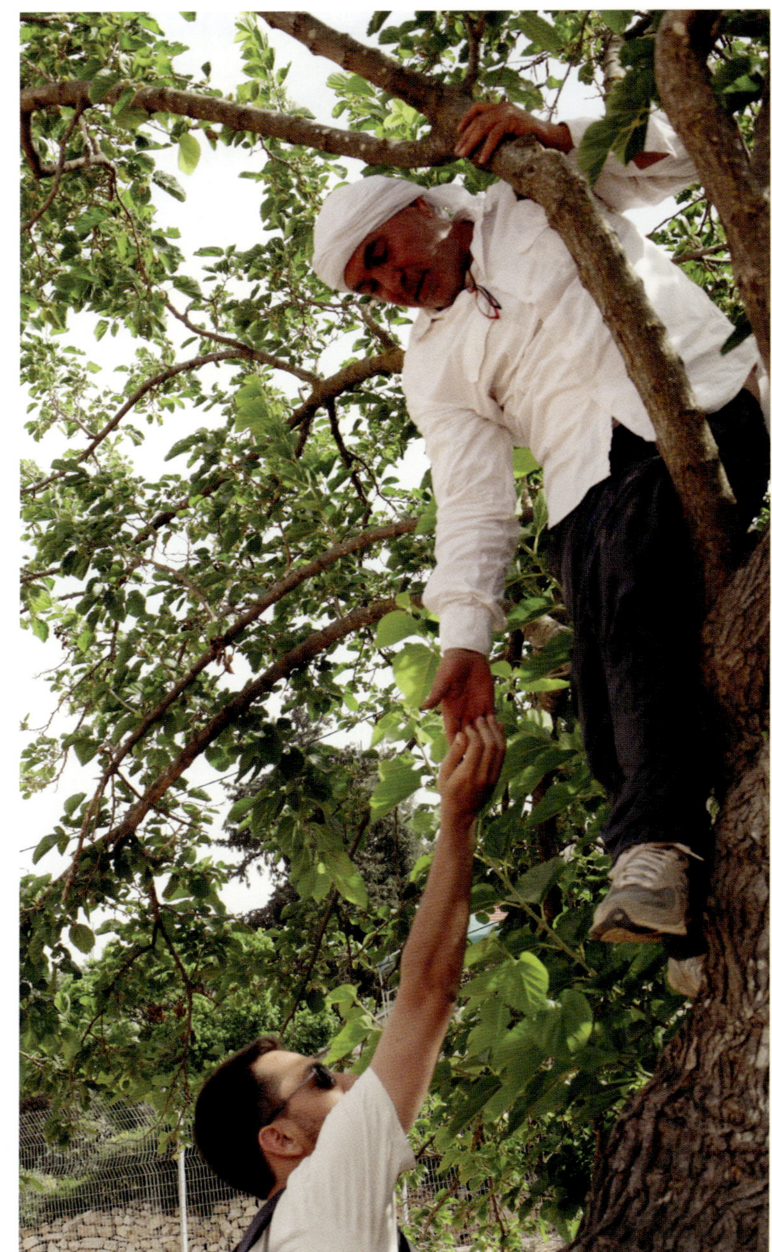

10.4 Zakariya lands, South Hebron Hills, May 2014.

how to use a shovel," he says. He knows. A few minutes later, the first step of stone, the entrance to the cave, comes to light. A lost world revealed.

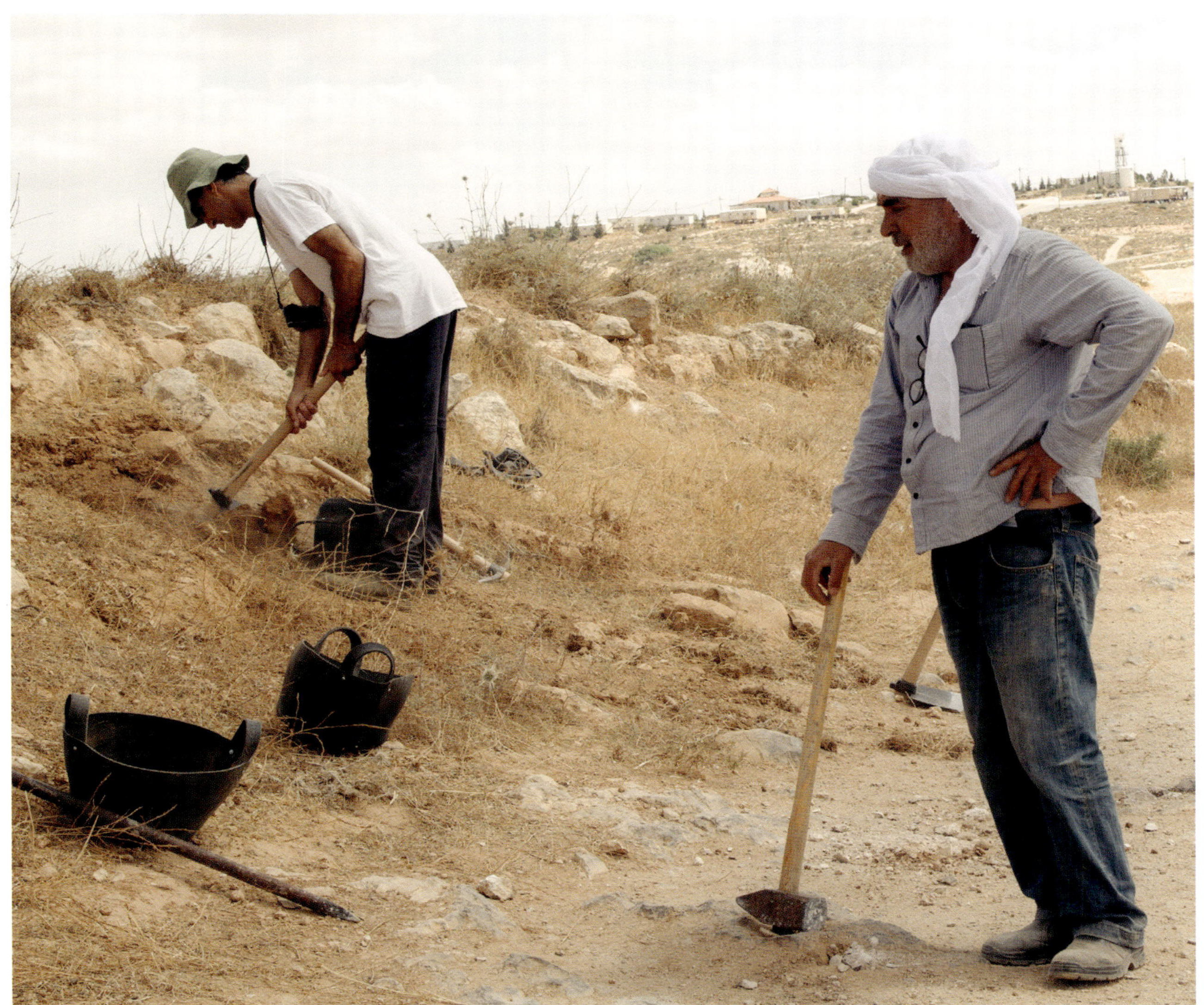

10.5 Bi'r al-'Id, South Hebron Hills, June 2015.

The tenderness that was always in him came out whenever he came across a donkey. "A horse," he would say, "is a prima donna, aloof and spoiled. Donkeys are unjustly scorned. They are faithful, kind, and never complain." Sometimes he would load his car with snacks that he knew the donkeys loved—potato chips, sweets—and offer them humbly before leaving South Hebron for home.

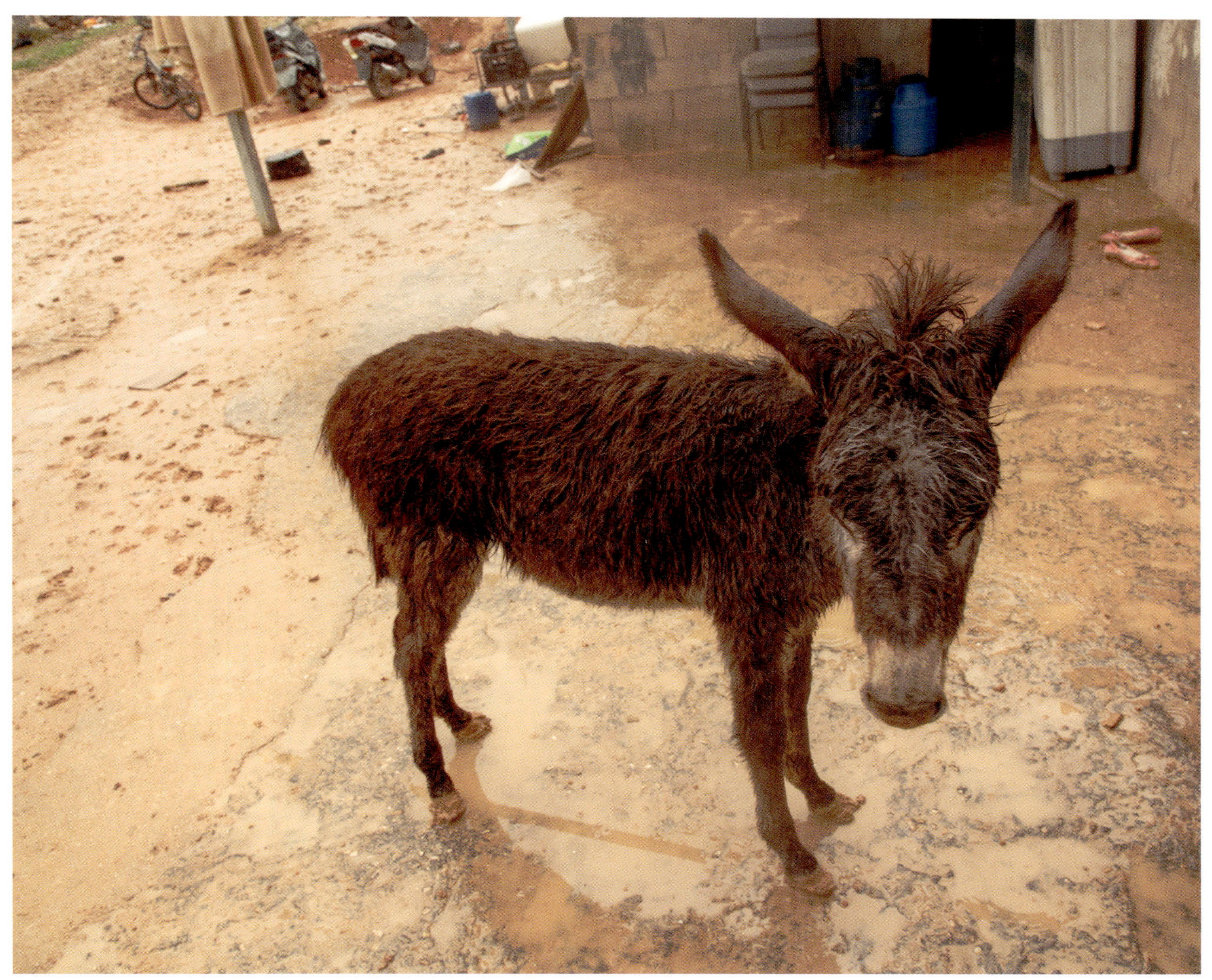

10.6 ‘Auja, January 2022.

Laḥza: Tea, Ar Rakiz

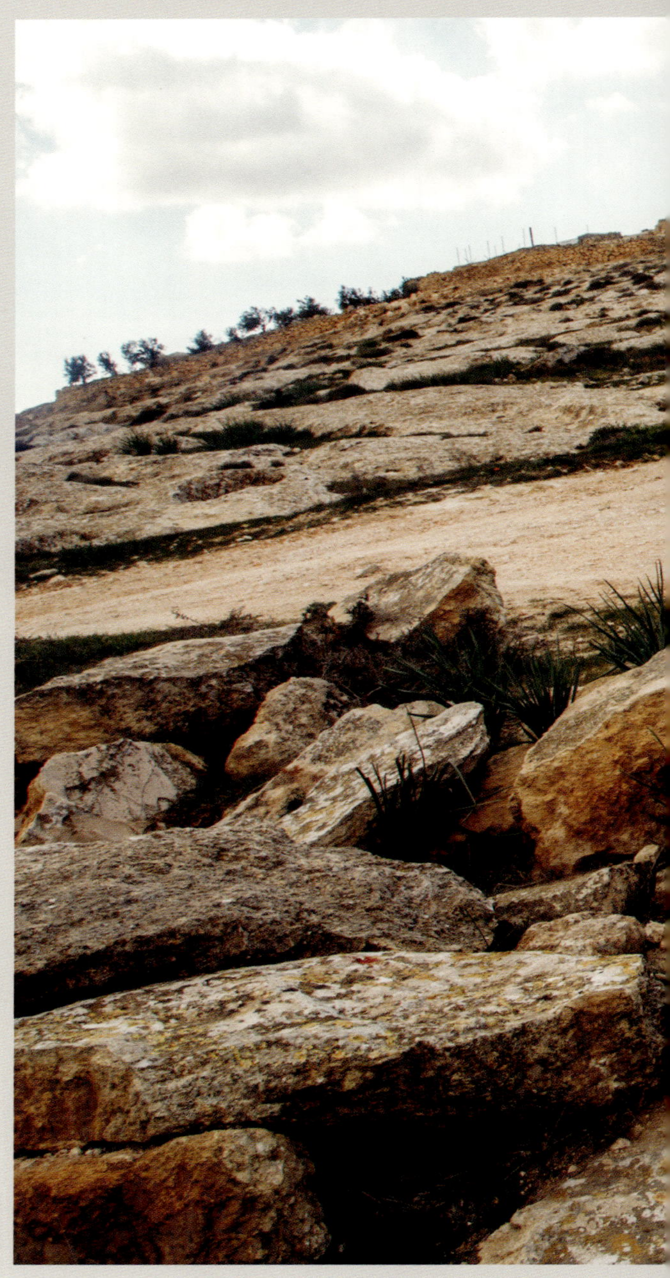

L.10 Ar-Rakiz, January 2022.

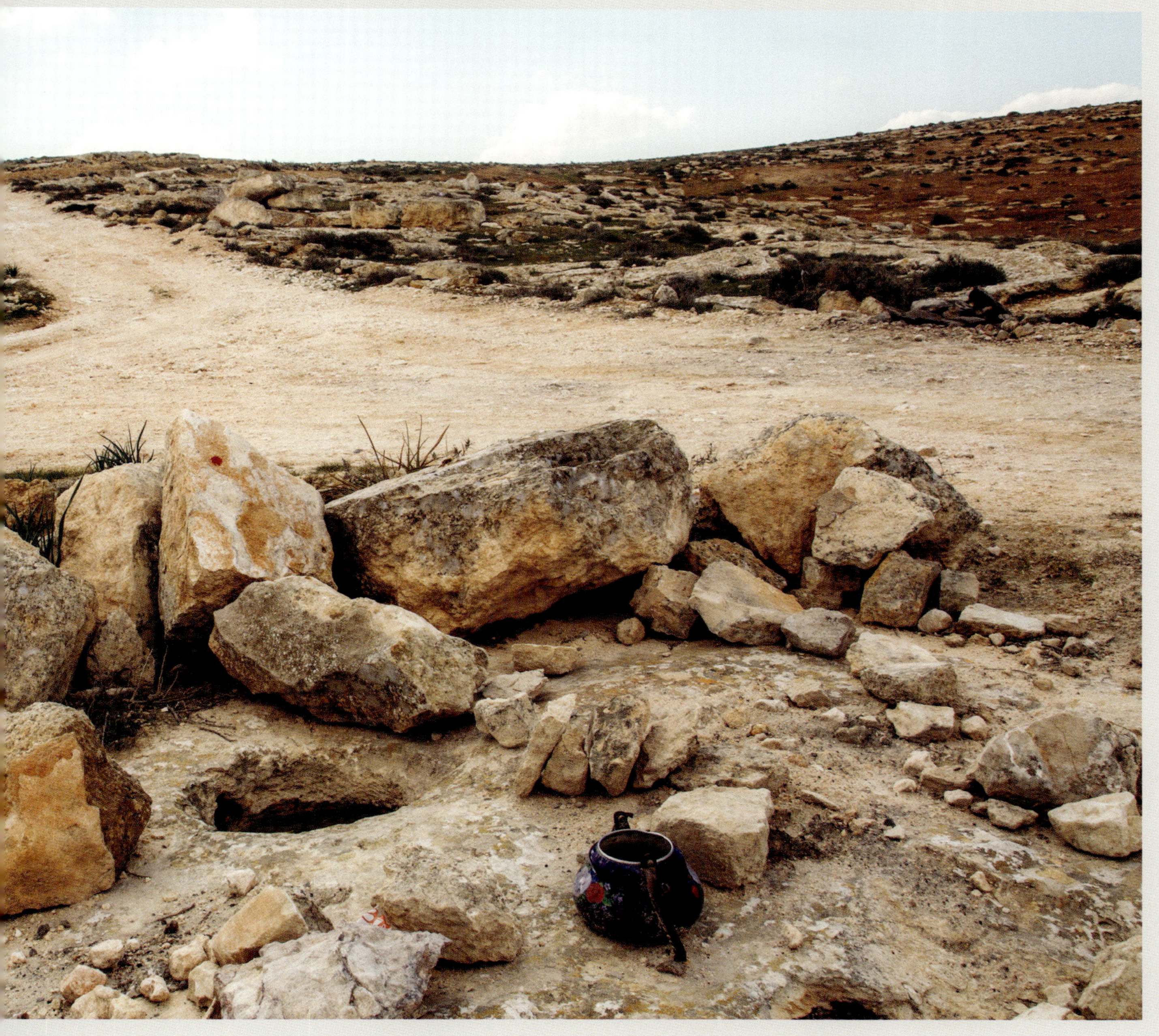

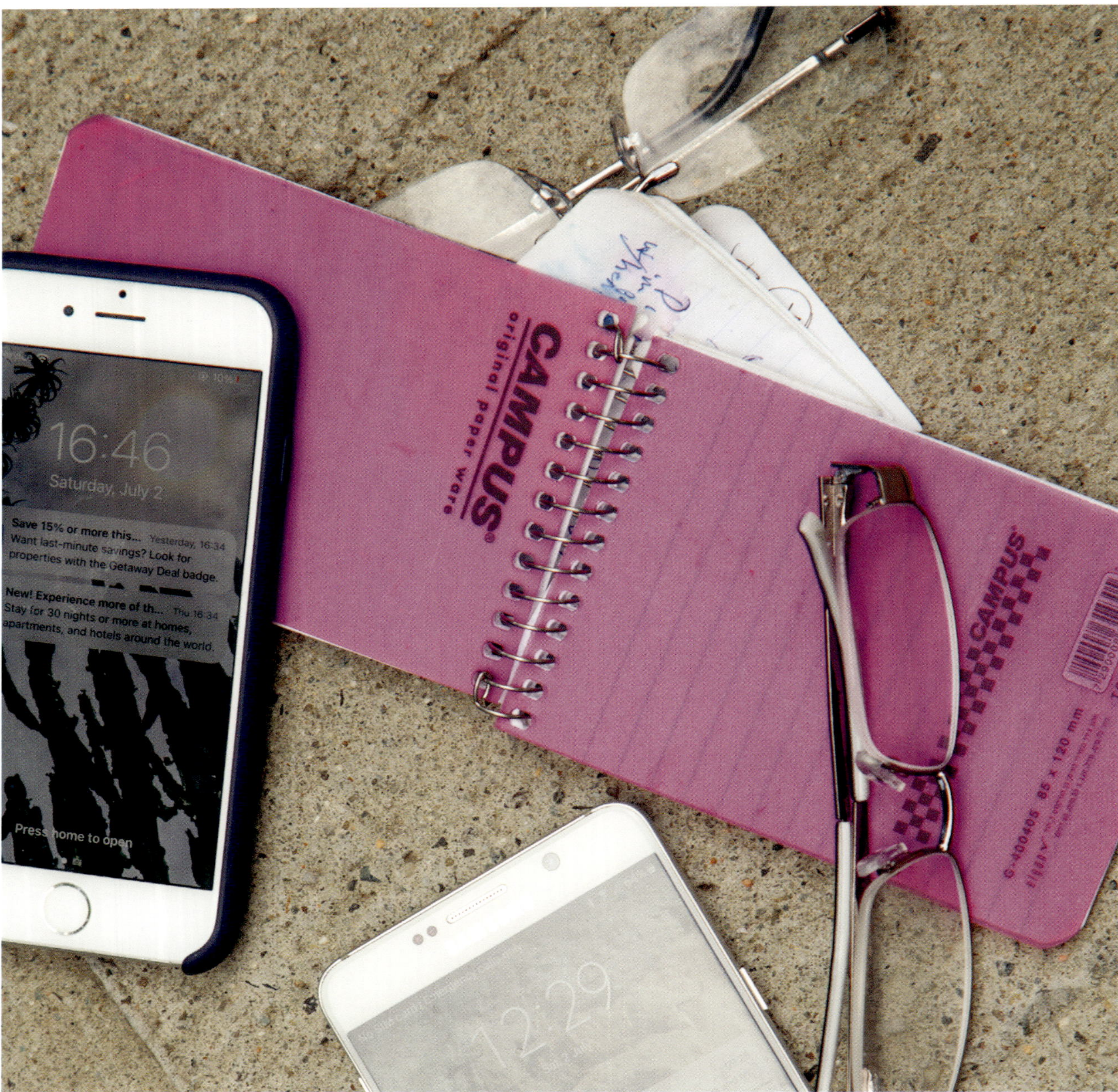
16:46
Saturday, July 2
Save 15% or more this...
Yesterday, 16:34
Want last-minute savings? Look for properties with the Getaway Deal badge.
New! Experience more of th...
Thu 16:34
Stay for 30 nights or more at homes, apartments, and hotels around the world.
Press home to open
CAMPUS®
original paper ware
CAMPUS®
G-400405
85 x 120 mm
12:29

11. Lost and Found

It is hard to lose something in Palestine.

Margaret:

I dropped a cellphone somewhere in East Jerusalem. I told the manager of the Educational Bookshop about my mishap. He said, "Let me try to get it back for you." Somehow, by the next day it was back, although by then it had drifted into a far corner of East Jerusalem. A Palestinian girl found it and brought it home to her mother, whom the bookstore manager found in turn. We had planned to call the woman who saved it for me, but we did not. The manager was angry because she requested a reward. "That's not the Palestinian way," he told me.

Then there was the cellphone I left on a minibus from Yatta to Hebron. The driver found it. He gave it to his son, who lives outside of East Jerusalem. The son messaged me. He did not ask for a reward, but he pleaded with me to find a way to get him a permit to reside in Jerusalem, with the woman he was in love with. It's a tall order. I asked around and came up with the name of a lawyer. Meanwhile, the phone was handed over to David at an intersection, late at night, by an unknown intermediary, and came back to me on my next visit. I don't know whether the residency permit ever materialized.

11.1 New Haven, CT, July 2022.

Two pairs of reading glasses from Superpharm made their way back to me, by circuitous routes, after more than two years. One

I dropped in a field stolen from its Palestinian owner by settlers; we were there to protect this man when he entered his own land. Some weeks later, he gave them to Amiel, who kept them in his house. The other pair lived peacefully in Arik Ascherman's car until I happened to pass him, one day, on the road back from 'Auja. He was, as so often, on the phone to the police or the civil administration, trying to get them to do their job, but he saw me and rushed over, still talking to whomever, to restore these precious spectacles to their owner.

One day, while I was sitting in a shepherd's tent in Rashash after the morning's grazing, another shepherd walked in, holding a small spiral notebook. He said he had found it out in the field, amidst the rocks, and he thought he had seen me writing in it. I wasn't aware that it had fallen from my pocket; it had lots of notes in it.

But then there was my lens . . .

Some Things are not Returned.

David:

There was my favorite watch, inscribed with Sanskrit numerals, that I bought in south India. It also noted the dates of important Hindu festivals. It fell off my wrist, probably somewhere in the olive groves or the terraces, during one of those moments when settlers attacked in Twaneh and we were rushing to protect the Palestinian farmers. Since then, I have lost any useful sense of time.

And there was the pocket schoolbook of *Odyssey Book IX*, with a very helpful Greek glossary, that I used to carry around on Ta'ayush days in case I got arrested. I lost it in Silwan when we were rebuilding terraces in a neighborhood slotted for demolition and expulsion. *Book IX* is the story of the Cyclops, a worthy precursor of Israeli soldiers and police.

One chilly April day in 2018 I forgot my blue jacket, with its long and checkered history, in the courtyard of Abu Rasmi's home in al-Hamma. I missed it for a while, though I was glad to think that it was warming up someone who needed it more than I did.

Margaret:

I would have gotten my lens back, too, if the Palestinians had not fled when the rock-throwing began that day in Asfar. Only the settlers were left, just outside the olive grove. Maybe one of them traded it in for some small sum, or he might still be using it on his own camera. I wasn't very sorry. It wasn't good enough or long enough to capture the rocks flying our way. Another photographer told me about a shop in Tel Aviv where I could get a better one, which I did. Since then, so far, I've never had occasion to photograph settlers throwing rocks at me.

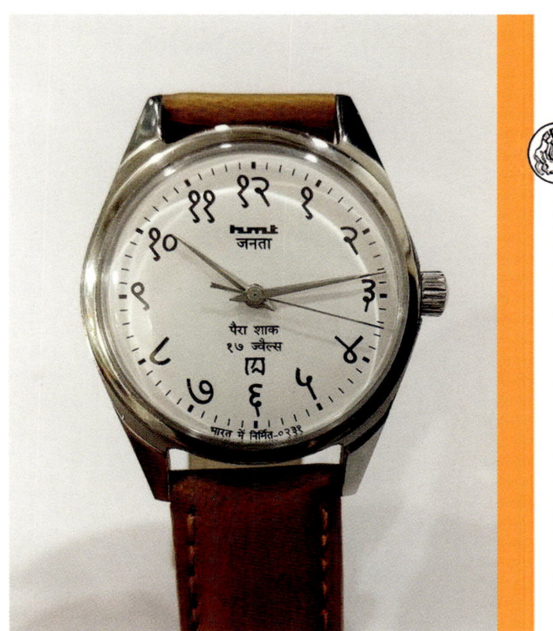

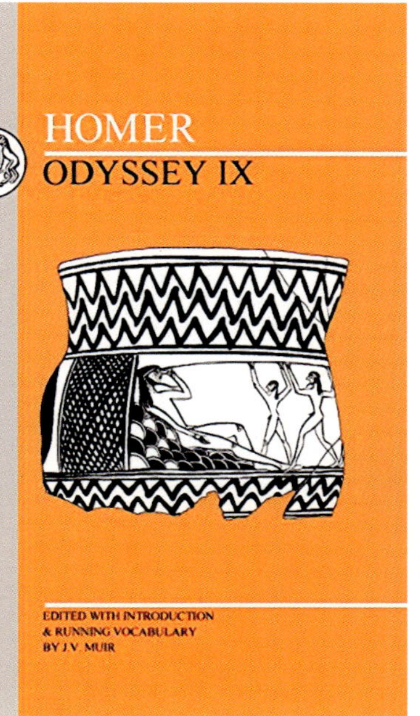

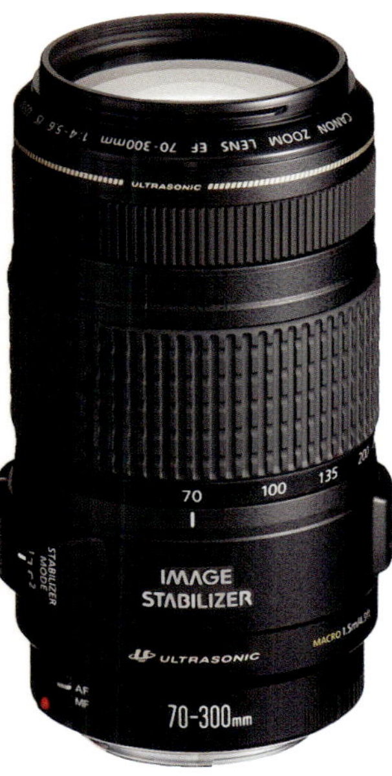

11.2 a–c
Unknown
date, origin.

Things Found in Palestine

Margaret:

1. A black hat (amidst the bags of spare clothes in the back of the Ta'ayush Toyota.)
2. And my sister-in-law, after reading our blog posts, said: "It's clear that you've found your calling."

11.3 Al-Hamme, April 2018.

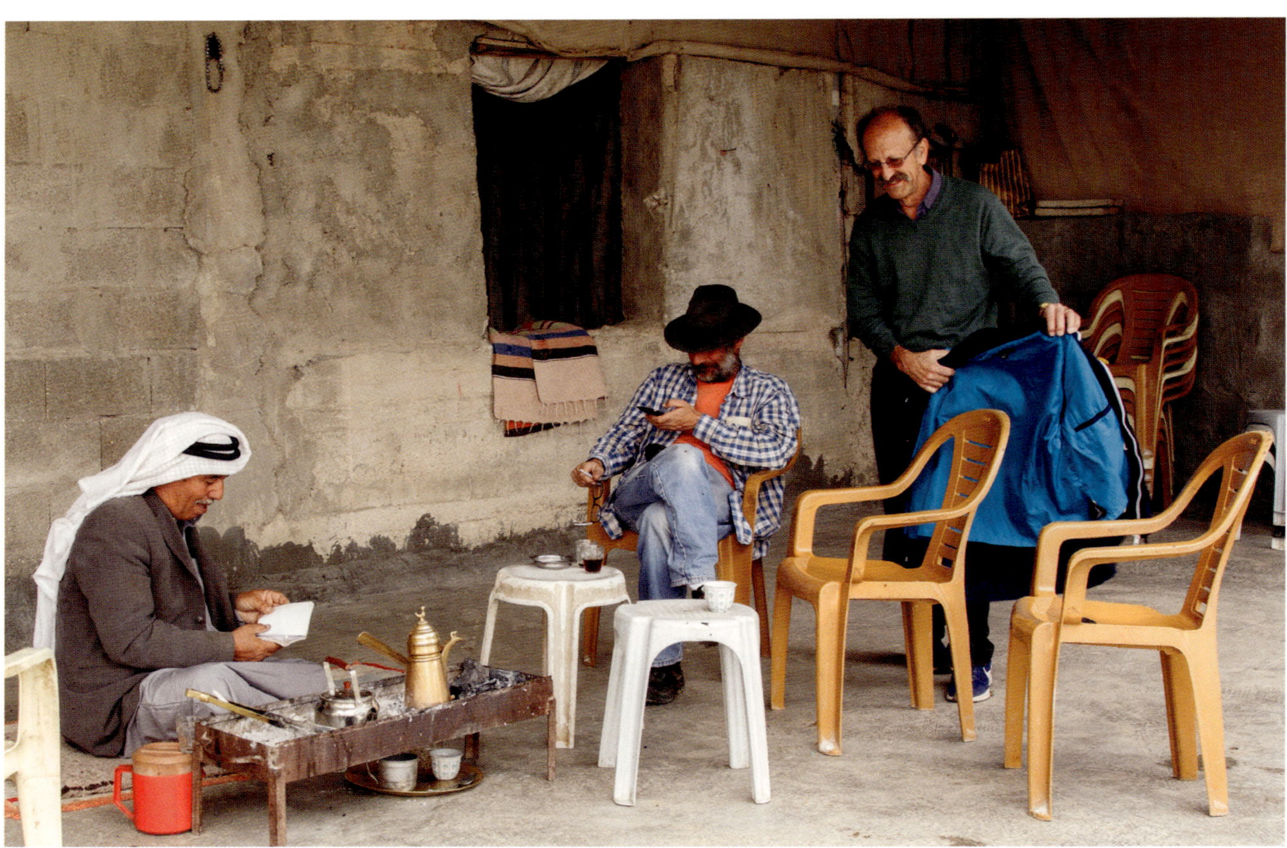

David:

3. A way to live.

11.4 'Auja, April 2018.
Photograph: Amir Bitan.

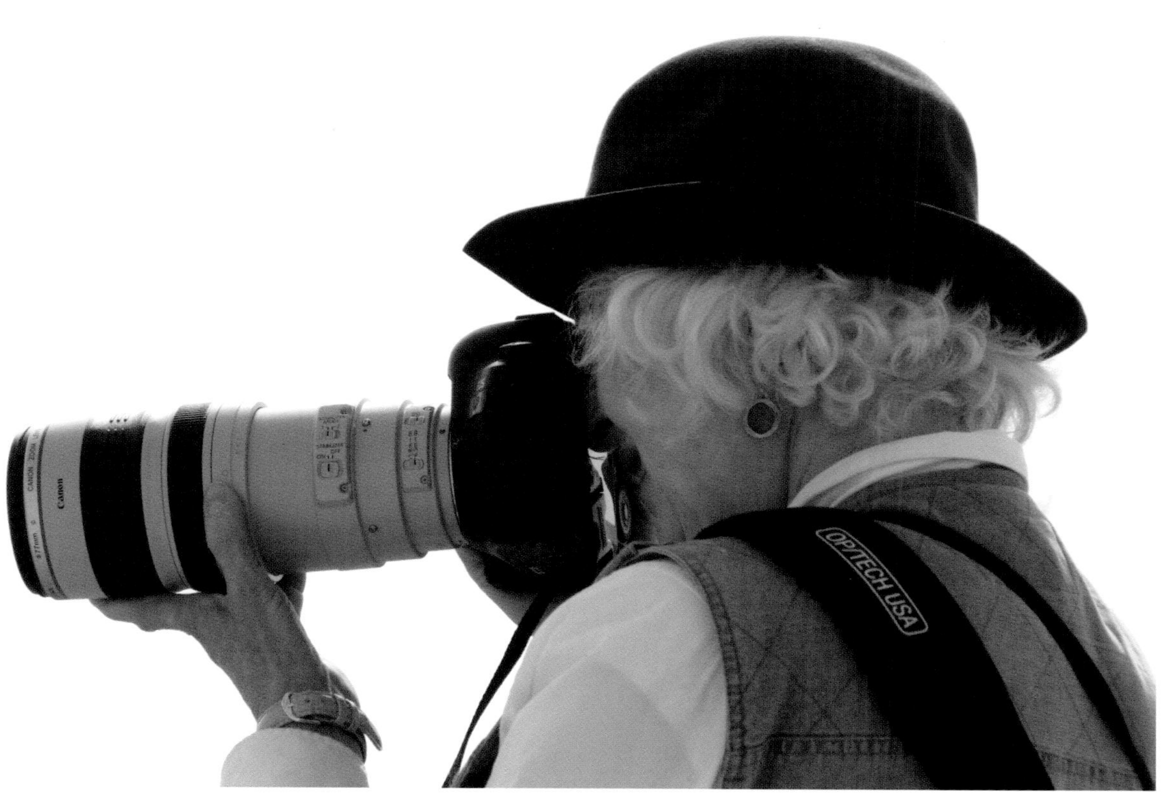

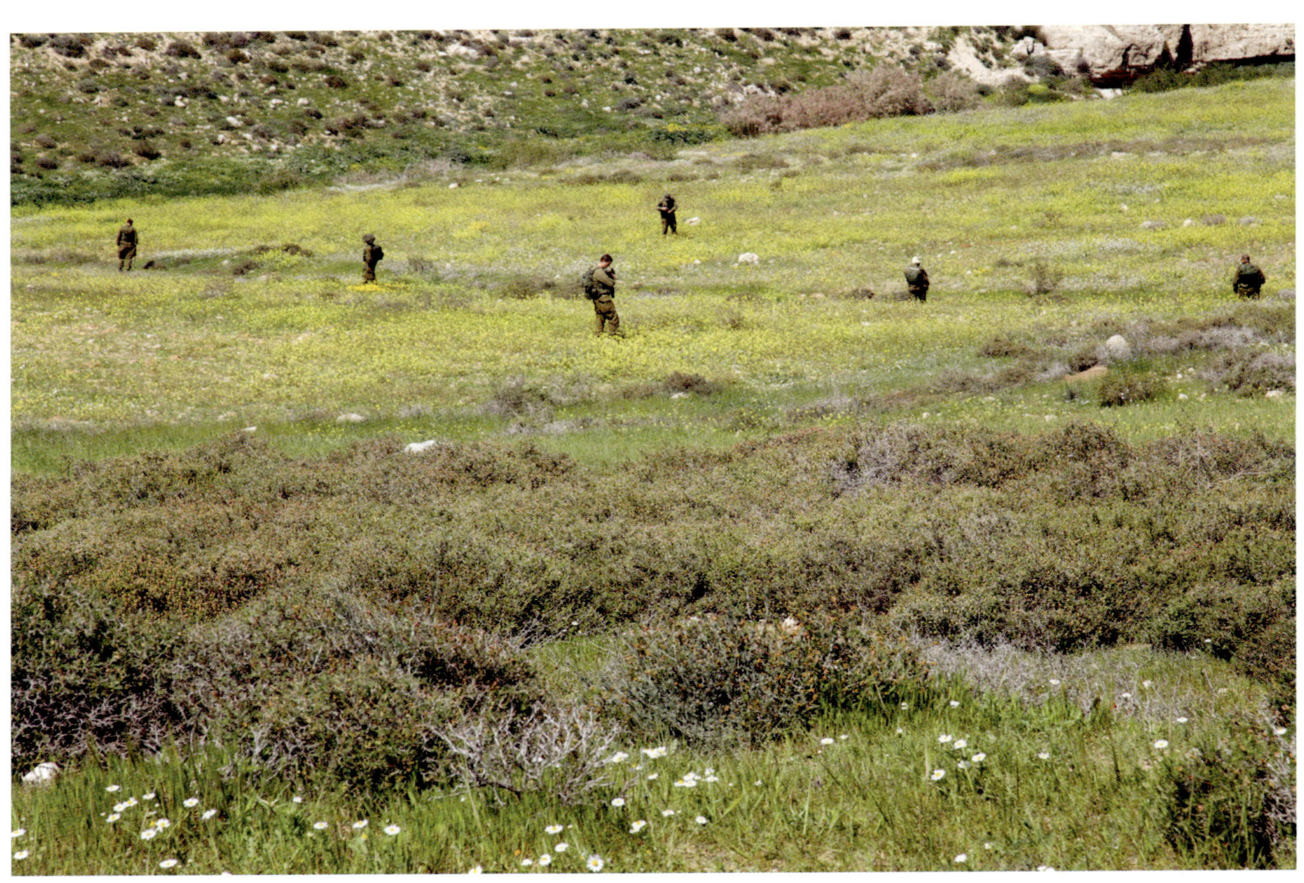

11.5 Zanuta, March 2015.

We won't even try to list the things Israeli soldiers lose in Palestinian, day by day. One day at Zanuta, we found a contingent of them poking with sticks through the tall grass as if they'd lost something of value there.

As indeed they had.

This litany of lost and found pales, however, beside the routine reality of Palestinian losses—home, fields, possessions, health, life itself.

All Palestinians in Area C live with the constant fear of losing everything.

Laḥza: ʿAuja

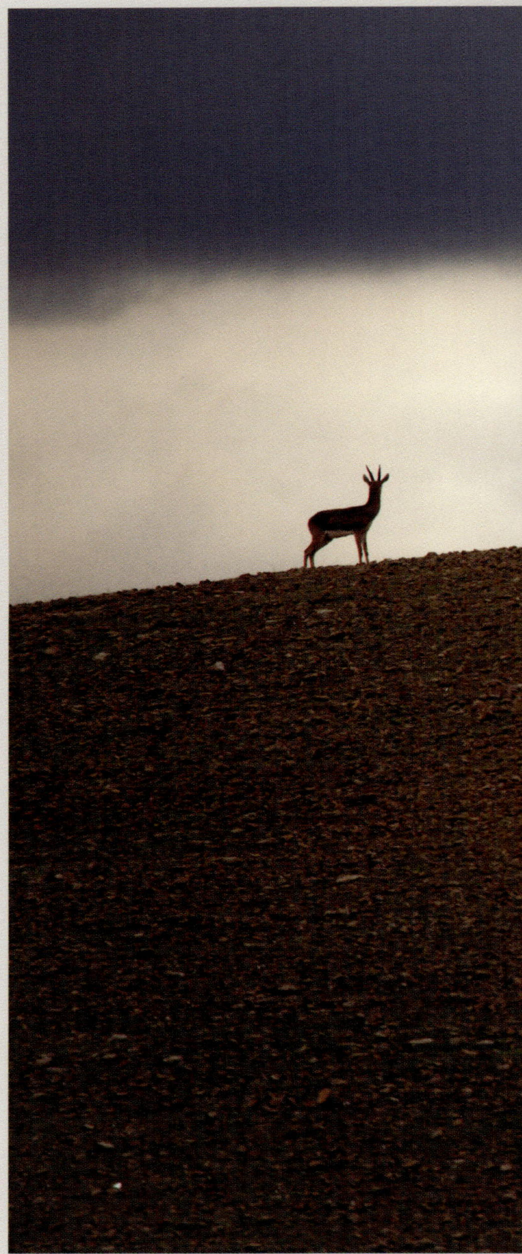

L.11: ʿAuja, January 2022.

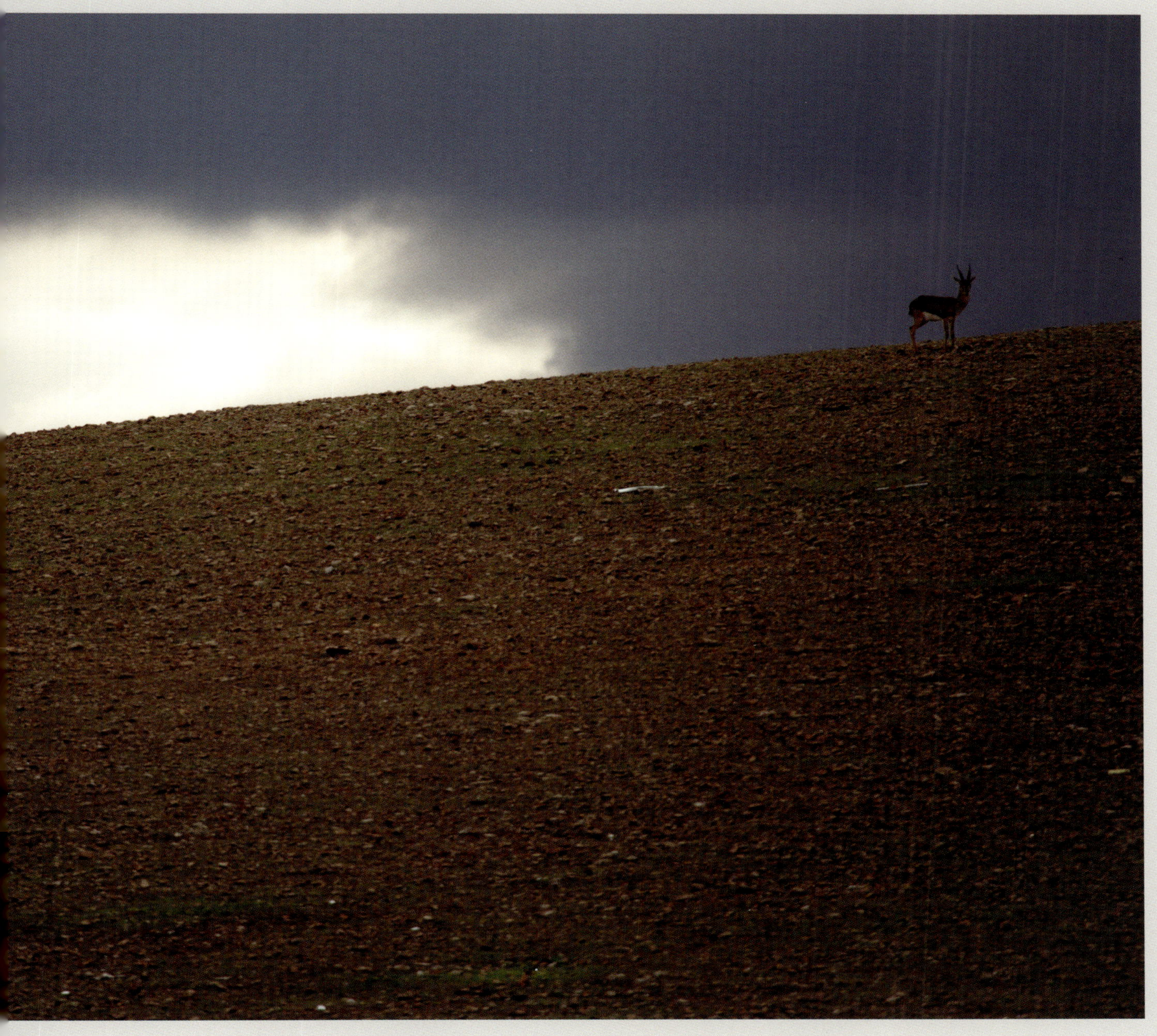

12.1 Susiya, February 2022.

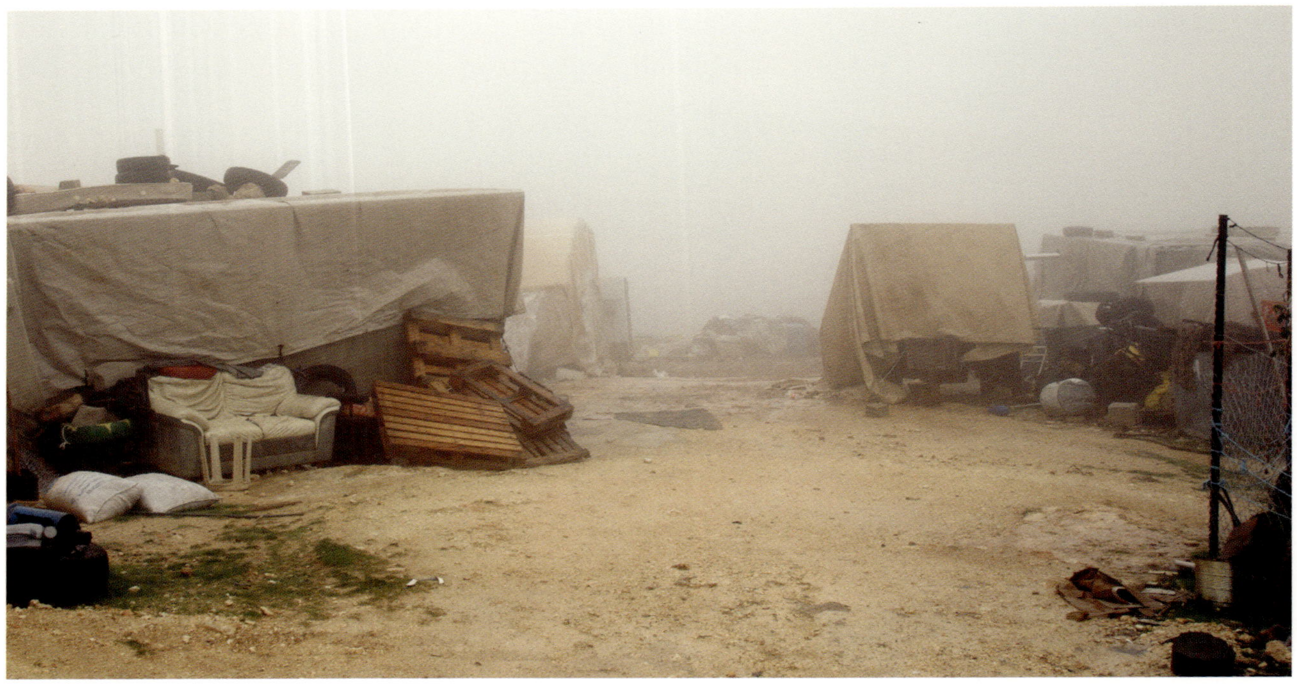

12. Voices

Nasser Nawaja', May, 2018

I am Nasser Muhammad Ahmad Nawajaʿ. I'm thirty-six years old, and I live in Qaryat Susiya in the South Hebron region of the West Bank.

We wanted to go back to our village over there (Susiya al-Qadima), but they wouldn't let us. Still, we are living here now on part of our farmlands. Now they want to destroy that, too, to wipe it out and with it the hope that we still have.

My grandfather was born in this region. Seven times they drove us out before 2001, in 1948, in 1986, all the other times, and they are always threatening to drive us out again.

There were two villages: Garitain, which was down below, in the valley, near the 1948 border, and Susiya, which is high and cool. Our family lived in both villages. In the winter, we would go down to Garitain, until the wheat harvest in July; then we would come up to Susiya for the rest of the summer, taking the sheep with us. Garitain has land that is good for wheat and lentils; Susiya is good for growing olives and grapes. In 1948, they drove us away from Garitain, but we were able still to go there until 1953, when there was some adjustment in the border.

I went to school in Yatta, walking eight kilometers each way. It was hard. In the morning, it was fine, but coming back in the afternoon, in summer, was terrible. I studied mathematics, Qur'an, a little English, literature, Arabic, history, poetry. I was good in school. I couldn't go to college or to university—maybe in some other, luckier life. But our children will go to university, *inshallah*. I have three children—Dalia, Layish, and Ahmad.

We live with many kinds of fear. Fear of demolitions, constant fear of the settlers, fear for our kids. In Twaneh, the kids go to school on the path that skirts the forest [of Chavat Maon]; the settlers come and attack them. The army provides a jeep to accompany them, but sometimes, the jeep is late. School gets out at 1:15, the kids should be home by around 1:35, but if the jeep isn't there, they wait, sometimes till 3:00. They're hungry and thirsty, and the mothers go crazy with fear, every day they pray, "Where are they?"

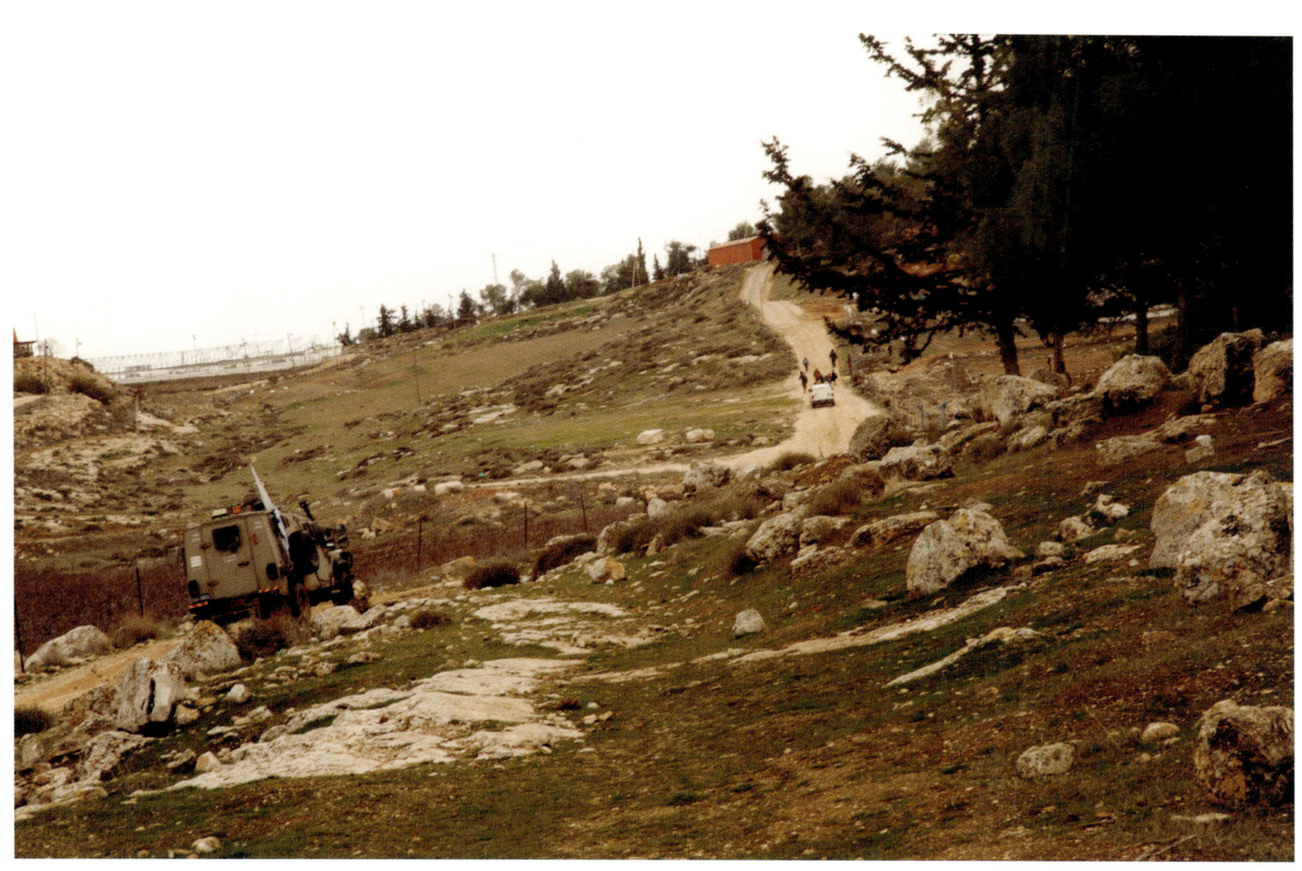

12.2 Twaneh, February 2022.

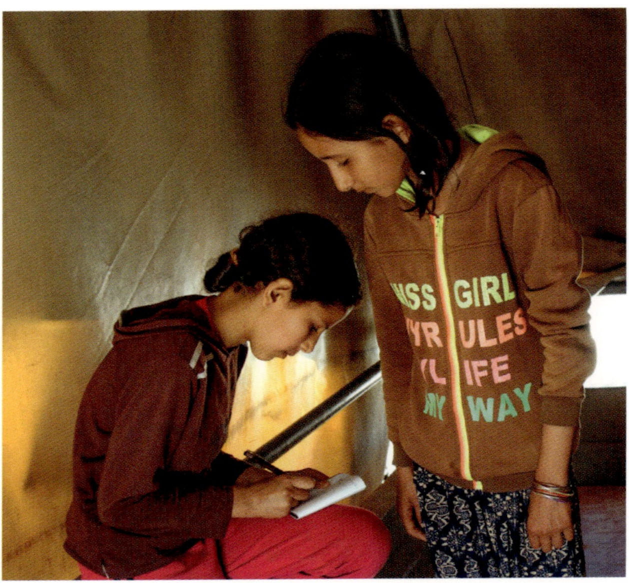

Tell me something. You talk about love: Of the land, of the place. Tell me something about love.

I grew up on the hills, we took water from our wells—not like in the city where you turn a faucet and water comes out.

We used to go out on these hills, we would take a ball and play. That was what we had, also pebbles to play hopscotch, there were no smart phones or anything like that. In the winter, we made channels for the water, for after the rains. We would plow the land, following the donkey. It's hard work, but we wanted to show that we were big. We did it out of love. See how much the land gives us, 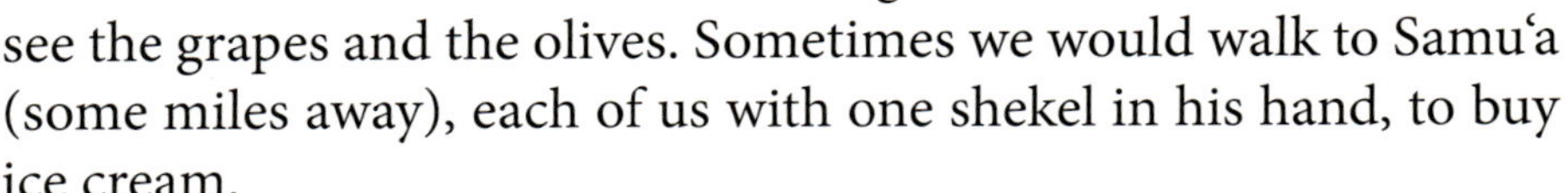 see the grapes and the olives. Sometimes we would walk to Samu'a (some miles away), each of us with one shekel in his hand, to buy ice cream.

12.3 Susiya, June 2015.

Nasser, I know you for many years, and quite often, despite everything, you look to me like a happy man. You smile when you are with the children, and also when you are in action.

You see the smile but you can't see what is inside. There is a lot of pain inside. I find it hard to speak about myself, but—there is a war inside between the good things and the bad things. Sometimes I think, Why do I need all this, I could maybe work in Israel, get away. If you think about the children, the future doesn't look good. The most important thing is the connection between Israelis and Palestinians here. It is the joint action with Israelis that has kept many communities alive.

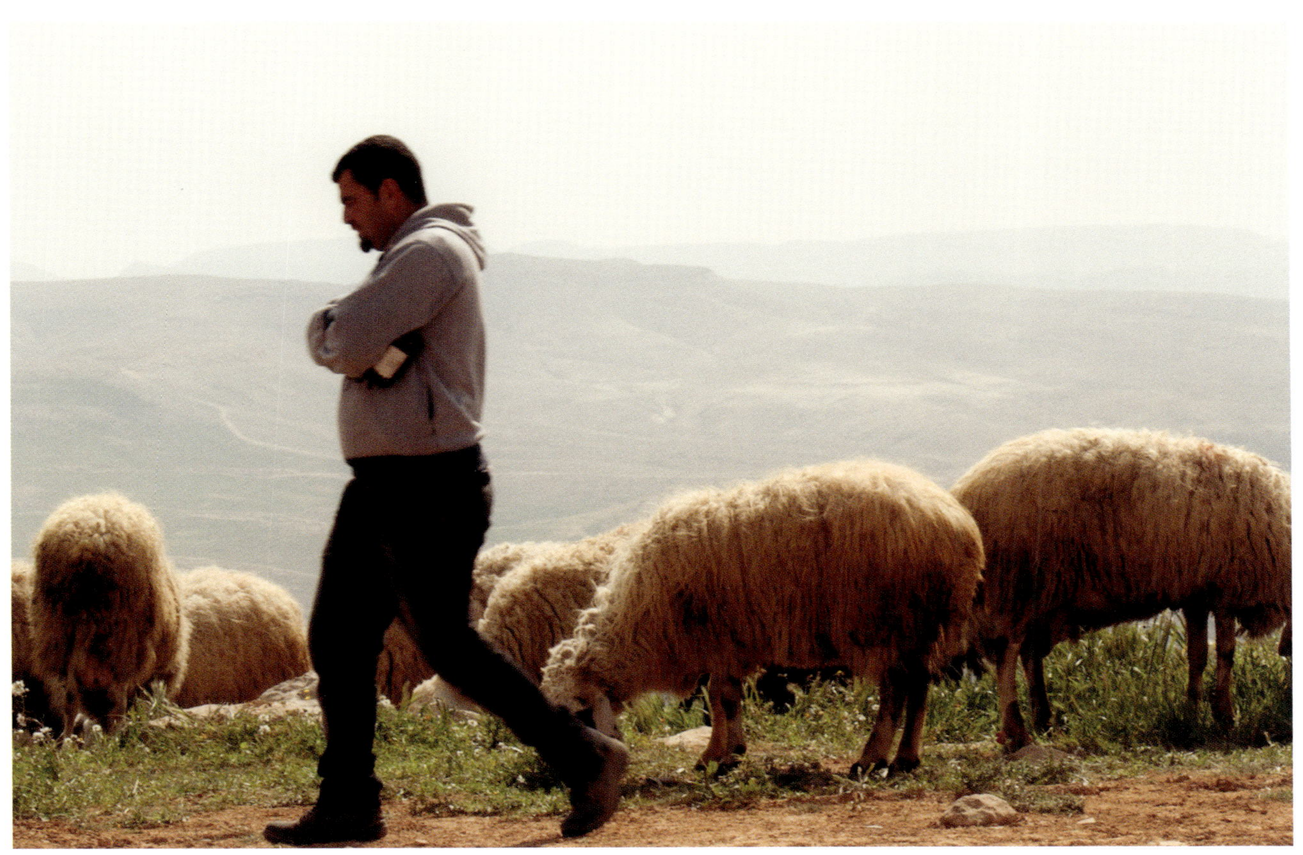

12.4 Path from Umm al-Ara'is
to Susiya, March 2015.

Opposing the Occupation is my life. When I sit in my tent on my land and don't leave, I am fighting the Occupation. It's not easy. There are people in the cities, in Ramallah, who are against what they call "normalization," *tatbi'*, which means working with Israelis. But our situation is better than in the north, where the settlers do whatever they want. Here, because of our joint action, if you oppose the Occupation and oppose terror, you can succeed.

Our whole project is non-violent, we oppose violence; we want to live like human beings on our own land.

Is there something else you want to tell us for our book?

One meeting is not enough for a book. A book is something really important for communicating the story of Susiya. Susiya is not just a bunch of tents on a hill. It's our land that we're living on. It's not that the land belongs to us; (it's that) we belong to the land. We eat her wheat, her vegetables, her fruits.

12.5 a and b Susiya, January 2017.

12.6 Susiya, February 2022.

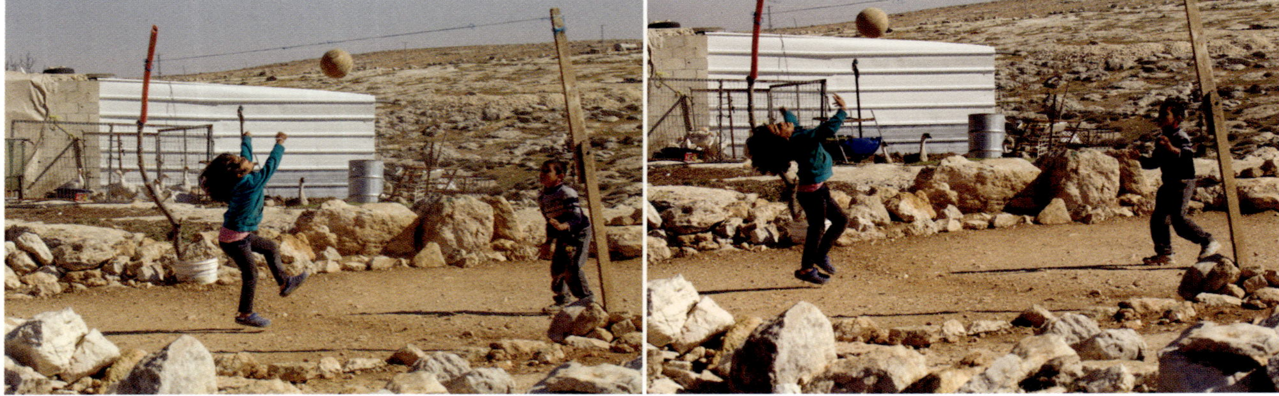

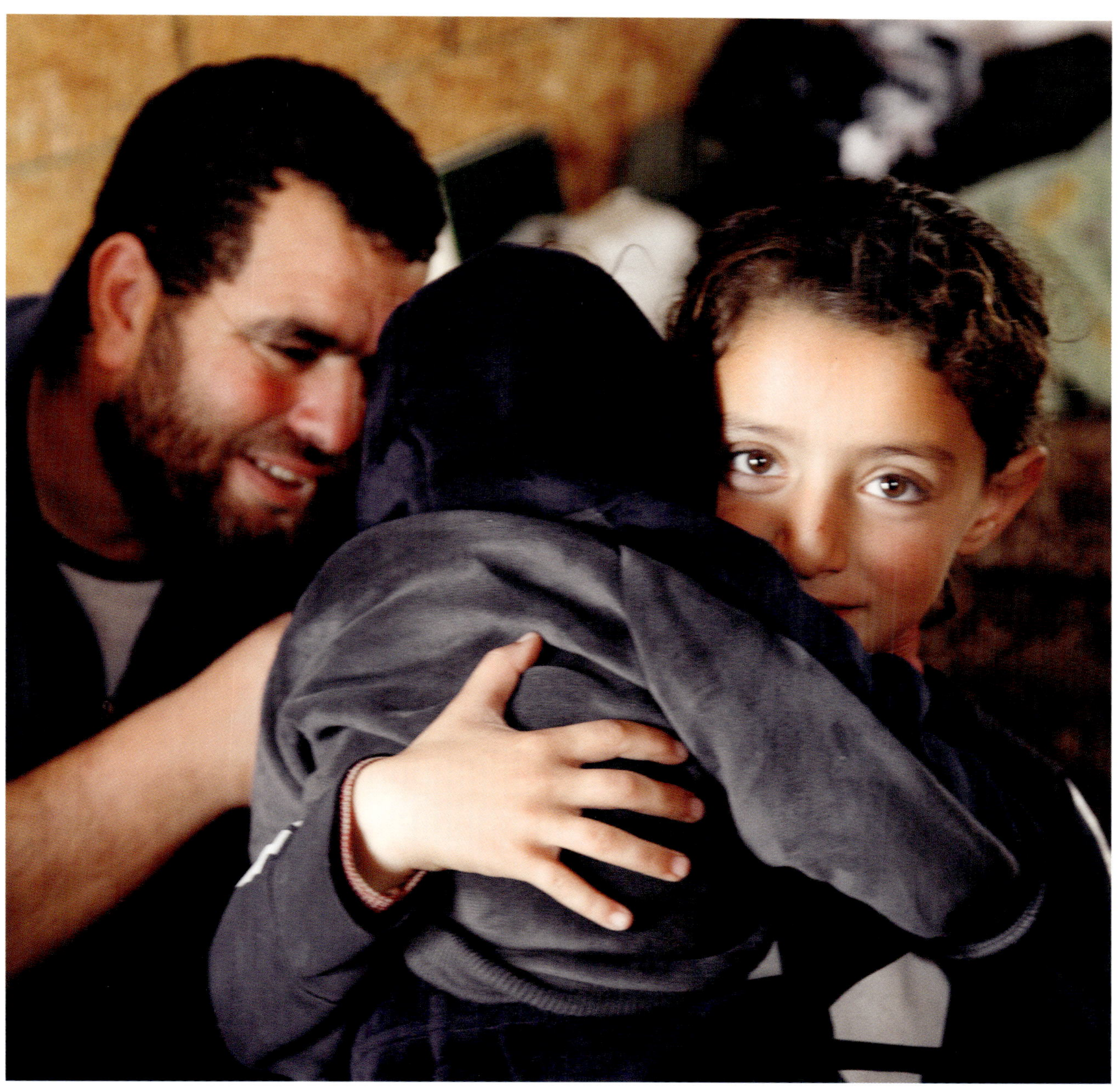

Fatma Nawaja', January, 2022

People around here, in Sha'ab al-Butum and Tuba and Umm al-Khair, say, "Listen to Fatma and do what she says, you'll be strong, *qawiyye*."

We are working with the women. We have a store where we sell wool, crafts items, labaneh, yoghurt, kuskus, maftul. Officially we are "The Rural Women's Organization." We have eighty members from all over South Hebron; some from Yatta.

We run summer camps, work days, and we are particularly committed to education. Every village has its teacher. We had 200 girls in the schools last year, grades 1–3. We also teach them about gender and sex education. We work with psychological counseling. In the corona times, we had meetings on zoom. We provide computers and iPads to the villages.

Our inspiration comes from the rocks, *btiji min al-hajar*.

The women are happy, but only half of the husbands like this. Change is always hard.

What is your biggest problem?

1. The Occupation.
2. The tradition and its rules.
3. Fear of fate, of what fate has in store. Where can we go?
4. The Occupation. The Occupation takes our land; embitters our life.

12.7 Al-Khan al-Ahmar, December 2018.

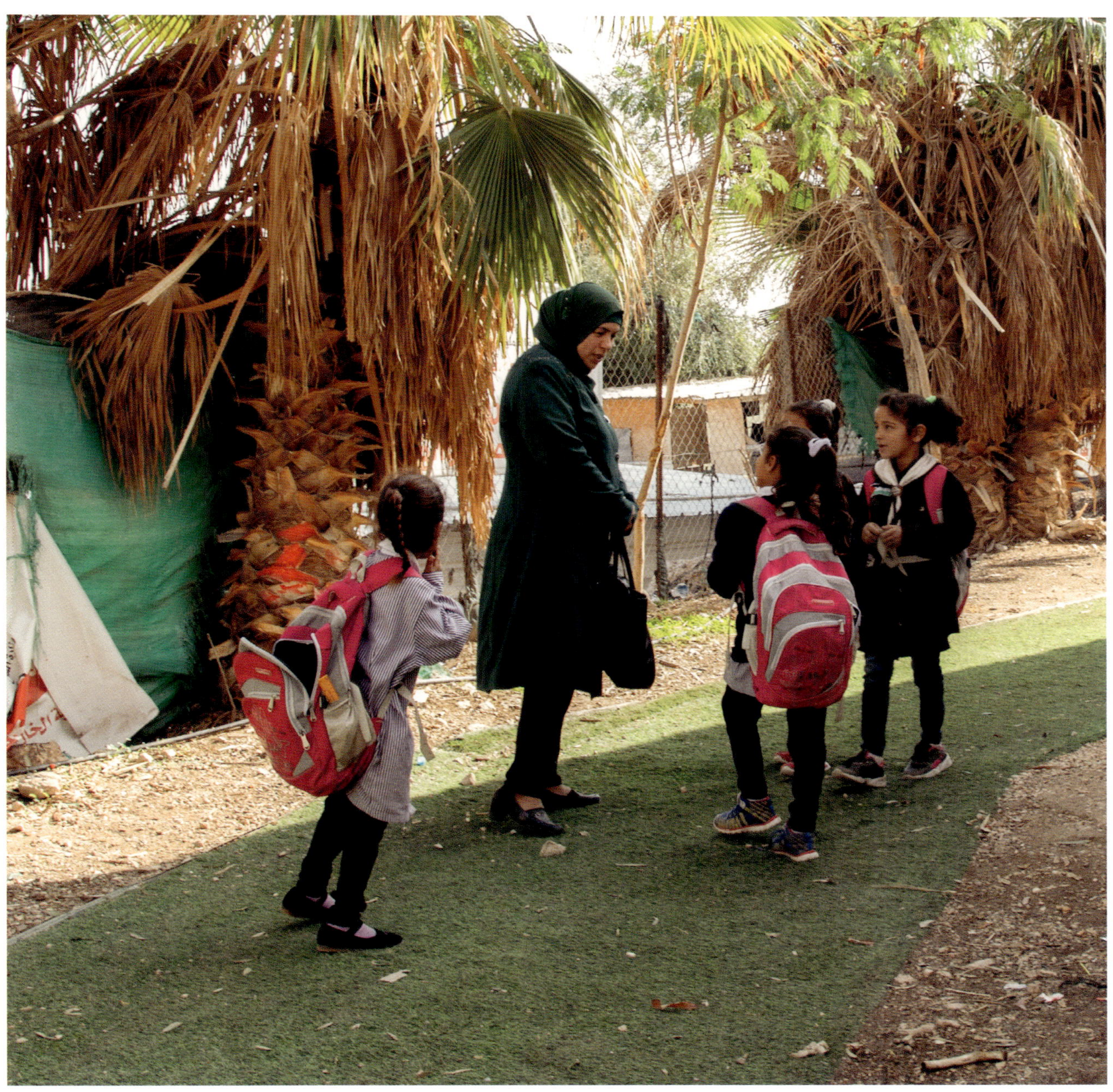

Sa'id 'Awad, February, 2022

I know every rock on my parents' lands. In 1998, the settlers first invaded. Every time, the suffering is great. We are farmers. For us, land is honor. We own wells in Gawawis. My grandfather had land in Tuba and many other places. We used to sow and harvest; there were celebrations at harvest time; people came from all over. The land gave us watermelons, huge olives, and so much more. Then in 1998, a settler turned up with a caravan.

What angers me is the uselessness and indifference of the Palestinian Authority. They give speeches, but they don't really care. They do nothing.

I am against violence of any kind.

I won't despair and I won't give up.

Note: On March 10, 2021, Israeli settlers attacked Sa'id and his family. They cracked his skull and broke his jaw while his wife and children tried to hide in their vehicle, which the settlers then smashed with rocks.

Guy Hirshfeld, April, 2018

Most people here who know me see me as extreme left wing. I believe in a two-state solution. Some people in Ta'ayush see me as right wing, because they believe in one state. But I have been in favor of a two-state solution since I was a kid. Once I was with the majority of the Israeli people.

I had a dream—to work in the Jordan Valley. The Jordan Valley was beneath the radar of everybody, except the army and the civil

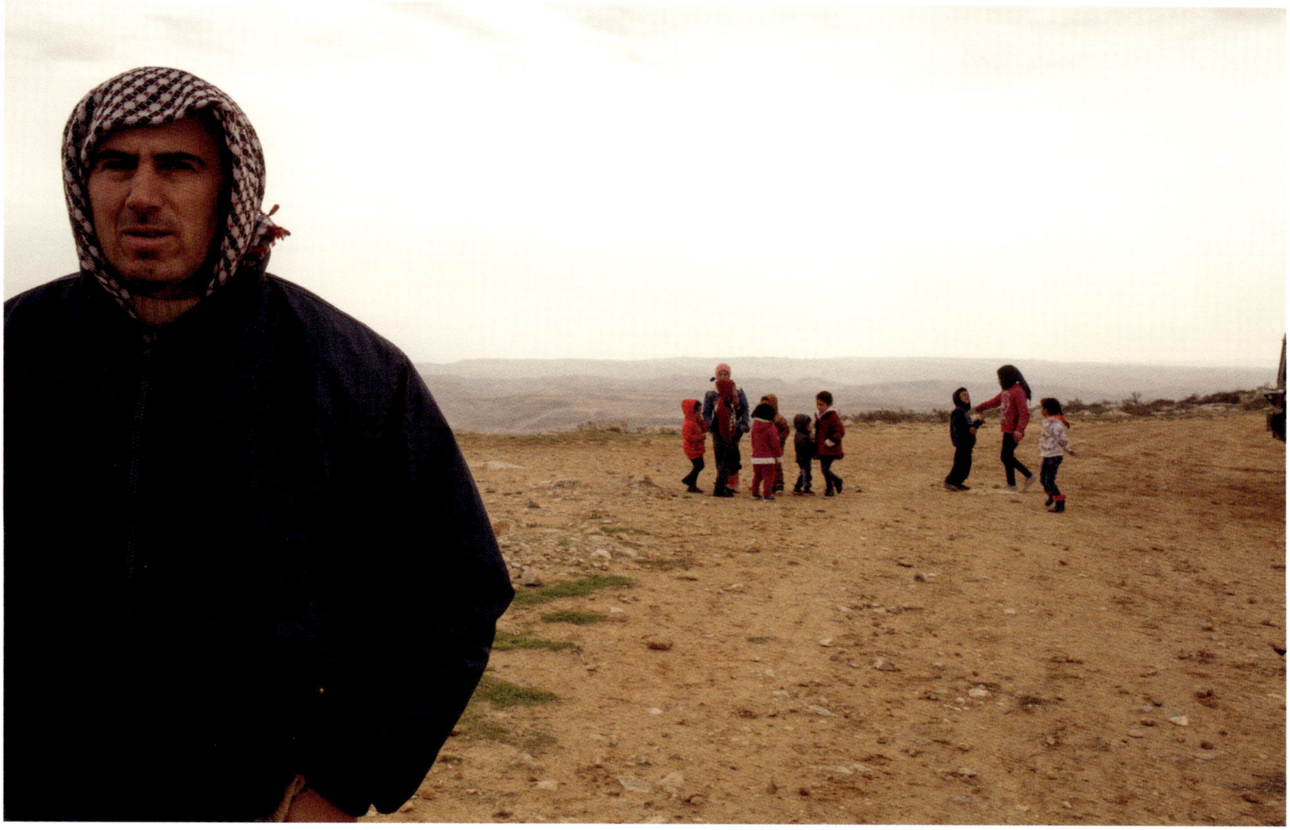

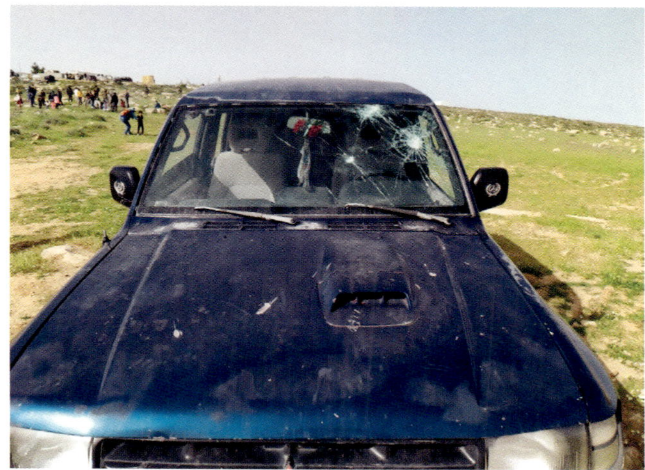

12.8 Umm al-Ara'is, January 2017.

12.9 Umm al-Ara'is, March 2021.
Photograph: Yigal Bronner.

administration. People said we don't have time and we don't have the activists. But getting the people—I knew we could do it. At the beginning, we'd just drink coffee, sit, listen to them. If they needed something, we tried to help. But not a lot. But then, after a few weeks or months, the settlers set up an outpost near Al-Hamma. So the Palestinians called us, and we started to work with them. Pretty soon the army demolished al-Hamma completely. We had to rebuild. The army demolished it again. And we rebuilt. After that, it was kind of quiet for a while. But there are problems everywhere.

12.10 Hamra, Northern Jordan Valley, May 2018.

The soldiers can come and show you a piece of paper that says you Palestinians have to leave, and sometimes there is no piece of paper, they tell you, "Get out, we have to train here." One of the bad things in the Jordan Valley is that nobody outside knows what's going on there. We are bringing it out into the open. And the way I speak to the soldiers and the commanders, they don't like it. If they see a soldier speaking with me or getting interested, I won't see him there the next time. They take him out. They don't want them to hear me.

I'm sensitive, in every encounter with the police I start to tremble, physically. You learn to live with this. I had a heart attack after they arrested me at Zanuta, in the summer, at the hottest time of day; they kept me for a long time in the command car. I came back to life after I resumed my activism.

Normally I'm a little depressive, but I know that we will see peace come. It could happen very quickly. And there's the fact that we're doing the right thing. I tell my daughters that one day they'll understand how important it was that there were people like us.

I always knew more or less what the Occupation meant, I knew the situation, but it all becomes crystal clear when you see it in the field.

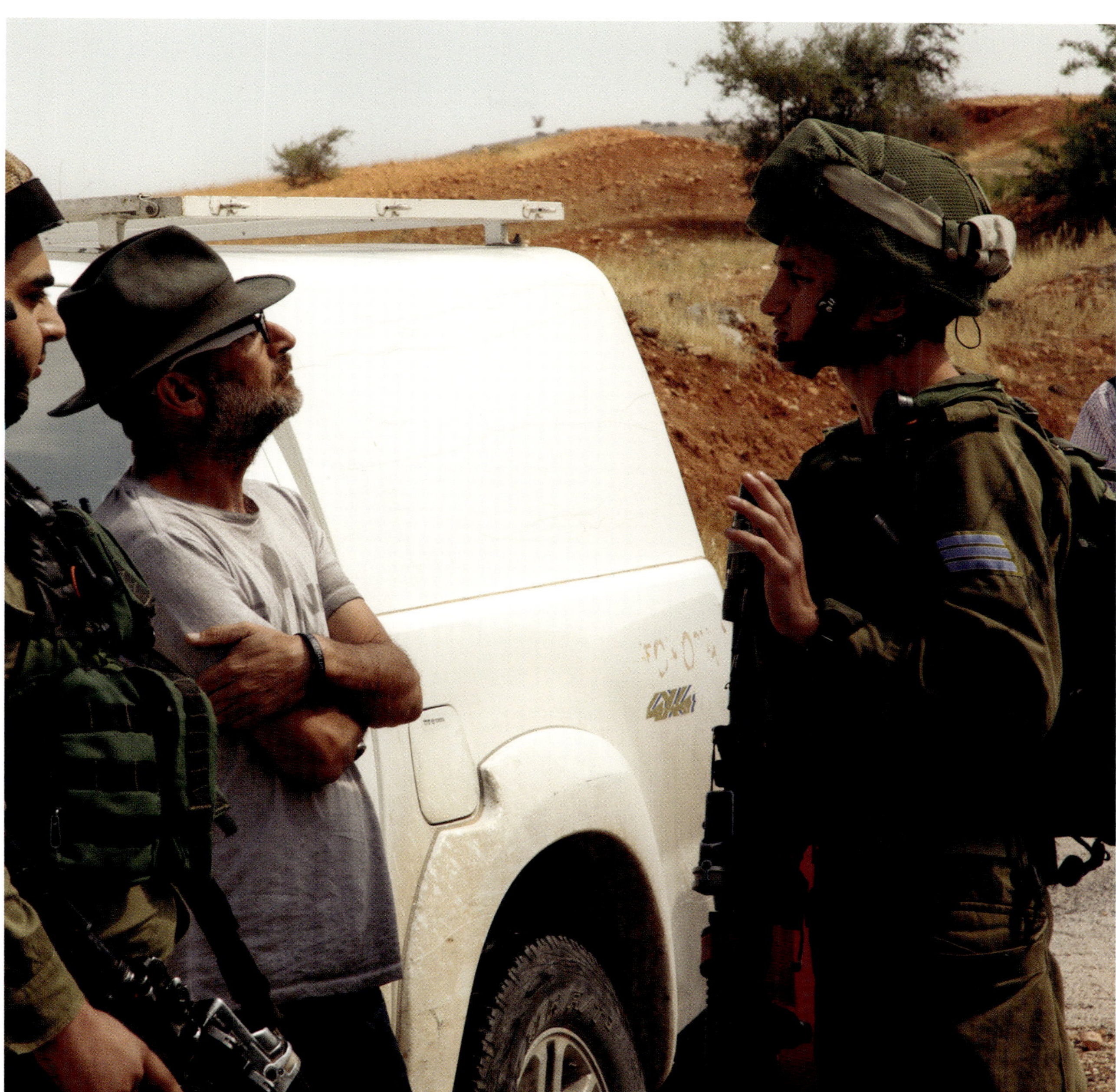

Kifah Adaraa, January, 2022

We had to build the school ourselves, with the army threatening us at every step.

We did it together. The men worked at night while the women stood guard on the hills to warn against soldiers arriving. The women worked during the day. The Civil Administration knew, of course, and soon there were demolition orders on the building, but Ta'ayush brought us lawyers, and eventually the court ruled that the school could not expand beyond three rooms, and that for ten years the army couldn't destroy it. Those were the years when I first encountered Ta'ayush, when I first met Jews. It was a big surprise. I learned that they were here to help us. I didn't know, before that, that it was possible to resist the occupation. Ezra [Nawi] encouraged us and taught us.

Still, when the three-room schoolhouse was ready, we had to face the soldiers who came to destroy it. And the same thing when we put up poles and wires so we would have electricity. Again, we worked night and day, and then the soldiers came and wanted to confiscate the poles and the wires and threatened to arrest the first person who tried to block their way. But we stood there in the road together, the women and children in front. We shouted to them, "You want to hit us because we want electricity!" The soldiers managed to steal two of the poles, the closest to the road, but we kept them from coming into the village to take the rest. Then something interesting happened. A woman soldier refused to hurt us. She went back and sat in the jeep, alone. She understood.

Eventually the court at Bet-El made the army bring back the two stolen poles, and on the first night of Ramadan, that year, 2009, we ate the Iftar meal in the light. A celebration.

And today the school has seven rooms.

We will continue our lives. There is no power in weapons. Power lies in the heart. *Mish al-quwwa bi'l silah. Al-quwwa bi'l-qalb.*

12.11 Twaneh, January 2022.

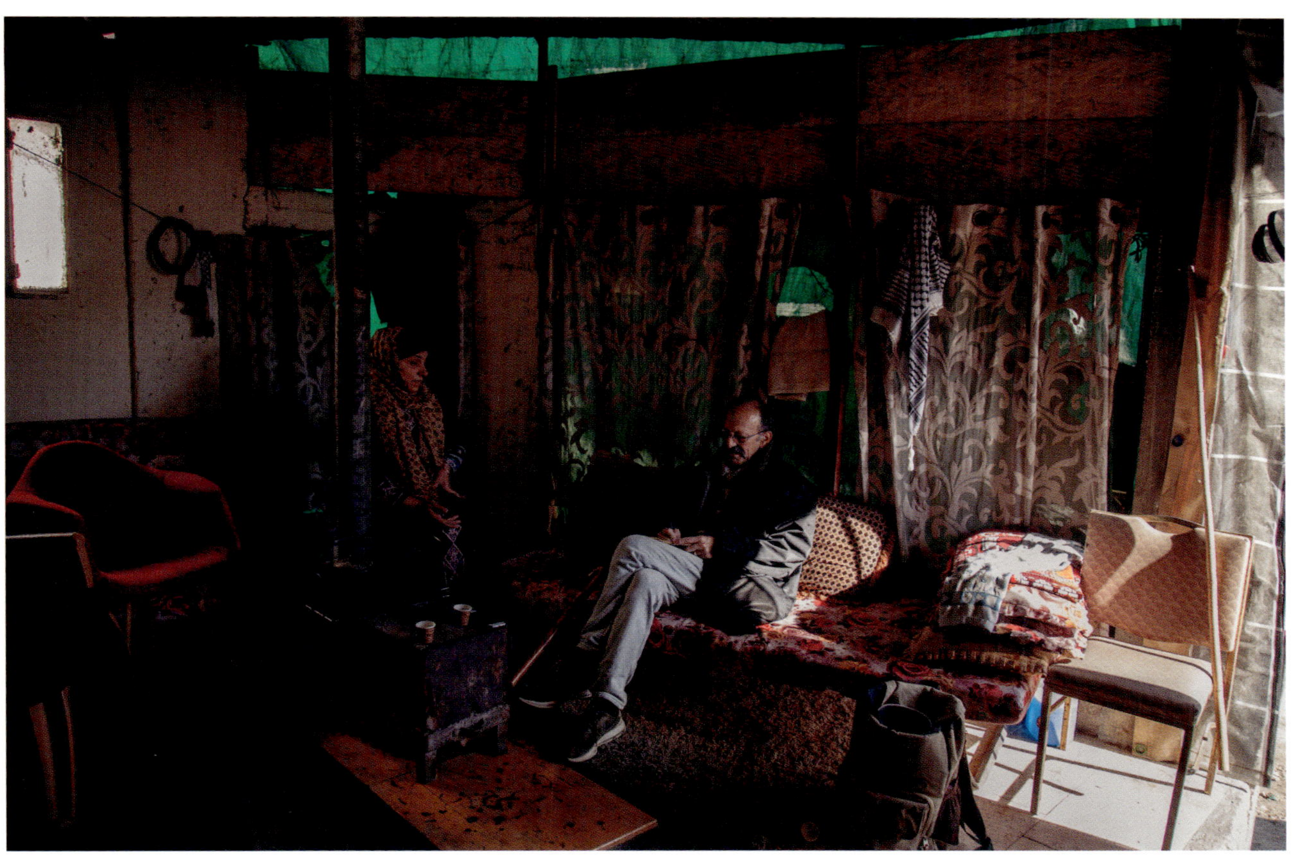

'Ali 'Awad, Tuba, January, 2022

I studied all twelve grades in the Twaneh school. I went there with the military escort from Tuba.

I'm a storyteller and a writer. I try to take my anger out by writing.

My family has land in Umm al-Khair as well as in Tuba. My grandfather was 'Ali Rashid Ibrahim; his grandfather was 'Ali 'Awad. He was living behind the hill of Tuba. In the nineteenth century, they lived in caves. 'Ali 'Awad founded the village.

Before Tuba—we are not sure of the family history. Some say we come from Jews in Saudi Arabia. We are shepherds; we cultivate a little barley, too.

Of course, I live with fear, permanent fear. *Hayat khauf da'iman.*

On June 1, 2021, the settlers came and burnt forty-one haystacks with fodder we had bought. We moved the other thirty-nine with our hands to cars, away from the settlers.

You have to stand up to it—to those who demolish my home or throw stones at me—no matter what happens. I can handle something that happens to me, but not to someone close to me. I have to think a thousand times before I have children. I have all the children of Masafer Yatta as my children.

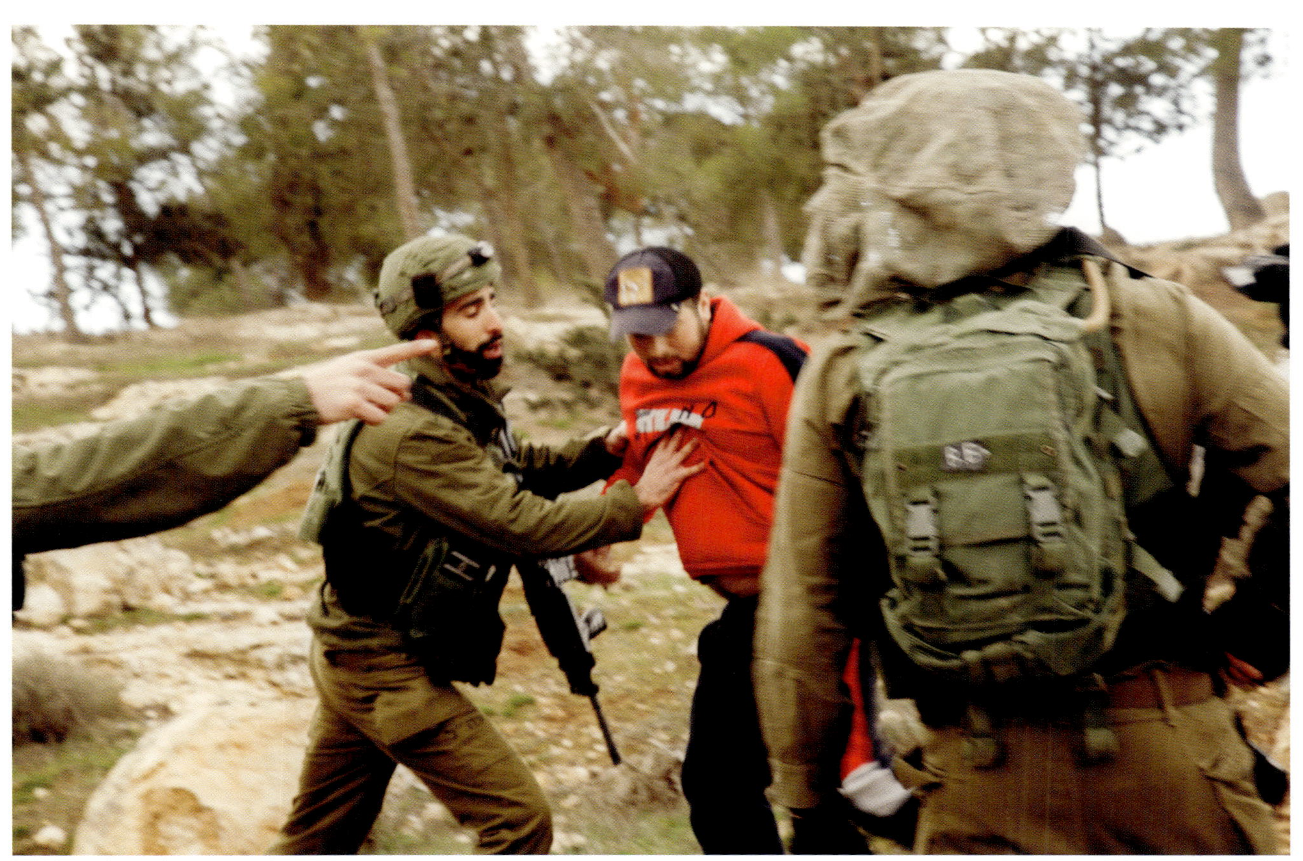

12.12 Twaneh, January 2022.

Guy Butavia, February, 2022

I remember seeing a military truck packed with handcuffed Palestinians. I was seven or eight years old. I asked my father. He was a Holocaust survivor, a partisan. He told me they were arrested. It was shocking for me. I understood that they were treated as if they were not regular human beings. Something is wrong here.

My father used to work with Palestinians, I knew them; we would go to Bethlehem and the Old City almost every day. Palestinians were human beings to me. I was alone with those feelings. I had a lot of fights with my father—he was very angry at me. I thought I was unloved. The family was very right wing. Many of my family were settlers in Kiryat Arba and other places. In fourth grade, they taught us that it's good to die for your country, but I told myself, No it's not. I also told myself, "Shut up."

As a child, my dream was to be a soldier. I was impressed by heavy machinery—trucks, tanks. Lego stuff. One of the worst days in my childhood was when they announced the peace with Egypt. I went to mother and asked, crying, "Does this mean I can't be a soldier?" Soon after that everything changed, and I understood.

I was arrested in 2016, after the TV show that framed Ezra. The rightist organization Ad Kan had planted a mole in Taʿayush. A few days after the screening, Ezra was arrested at the airport. It took them a week after that to arrest me. Nasir was arrested a few hours later.

At 4:30 in the afternoon, I heard knocking on the door. A civilian with a big gun. I called Amiel and told him to stay on the phone. There were three of them. It was very frightening.

On the way in the car, they talked about Ezra, cursing him. I knew I was in their hands, and I was very afraid. They accused us of killing a man, and of contact with a foreign agent. Ad Kan had

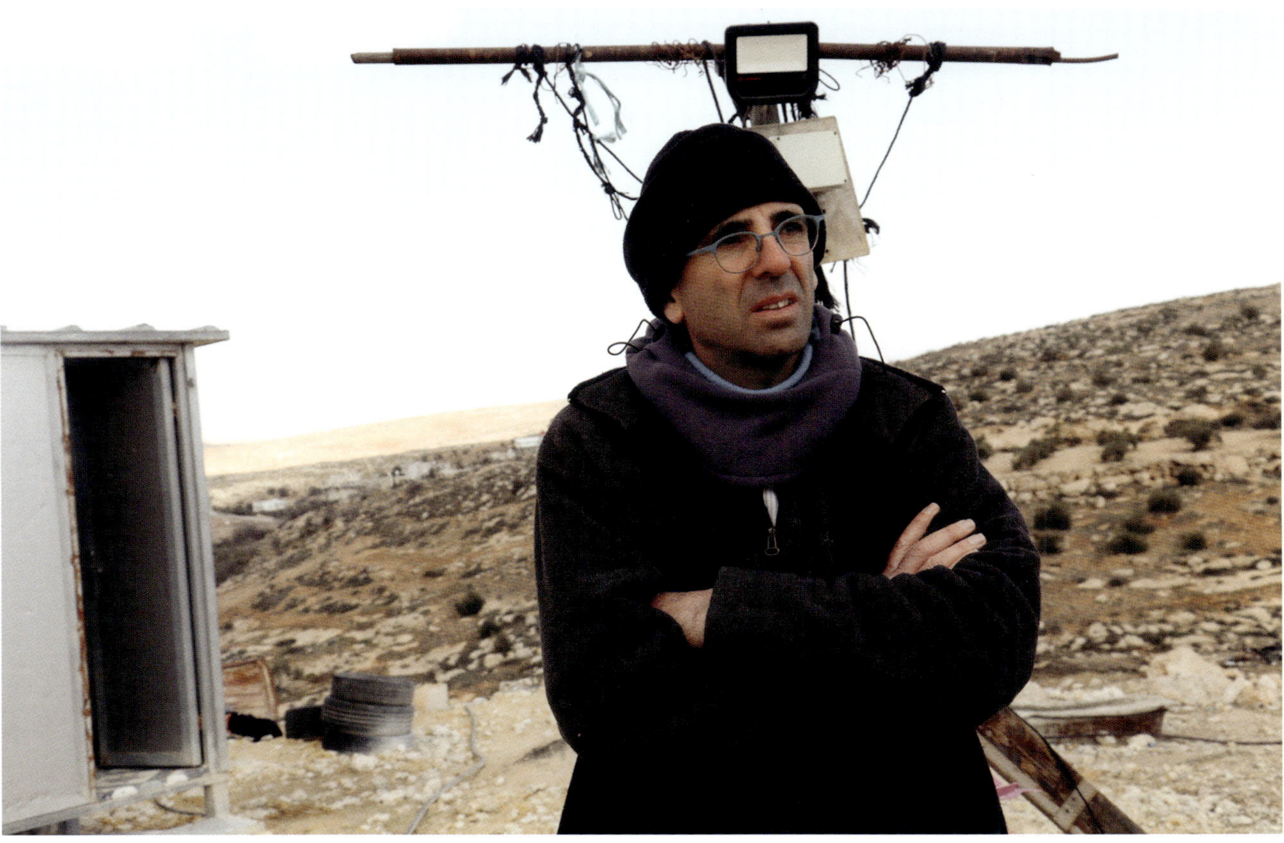

12.13
Ar-Rakiz,
January 2022.

files about many of the activists, including details of their personal lives. It was like fighting against enormous power. They were capable of controlling the police.

One of the interrogators, Yossi, was polite. The others were doing it with all their heart, pathologically. They are real monsters who think they have a mission to save their country. They were happy to take revenge. To do damage, to destroy us, break us.

It's been six years. It comes back almost every day. Images in my mind; nightmares. It can come out of nowhere. You see something, and it sets off a flashback.

My work is part of me. Sometimes there are only a few phone calls a day, sometimes it can be thirty calls. To try to get help, to get lawyers, to call the police, the army, the District Coordination

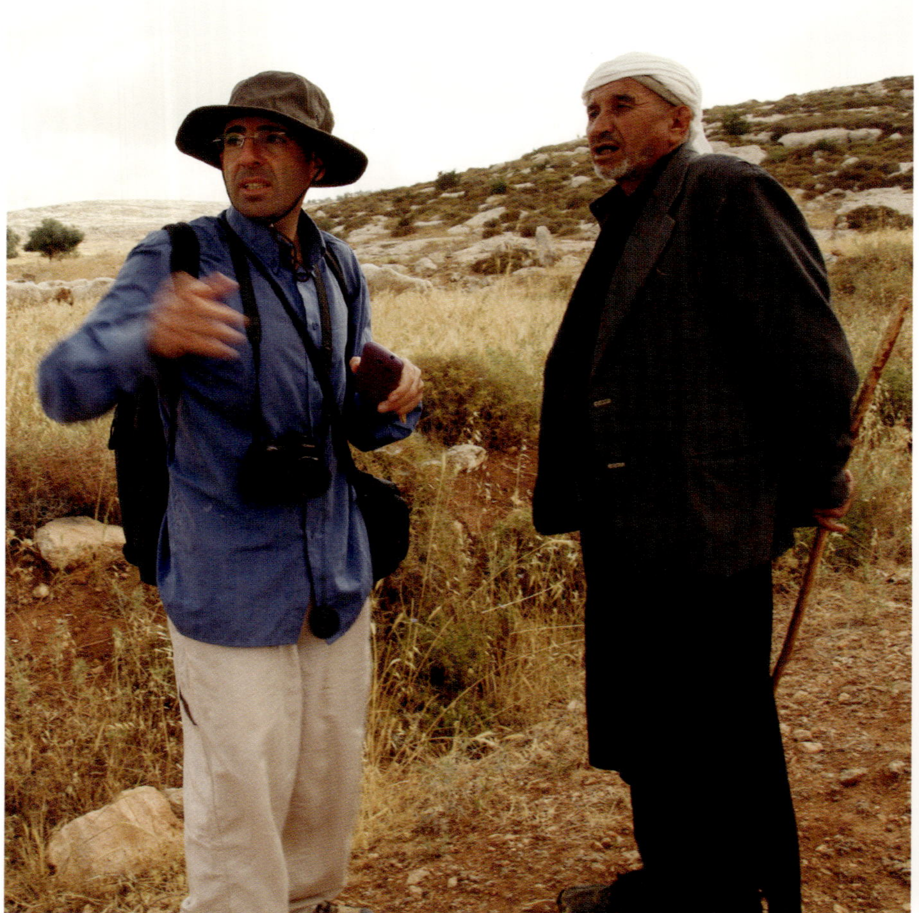

12.14 Umm al-Ammad, June 2014.

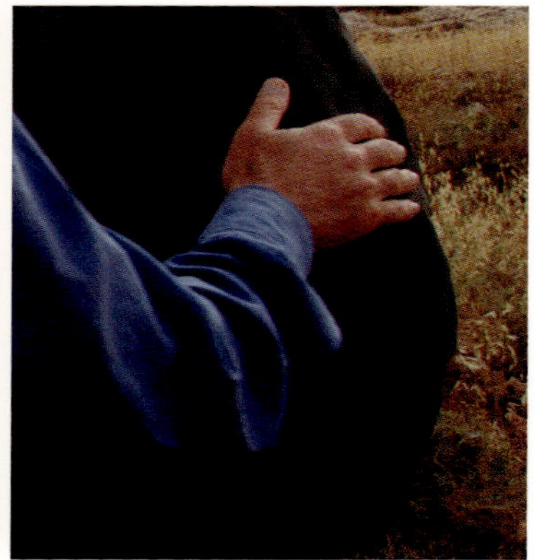

12.15 Umm al-Ammad, June 2014.

Office, to try anything. And many times it's not enough. You feel helpless. You feel responsible for what is going on. A shepherd is arrested, or attacked. . . . Sometimes I ask myself if I should stay here, if I can be useful.

And also there's the feeling that it's becoming more and more dangerous. Those knocks on the door: one is always waiting for that. And also you know that you're being followed.

Sometimes you choose your life, and sometimes life chooses you.

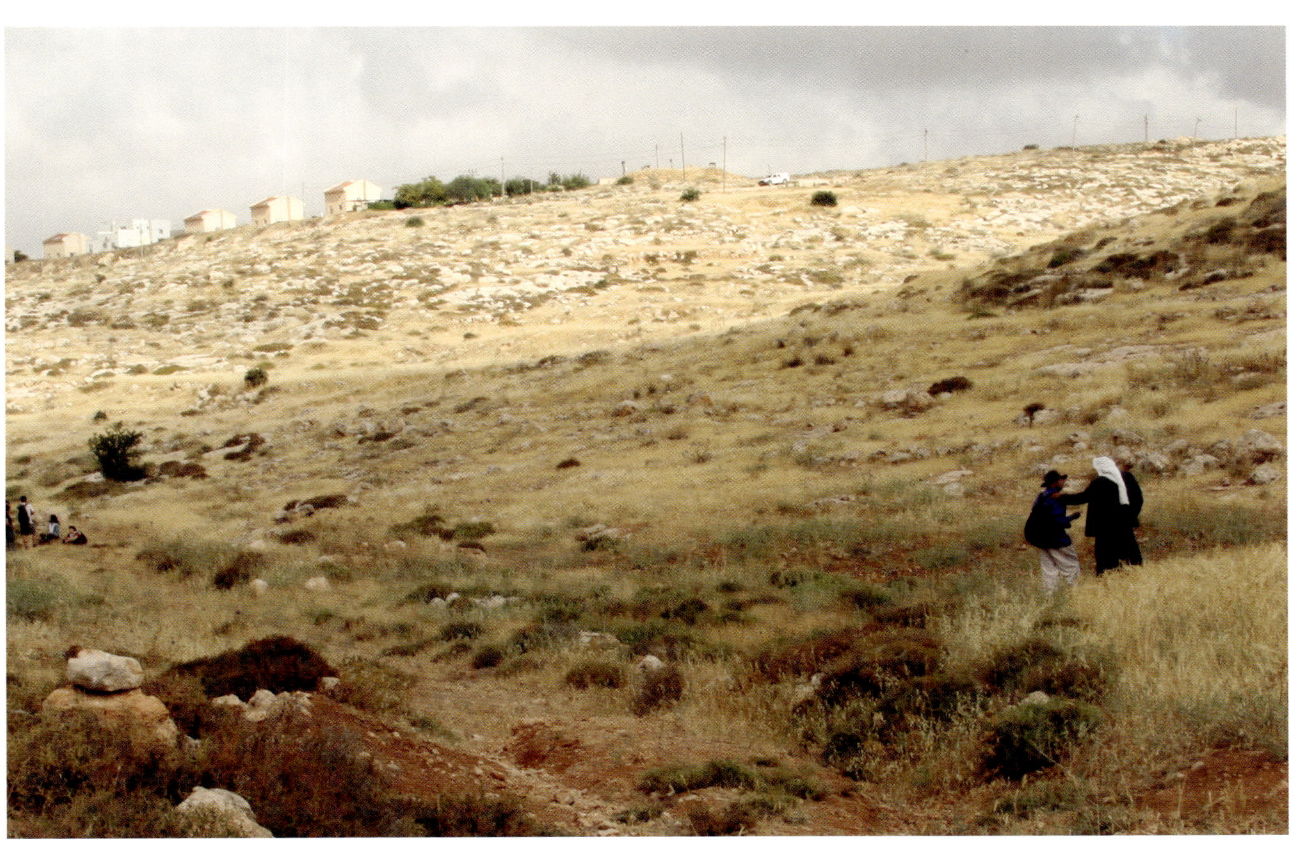

12.16 Umm al-Ammad, June 2014.

Basil Adaraa, February, 2022

Everything is activism. Coordinating, talking to people, workdays, demonstrations. For me, it comes with the DNA. If something happens and I'm not there, it's not good.

I remember being with my parents, with my mother Kifah, while they were building the school here. The army would come and try to stop them. The women quickly took the tools and ran to hide them in the olive trees. When that didn't seem to be enough, they sat down on top of them.

We had no electricity except for a generator for a few hours every day. We waited three or four years to get permission from the Civil Administration to build a tower for electric power. Then the army came, one late afternoon, to confiscate the tower. We put stones in front of the jeeps and trucks, then faced them—first children, in front; then women, including my mother. This inspired me.

We are six siblings. I am the second.

The recent attacks, like in Mufagara, are really scary. At Harat al-Dab', there was live fire; two people wounded. On Ramadan, they attacked our neighbor's house. I was close to the settlers, who were firing live bullets. They want to make us afraid because they can reach any place with their guns and slingshots and clubs. They come inside our houses with army and police alongside them.

We have to document and do what we can to stop it.

It's become more dangerous.

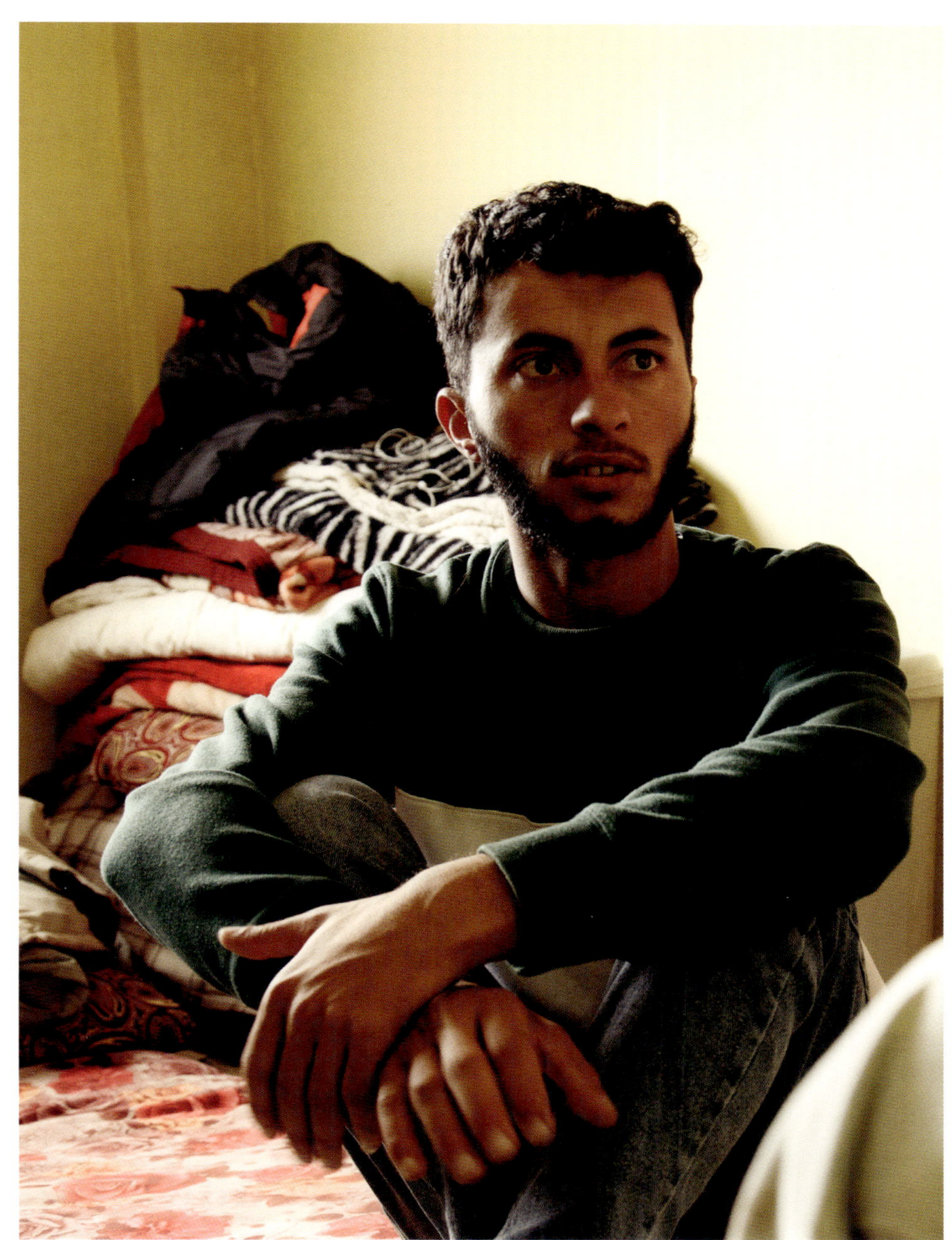

12.17 Twaneh,
February
2022.

'Azzam Yusuf Nawaja',February, 2022

I was imprisoned at the age of thirteen, for three months, in isolation. I was working in Ramleh, in the fields. On my way home on the bus, we ran into a roadblock of the Border Police. They came into the bus, checked things out, and said to me, "Get down." No reason. They took me to the Moskubiyya, the police compound in Jerusalem. I saw what I saw. I can't tell you. Don't ask.

They threw me naked into the zinzana, the police van, and then they put two dogs in with me, to scare me.

In the cell where I was supposed to sleep, there was no mattress, no bed, just the floor. Two buckets, next to one another—one to piss in, the other to drink from. Sometimes they would handcuff my hands behind me to the back of a chair, bending my body downward, for the entire night.

In 1986, they decided to clear out Old Susiya (*susiya al-qadima*), where we lived. They loaded us onto trucks in the middle of the night and drove us far north, past Zif. They destroyed our wells, our tents. It took years for us to return to Susiya. We had to start all over, dig wells; they wouldn't let us build anything. Mamnu'—it's forbidden. No electricity, no telephones. They wouldn't even let us drink water. They don't want us to breathe the air.

Once I was in Jerusalem and it snowed, and I saw Palestinian and Israeli police clearing the roads together. It warmed my heart.

If we don't help one another, why are we alive?

I write poems in the Bedouin dialect that I love. I may collect them into a diwan. I admire the words of Luqman al-Hakim, who is mentioned in the Qur'an. He said to keep Allah in your mind, and to speak truth. Sometimes my sons find the pages I scribble on, and they say, "More of Baba's silliness."

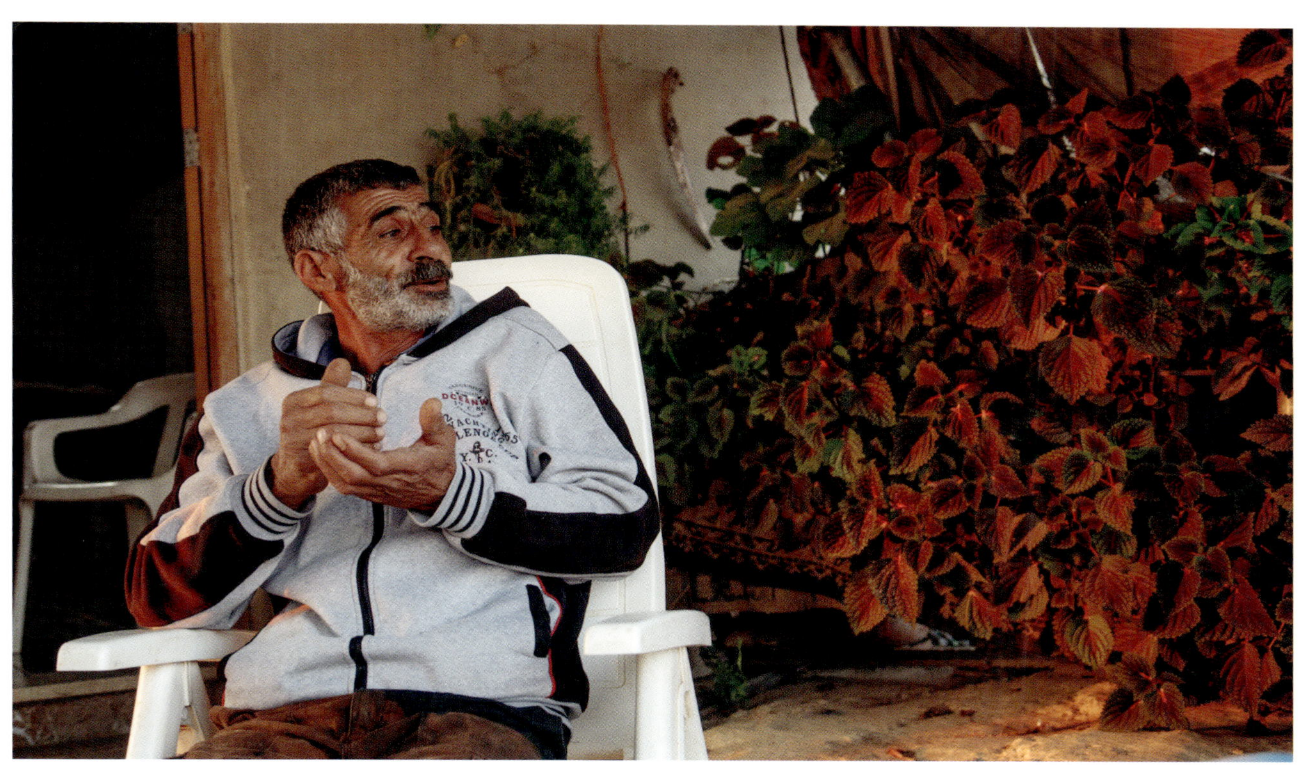

12.18 Susiya, November 2022.

I wrote a poem about a sheep. It's a true story. My mother once adopted an orphaned sheep with black eyes and brought her up. If the sheep were sick, Mother would pray to Allah to heal her. She loved that sheep. But one day when Mother went out to the sheepfold to feed her, the sheep knocked her over, from behind.

12.19 Susiya, February 2022.

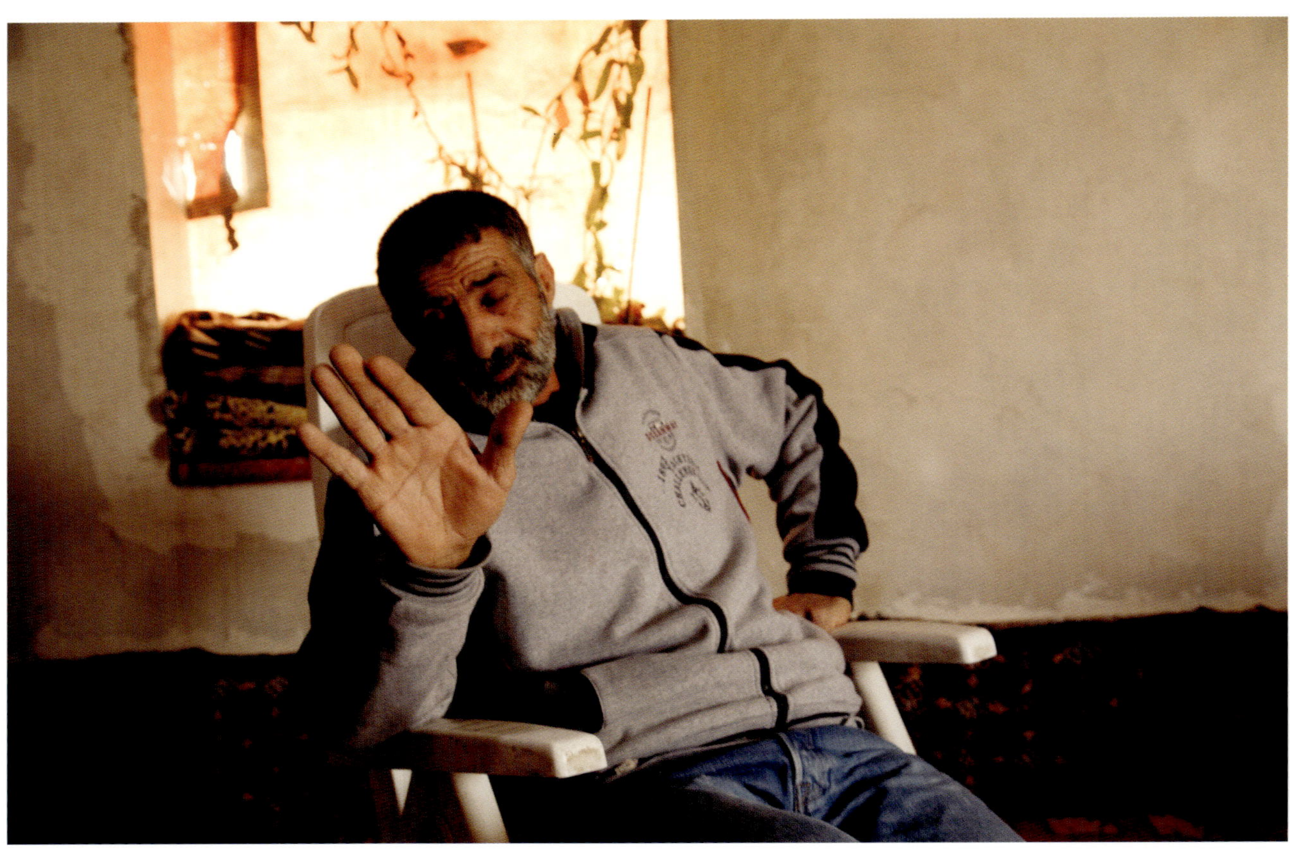

She hit her head and lost consciousness. She couldn't stand up. For fifteen days, she was in bed, screaming in pain. One day she said to me, "'Azzam, let's slaughter the sheep." I said, "How can we do that? You adopted her and cared for her." "Yes," Mother said, "but there is no forgiveness for traitors."

12.20 Susiya, February 2022.

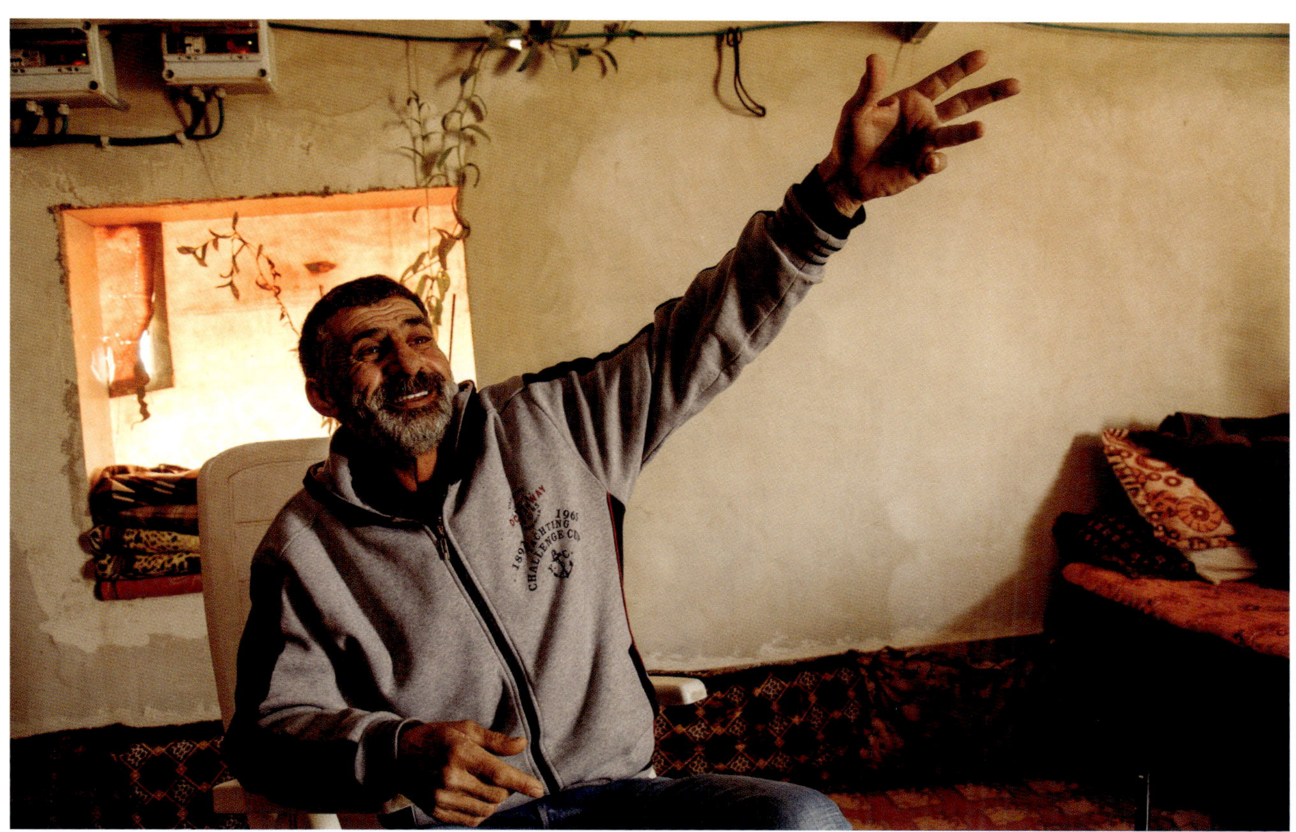

Michal Peleg, February, 2022

I was in Sheikh Jarrah when the first family was evicted. I couldn't bear the blatant injustice. How could I stand aside? I began to come regularly to Sheikh Jarrah. When Saleh went to jail we were there with him.

I met Ada and the others. From the first moment I heard about Taʿayush, I felt that this was the right thing. A real struggle that means not giving in to the settlers and the army. At first, I was very afraid, but then it became routine; you learn to face violence.

I remember especially one morning at Umm al-Ara'is, late autumn. It was SO cold. Na'il made a fire; we were standing there, with all the smoke in our faces, and Saʿid arrived and made tea and it was like a miracle—the special taste of tea that you can never get to at home because it's the smoke of the fire that gets into it and makes it exquisite.

So many times I was told by friends, even by soldiers and settlers: "You don't achieve anything, so why are you doing this? What's the point?" It makes me angry. It's part of this efficiency thinking. You are supposed to achieve something. I reject that way of thinking. It's important to resist what you think is evil. Of course I want to make a change, but it takes years, maybe centuries.

As long as there is someone saying no, there is hope.

12.21 Umm al-Ara'is, March 2015.

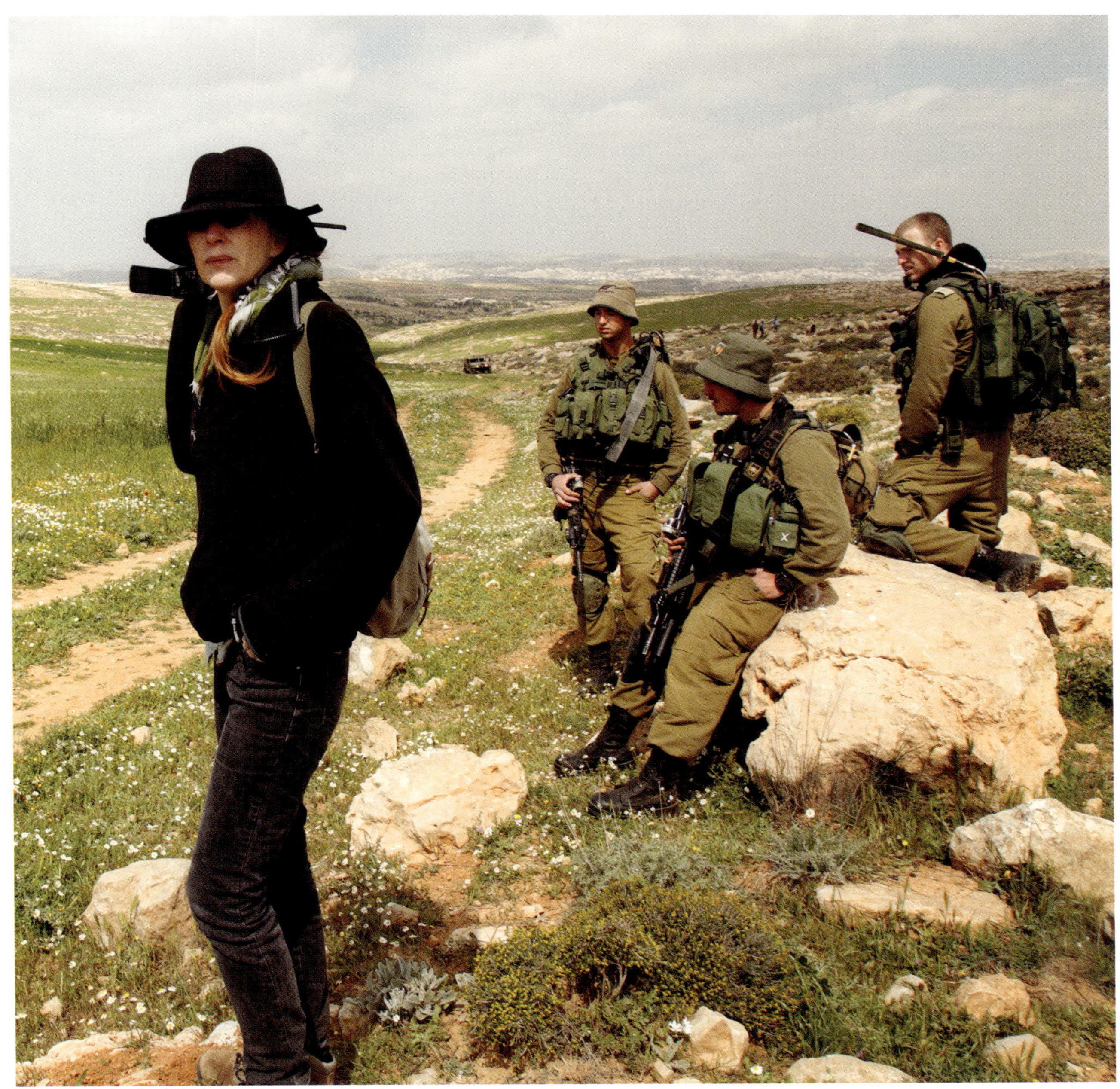

إِنَّمَا أَهْلُكِ جِيرَانٌ لَنَا　　　إِنَّمَا نَحْنُ وَهُمْ شَيْءٌ أَحَدْ

We are neighbors, your people and mine,
but in truth, we are one.

'Umar ibn Abi Rabi'ah, 7th century

13.
Friendship

13.1 Umm al-Ara'is, July 2017.

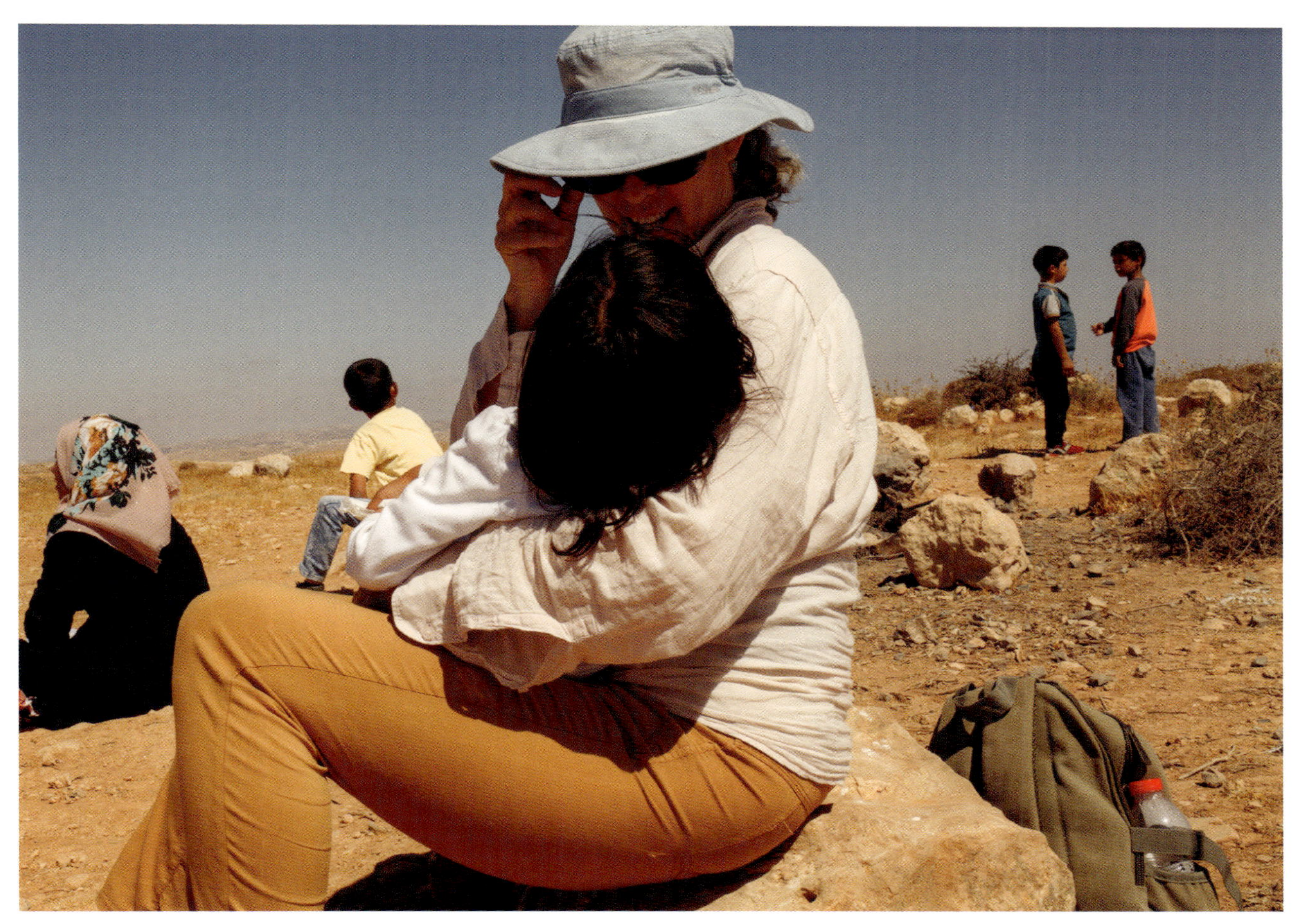

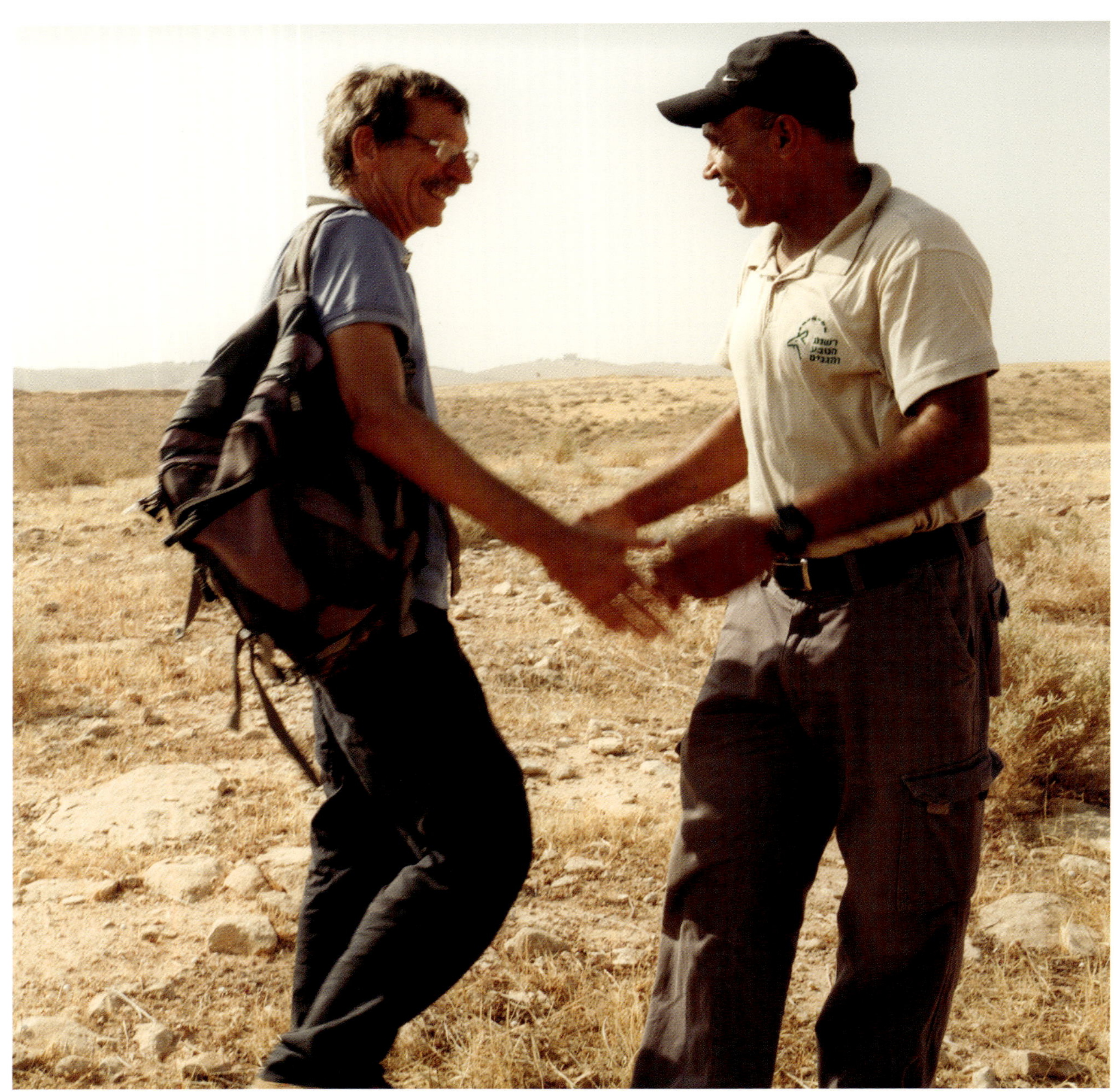
רשות
הטבע
והגנים

13.2 ‘Auja, July 2017.
13.3 Susiya, May 2018.

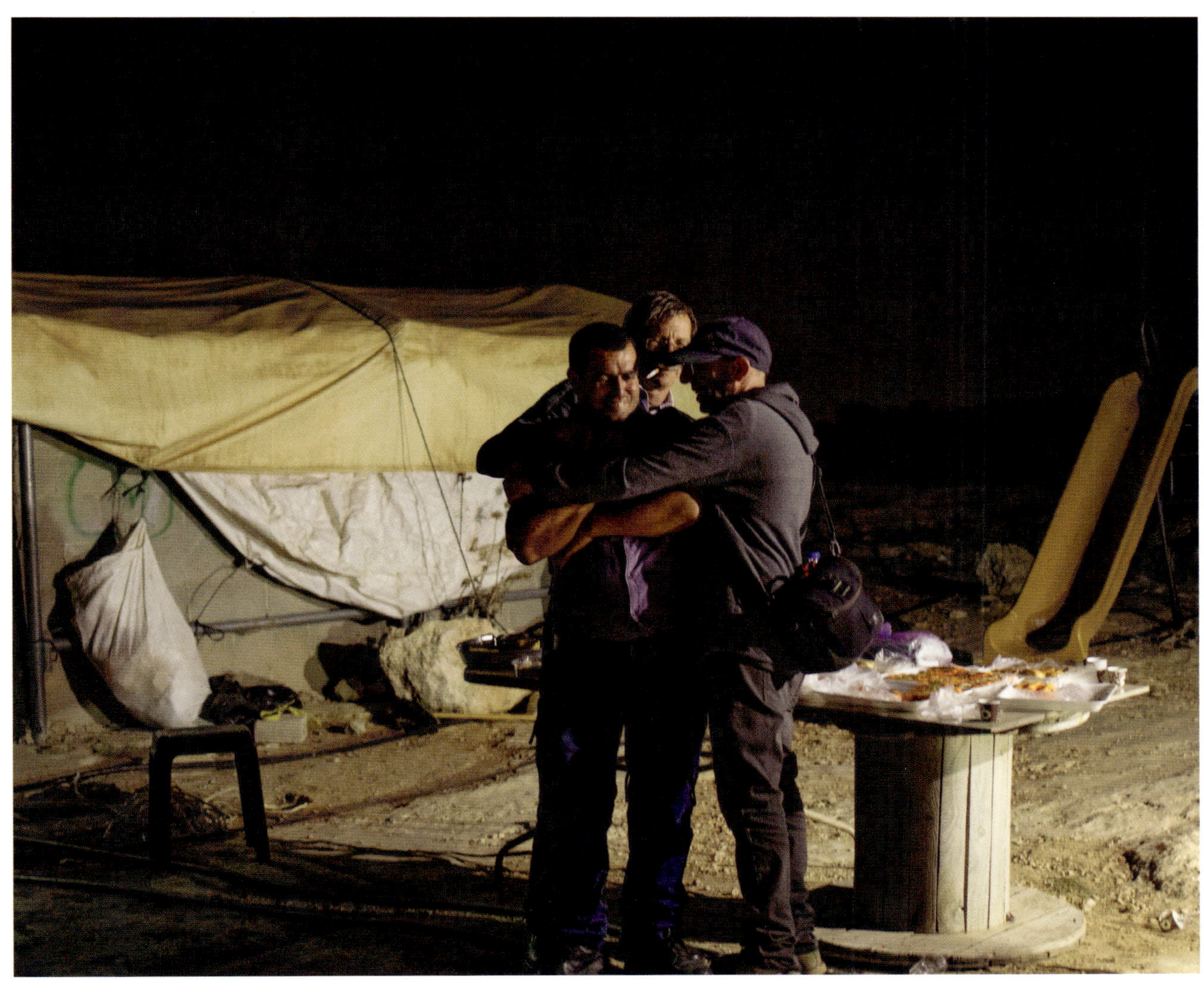

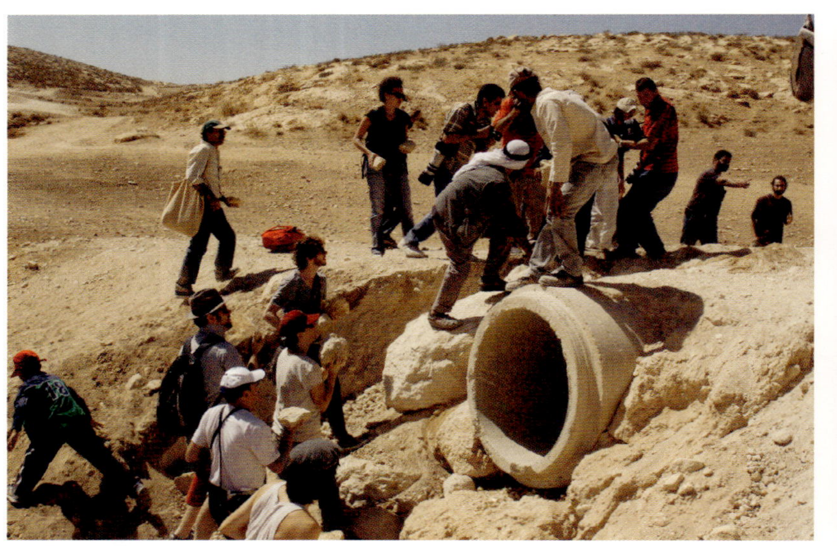

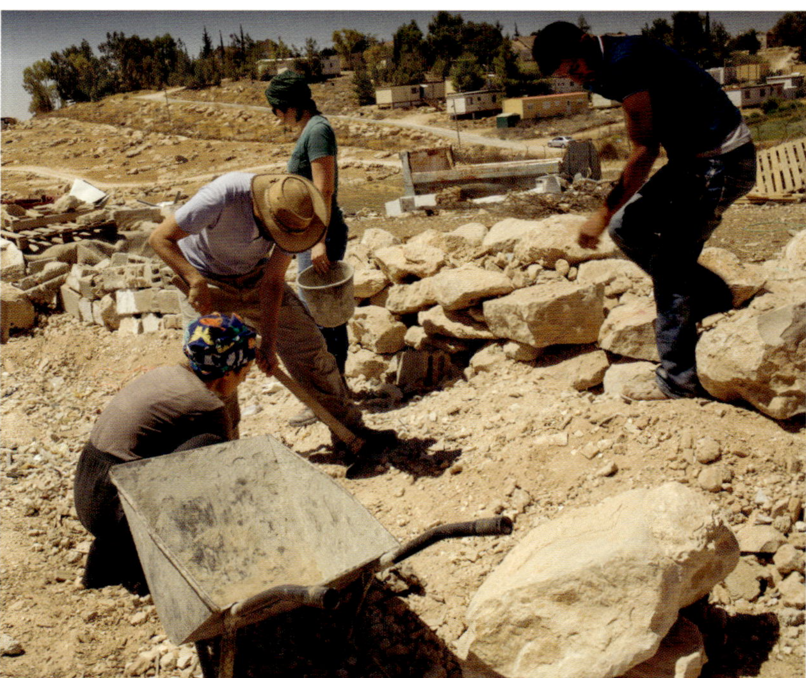

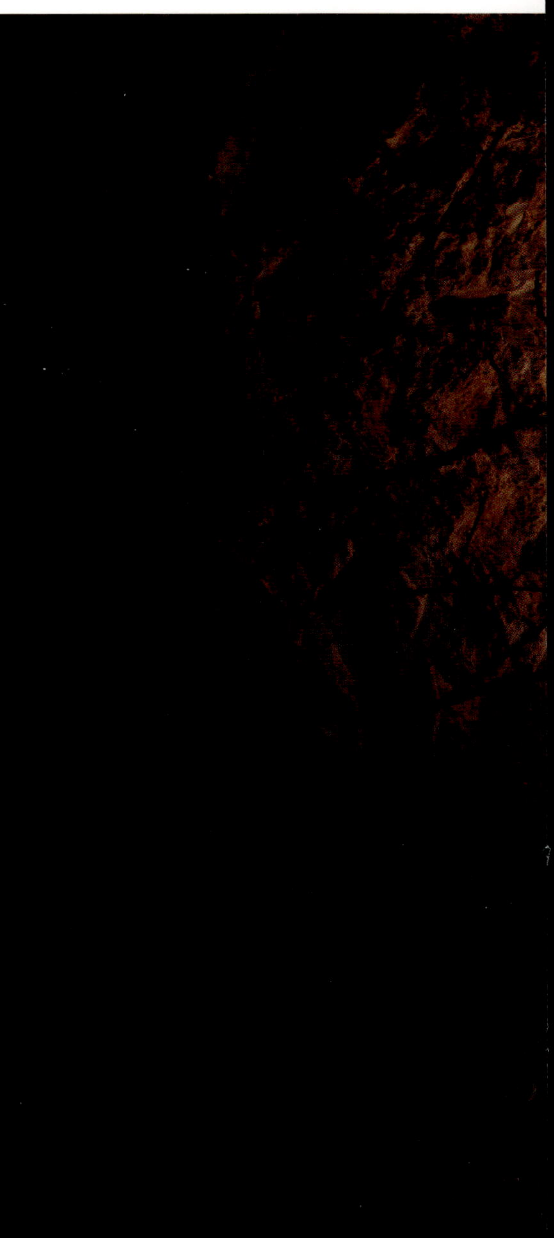

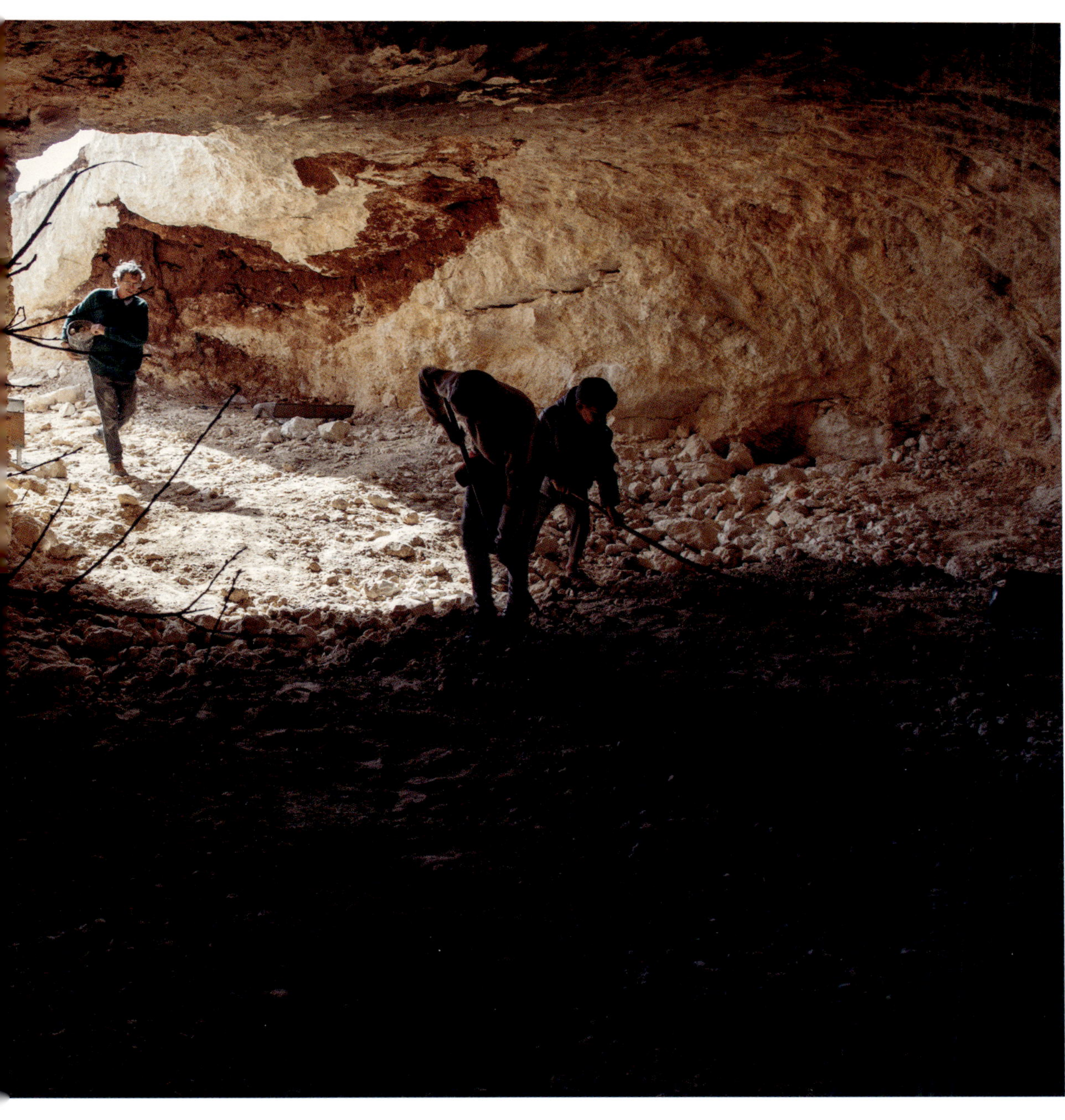

13.4 Road to Jinba, September 2009. Photograph: Istvan Perczel.

13.5 Umm al-Khair, July 2017.

13.6 Unknown location, December 2018.

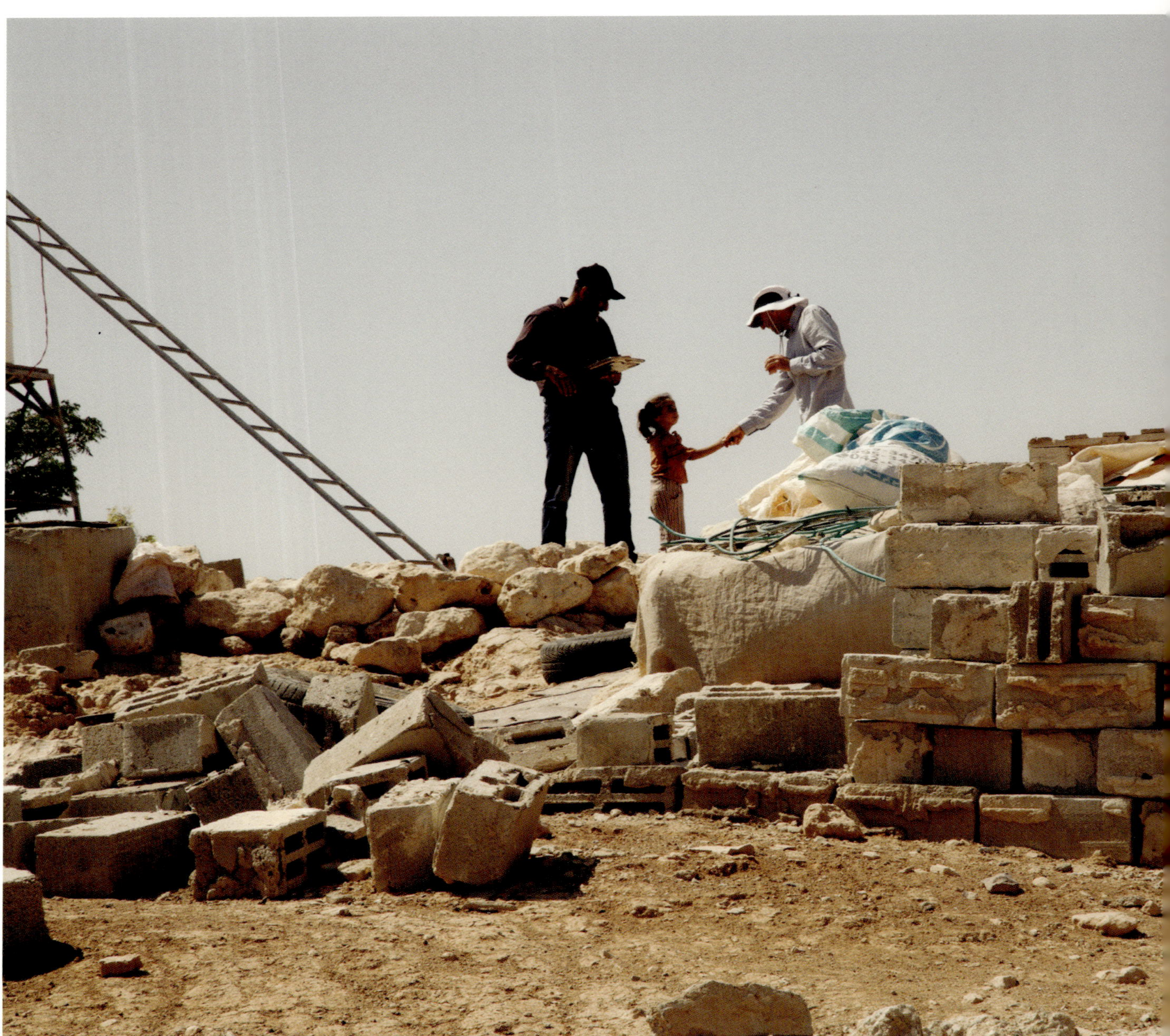

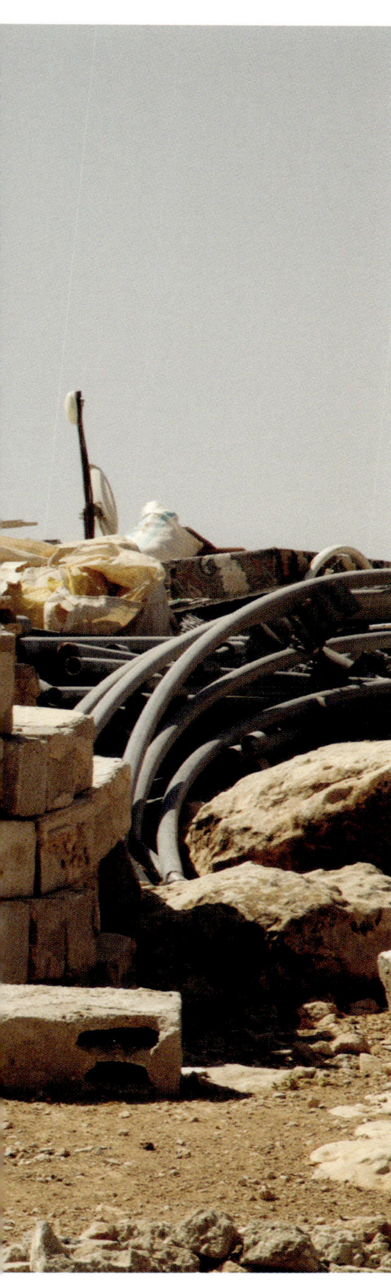

13.7 Fakheit,
June 2022.

Appendix 1
Timeline

November 29, 1947. United Nations Resolution 181 establishing two sovereign states in Palestine.

May 14, 1948. Ben Gurion reads the declaration of independence establishing the State of Israel, promising "complete equality of social and political rights to all its inhabitants irrespective of religion, race or sex."

May 1948–January 1949. War in Israel-Palestine. 700,000 Palestinian refugees flee or are driven out of the country, a catastrophe known in Arabic as the Nakba, or disaster.

January–July 1949. Armistice agreements with Egypt, Lebanon, Jordan, and Syria.

1949. Gaza Strip annexed by Egypt.

April 24, 1950. The West Bank annexed by Jordan.

June 5–10, 1967. The Six-Day War. Israel defeats the armies of Egypt, Jordan, and Syria and occupies the whole of pre-1967 Palestine and the Golan Heights.

June 27, 1967. Israel annexes East Jerusalem de facto.

1970–71. The first Jewish settlers move into Hebron. Foundation of Kiryat Arba urban settlement.

October 6, 1973. Egypt and Syria attack Israel, starting the Yom Kippur War.

July 1974. Right-wing Israeli settlers take over the Turkish Railway Station at Sebastia. They are evacuated by the army on the understanding that a permanent settlement will be established nearby at Elon Moreh. In the following years hundreds of Israeli settlements are established on the West Bank by government order.

September 17, 1978. Peace accords between Egypt and Israel are signed at Camp David, under the auspices of President Jimmy Carter.

Appendix 2
Suggestions for Further Reading

Alexandrowicz, Ra'anan. *The Law in These Parts*. film 1 hr 40 min; Israel, 2011.

Azoulay, Ariella Aisha, and Ophir, Adi. *The One-State Condition: Occupation and Democracy in Israel/Palestine*. Stanford University Press. 2012.

Breaking the Silence. *Our Harsh Logic: Israeli Soldiers' Testimonies from the Occupied Territories, 2000–2010*. New York: Metropolitan Books; Reprint edition. September 18, 2012.

Khalidi, Rashid. *The Hundred Years War on Palestine: A History of Settler Colonialism and Resistance, 1917–2017*. New York: Metropolitan Books. 2020.

Koudelka, Josef. *Wall*. New York: Aperture. 2013.

Krämer, Gudrun. *A History of Palestine: From the Ottoman Conquest to the Founding of the State of Israel*. Princeton, N.J.: Princeton University Press. 2011.

Kretzmer, David, and Ronen, Yaël, *The Occupation of Justice: The Supreme Court of Israel and the Occupied Territories*. Oxford: Oxford University Press; 2nd ed. 2021.

Nusseibeh, Sari. *Once Upon a Country: A Palestinian Life*, written with Anthony David. New York: Farrar, Straus and Giroux. London: Halban Publishers. 2007.

Said, Edward W. *The Question of Palestine*. New York: Vintage. 1992.

Sfard, Michael. *The Wall and the Gate: Israel, Palestine, and the Legal Battle for Human Rights*. New York: Metropolitan Books. 2018.

Shehadeh, Raja. *Palestinian Walks: Forays into a Vanishing Landscape*. New York: Scribner. 2008.

Shulman, David. *Freedom and Despair: Notes from the South Hebron Hills*. Chicago: University of Chicago Press. 2018.

Maps

By Tamar and Reuven Sofer

M.1 Central region of the Jordan Valley.
M.2 (next) Northern Jordan Valley.
M.3 (next) South Hebron HIlls.

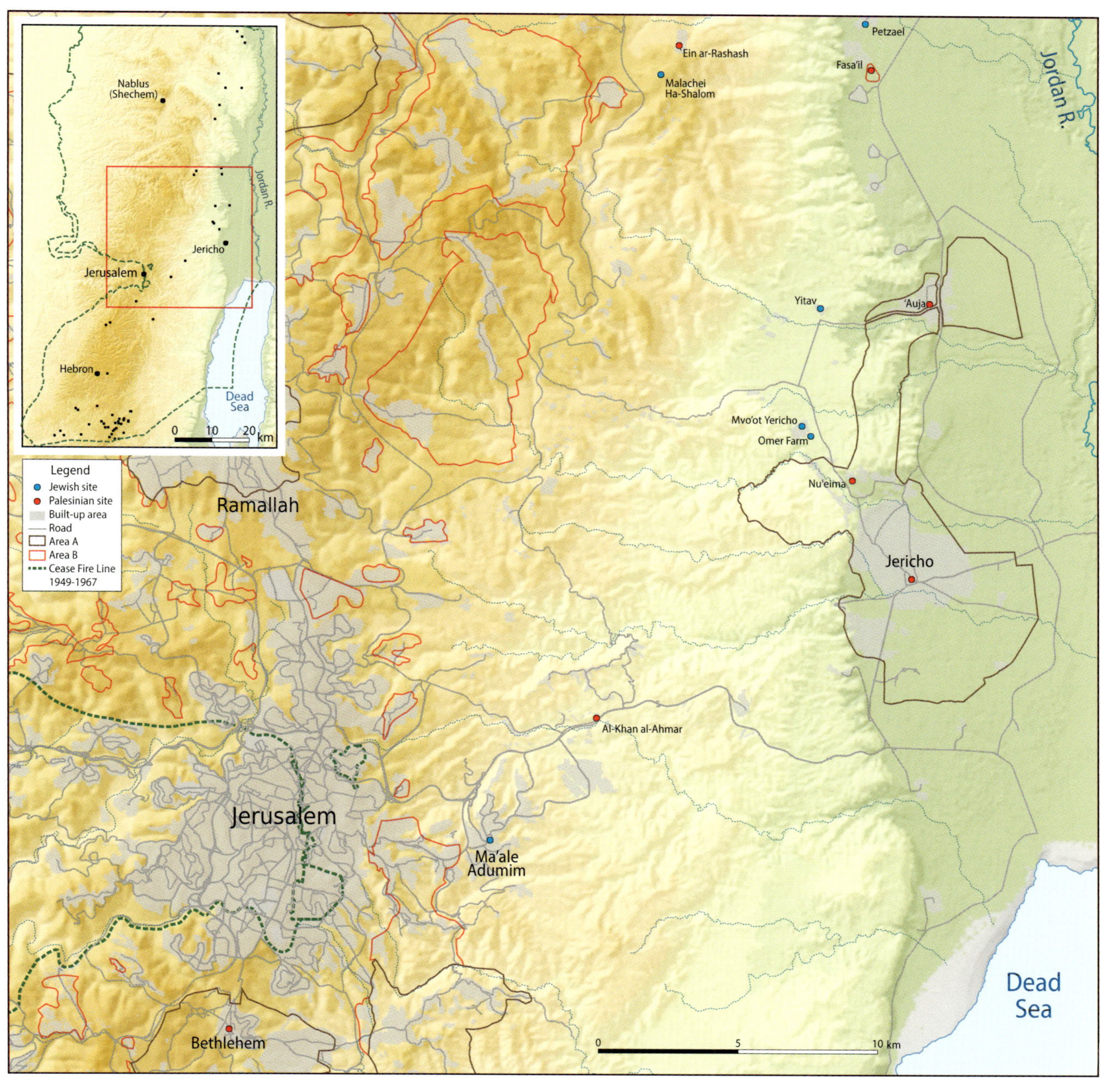

Nablus
(Shechem)
Jordan R.
Jericho
Jerusalem
Hebron
Dead
Sea
0
10
20
km
Legend
Jewish site
Palesinian site
Built-up area
Road
Area A
Area B
Cease Fire Line
1949-1967
Petzael
Ein ar-Rashash
Fasa'il
Malachei
Ha-Shalom
Jordan R.
Yitav
'Auja
Mvo'ot Yericho
Omer Farm
Nu'eima
Ramallah
Jericho
Al-Khan al-Ahmar
Jerusalem
Ma'ale
Adumim
Bethlehem
Dead
Sea
0
5
10 km

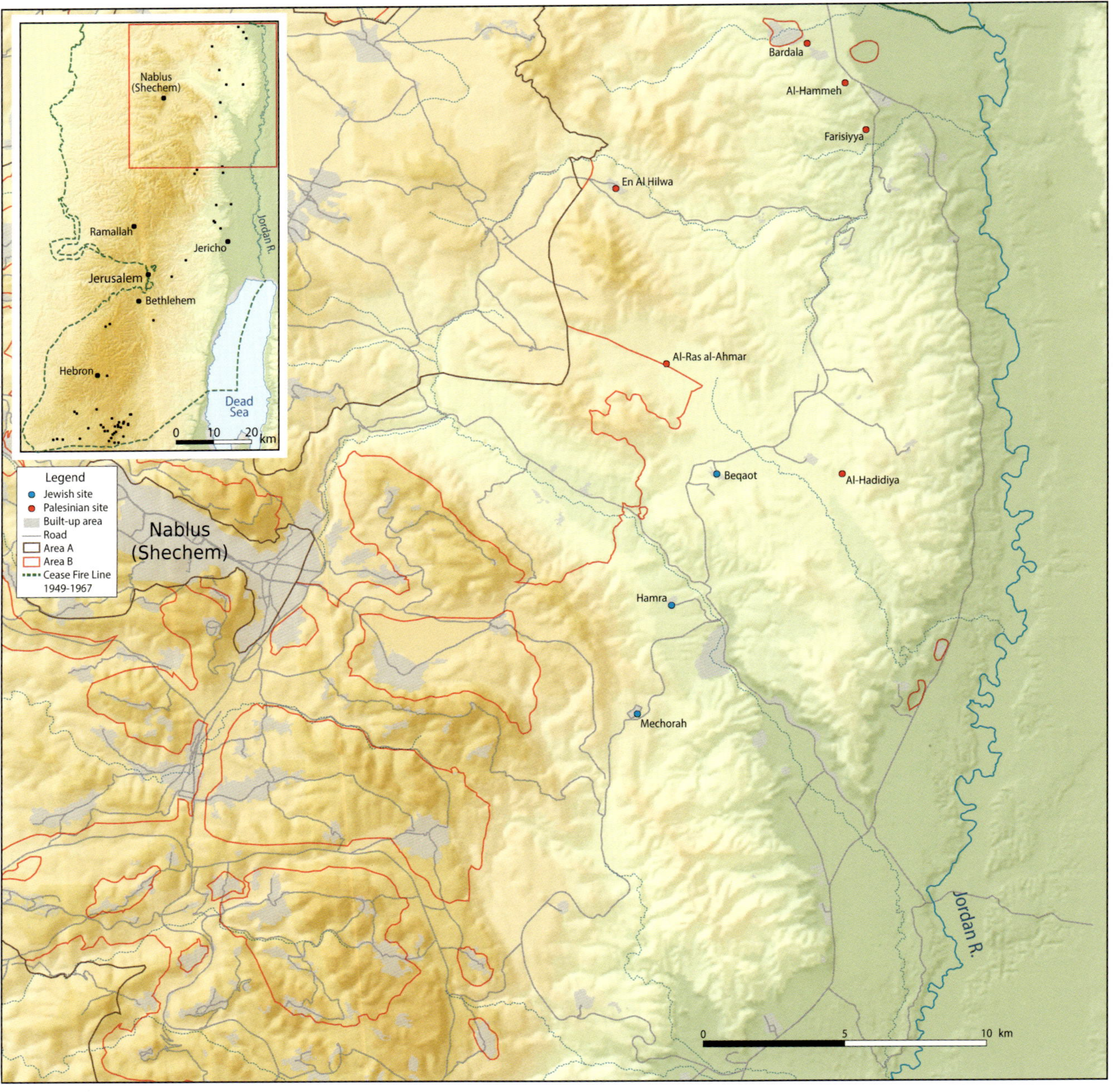

Nablus
(Shechem)
Ramallah
Jericho
Jordan R.
Jerusalem
Bethlehem
Hebron
Dead
Sea
0
10
20
km
Legend
Jewish site
Palesinian site
Built-up area
Road
Area A
Area B
Cease Fire Line
1949-1967
Nablus
(Shechem)
Bardala
Al-Hammeh
Farisiyya
En Al Hilwa
Al-Ras al-Ahmar
Beqaot
Al-Hadidiya
Hamra
Mechorah
Jordan R.
0
5
10 km

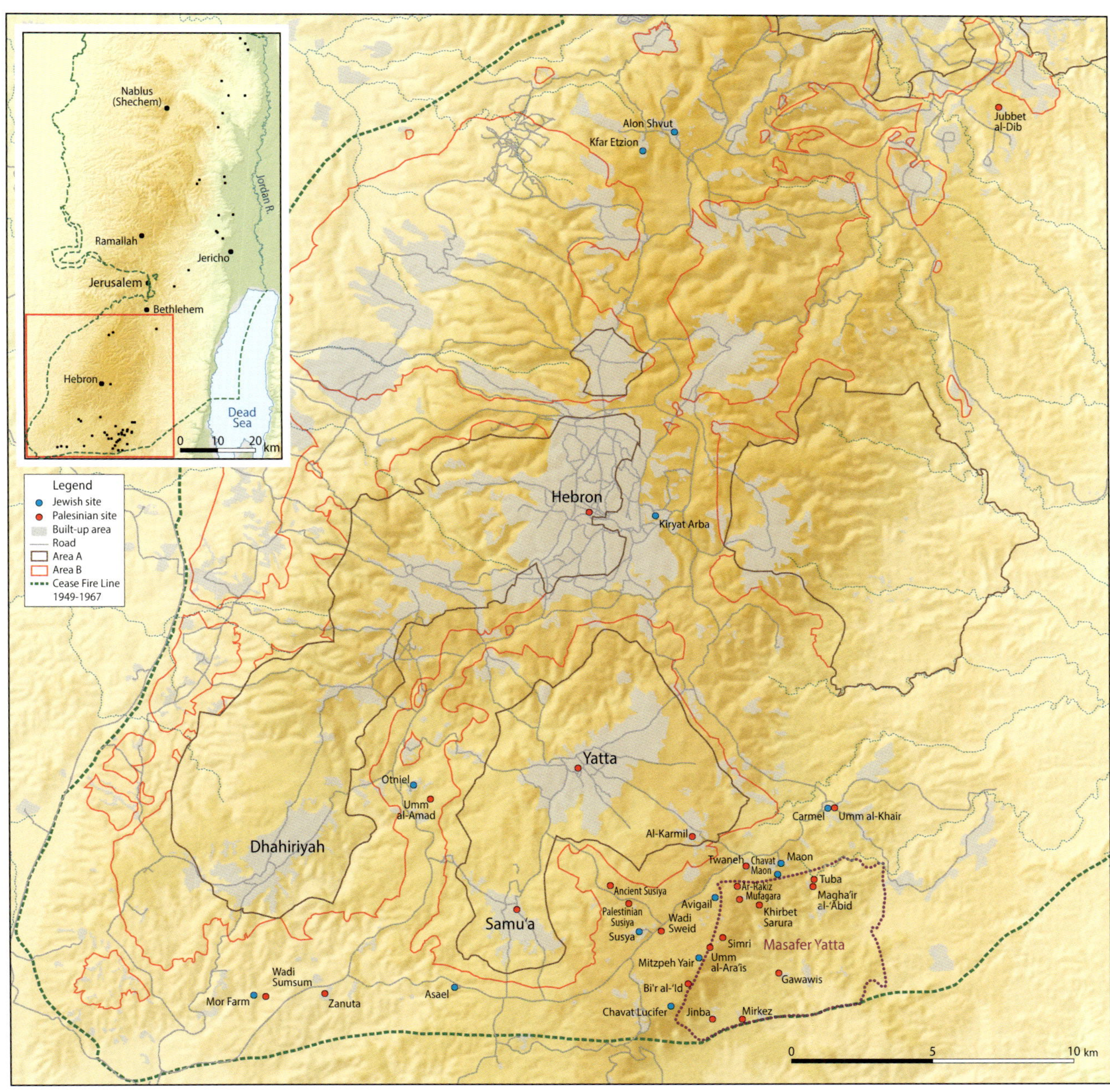

Nablus
(Shechem)
Jordan R.
Ramallah
Jericho
Jerusalem
Bethlehem
Hebron
Dead
Sea
0
10
20
km
Legend
Jewish site
Palestinian site
Built-up area
Road
Area A
Area B
Cease Fire Line
1949-1967
Alon Shvut
Kfar Etzion
Jubbet
al-Dib
Hebron
Kiryat Arba
Yatta
Otniel
Umm
al-Amad
Dhahiriyah
Carmel
Umm al-Khair
Al-Karmil
Twaneh
Chavat
Maon
Maon
Tuba
Ancient Susiya
At-Rakiz
Mufagara
Magha'ir
al-'Abid
Avigail
Palestinian
Susiya
Khirbet
Sarura
Samu'a
Wadi
Sweid
Susya
Simri
Masafer Yatta
Mitzpeh Yair
Umm
al-Ara'is
Wadi
Sumsum
Gawawis
Bi'r al-'Id
Mor Farm
Zanuta
Asael
Chavat Lucifer
Jinba
Mirkez
0
5
10 km

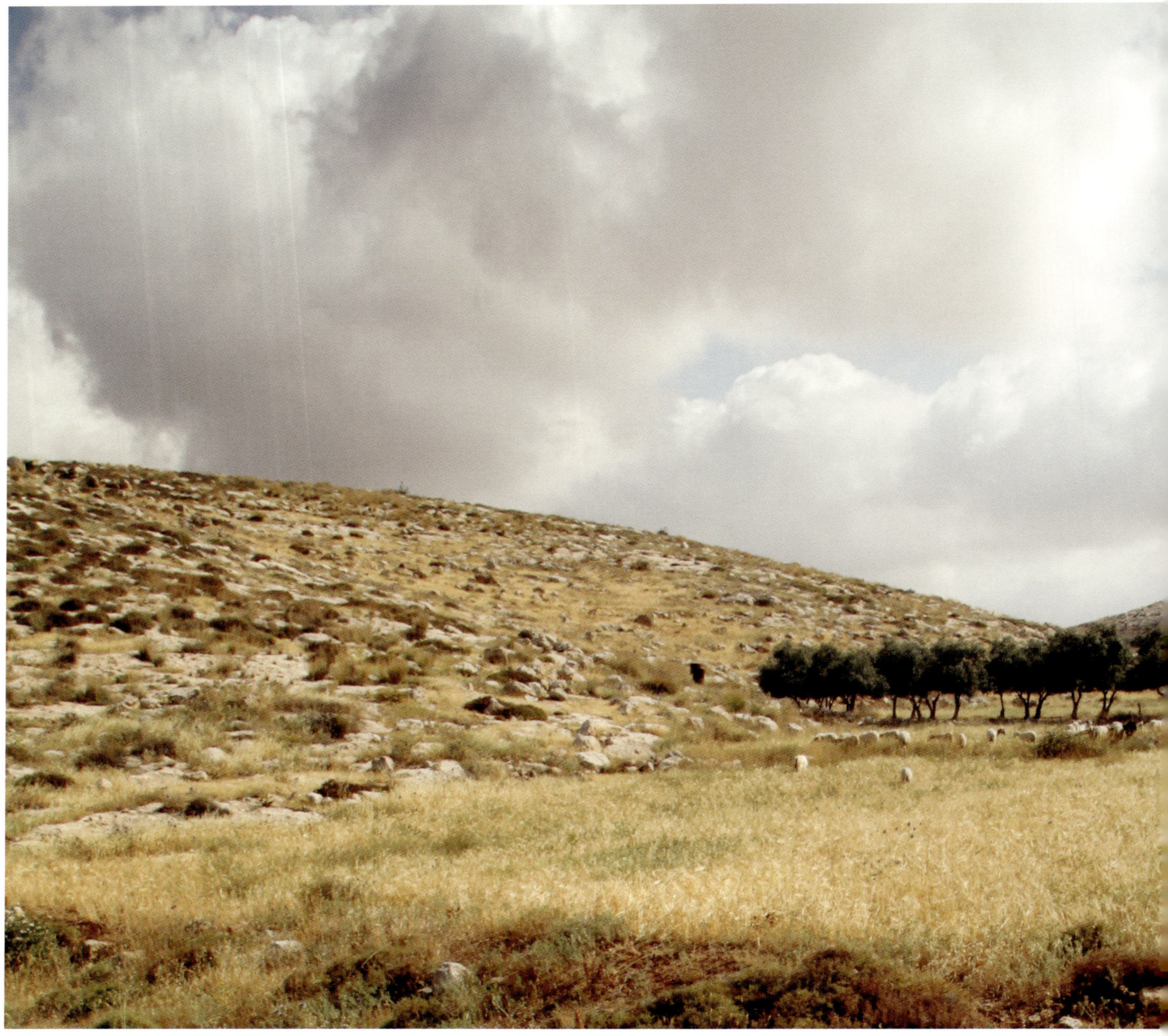

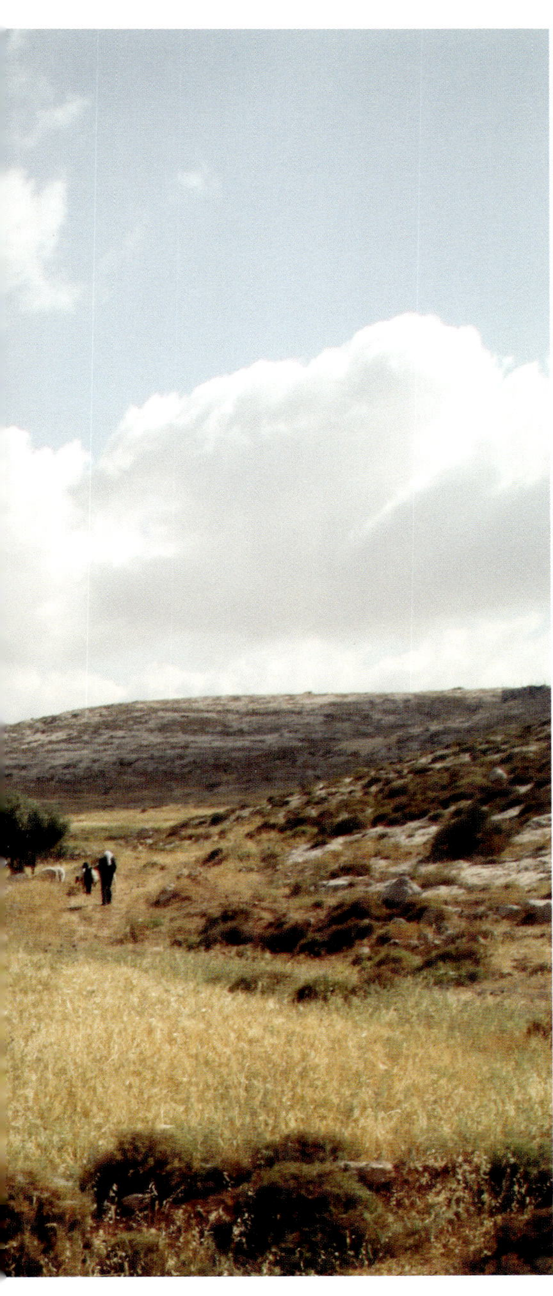

If the army had its way,
even the clouds would be prevented
from floating over this wadi.

E.1 Umm al-Ammad, June 2014.